MURDER
'Whatdunit'

'I focus not on whodunit, but on whatdunit'

Dr Milton Helpern (1902–77)
Chief Medical Examiner, New York City

'Murder has a magic of its own, its peculiar alchemy. Touched by that crimson wand, things base and sordid, things ugly and of ill report, are transformed into matters wondrous, weird and tragical. Dull streets become fraught with mystery, commonplace dwellings assume sinister aspects, everyone concerned, howsoever plain and ordinary, is invested with a new value and importance as the red light falls upon each. The moveless figure in the dock, the passing cloud of witnesses, even the poor and pitiful exhibits, all are endowed with a different character and hold for a space the popular attention ere they revert once again to their customary and homely selves.'

William Roughead (1870–1952)
Scottish lawyer and criminologist

MURDER
'Whatdunit'
An Illustrated Account of the Methods of Murder

J H H Gaute and Robin Odell
Authors of
THE MURDERERS' WHO'S WHO

With a Foreword by
Professor Keith Simpson CBE, MD

ST. MARTIN'S PRESS
New York

This book is dedicated to
PAULL HARRAP, CBE
publisher, colleague and dear friend

Library of Congress Cataloging in Publication Data

Gaute, J. H. H.
    Murder 'Whatdunit'.
    Bibliography: p.
    Includes index.

1. Murder – Dictionaries.   2. Murder – Bibliography.
I. Odell, Robin.   II. Title.
HV6515.G38   1983   364.1'523'0321   83–11194
ISBN 0-312-55326-9
First published in Great Britain by Harrap Limited.
First (U.S.) Edition
10 9 8 7 6 5 4 3 2 1

Contents

Foreword
by Professor Keith Simpson CBE, MD

The cry of 'Murder' is as likely as any in the English language to stop the conversation, for it contains ingredients of drama, passion, human cruelty, avarice, lust, hatred and violence — and sometimes the horror of disposal in secret of the dead body . . . elements that no other event can claim, not even the horrors of pestilence and war. There is no other word for this crime, and no historian or lawyer, not even the crime writer with his Roget's *Thesaurus* at his elbow, has a synonym to match it. Assault, battery, mugging, the cruelty of torture or starvation, horrors of politically inspired outrages with explosive devices, mass killings like those of the religious maniac Jones — the kaleidoscopic colours of 'Murder', and its infinite ingenuity and drama, transcend all.

Every journalist knows this, and a long succession of distinguished crime writers have flourished on it, from Edgar Allan Poe to Agatha Christie, P. D. James and Georges Simenon. Scholarly analyses of murder by Colin Wilson and Julian Symons and encyclopaedias like those of Spencer Shew — and more recently *The Murderers' Who's Who* of the present authors, Messrs Gaute and Odell — have been devoured by a public who remain avid for more. It is a fascinating world, filled with fascinating characters whose names will always lurk in the shadows of dark alleys and 'la Rue Morgue'. And the exciting thing about real-life crime is that indeed it is truer than fiction: the dramas of Dr Crippen, of Haigh with his 'acid-bath' and of Christie outdo all the imaginings of the crime writers. Who has ever matched Landru, Vaquier, Rouse, Seddon, Peter Kürten and the rest? As Shakespeare wrote in *Hamlet*, 'For murder, though it have no tongue, will speak with most miraculous organ.' Indeed, the truth has outdone fiction — and still does.

Only in the creation of the fictional detectives of fame have crime writers succeeded in equalling those of the 'Sûreté', 'The Yard' and the FBI. Sherlock Holmes may never lose his remarkable abilities, or Hercule Poirot that gift for smelling out the guilty party, and, as each showed, through the delicate tracery of clues, deductions and reasoning.

Now this new work has attempted something never before set in print, for it not only gathers, in easily located alphabetical order, the main topics of criminological interest: *it acquaints the ordinary public reader with the tools and methods of crime investigation*. It is in effect an Izaak Walton on Crime and

Criminality of astonishing accuracy, written in a language that everyone can understand, whether the subject is Ruxton or Reconstruction of Remains, Smith or Secretors: Disposal of the Body vies in importance with Dobkin and Deeming. We are introduced to what goes on in modern laboratory analysis for poisons, not just to the Maybricks or Armstrongs . . . and the authors' enthusiasm for their subject — in which each has shown a lifetime of profound interest by their earlier writings — manifests itself on every page.

Even after fifty years of work in the field of crime-detection, and my encounters with the horrors of cold, calculating murders in the routines of a professional pathologist, I found this vast text arresting in its grasp of 'the real thing' and its fascinating colour. After a lifetime of experience in well over 100,000 autopsies of all kinds and colours in many parts of the world, this can only mean that Joe Gaute and Robin Odell have 'done it again'. And there can be no doubt they have. No one who takes this book up and starts to turn over its pages will find it easy to put down. It is a *vade mecum* every amateur — and not a few professional criminologists — will find constantly jogging his elbow, an essential reference work for the crime writer and an accurate encyclopaedia of world history in the subject. It is a *tour de force*.

Preface

The most obvious question to ask about a murder is 'Who did it?' The law needs to know the answer for society's protection, and the public, for its own sense of well-being, requires offenders to be brought to account. The drama created by murder and sudden death, and the mystery of identifying the perpetrator, have traditionally combined to form the ever popular 'Whodunit?' of crime fiction. The cunning criminal and the questing detective pitting their wits against each other in the struggle for truth and justice, with the murderer's identity as the prize, are the very stuff of the 'Whodunit?'

But 'Whodunit?' is not always easy to answer without first inquiring 'What?' 'What was the cause of death?', 'What was the motive?' and 'What took place at the scene of the crime?' The late Dr Milton Helpern, Chief Medical Examiner of the City of New York, when asked about the nature of his work replied, 'I focus not on whodunit but on whatdunit.' This book is about the 'whatdunit?' of murder.

Every murder has a cause and effect — a perpetrator and a victim. Linking them is method — the poisoned cup, the dagger drawn or the pointed gun. In murder, as in cricket, there are a set number of ways of 'getting out'. In strict terms of arresting the life force, shooting, stabbing, burning, bludgeoning, asphyxiation, poisoning, omission or neglect and explosion are the pre-eminent 'causes of death', which encompass all the well-known and deadly forms.

To the extent that asphyxia may result from strangulation, drowning, suffocation, gassing or hanging, and that murder by poisoning is possible using many different agents, it can be appreciated that murder methods form a complex field of study. A special place is reserved for the medical fraternity who, when they embrace the idea of murder, almost invariably choose poison. We show how wide this choice has been, ranging from straightforward arsenical weed-killer to sophisticated drugs such as succinylcholine chloride. It remains one of the paradoxes of murder investigation that doctors, the group which might be expected to exercise impeccable technical judgment, frequently bungle their efforts at murder.

Method is one element in the classic trio of characteristics — motive, method and opportunity — which enter into every murder. In her book *Murder and its Motives*, first published in 1924, F. Tennyson Jesse set out six categories of motive: gain, revenge, elimination, jealousy, lust and conviction. These groups have withstood the passage of time fairly well, for 'lust of killing' and 'conviction' are capable of assimilating the modern social phenomena of stranger-to-stranger and sado-masochistic murders. It remains true, though, that the majority of murders are domestic in origin and the motives are usually jealousy and elimination. Opportunity, the third characteristic of murder, is a less tangible subject which is a matter of timing, circumstance and luck for the murderer. Victimology, the idea that some individuals put themselves at risk as victims of murder, also plays a part.

We have attempted to bring together the work of the pathologist, scientist, detective and prosecutor in examining the problems of motive and method which have led to murder. This book is a companion volume to *The Murderers' Who's Who*, and like that work it uses a selection of entries in a reference format to give the flavour of murder investigation. We have tried to make it as complete as any single volume for the general reader can be on so diverse a subject. It is intended to give concepts and working details of the forensic aspects of murder investigation, but it is not a text-book.

Murder: Whatdunit does not seek to give any ideas or comfort to the criminally minded. Sir Bernard Spilsbury's biographers observed that, 'A manual for murderers would include two strongly worded sections on the dangers of being too greedy and of antagonising the victim's relatives and friends.' What we hope comes over strongly is the relentless advance of forensic medicine, which exposes the ineptitude of most murderers and for the greater part leaves their success hingeing mainly on luck. We record the development of many of the most important advances in scientific criminology, from the simple Marsh Test for arsenic to the complexities of fingerprint identification. The traditional role of the doctor acting as police surgeon, and that of the forensic pathologist providing technical assistance to the police, has been strengthened by the addition of other areas of expert knowledge: dentistry, chemistry, biology, firearms and document examination and psychiatry. Forensic science as a whole is a powerful tool in the hands of today's criminal investigators who defeat the murderers' methods with their own counter-measures. One of the most valuable aspects of forensic science is the study of contact traces — working on the principle that every encounter between a murderer and a victim results in the transfer of often minute traces of evidence such as fingerprints, hair, fibres or blood.

The growth of the legal process, from the definition of murder to the concepts of common law and trial, is shown, as also are the developments in execution demonstrated by the odd national diversity of methods: guillotine for the French, hanging for the English, and the gas chamber or electric chair for the Americans. This is all part of the background to murder, as is the process of establishing the truth about a crime. Interrogation, with its origins in coercion by torture and ordeal, leads through voluntary confession to modern methods of drug or hypnotically induced truth and lie detectors.

A much debated aspect of murder is the mental state of the murderer, which Dr Lindesay Neustatter in his *The Mind of the Murderer* noted is 'by no means so different from the so-called normal man as is sometimes supposed'. This remains frontier territory in forensic psychiatry, despite the agonizing that has gone into forming rules by which insanity and non-responsibility may be tested. Hypnosis, amnesia and automatism are all conditions which can affect behaviour, and possibly result in criminality. To these conditions must be added schizophrenia, the alleged affliction of the Son of Sam (David Berkowitz) and the Yorkshire Ripper (Peter Sutcliffe). They both claimed to have heard voices urging them to kill, but how should society judge and sentence them? The former pleaded guilty, and was sentenced to 365 years' imprisonment; the latter pleaded not guilty to murder, but was found guilty and received a life sentence. A cynical journalist at Sutcliffe's trial was said to have remarked, 'When you speak to God it's called praying, but when God speaks to you, it's called schizophrenia!'

A number of cases that appear in *The Murderers' Who's Who* are touched on briefly here, but their treatment is different. For instance, no entry on ACID could be complete without reference to John George Haigh, or any entry on BURNING without reference to Alfred Arthur Rouse. But the purpose is to draw out the forensic aspects of the cases referred to in order to illustrate the mode of murder. Many new cases are used in the present work, especially from English and American murder trials, which enhance the combined reference value of the two books.

People are also featured in another way, with references to many of the great personalities who have devoted their efforts and genius to methods of investigating murder. Their names appear throughout the book in relation to those aspects of murder with which they are most closely associated. They, and many others, contributed immeasurably to the sum of criminological knowledge and provided answers to 'Whatdunit?'

New trends continue to develop in the study of murder, and the video recording of criminal-trial proceedings in the USA is one of the latest developments. It highlights the continuing fascination of murder and especially of the detailed mechanics of its commission and discovery. The ever-increasing use of firearms continues to numb the senses with its statistics. Of America's 23,000 murders committed annually, 70 per cent are carried out with guns. The existence of 55 million handguns in private ownership, coupled with increasing use of drugs, provides a dangerous acceleration of crime in her large cities — five murders a day, for example, in New York City.

For crime readers an attempt has been made to explain some of the intricacies of sudden death, and a comprehensive index and bibliography are provided in the event that they may wish to go further. We do not profess to have plumbed the unfathomable depths of the subject, but we hope to have provided insights for those who would be fascinated, and information for those who are simply interested — perhaps it even provides deterrence for any who might be tempted!

Many of the titles mentioned in the bibliography may be difficult to obtain, so we have included at the end of the book a list of booksellers who specialize in second-hand crime books, and who will be delighted to try to obtain any titles required. We have also mentioned three crime monthlies for those who like to read more widely about murder cases.

In compiling this work the major task, the forensic side, has been undertaken by Robin Odell, with Joe Gaute looking after the case details.

J. H. H. Gaute   **R. I. Odell**
Pyrford, Surrey   Sonning Common, Berkshire

Acknowledgments

First of all we must thank Professor Keith Simpson, who, though a very busy man, somehow found time to read the proofs and give us the benefit of his great knowledge, as well as honouring this book with a foreword. We are also grateful to Dr John Thompson for forensic advice and illustrations, and to those who have willingly granted permission to use copyright illustrations. If we have failed to trace any copyright-holders we apologize.

Our thanks go to Richard Butterworth for his excellent handling of production and publicity matters; to Michael R. Carter for his enthusiastic approach to design; and to Roy Minton for his expert editing and valuable advice. Our gratitude is due also to Ann Aston, who typed much of the script, to Debbie Sutcliffe for her preparation of the line illustrations and to Richard Whittington-Egan who has carefully read the final proofs. Last, but certainly not least, we thank our wives for their constant help and encouragement during the long period of the preparation and writing of *Murder: Whatdunit*.

Notes

Within some of the entries there has been reference on occasion (by the use of capital letters) to other entries in this book, where it has seemed to the authors that similarities or comparisons might interest the reader. At the foot of each entry is a list of numbers which refer to the comprehensive bibliography included at the end of the book. Numbers in italics denote relevant murder cases which readers might wish to pursue in greater detail. The numbers in bold type indicate books giving mainly technical information.

A

ACID

The destructive power of acid has attracted the attention of a number of murderers with a view to its use for disposing of unwanted corpses. It is a matter of some amazement how doctors and even lawyers, persons trained in the exercise of judgment, turn their minds to murder and employ the most extraordinary methods. In 1933 a French lawyer of dubious reputation, Maître Georges Sarret, devised a get-rich-quick scheme based on an elaborate insurance fraud. He successfully carried out his plan with the aid of two female accomplices, the sisters Catherine and Philomène Schmidt, and a man called Chambon. Having netted 100,000 francs, the villains fell out, and Chambon attempted blackmail. Sarret and the Schmidt girls lured the blackmailer and his mistress into a trap, and the Maître shot them while the Schmidts ran a motor-cycle engine to drown the noise.

Faced with the DISPOSAL OF THE BODIES, Sarret put the corpses into a bath and poured 25 gallons of sulphuric acid over them, quickly reducing the flesh to sludge. Fired with this success, the deadly trio tried to repeat their fraud tactics for larger stakes — 1,750,000 francs. One of the girls was caught before the crime was perpetrated, and the three were soon brought to trial, when the story of the shooting and acid bath came to light. The two Schmidts each received ten-year prison sentences and Maître Sarret was executed in Marseilles in April 1934.

Probably the most celebrated user of acid was self-styled engineer John George Haigh, who in 1949 earned fame as the acid-bath murderer. His victim was Mrs Henrietta Durand-Deacon, a well-off widow who lived in a London hotel where she met Haigh. She told him of her plans to market a cosmetic product, and he responded by inviting her to visit his factory.

On 18 February 1949 Haigh drove Mrs Durand-Deacon to his 'factory' in Crawley, Sussex, which was no more than a store-room attached to another building. There he shot her in the back of the head and tipped the corpse into a drum which he filled with sulphuric acid. Later the same day Haigh disposed of the watch and jewellery which he had taken from his victim. He made several trips to Crawley during the next few days to see how far the digestion had gone.

When Mrs Durand-Deacon was reported missing Haigh was one of the first to show concern, and went with another person to make a report at Chelsea police-station. His glib tongue made the police suspicious, and they quickly discovered that Haigh had a criminal record. Inquiries led investigating officers to the Crawley factory, where they found some of the missing woman's clothing, traces of BLOOD and a recently fired .38 revolver. Haigh was arrested, and in cocksure mood told the police, 'Mrs Durand-Deacon no longer exists — I've destroyed her with acid. How can you prove murder if there is no body?' He was wrong, as subsequent events were to prove.

When arrested Haigh boasted that he had killed eight other people and disposed of their corpses in drums of acid. While the acid had reduced his last victim's body to sludge, there were sufficient identifiable traces remaining to bring the murder home to its perpetrator. Dr Keith Simpson found a gallstone on the rough ground outside the Crawley factory where Haigh had dumped his concoction of sludge. He also discovered some remnants of bones from a human foot, and about 28 pounds of body fat. Undoubtedly a human body had been

1

Haigh's 'factory' showing acid carboys .

destroyed in that workshop, but the most important discovery was a set of acrylic dentures. These TEETH were positively identified as belonging to Mrs Durand-Deacon by her dentist. Haigh was convicted of murder, and was executed in August 1949.

The police were unsure at the time whether sulphuric acid was capable of completely destroying a human body. Sulphuric acid — or vitriol, as it is commonly called — is a highly corrosive substance extensively used in industrial processes in its concentrated form. It is also used as a 30 per cent solution in battery acid. The most common criminal uses of vitriol are in bomb-making and assault by acid-throwing. Fatal poisoning by sulphuric acid has been recorded when the acid has been swallowed accidentally or suicidally. As an acid bath to dispose of human remains, sulphuric acid acts by extracting water from the tissues, and in the process generates considerable heat — Mr Haigh's drum of acid would have been very hot to the touch. On parts of the body exposed to the air sulphuric acid has a charring effect like a burn. If a human body is entirely immersed it will be completely digested (bones and all) by the acid.

Haigh's victim was consumed, save for a few bones of the feet, which probably protruded above the level of the acid when the body was upended in it. The tell-tale plastic denture survived because of the slowness with which acrylic resin dissolves within sulphuric acid. The gallstones — compacted bile-sand covered with a fatty substance — also resisted the acid test.

Procuring murder by means of acid is rare except through poisoning by prussic acid or CYANIDE, although an extraordinary form of torture with acid which resulted in murder was devised by a California doctor. In August 1962 Dr Geza de Kaplany and his new bride, a beautiful girl called Hajna, moved into an apartment block in San José. During the evening of 28 August fellow-residents heard the sound of running water and classical music played at high volume. These noises came from the de Kaplany apartment, and appeared to override a wailing sound. When the police were called late in the evening because of the nuisance to other residents the music stopped, and a horrifying human wail was distinctly audible. An ambulance was sent for, and Hajna was taken to hospital — onlookers thought they could smell acid fumes in the air.

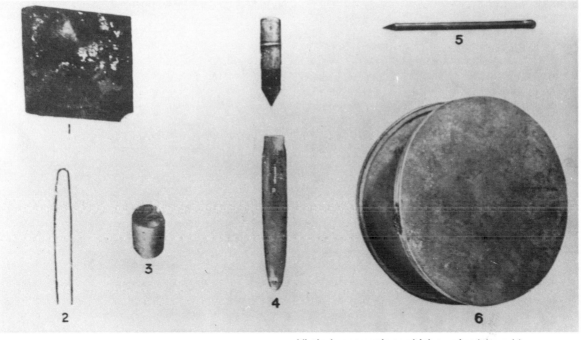

Victim's possessions which survived the acid

When Hajna de Kaplany was admitted to hospital she was found to have third-degree corrosive burns covering 60 per cent of her body. Her eyes were so burned that the pupils could not be seen, and her breasts and genitals in particular had been subjected to corrosive burning. After a month of agonizing suffering the poor woman died of her injuries. The de Kaplanys' bedroom was a virtual torture chamber. There was a large hole in the carpet where acid had burned through, and on the floor was a heap of disintegrating, yellow-stained bed-clothes. A pair of rubber gloves lay near a leather carrying-case containing three pint bottles of sulphuric, hydrochloric and nitric acid — the last one was two-thirds empty. A note written on a medical prescription form was found in the bedroom. It read: 'If you want to live — do not shout; do what I tell you; or else you will die.' Dr de Kaplany told police that he had attacked his wife of five weeks to take away her beauty and to warn her against adultery. He was charged with murder by torture, and tried in San José in 1963. The 'acid doctor', as he became known, was found guilty and sentenced to life imprisonment. He served thirteen years of his sentence, being released in 1975 to work as a medical missionary in Taiwan.

1, 19, 27, 95, 110, 178, 211, 313, 329, 374, 375, 407, 412, 427, 454, 481, 504, 518, 546, 575, 626, 637, 710.

ACONITINE

While giving evidence on poisons in a criminal case, it is said that Professor Robert Christison, one of the foremost experts in toxicology of his time, remarked to the judge, 'My Lord, there is but one deadly agent of this kind which we cannot satisfactorily trace in the human body after death, and that is —' At this point he was stopped by the judge, who thought that public interest would best be served by not mentioning the name of the poison. The agent Christison had in mind was aconitine, a vegetable poison derived from the monkshood plant, which was to feature at a later date in a famous murder case involving George Lamson, one of the professor's medical students.

Aconitine is a vegetable alkaloid obtained from the root and leaves of the monkshood or wolfsbane plant (*Aconitum napellus*). Its leaf may be mistaken for parsley, and its root for horse-radish. It has an earthy, bitter taste, a depressant effect on the central nervous system, and was used medicinally in liniments and tinctures for relieving toothache, neuralgia and rheumatism. It is, however, highly toxic, and can be absorbed through the skin. Aconitine was a favourite poison in ancient times, being widely used in Greece and Rome for the elimination of political enemies. The Greeks called it 'stepmother's poison', and the Emperor Trajan forbade Romans to grow wolfsbane in their gardens. The chief symptoms of aconitine poisoning are a tingling feeling in the mouth, accompanied by numbness and increase in body temperature. There may be nausea, vomiting, visual disturbance, feeble pulse and loss of muscular power. Paralysis sets in, and death results from respiratory or heart failure. The poison is fast-acting, and death may result within eight minutes from a lethal dose of 1–2mg.

George Henry Lamson, apart from being a physician, was also a dabbler in drugs. He became a MORPHINE addict while serving as an army doctor in Serbia during the Russo-Turkish War of 1876–7. When he returned to England he set up in general practice and married a woman who with her brothers, Herbert and Percy John, had inherited their father's estate. In 1879 Herbert died, and his will enabled Lamson to pay off his debts and buy a better practice. The remaining brother, Percy, was a disabled lad of eighteen who was fond of his sister and liked to visit her during the school holidays. On one such occasion it is thought that Lamson made an attempt on the young man's life by administering aconitine (which he pretended was quinine) to him.

In December 1881 Lamson turned up at Percy's school in Wimbledon, where in the presence of the headmaster he produced a ready-sliced Dundee cake which he offered round. Shortly after the visitor left Percy was taken ill, and within four hours was dead. Lamson had fled to Paris, but decided to return after a few days when he reported to SCOTLAND YARD. He was arrested and put on trial for the murder of Percy John. He was accused of administering aconitine, still a little-known drug at that time. The methods available for detecting alkaloid poisons were primitive, and the expert witness at the trial, Dr Thomas Stevenson, lecturer in MEDICAL JURISPRUDENCE at Guy's Hospital, identified them by taste. He testified that he had made extracts to isolate the poison from the dead youth's body organs. 'Some of this extract I placed on my tongue,' he said, 'and it produced the effect of aconitia.' Lamson was known to have bought from a London druggist sufficient aconitine to kill a hundred people. It was suggested that he injected some of the poison into a raisin, which he then pushed into the slice of cake earmarked for his victim. His MOTIVE was gain, his ambition being to inherit his brother-in-law's wealth through his wife. Dr Lamson, one in a long line of medical

poisoners, was found guilty and sentenced to death. He made a CONFESSION to the prison chaplain before he was executed in April 1882.
1, 62, 72, 98, 103, 177, 200, 256, 309, 311, 491, 536, 589, 644, 675.

ACTUS REUS

Criminal responsibility is defined by the terms *actus reus*, which in murder is the physical act of killing a person, and MENS REA, which is the guilty mind or intent. It is held in COMMON LAW that simply committing an act does not of itself constitute guilt unless there is guilty intent. Thus every crime has two parts — the actus reus and the mens rea.

The law therefore does not prosecute a person for criminal intent alone; only where the guilty mind actuates the commission of a crime. The *actus reus* of MURDER is the death of the victim resulting from an intentional act or from wilful omission.
162, 510.

ADIPOCERE

A condition of the human corpse which occurs in damp conditions when the natural body fats solidify and form a yellowish-white waxy substance. The adipocere adheres to the bone, and helps to retain the recognizable shape of the parts of the body.

Adipocere may occur in a body immersed in water or in contact with damp soil. Its formation is a slow process, usually developing over several months, in which neutral body fats are hydrolysed into a mixture of fatty acids and soap. The process is also known as saponification. The condition does not usually affect the whole body — the limbs, chest wall and sometimes the face being common sites. But once adipocere is formed it may remain stable for many years and keep the body shape intact.

The Hopetoun Quarry murder case in Scotland in 1913 was notable for the discovery of two almost completely adipocerous bodies. The remains of two small boys were found in a water-filled quarry, and the fact that they were tied together with sash cord suggested foul-play. Sir Sydney Smith, who examined the bodies with a view to identifying them, thought they had been in the water about two years. From an examination of the TEETH he

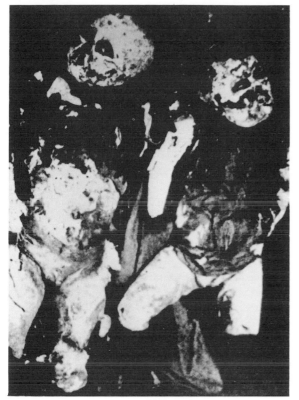

Bodies of the Hopetoun Quarry children

October 1913, two years after he had sent his sons to a watery and adipocerous grave.
625, *632.*

ALIBI

The favourite defence of the crime suspect in both fact and fiction is to show that he was elsewhere at the time the alleged offence was committed — in other words, to prove an alibi (Latin for 'elsewhere'). The device is frequently worked in detective fiction to save the hero, and to condemn the villain by showing up his false alibi.

In real life the idea has been so overworked in the courts, with suspects 'springing' last-minute alibis and producing supporting witnesses, that the law has taken steps to regulate the practice. For example, modern police investigators take statements from all persons likely to be called to speak for an accused in court before the question of establishing an alibi is raised. In this way any subsequent attempts by witnesses to mislead can easily be checked. English law also requires that notice of an alibi is given in advance of a trial on indictment, and the names of any persons called to testify must also be given.

Hans Gross, the pioneering Austrian criminologist, said that the false alibi is 'certainly the most dangerous obstacle to the conviction of the real malefactor'. The false alibi is more easily rebutted by modern investigative procedures, but the defence of 'being elsewhere' has featured prominently in a number of murder trials. James Hanratty was convicted of the A6 Murder after a trial involving controversial identification and alibi evidence. On 22 August 1961 a married man and his lover in their parked car were surprised by a man who threatened them with a gun and ordered them to drive to a lay-by on the A6 road at Deadman's Hill. There the man was shot dead, and his girl-friend raped and severely wounded.

James Hanratty was arrested in Blackpool. He was put on trial for murder, and his fate hinged on doubts about IDENTIFICATION and on his alibi, which placed him in Liverpool at the time the murder was committed. On the grounds that he did not want to betray their trust, Hanratty refused to name the friends who could substantiate his alibi. Then he inexplicably changed — and thereby weakened — his alibi story by saying he stayed not at Liverpool but at Rhyl in North Wales. Again there were no witnesses. The man whose identification as the murderer was in doubt,

established their ages as about six to seven and three to four. The adipocere (which was complete, save for the feet) had also preserved their stomachs and internal organs. The STOMACH CONTENTS in each case contained vegetables which were recognizable ingredients of Scotch broth. This discovery, combined with the extensive adipocerous formation, enabled the pathologist to speculate about TIME OF DEATH; he thought they had probably taken their last meal about one hour before they died, and that death had occurred during the late summer or early autumn of 1911. Smith believed the boys lived locally, and surmised that they had walked to the quarry unsuspectingly with their killer.

He advised the police of these findings, and within days the boys were identified as two children missing from the district, and their father, Patrick Higgins, a widower, was arrested. Higgins was tried for murder at Edinburgh in controversial proceedings which centred on his state of mind and a defence based on a history of EPILEPSY. Despite the contention that he killed while the balance of his mind was disturbed, he was found guilty and sentenced to death. Higgins was hanged in

and whose alibi if properly corroborated might have saved him, was found guilty and later hanged.

Another murder trial in which the accused man's alibi was a central feature was the Wallace case. William Herbert Wallace, a quiet man who worked as an insurance agent in Liverpool, returned home on 20 January 1931 to find his wife's brutally murdered body. Wallace was the chief suspect, and he was duly sent for trial. The controversial elements of his court ordeal were evidence concerning RIGOR MORTIS of the victim and his alibi.

A message was left the previous evening at his Chess Club asking that he call on a person named R. M. Qualtrough, whose address was given as 25 Menlove Gardens East in Liverpool's Mossley Hill district. Wallace claimed that he knew neither the name nor the address, but assuming the message was in connection with insurance business, set out to find Qualtrough. After nearly two hours of fruitless searching for the address he gave up and returned home to find his wife dead in the parlour.

There was no street in Liverpool called Menlove Gardens East, although Menlove Gardens West, North and South did exist, and no person by the name of Qualtrough could be traced. There was no doubt, however, that a man had telephoned the Chess Club and left the message for Wallace. The prosecution contended that Wallace contrived the story in order to provide an alibi for the time of the murder. Key elements in the period leading up to the murder were the pathologist's estimate of the time of death (nearer 6.0 p.m. than 7.0 p.m.), the milk-boy's evidence that he had seen Mrs Wallace alive at 6.30 p.m. and witnesses who had seen Wallace during his search for Menlove Gardens East. The milk-boy's evidence plainly contradicted the pathologist, and when the timings are set out graphically it can be seen that Wallace appeared to have a mere 18 minutes in which to murder his wife and tidy up.

Despite the defence claim that the prosecution's case was based on CIRCUMSTANTIAL EVIDENCE, Wallace's alibi failed, and the trial jury found him

TIME	WITNESSES' EVIDENCE	WALLACE'S EVIDENCE
5.55 p.m.	Wallace dealing with insurance business in Eastman Road	
6.05		Wallace arrived home for tea
*6.30	Milk-boy saw Mrs Wallace alive	
*6.45		Wallace left home to look for Menlove Gardens East
7.06	Wallace seen boarding a tram two miles from his home	
7.15	Wallace seen boarding another tram heading for the Menlove Gardens area	
7.45	Wallace asked directions from a police constable	
7.52	Wallace consulted a street directory in a newspaper shop	
8.45	Wallace returned home, spoke to his neighbours and found his wife dead	

*These are the vital times. A reconstruction of the milk-boy's round put his sighting of Mrs Wallace at 6.31 — it might have been later — and the latest that Wallace could have left home to catch the tram was 6.49 — leaving eighteen minutes for him to commit murder.

Reginald Gordon Parry: did he kill Julia Wallace?

guilty. He was sentenced to death, but, in a decision which made legal history in Britain, his conviction was quashed on appeal. The grounds were that the trial verdict was not supported by the evidence. Wallace became a free man, but also the subject of malicious gossip. He died of kidney disease in 1933.

In 1981, fifty years after Wallace had been tried for murder, the name of the likely murderer of his wife came to light. In a radio programme devoted to the case by Liverpool's Radio City, John Parks, an elderly contemporary of Wallace, reiterated publicly what he had told the police in 1931. In the early hours of the morning following Julia Wallace's death a man brought a car into the all-night garage where he worked, and instructed him to clean it inside and out. The car-owner was 22-year-old Richard Gordon Parry, an insurance agent and local 'wide-boy'. Parry appeared agitated. There was blood in the car, and when Parks came across a bloodstained glove Parry snatched it from him, declaring, 'If the police

found that it would hang me.' He also blurted out that he had dropped an iron bar down a grating in Priory Street.

After Parry had driven off in his clean car and news broke of the murder which had transpired earlier, Parks told his employer about the incident which had occurred at the garage. The police were

Parry's signature

informed, and an officer visited the garage to question Parks. Wallace also mentioned Parry's name to the police, but for a different reason. The two men had worked for the same insurance company until Wallace discovered that the younger man had defrauded the agents' collection money of £30, as a result of which Parry was dismissed. This easily corroborated incident provided a possible grudge MOTIVE and, coupled with Parks's statement, caused the police to question Parry and search his home. Parry's alibi was that he was with his girl-friend at the material time. Although she substantiated this story initially, her support for it was later withdrawn. Independent witnesses confirmed that Parks had told the police of his suspicions, but in the event the authorities chose to believe Parry's alibi and discount Wallace's.

Parry retired to Wales in the mid 1970s where he died, leaving no account of his own to clear up the mystery. The police refused the radio programme access to the case files, so that it was not possible to confirm Parry's guilt and take the case out of the ranks of UNSOLVED MURDERS. There remains the strong feeling that an innocent man was hounded to an early grave while the real murderer was let off the hook.

9, 16, 54, 87, 139, 182, 194, 218, 222, 229, 242, 265, 356, 387, 438, 455, 457, 500, 503, 525, 591, 598, 622, 694, 754.

AMNESIA

The attractions of answering a criminal charge by saying, 'I don't remember' have doubtless occurred to many felons as a first line of defence. In itself it is no answer, but genuine loss of control caused by an illness such as EPILEPSY has been successfully argued in a murder trial. So too has the possibility of someone being killed by a person who is asleep — in effect, in an amnesic state.

A case which made legal history in England was the trial for murder of Günter Fritz Podola, a German-born petty criminal, who killed a police officer in London. In July 1959 Podola burgled a flat in South Kensington, stealing jewellery and furs, and later tried to blackmail the owner. He posed as a private detective, and hoped to cause

The room in which police seized Podola

embarrassment with photographs and tape-recordings. The lady in question simply called the police, and when the would-be blackmailer phoned again his call was traced. Within minutes two detectives were at the call-box. Podola spotted them, and ran off towards a near-by block of flats where he was caught. While his companion went off to fetch their patrol car Detective Sergeant Raymond Purdy stayed with Podola, who pulled a gun, shot him dead and escaped.

IDENTIFICATION was made by palm-prints left by Podola on a window-ledge at the block of flats, and he was traced to a hotel in South Kensington. On 16 July a number of policemen approached the door of his room and shouted, 'Police! Open the door.' No reply was given, so the door was broken down and after a struggle Podola, who had been knocked over, was taken to hospital apparently suffering partial loss of consciousness. When he recovered he said he could remember nothing of the murder on account of amnesia resulting from the injuries he received at the time of capture.

At his trial for murder in September Podola's counsel entered a plea, never before raised in an English court, that the accused was unfit to plead on the grounds of amnesia. This matter had to be settled before the trial could begin, and a jury was especially empanelled for the task. The evidence put forward was that the defendant was suffering a genuine loss of memory which had expunged from his mind the events of 16 July 1959, and also blotted out memories of thirty years of his life. Specialists could find no evidence of any structural damage to his brain, and it was argued that his condition was dissociation of memory, a state which it was not in the patient's power to control. Of the six doctors who examined Podola, four considered he was suffering from amnesia and two thought he was malingering. All agreed he was sane. The jury concluded that the accused was not suffering from genuine loss of memory, and Mr Justice Edmund Davies directed them to find Podola fit to stand trial. A second jury was then empanelled for the trial proceedings, which turned out to be brief. Podola continued to insist that he was suffering from loss of memory, and consequently was unable to brief his counsel on any new line of defence. At the conclusion of the prosecution's case against him he made a statement in which he said, 'All I can say in my defence is that I do not remember having committed the crime I stand accused of.' After an absence of little more than half an hour the jury returned a guilty verdict and Podola was sentenced to death.

Between the trial and appeal, and again while in the death cell, Podola conveniently regained his memory. In any case, it was a widely held opinion that he had given himself away in a letter written while he was in custody. In dismissing his appeal the judge said, 'Even if the loss of memory had been a genuine loss of memory, that did not itself render the appellant insane.' Podola was hanged in November 1959.

202, 233, 241, 291, 367, 369, 389, 709.

ANTIMONY

'Now, gentlemen, antimony is a well-known poison, but although in the pharmacopoeia it is rarely used now, its effects are well-known. It is spoken of as a poison that has certain fine and well-known characteristics, and it is generally used in the form of tartar emetic. . . .' declared Mr Justice Graham in his summing up to the JURY at the trial of George Chapman for murder in 1903. Chapman, a powerful, Nietzschean-looking figure in the dock, was the son of a Polish carpenter whose real name was Severin Klosowski. He was a sinister character with experience as a barber-surgeon which had led to the speculation that he was JACK THE RIPPER.

What is certain is that he bought a quantity of tartar emetic in 1895, which he signed for in the poisons book of a Hastings chemist. Shortly before this, while working at Leytonstone as a barber, he had gone through a form of marriage with Mary Isabella Spink, who had separated from her husband. Mrs Spink had private means which enabled Chapman to set up his own shop in Hastings and then to take the lease of the Prince of Wales Tavern in Bartholomew Square, off the City Road in London's East End. After a few months of this new life Mary Spink's health began to deteriorate. She suffered severe attacks of vomiting and diarrhoea, and after becoming extremely weak died on Christmas Day 1897. The grieving Chapman received a wreath for his late wife subscribed to by the Prince of Wales's customers.

A few months later Chapman advertised for a barmaid, and he appointed Bessie Taylor to the position. This healthy young woman was 'married' to Chapman, and they moved first to Bishop's Stortford and then back to London to run the Monument Tavern in Union Street, Borough. Bessie's health now began to fail — she grew thinner, and Chapman was violent toward her. She suffered vomiting and diarrhoea, and her doctor appeared helpless. She died of exhaustion on 13 February 1901. Six months later Chapman advertised for a barmaid, and took on Maud Marsh, who in no time at all reported to her father that her employer was 'paying her attentions'. In due course the customers at the Monument were able to celebrate the landlord's 'marriage' to Maud.

Soon 'Mrs Chapman' began to suffer from vomiting, diarrhoea and abdominal pains which mysteriously abated when she was admitted to hospital, although the doctors were unable to specify the cause. The distressing symptoms returned when she was restored to her 'husband', and she grew so weak that she was unable to swallow any solid food at all. Her mother came to look after her, and was taken ill after sipping a brandy and soda prepared by Chapman for Maud, but which the sick woman declined to drink. The first small seed of suspicion was thus sown. By this time Chapman had moved to the Crown in Union Street, Borough, and it was there that Maud died on 22 October 1902. Suspicion that she had been poisoned strengthened, and the doctor refused to issue a DEATH CERTIFICATE. An unofficial POST-MORTEM examination was carried out, and after arsenic was found in the stomach of the dead woman the authorities were informed.

A second post-mortem was carried out, and Dr Thomas Stevenson, Home Office analyst, concluded that death had been caused by antimony poisoning. The earlier finding of ARSENIC was correct up to a point, for the poison was present in a small quantity as an impurity in the antimony — it was not in itself the fatal agent. Dr Stevenson in his report made reference to the remarkable state of preservation of the body. This was the first occasion on which this characteristic of antimony — which it shares with arsenic — had been recorded.

The effects of arsenical and antimonial poisoning are similar. Both poisons are irritants, and give rise to symptoms easily mistaken for gastro-enteritis. Antimony is colourless, odourless and practically tasteless, and as tartar emetic is easily soluble in water. Tartar emetic (potassium antimonyl tartrate) was the most readily available form of antimony in Chapman's day. It was used in weak doses (1/24th of a grain) to ease coughing, to move bowels and to stimulate perspiration; in larger doses, as its name suggests, it produces vomiting. These characteristics of its action were important to the would-be poisoner, for if too large a dose was given vomiting would result, and the poison itself would be expelled from the victim's stomach, with little harm resulting. Consequently, the successful antimony poisoner works with small doses.

The fatal dose of antimony varies considerably; 1·5 grains has caused death, but instances have been recorded where as much as 400 grains have been taken without fatal effect. Antimony is excreted more rapidly than arsenic, so the cumulative effect is less. In chronic poisoning repeated small doses cause loss of appetite, which combined with vomiting and purging leads to emaciation and general debilitation. The poison also depresses the heart and breathing action, with death likely to occur as a result of heart-failure. The catalogue of symptoms is more violent than in arsenical poisoning, with constriction of the throat and muscle cramps adding to the victim's distress.

Chapman's systematic use of antimony produced these symptoms in all three of his victims. The bodies of Mary Spink and Bessie Taylor were exhumed — 3·83 grains of antimony were found in the former, and 29·12 in the latter. Maud Marsh had 20·12 grains of poison in her body. The Reinsch and Marsh Tests used for arsenic also apply to antimony. George Chapman was tried for the murder of Maud Marsh, and was convicted. He protested his innocence to the last, but he was hanged in April 1903.

Antimony poisoning is comparatively rare, but the few murder cases involving its use have been notable. Doctors Palmer and Pritchard employed it for HOMICIDE when its effects were not too well understood, and it appeared a safer poison than arsenic. The trials of both doctors brought together some powerful figures from the world of forensic medicine. In the case of Palmer, the financially embarrassed race-goer, whom the English regard as specially infamous, Dr Alfred Swaine Taylor and Professor Robert Christison gave expert testimony. Their evidence was that although 0·5 grains of antimony were found in the body of the murdered man, John Parsons Cook, his symptoms were those of STRYCHNINE poisoning. In the case of Pritchard, the ex-assistant naval surgeon with an excess of vanity, two celebrated Edinburgh experts appeared for his prosecutors, Professor Douglas Maclagan and Dr Henry Littlejohn.

In October 1864 Mrs Mary Jane Pritchard, a hitherto healthy woman aged thirty-eight, fell ill

The letter which pointed suspicion at Dr Pritchard

Glasgow March 18th 1865

Sir

Dr Pritchards' Mother in law
died Suddenly and unexpectedly
about three weeks ago in his house
Sauchiehall Street Glasgow under
Circumstances at least very Suspicious
His Wife died to-day also suddenly
and unexpectedly and under circumstances equally Suspicious. We think
it right to draw Your attention to
the above as the proper person to
take action in the matter and See
justice done,

To Hunt Esq

Yours &
Amor Justitiae

with headaches, vomiting and cramps. She was treated by her husband, who decided to call in a second opinion. Gastric fever was suggested, but the other doctor was puzzled. As Mrs Pritchard's condition failed to improve, her mother, Mrs Taylor, decided to come to Glasgow to nurse her. Within two weeks of arriving in the Pritchard household, this once sturdy lady of seventy years was dead of a seizure. Again, Pritchard had called in another doctor, James Paterson, who lived close by, and who was told that Mrs Taylor 'was in the habit of taking a drop'. Dr Paterson did not think Mrs Taylor was drunk when she was taken ill, but he did think she might have been drugged with opium. After Mrs Taylor's demise on 25 February 1865 Pritchard asked Dr Paterson to issue a death certificate. This he declined to do, and instead wrote to the District Registrar saying that the death 'was sudden, unexpected and to me mysterious'. No notice was taken of this warning, and to all intents and purposes Mrs Taylor had died of gastric fever.

Having buried his mother-in-law, Pritchard now resumed nursing his wife, who continued to complain of a burning sensation in the throat, of intense thirst and vomiting. Her deterioration was quick, and on 18 March, with her husband lying in bed beside her, Mrs Pritchard died. Her death was certified by her husband as gastric fever, but before Pritchard could get her buried an anonymous letter arrived on the desk of the Procurator-Fiscal. This simply drew attention to the two SUDDEN DEATHS which had occurred in Pritchard's house. The doctor was arrested, and Maclagan and Littlejohn carried out a POST-MORTEM on his wife's body — organs were removed for analysis. By means of the Reinsch Test antimony in the form of tartar emetic was found in the urine, bile, blood, liver, kidneys and other organs.

Mrs Taylor's body was exhumed, and various organs and body fluids were analysed — again quantities of antimony as tartar emetic were found. The presentation of the scientific evidence at Pritchard's trial for murder, which began in Edinburgh on 3 July 1865, was meticulous, and left no doubt that Mrs Pritchard had died as a result of antimony given in the form of small doses of tartar emetic over a long period. There was ample evidence of the doctor's purchase of poison in a Glasgow apothecary's records which showed two sales, each for an ounce of tartar emetic, on 16 November 1864 and 7 February 1865. Dr Pritchard was convicted, and while in the death cell made three CONFESSIONS. In the last of these

he said, 'I am guilty of the death of my mother-in-law, Mrs Taylor, and of my wife', adding, 'I can assign no motive for the conduct which actuated me, beyond a species of "terrible madness".' He was hanged in Glasgow in July 1865 before a large crowd — the last man to be publicly executed in Scotland.

Another great Victorian poisoning case involving antimony was the Bravo affair. Charles Bravo was taken ill in his home, The Priory, Balham, on the night of 18 April 1876, after he had retired to bed in the room which he occupied separately from his wife Florence. Bravo was heard calling loudly for his wife to fetch hot water. The maid answered the call, and found her master distressed, after having vomited violently. Mrs Cox, Florence Bravo's living-in companion, also appeared on the scene, and Bravo collapsed unconscious. Mrs Bravo was roused from her sleep, and the doctor was sent for. He suspected POISONING, but was unable to identify the cause — Mrs Cox had informed him that Bravo told her he had taken poison, and CHLOROFORM was mentioned. Chloroform, laudanum and camphor liniment were the only medicines known to be in the house. Other doctors were called — all were convinced Bravo was dying from the effects of an irritant poison. When the sick man recovered consciousness all he would say in answer to questions was that he had rubbed his gums with laudanum. 'That won't explain your symptoms,' he was told firmly.

Bravo continued to suffer severe abdominal pain, accompanied by vomiting and diarrhoea — vomited matter was tested for arsenic, but with negative results. In all five doctors were consulted, but their efforts combined with those of his wife could not ascertain from the stricken man what he had taken. In desperation Florence Bravo called in Sir William Gull, who had distinguished himself by diagnosing the Prince of Wales's illness a few years earlier. Gull told Bravo, 'This is not a disease. You are poisoned; pray tell me how you came by it?' The great man received the same reply as his colleagues — laudanum. The fight to save Bravo finished when he died on 21 April after days of intense suffering. No death-certificate was issued, and an inquest was ordered.

Following a post-mortem examination, an analysis was made of vomited matter taken from the sick-room and fluid from the dead man's intestines. Professor Theophilus Redwood of the Pharmaceutical Society of Great Britain reported that death had resulted from antimony in the form of tartar emetic taken in a single dose of between 20 and 30 grains. The first inquest returned a verdict consistent with the analytical findings, but concluded there was insufficient evidence to show how the poison had entered the body. It was widely concluded that Charles Bravo had committed suicide.

A second inquest was conducted which practically developed into a trial of Florence Bravo and Mrs Cox, with evidence heavy in domestic intrigue. It became known that Mrs Bravo had an affair with an elderly physician, Doctor Gully, and that Mrs Cox had quarrelled with Charles Bravo. A verdict of wilful murder was returned, with the rider that the evidence was insufficient to fix the guilt upon any person or persons. That tartar emetic was used at the Priory was established when it was shown that two ounces of the drug had been bought by Mrs Bravo's coachman from a Malvern chemist. The coachman, whom Mrs Bravo had dismissed in January 1876, said he used the substance as 'horse medicine', in accordance with farriers' practice, to condition their animals.

Man's use of antimony predates the Christian era by thousands of years. Egyptian women employed it in cosmetics, and in a later era monks used it to deal with the effects of fasting by reducing the appetite, frequently being fatally poisoned in the process!

1, 14, 25, 79, 88, 98, 112, 161, 169, 177, 196, 200, 206, 225, 256, 304, 309, 315, 337, 347, 357, 415, 469, 491, 536, 541, 581, 582, 589, 666, 696, 734.

ARSENIC

A metallic poison known since ancient times which became the poisoner's favourite agent. An eighth-century Arab alchemist produced arsenious oxide, a white, odourless powder with highly poisonous qualities, from realgar, a naturally occurring ore found in lead and iron mining. He thus made available one of history's most widely administered poisons. A form of arsenic had been used in Imperial Rome to such an extent that men of affairs found it necessary to employ food-tasters, and during the Italian Renaissance it became the poison of princes in the hands of the Borgias. The terrible reputation of the poison was such that in France it became known as *poudre de succession*, or 'inheritance powder'.

Arsenic possesses numerous qualities which endear it to the calculating mind of the poisoner. It looks harmless, passing for flour or sugar, and its virtual lack of taste makes it easy to disguise in food. The symptoms it produces in the victim — vomiting and diarrhoea — are characteristic of a number of ordinary illnesses. Moreover, its effect is cumulative, so that the poisoner does not have to rely on one large, fatal dose: he can give it little and often, thereby weakening his victim by stages before delivering the fatal dose. Again, the symptoms of chronic arsenical poisoning — stomach upsets, dermatitis and discoloration — may easily be attributed to other causes. For centuries there was no means of detecting arsenic in the body of a suspected victim, while prosecution was not possible unless there was clear evidence linking the purchase or administration of the poison to the suspect.

In time arsenic acquired further useful attributes by being widely available in a number of household products, such as the green dye in wallpaper, in rat-poison, weed-killer and fly-papers, and in medicinal tonics and cosmetic preparations. It also found uses in glass-making, sheep-dips, taxidermy and dyeing. Thus a most effective poison was within any person's grasp, and the poisoner need exercise no special ingenuity to obtain it.

Arsenic has featured in many celebrated murder cases around the world, most usually in domestic situations for the removal of an unwanted spouse or rival. Each case has pushed the science of detection to new limits, and to a point where arsenic, once the king of poisons, has been deposed. In 1752 31-year-old spinster Mary Blandy was tried at Oxford for murdering her father with poison. She admitted putting powder into his tea to 'procure his love' — powder which she claimed to be a philtre to sweeten the old man's attitude to her liaison with her lover, Captain William Cranstoun. Her court appearance was the first trial for murder by poison at which medical evidence was called in regard to the cause of death. Dr Anthony Addington did not possess the knowledge to analyse the victim's organs for poison, nor was he able to use chemical tests to prove that the powder Mary used was arsenic. Nevertheless, on the basis of simple comparison he convinced the court that the powder was arsenic, and Mary Blandy was convicted and sentenced to death.

Twenty-three years after Mary was hanged — not too high 'for the sake of decency', as she instructed the hangman — a Swedish chemist made an important discovery. Karl Wilhelm Scheele found that he could change arsenious

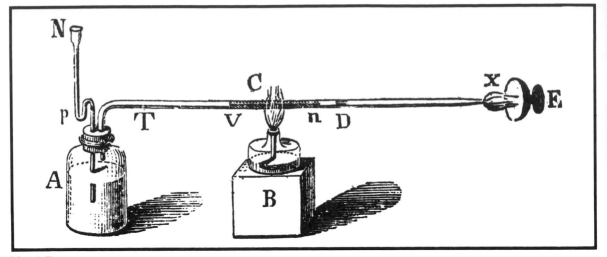

Marsh Test apparatus

oxide to arsenious acid, which in contact with zinc produced arsine, a highly poisonous gas. This discovery was later to play a great part in the arsenic story, but in the meantime the chemistry of poisons was being developed in France by Dr Mathieu Orfila. In 1813 he published his *Traité des poisons*, which quickly became an authoritative work, and eventually won its author recognition as the father of the new science of toxicology.

Scheele's work was pursued by scientists in Germany, but the break-through was provided by an English chemist, James Marsh. In 1836 he published a method for converting arsenic in body tissues and fluids into arsine gas by means of a simple apparatus which recovered the poison as a metallic mirror on a piece of porcelain. The process was unbelievably sensitive, making it possible to detect as little as a fiftieth of a milligram of arsenic (three-thousandths of a grain). The Marsh Test revolutionized the investigation of poisoning, and it was quickly taken up by crime scientists.

In 1840 the Marsh Test was used in the celebrated Lafarge poisoning case. In January of that year Charles Lafarge, a minor French industrialist, died of suspected poisoning at his home in Le Glandier. Arsenious acid was found in his stomach, and it became known that his wife, Marie, had bought arsenic as rat-poison. She was arrested and sent for trial. The application of new scientific methods proved traumatic, for when the Marsh Test was applied to corroborate earlier findings of arsenic by traditional methods the results proved negative. The elation of the defence was short-lived, as the experts declared that the

test worked better on organs other than the stomach. EXHUMATION of Lafarge's body was carried out for the purpose of retrieving these other organs for testing. Once again the Marsh Test proved negative, although arsenic was found in various foodstuffs taken from the house at Le Glandier, including 'enough to poison at least ten persons' in some egg-nog.

With the proceedings apparently at stalemate, the court sent word to Orfila requesting him to give his opinion. He gathered together all the experts who had worked on the case, and re-examined all the vital materials with the original test reagents. Behind the locked doors of an anteroom in the courthouse he applied the Marsh Test correctly, whereas his predecessors had bungled the procedure, and demonstrated the undoubted presence of arsenic in all the test organs.

Orfila's report was a model of its kind, and it sealed Marie Lafarge's fate. 'I shall prove,' he said, 'first, that there is arsenic in the body of Lafarge; second, that this arsenic comes neither from the reagents with which we worked nor from the earth surrounding the coffin; also, that the arsenic we found is not the arsenic component which is naturally found in every human body.' The great man had spoken, and the court had no difficulty in finding Marie Lafarge guilty.

In an attempt to control the availability of poison Britain passed the Arsenic Act in 1851. This restricted shop sales to persons over the age of twenty-one and known to the seller. The details of every purchase were to be recorded in a poisons book, and — most importantly — before sale arsenic must be coloured with soot or indigo in the proportions of at least one ounce to a pound of arsenic. This did not prevent Madeleine Smith buying arsenic 'for the garden and country house' from a Glasgow chemist in 1857. The chemist subsequently reported that '. . . it was common white arsenic, mixed with soot in the proportion required by the Act'.

When Pierre L'Angelier, Madeleine's lover, was taken ill for the third time at his lodgings he demonstrated all the symptoms associated with acute arsenical poisoning — vomiting, diarrhoea, general weakness, jaundice and a quick pulse. After he died a miserable, lonely death in March his stomach was removed at a POST-MORTEM, and the organ and its contents were examined by Dr Frederick Penny, Professor of Chemistry in Glasgow's Andersonian University. He found 82 grains of arsenic in the stomach — one of the largest doses ever recorded. This discovery triggered off one of the most celebrated and controversial poison cases brought to trial.

Incriminating letters from Madeleine found among the dead man's possessions pointed the finger of suspicion at the girl. A picture emerged of a tormented love-affair, with marriage between an architect's daughter and a lowly packing-clerk absolutely ruled out. The threat of exposure hung over Madeleine after she had ignored her father's instructions not to see L'Angelier, and also continued the flow of damaging correspondence. Moreover, in accordance with her parents' wishes she had promised herself to another man.

With passions aroused, and the air thick with L'Angelier's recriminations and threats, Madeleine had a motive for murder. But like James Maybrick — who was later to follow him to a poison victim's grave — L'Angelier had a liking for drug-taking, including arsenic-eating. He told acquaintances that he took arsenic regularly, presumably to improve the complexion and give an outward appearance of robust health. Certainly this would have been consistent with his vain nature. If it could be shown that L'Angelier possessed arsenic for his own use it became possible to suggest that he took his own life in desperation at the prospect of losing Madeleine. In any event, despite the blackening of her character in court, the gentle-looking Miss Smith created sufficient doubt in the minds of the Scottish jury to bring in a verdict of NOT PROVEN.

That regular use of arsenic builds up a tolerance without causing harm has been borne out by the arsenic-eating habits of Austrian miners in the province of Styria. Iron has been mined in this area since Roman times, and with it realgar, an arsenic-bearing ore. It was common practice in Styrian mining communities in the nineteenth century for the men to eat arsenic for strength and the women to improve their complexions. An instance was reported in 1880 of a Styrian woodcutter who regularly ate five grains of white arsenic without coming to any harm — two grains (130 milligrams) is a recognized fatal dose. Arsenical cosmetic preparations grew in popularity throughout Europe, and many women applied lotions and creams to their skin to improve its tone and remove blemishes. Fowler's Solution (weak arsenious acid, originally used as a treatment for intermittent fever) came into vogue as a tonic, and was widely prescribed for both sexes.

James Maybrick, a Liverpool business-man, believed that arsenic was an aphrodisiac, and he told his friends that he took it regularly: 'It is meat and liquor to me,' he said. Against the wishes of his family, he married an American woman twenty-four years younger than himself. Florie was a lively person who took none too kindly to her husband's double standards when she found out that he had a mistress. There were arguments, and Maybrick threatened to cut Florie out of his will. Their marriage suffered, and in 1889 Florie sought the warm embraces of a lover. Her pompous husband was furious when he found out, and he gave her a black eye.

A short while after this episode Florie bought a dozen fly-papers from a local chemist, followed by a further two dozen bought five days later at another shop. On 28 April 1889 James Maybrick was taken ill, and he died on 11 May; Florie mentioned to the doctor that he had been taking a 'white powder'. Arsenic was found in Maybrick's stomach, and following the discovery in Florie's room of a packet labelled 'Arsenic: Poison for cats' his wife was arrested and charged with murder.

Florence Maybrick was tried at Liverpool, and in addition to the hostility of her late husband's family she suffered the humiliation of being branded an unfaithful wife. Her defence was that Maybrick had died as a result of his own hypochondriac dosing — traces of STRYCHNINE, HYOSCINE and MORPHINE were found in his body. But there was damning evidence against her. A bottle of Valentine's beef juice used to feed the sick man had been subjected to the Marsh Test and found to be positive for arsenic. Florie explained that her husband had begged her to give him some

Mrs Maybrick's prescription for an arsenical face-wash

of the white powder he was in the habit of taking. At first she refused him, but then she relented and, not knowing what the powder was, put some into the bottle. With regard to the fly-papers Florie said she used them to prepare a face-wash which had been prescribed for her by an American doctor as a treatment for a 'slight eruption of the face'. As the analyst told the grand jury, one fly-paper soaked in water for twenty-four hours produced enough arsenic in solution to poison any ordinary person.

Less than half a grain of arsenic was found in Maybrick's body, but this was sufficient to condemn his wife. Statements attesting to Maybrick's affinity for arsenic (including the sensational admission made to a person who saw him sprinkling powder on his food: 'I take this arsenic once in a while because I find it strengthens me') won no favours with the judge, Sir James Fitzjames Stephen. He summed up against Florence Maybrick and she was found guilty, sentence of death being commuted to life imprisonment. She was not released for fifteen years, and like Madeleine Smith she died in America.

Despite improvements in the detection of poisons, the twentieth century has seen a number of murders by arsenical poisoning. Certainly there has seemed to be little difficulty in obtaining supplies of the poison. Arsenical fly-papers featured in the Seddon case (1912), weed-killer in

the trials of Greenwood (1920), Armstrong (1922) and Bryant (1936), cat-poison in the case of de Melker (1932), ant-poison in the trial of Groesbeek (1969), while in the case of Besnard (1952–61) there was definitely no shortage of arsenic. Perhaps the two most outstanding cases were those of Armstrong and Besnard, the former on account of the strength of the expert evidence and the latter because of its weakness.

Herbert Rowse Armstrong, an ex-Army officer, was a practising solicitor in Hay-on-Wye. His wife Katharine was a hypochondriac and a nagger, so he slowly poisoned her; she died on 22 February 1921. Although in retrospect Mrs Armstrong's illness bore all the signs of chronic arsenical poisoning — loss of weight, nausea, diarrhoea, loss of hair, peripheral neuritis and pigmentation of the skin — her death was recorded as due to gastritis and she was buried without fuss.

Later in the year, Major Armstrong found himself in dispute with a fellow Hay solicitor, Oswald Martin, and made an attempt on his life with a poisoned scone. Suspicion aroused by Martin's illness was heightened by the knowledge that Armstrong had bought arsenic from the local chemist, who also happened to be Martin's father-in-law. The local doctor who had attended Mrs Armstrong was called in and, with the knowledge that arsenic is excreted from the body principally through the kidneys, a sample of Martin's urine was taken for analysis. This proved positive for arsenic, and the mechanics of a major investigation were set in motion.

An EXHUMATION order was granted, and a POST-MORTEM performed on Mrs Armstrong's body by Sir Bernard Spilsbury showed that she was riddled with arsenic — a total of 208 milligrams was found. The body was in a remarkable state of preservation, bearing in mind that it had lain buried for ten months. This too is a feature of arsenical poisoning, which has the effect of partly mummifying the corpse. Armstrong — already in custody for the attempted murder of Martin — was tried for wife-murder. Masterly medical evidence was presented by Spilsbury, supported by Sir William Willcox, Medical Adviser to the Home Office.

The Major went into the witness-box, but gave a poor account of his use of arsenic for killing weeds. Above all, he was unable to account convincingly for a packet of arsenic found in his coat-pocket when he was arrested. The inescapable conclusion was that he had this ready for a further attempt on the life of Martin, whom he had been pestering with invitations to tea. Armstrong was found guilty, and gained the doubtful distinction of being the only solicitor to be hanged for murder in Britain (in May 1922).

If the scientific evidence in the Armstrong trial was assured, that in the Besnard case faltered from the beginning. The 55-year-old Marie Besnard, whom the Press called 'The black widow of Loudon', was charged with twelve murders by arsenic, and subjected to three trials in the space of ten years before being acquitted. It was an extraordinary case from any point of view. Madame Besnard's second husband died of a heart-attack in 1947. His demise was followed by an anonymous letter sent to the public prosecutor alleging that Léon Besnard had confided his fear that he was being poisoned by his wife. His body was exhumed, and arsenic found. Suspicion now loomed large in the minds of the French authorities, and a spate of exhumations ensued. These included Marie Besnard's first husband, her mother, father, mother-in-law, father-in-law and other relatives and acquaintances — in each case arsenic was found.

Marie Besnard was tried for murder on twelve counts at Poitiers in 1952. Despite a great deal of malicious rumour, no one was able to come forward and testify that she had been seen using arsenic. The greater part of the proceedings was taken up by expert evidence. Dr George Béroud, Director of the Police Laboratory at Marseilles, described the long series of analyses he had undertaken, using the Marsh Test and other methods. Maître Albert Gautrat, defending Madame Besnard, set out to discredit the toxicological evidence. He asserted that the specimen jars used to collect the various test samples were dirty, and he trapped Béroud into saying that he could distinguish between arsenic and ANTIMONY with the naked eye, and then demonstrated in court that he could not!

The first round of scientific evidence was thus discredited, and the court appointed new experts to study the case. Fresh exhumations were ordered to obtain new test materials under the supervision of Professor René Piédelièvre, a distinguished forensic scientist. Two years later Marie Besnard was put on trial again. In reality it was more a trial of scientific methods and the skills of the lawyers. Doubt was again cast on the toxicological methods used, principally the application of new radio-chemical techniques to establish the presence of

fatal quantities of arsenic in the hair of the exhumed bodies. The challenge was made on the grounds that this new method was untried, and Gautrat introduced testimony showing it was possible, as a result of bacterial activity, for arsenic to be assimilated by hair from the soil in a grave. Deadlock was reached again.

The court decided to assemble a fresh set of experts, and Frédéric Joliot-Curie, the Nobel Prize winner, was asked to check the earlier radio-chemical analysis for arsenic. He concluded that there had been inaccuracies; the arguments about arsenic in the soil of Loudon dragged on for another seven years. Finally, in 1961, a third trial was held. It was quite clear that the whole affair had become an argument between experts about research findings. Marie Besnard's defence lawyers pressed the point that there was no direct evidence to incriminate her, and contended that fourteen years of inquiry had led to one conclusion — the only explanation for arsenic in the bodies exhumed at Loudon was that it came from the soil in the cemetery. Marie Besnard was acquitted of the charges of murder.

'One of the coolest murders by arsenic that ever came to lie in my crime files' was how Professor Keith Simpson described the Radford case. In 1949 Margery Radford had suffered for seven years from tuberculosis, and lay near to death in a Surrey sanatorium. A few days before she died Mrs Radford had been ill with vomiting after eating food bought specially for her by her husband. The latest was a fruit-pie, and knowing that her husband was consorting with another woman, and possibly wanted to hasten her end, she spoke to a friend. 'I am sure it has been poisoned,' she said, referring to the pie, and asked for the remaining piece to be analysed. The friend sent the pie to the superintendent of the sanatorium, and posted a letter separately explaining the circumstances. On finding a piece of fruit-pie in his office the unsuspecting superintendent ate some of it with near-disastrous consequences. He was extremely ill, and when he returned to work and read the letter waiting for him he immediately called the police.

The remains of the pie were analysed, and found to contain 3·25 grains of potassium arsenite. Mrs Radford — who had died in the meantime — had 6·5 grains of arsenic in her body. The tendency of arsenic to linger in the HAIR provides a calendar of the period over which poisoning has taken place. Mrs Radford's hair contained arsenic extending for a distance of five centimetres from the base. As

SOME FAMOUS ARSENIC POISON CASES

YEAR	COUNTRY	PERSONS ACCUSED	VICTIMS	FATE
1676	France	Marquise de BRINVILLIERS	100+	Decapitated
1752	England	Mary BLANDY	1 (father)	Hanged
1811	Germany	Anne Marie ZWANZIGER	11	Beheaded
1840	France	Marie LAFARGE	1 (husband)	Imprisoned
1844	Scotland	Christina GILMOUR	1 (husband)	Not proven
1851	France	Hélène JEGADO	23	Guillotined
1857	Scotland	Madeleine SMITH	1 (lover)	Not proven
1859	Canada	Dr William KING	1 (wife)	Hanged
1859	England	Dr Thomas SMETHURST	1 (lodger)	Pardoned
1873	England	Mary Ann COTTON	20	Hanged
1887	Ireland	Dr Philip CROSS	1 (wife)	Hanged
1889	England	Florence MAYBRICK	1 (husband)	Imprisoned
1896	Japan	Edith CAREW	1 (husband)	Penal Servitude
1898	USA	Cordelia BOTKIN	2	Imprisoned
1905	USA	Johann HOCH	15 (wives)	Hanged
1911	India	Henry CLARK and Augusta FULLAM	1 (husband)	Hanged Imprisoned
1911	England	BINGHAM POISONING CASE	3 (same family)	Unsolved
1912	England	Frederick SEDDON	1 (lodger)	Hanged
1920	England	Harold GREENWOOD	1 (wife)	Acquitted
1922	England	Herbert Rowse ARMSTRONG	1 (wife)	Hanged
1922	England	Edward Ernest BLACK	1 (wife)	Hanged
1928	Australia	Ronald Geeves GRIGGS	1 (wife)	Acquitted
1928/9	England	CROYDON POISONINGS	3 (same family)	Unsolved
1931	England	Annie HEARN	1 (neighbour)	Acquitted
1932	South Africa	Daisy de MELKER	3 (2 husbands and son)	Hanged
1936	England	Charlotte BRYANT	1 (husband)	Hanged
1936	USA	Mary CREIGHTON and Everett APPELGATE	1 (wife)	Electrocuted
1949	UK	Frederick RADFORD	1 (wife)	Suicide
1958	UK	Marcus MARYMONT	1 (wife)	Imprisoned
1961	France	Marie BESNARD	12	Acquitted
1969	South Africa	Maria GROESBEEK	1 (husband)	Hanged

Note: The numbers of victims are not substantiated in every case, but the commonly accepted figure is given.

hair grows at a rate of about 0·44 millimetres a day, it was ascertained that she received her first dose of arsenic 100–120 days before she died.

Suspicion immediately fell on her husband Frederick, who admitted buying the pie but asked, 'Why should I want to kill my wife? I knew she was going to die anyway.' The day after he was questioned by police Radford was found dead in his home — he had taken his own life with CYANIDE. Had Mrs Radford not set off a chain of events by asking for the pie to be analysed there is no doubt that the world would have believed her death was entirely due to tuberculosis, and a perfect murder would have been committed.

The Marsh Test for arsenic is still used, but analysts today prefer the Reinsch and Gutzeit Tests, which employ the same principle of reducing arsenic to arsine gas but are easier to conduct. Hugo Reinsch, a German chemist, developed his test in 1842, but while it is in some ways easier it has its pitfalls. The reagents used must be scrupulously checked to ensure that they are arsenic-free. Failure to do this blemished the evidence in the Smethurst case (1859) and caused no small embarrassment at the time to Dr Alfred Swaine Taylor.

*1, 14, 25, 31, 37, 62, 69, 75, 77, 78, 97, 98, 101, 112, 132, 161, 169, 179, 196, 225, 256, 269, 270, 275, 283, 284, 294, 301, 315, 347, 354, 370, 398, 415, 430, **445**, 456, 457, 461, 479, 480, 491, 500, 501, 503, 507, 508, 521, 535, 539, 564, 567, 581, 587, 588, 600, 607, 620, **625**, 626, 675, 689, 696, 699, 713, 729, 736, 741, 742, 748.*

ASPHYXIA

Obstruction of the body's respiratory function, reducing or cutting off the air-supply to the lungs, results in a condition known as asphyxia. This is characterized by common features, although the cause may vary. The word 'asphyxia' comes from the Greek, and means 'without pulse' — that is, the condition in which the action of the heart and lungs is stopped and death results.

Some medical authorities class as asphyxia a number of disorders not resulting from obstruction, such as poisoning with CYANIDE or carbon monoxide (see under GASSING), which affect the oxygen-carrying capacity of the BLOOD. In forensic work, especially related to homicide, asphyxia is generally taken to refer to the effects of interference with the mechanics of breathing resulting from strangulation, choking, suffocation, overlaying and crush asphyxia. The common characteristics of these are blueness of the skin

(cyanosis), congestion of the face and burst blood capillaries (petechiae) in the heart and lungs and also in the EYES.

These features develop in three stages during the victim's struggle to breathe against the obstructing force:

1. Increase in pulse rate, rise in blood pressure and gasping for breath.
2. The face becomes congested, cyanosis develops, the eyes bulge, consciousness begins to ebb and there are general convulsions.
3. Respiration becomes shallow, unconsciousness is complete and the muscles twitch involuntarily as death occurs. Vomiting, and voiding of the bladder and rectum, is common.

The process may take up to five minutes, the exact time depending on a number of factors such as compression of the neck, which may trigger vagal inhibition and stop the heart in advance of complete asphyxia. Sudden immersion in cold water may also result in vagal inhibition and death without the appearances of drowning. Asphyxia may also result from accidental means, such as a mother unintentionally overlaying her baby and smothering it, or the drunk who inhales his vomit and chokes.

Air may be excluded from the lungs by various mechanical means: by obstructing the nose and mouth (suffocation); by blocking the entry to the upper air passages inside the throat (choking); by constricting the neck (strangulation and hanging); by compressing the chest wall (crush asphyxia); and by filling the air passages with fluid (drowning). Death by these means frequently involves MURDER, and the subjects of SUFFOCATION, STRANGULATION and DROWNING are dealt with extensively as separate entries.

HANGING is usually suicidal, although it has been simulated in an unusual murder case. Suicide committed by self-suspension from a rope or cord rarely involves the sort of drop contrived in judicial hanging by the executioner. In such cases the weight of the body jerking to a stop at the end of the rope causes the neck to break and ruptures the spinal cord, whereas in hanging resulting from suicide or by accident in acts of MASOCHISM the tightness of the noose is sufficient to cause death by compression of the neck.

An unusual case of simulated hanging occurred in 1953 and involved two sergeants serving with the British Army in Germany. One of the men apparently committed suicide by hanging himself from the stairs in a barrack block. He had severe bruising around the throat, and the windpipe had been perforated by the broken thyroid cartilage. It then emerged that a fellow-sergeant named Emmett-Dunne had quarrelled with the dead man, and persistent rumours that the victim had not committed suicide led to the case being reopened. Following the EXHUMATION of the body and a second POST-MORTEM by Professor F. E. Camps, it was concluded that the dead man had been killed by a deliberate blow to the throat and that his body was arranged to simulate death by hanging.

The sergeant was arrested and sent for trial in June 1955. The new medical evidence proved that death by hanging could be ruled out, and it was shown that the victim had died of shock after receiving a karate type of blow, delivered to the throat with the side of the hand with sufficient force to split the thyroid cartilage. The accused admitted that a blow was struck, but only in self-defence, and that death was accidental. The sergeant was found guilty of murder, and received a sentence of life imprisonment.

Crush asphyxia — also called traumatic asphyxia — is caused by compression of the chest, and is a type of injury commonly encountered in trench collapses and mining accidents when a person is pinned down by a heavy weight. Many of the deaths resulting from the collapse of crowd barriers at Ibrox Park football stadium in 1971 were of this type. The chest is compressed and the diaphragm becomes fixed so that the action of the lungs is stopped. This form of asphyxia is rarely encountered in the investigation of murder, but as a method of killing it has two historical users in Burke and Hare. These were the Irish labourers who provided cadavers for Edinburgh's medical schools in the early nineteenth century by the novel method of BODY-SNATCHING. The technique they used was to crush the life out of their usually drunken victims by sitting on their chests. This deflated the lungs, and by covering the mouth and nostrils at the same time the breathing mechanism was violently arrested.

Asphyxia is a large subject with many different aspects, and is one of the most widely encountered conditions in the investigation of murder. *369, 372, 548,* **625***, 728.*

ASSASSINATION

Killing by violent means for political or religious reasons is generally termed assassination, as opposed to MURDER. A characteristic of assassination is the use of treachery to bring the assassin close to his target. This was amply demonstrated in the killing of President Sadat of Egypt in October 1981, when his assassins posed as loyal soldiers and killed him at point-blank range.

The word assassin derives from *hashishin*, a person who takes hashish, and is bound up with Arab politics in the eleventh and twelfth centuries. The original Assassins were members of the Ismailis, a breakaway Moslem sect, which adopted the practice of murdering its enemies as a sacred religious duty. The Assassins were alleged to take hashish to inspire them with visions of paradise before setting out on their murderous missions and probable martyrdom. Key elements in their attacks were disguise and the betrayal of trust. The concept of assassination probably reached Europe by way of the returning Crusaders who related stories of a Christian knight struck down in 1192 in Syria by two Assassins disguised as monks. The Assassins ceased to exist as a political entity by 1300, but their descendants exist today in small enclaves, chiefly in India and Pakistan, and give their allegiance to the Aga Khan.

In modern times kings and presidents have suffered violent fates at the hands of assassins. Four presidents of the United States of America have been assassinated, and attempts have been made on the lives of several others, including in recent times the wounding of President Ronald Reagan. The list of prominent public figures struck down by the assassin's violence contains such important names of monarchs, dukes, politicians and peace-makers as Robert Kennedy, Mahatma Gandhi, Leon Trotsky, Emperor Alexander II of Russia, Martin Luther King, President Anwar Sadat and Archduke Franz Ferdinand. In some instances these assassinations have been attempts to change history, but more often than not the assassin is a lone individual asking the world to take notice of him. John Wilkes Booth (who killed President Lincoln) said he did it not for the money but 'for notoriety's sake'.

Assassination of public figures has been less fashionable in England, and attempts have usually been the work of unbalanced individuals. James Hadfield, who tried to kill King George III in 1800, was acquitted of the crime on the grounds of insanity. The only successful assassination of a

Assassins strike:
(*top*) Tsar Alexander II is killed by a bomb; (*bottom*) Bellingham shoots Prime Minister, Spencer Perceval

British Prime Minister took place in May 1812 when Spencer Perceval was shot dead by John Bellingham as he entered the central lobby of the House of Commons. Bellingham made no attempt to escape. 'I am the unfortunate man who has shot Mr Perceval', he said. 'I know what I have done. It was a private injury, a denial of justice on the part of the Government.' This was the assassin's motive — a grudge against authority following an abortive business venture in Russia when he tried but failed to gain support from the British Government to rescue him from his difficulties.

Bellingham pleaded guilty at his trial for murder and made a long statement about his grievances. The judge ruled that the accused clearly understood that what he was doing was wrong, and sentenced him to death. John Bellingham was hanged in Newgate within a week of committing his act.

In 1843 Daniel M'Naghten, intent on killing the Prime Minister, mistakenly shot his secretary, and in the aftermath lent his name to the M'NAGHTEN RULES,.which to this day are used in many courts as the touchstone of insanity defences.

While controversy continues over whether the assassination of President John F. Kennedy was the lone act of Lee Harvey Oswald or the result of a CONSPIRACY, it is the case that most assassins act alone out of some sense of conviction. Two of the killers of US Presidents, Charles Guiteau and Leon Czolgosz, were thought to be suffering from SCHIZOPHRENIA, an affliction also imputed to Lee Harvey Oswald. Colin Wilson, in writing about the psychology of murder, described the assassin as 'a man for whom murder is not only an ultimate purpose, but also a means of self-fulfilment, a creative act'. With this consideration in mind, he placed John Wilkes Booth, JACK THE RIPPER and Charles Manson in the same class of individuals who committed murder for its own sake. The Manson murders with their background of drug-taking make an interesting comparison with the original concept of the assassin high on hashish.

In the aftermath of the death of President Kennedy, a US National Commission on the Causes and Prevention of Violence compiled a profile of the presidential assassin type. This was a young man alienated from his home and parents, unsuccessful in marriage, often without a job, and generally a social misfit contemplating murder of a public figure as a means of securing an identity. The theory stood up well in practice when a young man much resembling this picture attempted the life of President Reagan. Even more sinister in what is called the politics of homicide is the suggestion that Sirhan Sirhan, the Palestinian jailed for assassinating Robert Kennedy, was programmed for his violent act by HYPNOSIS.
188, 418, 467, 556, 732, 738.

ATTEMPTED MURDER

An attempt to commit murder is an offence under COMMON LAW and is regarded as seriously as murder itself. A person who attempts murder is judged to have the MENS REA or guilty intent to complete the crime. In essence, an attempt is the same as actually committing the murder, although intent alone is not sufficient. Conviction depends on proving that an accused person carried out some action as part of the criminal attempt (see under ACTUS REUS).

Attempted murder was one of a number of offences exempted from capital punishment in England by an Act of Parliament passed in 1837, although, according to *The Hangman's Record*, the last person to be executed for 'barbarous attempted murder' was Martin Doyle, who was hanged at Chester in 1861.

The accusation of attempted murder has usually been the prelude to a full murder charge when a hitherto unknown killing comes to light, as in the case of Major Armstrong (see under ARSENIC), or when the victim subsequently dies of his injuries. An unusual case of attempted murder was provided by the trial of Claus von Bülow, who was convicted while his victim lay in a drug-induced coma. This case also provided an interesting link with Kenneth Barlow, who committed the first insulin murder (see under POST-MORTEM), for it was noted that von Bülow during his training in Britain as a lawyer worked in the same chambers in 1957 as the judge who tried Barlow.

Claus von Bülow, a Danish aristocrat, married a wealthy American heiress, and the couple were part of the social élite in Newport, Rhode Island, where they had a mansion. After Maria von Bülow went into a permanent coma in December 1980 suspicion began to focus on Claus, who appeared to have been reluctant to call a doctor. Maria — also known as 'Sunny' — went into hypoglycaemic shock as a result of a dramatic drop in her blood sugar. There was no evidence of pancreatic or liver disorder to account for the high levels of insulin found in her body. When Maria Schralhammer, the sick woman's maid for twenty-two years, found a bag containing used syringes and a bottle of insulin in Claus von Bülow's closet questions were asked.

What followed became known as the 'Sleeping Beauty Case', with von Bülow being tried for attempted murder in front of court-room television cameras at the same time as his wife lay comatose in a New York hospital. The prosecution argued that von Bülow tried to murder his wife 'with a drug that until a few years ago was undetectable in the human body'. The suggested motive was his desire to secure his wife's fortune and to make himself free to marry his mistress, a former actress.

The defence countered that Mrs von Bülow was a suicidally inclined alcoholic who had destroyed herself by excessive drinking and use of barbiturate drugs. The crucial evidence was that of Maria Schralhammer, who found the insulin and syringes — 'Insulin? For what insulin?' she had asked with the anxiety of a long-standing servant familiar with all her mistress's ways. By finding Claus von Bülow guilty of two counts of assault with intent to murder, the Rhode Island jury provided their answer.
117, *675*.

AUTOMATISM

Where a crime is committed by a person acting as an automaton, with no knowledge of his acts at the time or afterwards, it may be argued that there is no guilty intent (MENS REA), and hence no criminal responsibility. If the JURY accepts the defence of automatism it is entitled to give a not guilty verdict.

Automatism has been added to English CRIMINAL LAW during the last thirty years, and two forms of the defence are recognized — sane automatism and insane automatism. The former discounts any mental abnormality and applies in a case where a crime might have been committed in a state of unconsciousness or amnesia following, for example, a blow on the head. Insane automatism assumes that the defendant had no memory of his act because of a mental defect or abnormality, and consequently could not know that he was doing wrong. In such a case he might be found not guilty by reason of insanity, or be acquitted on grounds of DIMINISHED RESPONSIBILITY. A person committing a criminal act while in the grip of EPILEPSY might be defended in this way. A brain tumour might also give rise to a defence of insane automatism.

The automatism defence has been successfully used to contest a murder charge where it was shown that the accused acted while sleep-walking. **117**, *338, 576*.

AXE MURDERS

Probably the most famous axe murders are those attributed to Lizzie Borden, who according to the famous rhyme 'gave her mother forty whacks' and 'her father forty-one'. The axe — possibly because of its association with beheading and the medieval executioner — holds a special place in the annals of murder. It is a particularly savage weapon, for it combines bluntness and sharpness in the same instrument. In the age which preceded central heating most homes were furnished with a wood-axe to prepare kindling or logs for the fire. Thus, like the BLUNT INSTRUMENT, an axe was ready to hand when murderous rage erupted.

While Lizzie Borden was acquitted of murdering her father and stepmother at Fall River, Massachusetts, in 1893, others charged with wielding axes have been less successful. Kate Webster, whose MOTIVE was simple gain, disposed of her mistress in her house at Richmond in 1879. She felled her with a cleaver, then chopped the body into pieces which she boiled and placed in a wooden box. This was deposited in the river Thames, from whence it subsequently surfaced to give the game away. The head, which Kate carried around for a while in a carpet bag, was never found. The murderess, confessing her guilt but pleading she had been ill-used by the world, was hanged.

Bloody imprint made by an axe

This case had distant echoes across the Atlantic ten years later, when Roxana Druse took up the family axe and killed her husband. She was the overbearing, sharp-tongued wife of elderly John Druse, a well-liked farmer at Little Falls, New York. In the winter of 1889 neighbours thought the Druse farm was uncommonly quiet, and became disturbed by the dense black smoke emitted by the farmhouse chimney. Roxana explained that her husband was away visiting relatives, but curious neighbours buttonholed her young son, who poured out a story of murder and sinister goings-on.

Confronted by an accusation of murder, Roxana admitted killing her husband with an axe and severing his head, which for a time lay on a plate in the pantry. Her reason was simply one of bitterness at being turned into a drudge by the grinding hard work of the farm. Aided by her mentally retarded daughter, she set about DISPOSAL OF THE BODY. The corpse was first dismembered and the pieces boiled. These *disjecta membra* were then burned piece by piece on the kitchen fire. All were consumed by the flames except the head, which like that of Kate Webster's victim was never found. The murder weapon was found at the bottom of a pond on the farm. Roxana and her daughter were convicted of murder, the latter being sentenced to life imprisonment while her mother was hanged.

As Mrs Druse demonstrated, the axe is a dual-purpose weapon — once its bluntness has been employed to strike down the victim, its edge can be used to hack the body into pieces to aid dismemberment. It is interesting to observe how Mesdames Druse and Webster, enticed by the homely feel of the axe, quickly lapsed into a kind of culinary disposal of their victim's bodies.

The masculine approach to the axe has been somewhat different. Louis Wagner, a German immigrant fisherman, made a round trip of twenty miles in a rowing-boat from Portsmouth, New Hampshire, to Smutty Nose Island. There on the lonely island on the night of 5 March 1873 he brutally killed two women by smashing their heads with an axe, breaking the weapon's handle in the process. His crime earned him twenty dollars, blistered hands and a hanging.

The Axe-man of New Orleans, while choosing a crude weapon, used sufficient guile to escape detection. He created a reign of terror between 1911 and 1919 which has been likened to that produced in London by JACK THE RIPPER. The Axe-man's MODUS OPERANDI was to gain access to his victim's home by breaking through the door

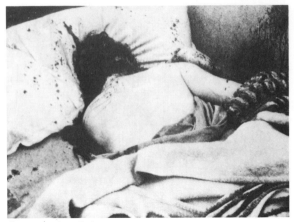

Axe-murder victim

with an axe, which he then used to smite the occupants. The murder weapon, which often belonged to the victim, was invariably left at the scene of the crime. At least nine people were murdered in this fashion, and despite numerous DYING DECLARATIONS and false accusations, the axe murderer was never caught. His motive was not robbery, for money which could easily have been stolen was left untouched at the crime scenes.

The head is a favourite target for the axe murderer, who inflicts severe lacerated wounds, achieving penetration of the SKULL if the weapon's edge is sharp. The axe attacker usually uses both hands, and the victim's forearms may exhibit defence wounds as evidence of attempts to fend off the blows. As self-inflicted head wounds with an axe are not unknown, the crime investigator looks for corroborating signs of a murderous assault. The position of the body, evidence of a struggle and the nature of BLOOD-splashes are especially significant. Finding the likely murder weapon is of prime importance, and once it is found it must be matched to the crime. Where an axe or bludgeon has been used this is often difficult, because of the destructive nature of the injuries.

Among the varieties of murder which featured in Sir Bernard Spilsbury's records was at least one axe murder. In June 1931 a labourer passing a smouldering rubbish-tip by some railway sidings near Elstree noticed a human hand sticking out of the refuse. The burned body of a middle-aged man was dragged out, and from its condition Spilsbury judged that death had been caused by a severe blow to the head. There was a rectangular-shaped fracture of the skull, and the man's left hand was bruised. The left forearm bore a tattoo from which it was possible to identify the victim. He was

Herbert Ayres, otherwise known as 'Pig-sticker', a casual labourer and one of a band of men who lived rough and were known only by their nicknames.

One of these men volunteered information to the police from which they ascertained that two men called 'Moosh' and 'Tiggy' had been seen beating up a third man. A bloodstained axe was found under the floor of their hut, and they were arrested under their real names of Oliver Newman and William Shelley. Spilsbury found that the squared back of the axe-head fitted neatly into the fracture in the dead man's skull. Newman and Shelley admitted attacking 'Pig-sticker', who they thought had stolen food from their hut. An axe was conveniently to hand, and a lesson meted out to punish theft turned into murder. The two men were convicted at the Old Bailey, and later hanged.

1, 78, 97, 196, 432, 455, 457, 515, 539, 540, 542, 561, 626, 654, 660.

B

BACTERIAL POISONING

Joan Robinson Hill, a distinguished horsewoman and a person well known in Texas social circles, died in 1969 from what newspapers described as 'a massive, fulminating infection of unknown origin'. Although no traces of toxic material were found in her body, her husband, John Hill — who practised as a plastic surgeon in Houston — was charged with her murder. He was charged specifically with 'murder by omission', which under Texas law meant that he was accused of causing his wife's death by deliberately withholding medical treatment.

Joan Hill, the adopted daughter of wealthy oil-man Ash Robinson, became ill at a time when her marriage was crumbling. After treating her for four days at home, Dr Hill took her to hospital, where she died. A hurried POST-MORTEM was carried out, and the body was buried before proper cause of death had been certified. This provoked the first of many arguments, and although a liver infection was said to have caused death, Ash Robinson refused to accept this explanation. He began openly to accuse John Hill of allowing his wife to die, and these allegations became the subject of a 5 million dollar suit for slander. When Hill married again after only three months the accusations of foul play against his first wife were renewed.

Joan Hill's body was subjected to EXHUMATION, and a second post-mortem was carried out. Doctors concluded that the brain, preserved from the first autopsy, showed signs of meningitis. However, it was pointed out that the brain stem in the body gave no such indication, and it was suggested that the pickled brain was not Mrs Hill's. The controversy surrounding the case continued when it took three grand jury sittings to reach an indictment against John Hill.

The plastic surgeon was tried for murder in 1971, when his second wife, Ann Kurth, whom he had since divorced, testified against him. She alleged that he had tried to kill her with his car (see under HIT-AND-RUN) and further testified that he told her how he killed his first wife. All this resulted in a mistrial, but the accusation was made public that Dr Hill had injected his wife with a bacterial culture made from 'every form of human excretion ... urine, faeces' and even 'pus taken from a boil on a patient's back'. He injected this concoction mixed with an antibiotic and remarked, 'By the time I took her to the hospital she was in irreversible shock.' Before a second trial could be held John Hill was shot dead in his house by a hired gunman, who in his turn was shot and killed by a police officer.

The idea that bacteria could be used as unseen messengers of murder was hit on by a Frenchman, Henri Girard, the first so-called scientific murderer. He developed cultures of typhoid bacteria to further his criminal ambitions. Girard was a financial manipulator who thought out a get-rich-quick insurance scheme. In 1912 he insured an acquaintance, Louis Pernotte, for 300,000 francs, and then attempted to procure his death. In the process he made the whole Pernotte family ill with typhoid, and finally had to concentrate his efforts on Louis, whom he plied with daily injections — allegedly of camomile — until he eventually succumbed.

Girard also experimented with the poisonous mushroom *Amanita phalloides* (Death Cap), but his intended pre-insured victims proved too resilient. He succeeded eventually when in 1918 he murdered a widow with a poisoned drink. The insurance companies had grown suspicious of Girard's association with some of their clients, and an inquiry was begun which led to his arrest. Claiming that no one understood him, Girard swallowed one of his own bacterial cocktails and died in custody.

News of Girard's scientific methods of murder no doubt crossed the Atlantic. At any rate, a notoriously worthy successor was found in Dr Arthur Warren Waite, a young New York dentist. Waite married the daughter of timber millionaire John Peck. Despite a lavish home and a doting wife, Waite neglected his dental practice, preferring to play tennis and engage in passionate affairs. This extravagant life-style required a large income, and the Pecks made it clear they would not subsidize their son-in-law. He therefore decided to murder them in order to secure a million-dollar inheritance.

Waite first invited Mrs Peck to stay with him and his wife in New York. Within ten days of arriving in December 1915 she was dead, supposedly of kidney disease. Her distressed son-in-law arranged for a speedy cremation, and then, after the passage of a few weeks, invited Mr Peck for a visit. In less than a month he too was dead. The sorrowing son-in-law again urged a speedy cremation, but this was vetoed by Peck's son, who demanded the return of his father's body to Grand Rapids for proper burial. In the meantime an anonymous letter pointed suspicion at Waite, and a post-mortem examination was called for. Mr Peck was found to have been poisoned with ARSENIC and CHLOROFORM.

At first Waite denied the charge of murder, but his protestations of innocence subsided when police officers produced a medicinal nasal spray taken from his New York flat. He had used the spray to treat his in-laws, but instead of being charged with drugs it contained typhoid and anthrax germs. He confessed in due course, and admitted using diphtheria, tuberculosis and influenza germs on Mrs Peck. The old man was made of sterner stuff, and in addition to the germs required poisoning with arsenic to secure his death. 'A bad man from Egypt dwells in my body. He makes me do bad things,' Waite told the police.

Master of the quip, Waite was asked at his trial if he was crazy. 'I think not,' he replied, 'unless it is crazy to want money.' Following his conviction for murder he was sent to the ELECTRIC CHAIR in 1917. 'Is this all there is to it?' he inquired of his incredulous warders as they strapped on the electrodes.

324, 396, 411, 421, 515, 651, 665, 668, 690.

BLOOD

Shedding of blood is the dramatic accompaniment to murder committed by violent means. Blood accounts for about 9 per cent of a healthy person's body-weight and as many murderers have discovered to their cost, when it is spilled a little goes a long way. Once blood is shed in any quantity, and especially when it starts to clot, it becomes very difficult to deal with. Murderers' attempts to clean up after their violent handiwork often fail because of blood-traces which adhere tenaciously to their clothing or to the murder weapon. Blood found at the scene of the crime has trapped many killers who thought they had removed all incriminating traces. A sensational demonstration of this was provided by the French detective Gustave Macé in 1869, when he was interrogating a murder suspect in the room which he believed had been the scene of a ghastly crime involving the dismemberment of the victim. Convinced that a great deal of blood must have been shed, Macé looked about the room but could see no obvious traces. Then he noticed a marked hollow in the tiled floor. With the suspect looking on in astonishment, the detective took a jug of water and tipped the contents on the floor — the water collected in the hollow area, and when the tiles were lifted their under-surfaces were found to be caked with dried blood. This discovery led to a murder confession by Pierre Voirbo and to a triumph of detection for Macé.

Blood is important forensically, and can yield a great deal of information to the investigator. The first task in examining suspicious stains is to determine whether they are blood, and if so, are they human? Once this is established stains are examined for age, sex and blood-group. The shape and pattern of liquid blood-splashes can help in reconstructing the murder; bloody FINGERPRINTS and palm-prints tell their own story; dried blood on a suspect's clothing can be related to the victim, the crime scene and the murder weapon; blood and tissue forced under the fingernails of the victim during a violent struggle can be linked to the assailant.

Thus a single blood-trace can provide a wealth of information, and analytical techniques are improving all the time. For example, traces of drugs found in a bloodstain indicate medical treatment which a person might be receiving. While such procedures improve the scope of detection, it is not yet possible to identify an individual by his blood as it is by his fingerprints. Nevertheless, forensic serology, which in addition to blood deals with other body fluids such as saliva and semen, is important not only for narrowing suspicion on the guilty but also in showing a suspect's innocence. As in many other aspects of forensic investigation, bloodstains are taken into account with a variety of other evidence to build up a pattern of crime.

A number of substances such as fruit-stains or dye-stuff may soil clothing and take on the appearance of bloodstains. The benzidine test — used for many years to confirm the presence of blood — has been discontinued because the reagent is carcinogenic. It has largely been replaced by the Kastle-Meyer test, using a solution of phenolphthalein which turns pink in contact with even small traces of blood. The test works by detecting the presence of the enzyme peroxidase in the blood. However, as this substance is also present in other biological materials, the Kastle-Meyer test is regarded as a screening procedure. It is highly sensitive, and a positive reaction is judged presumptive of blood, and further confirmatory tests are carried out. These are usually chemical and microscopical procedures to identify blood by its pigments and cellular structures.

Once a stain has been confirmed as blood it has to be determined whether it is human or animal. The precipitin test is used for this purpose. Blood of every animal species contains different proteins, and blood from one species will not accept proteins from a different species. Blood develops antibodies as a protective measure against disease and foreign matter to render them harmless. The serum containing antibodies produced by this reaction provides immunity from disease.

This principle is used to test whether bloodstains are human or not. Serum for the precipitin test is obtained from rabbits which have produced antibodies to destroy a small quantity of human blood injected into them. A drop of this anti-human serum is added to suspect blood, which will precipitate its protein if it is of human origin. Police laboratories hold anti-sera for most common animals, thus allowing the crime investigator to confirm or disprove statements made by suspects about the origin of suspicious bloodstains. The precipitin test is sensitive, and will work on small traces of blood. The test is also known as the Uhlenhuth test after the German scientist who developed it in 1901.

The colour of dried blood changes in time from red to brown, and the peroxidase test takes longer to develop with an old stain. An experienced observer considering these factors might be able to give an opinion as to the age of a particular stain, but it is now possible to measure colour-change scientifically. Spectrophotometric analysis of bloodstains allows them to be aged within the range of one day to three weeks.

In 1949 two British scientists observed that the nuclei in the cells of female tissues usually contained a distinctive drumstick-like structure which was rare in males. This structure, called a Barr body after one of its discoverers, is most noticeable in white blood cells and in the epithelial cells lining the mouth. Barr bodies are associated with the differences in chromosomes between males and females, and their appearance in blood of unknown origin is a basis for identifying it as from a female.

Determination of the blood-group characteristics of stains found on clothing or a suspected murder weapon is another powerful link in the chain of evidence which can be built up in a case of violent death. Blood-grouping is a developing science in its own right, and while it cannot provide information as certain as a fingerprint, it can provide CIRCUMSTANTIAL EVIDENCE establishing contact between a suspect and the victim.

Blood has one factor in common with fingerprints — it occurs in unalterable types. Every person's blood falls into one of the four international blood groups identified in 1900 by Dr Karl Landsteiner. The ABO blood-grouping system is a function of the red blood cells, and the presence in them of a substance known as agglutinogen. A Group contains A agglutinogen, B Group has B agglutinogen, AB Group contains both and O Group has neither. These factors are found in specific proportions among white populations.

Group	Agglutinogen in red cells	Distribution in white population in %
O	neither	46
A	A	42
B	B	9
AB	both	3

In 1927 Dr Landsteiner and a fellow-worker discovered further factors which occurred separately in human blood and were distributed in specific proportions among the population. These are the M, N, and MN factors, to which was added the P factor and in 1940 the Rhesus factor. The knowledge that each person's ABO and MN blood-group characteristics are inherited and fixed for life has made the examination of blood an important part of crime investigation. It is possible to place an individual in one of 288 different blood-groupings, but forensic serologists are not able to say that a particular blood-trace originated in a particular individual. The value of blood-grouping procedures in crime work is that many potential suspects can be eliminated from an inquiry, thereby allowing the investigation to be narrowed down. About 80 per cent of the population are SECRETORS which means that their blood cells are present in such body fluids as semen and saliva. It is possible, therefore, to determine blood-groupings by examining these fluids.

Examination and interpretation of bloodstains on and around the body, and of blood-spots, splashes and smears at the scene of the crime, are an essential part of a murder investigation. The position and appearance of blood-marks on the body and its immediate surroundings will help the investigator to reconstruct the crime.

An illustration of how evidence provided by blood-marks upon the victim could guide murder detectives occurred in the Bahamas in 1943, when Sir Harry Oakes was found dead. The millionaire was discovered lying on his bed: he had been bludgeoned to death, and an attempt made to burn the body. The corpse lay on its back, and a trickle of blood was evident on the face between the ear and the nose. This had resulted from an injury close to the ear, and as blood cannot flow uphill it was obvious that the wound had been caused before the body was placed where it was found.

A great deal can be gleaned from the shape of blood spots and splashes found on surfaces such as floor, walls, ceiling, woodwork and furniture. The French criminologist Alexandre Lacassagne noted the correlation between the shape of blood-spots and the postion of the victim. Blood dropping vertically on to a flat surface forms a circular mark

Shape made by blood dropping vertically

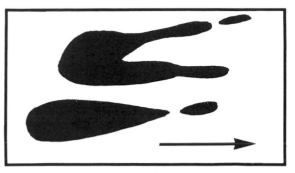

Shapes made by blood dropping at an angle

with crenated edges, and denotes that the source was stationary at the time. Drops of blood falling from a moving object hit a flat surface obliquely and leave a spot shaped like an exclamation mark, with the smaller spot indicating the direction of travel.

It is possible to estimate the height at which a blood-drop fell vertically on to a flat surface by closely examining its edges. Up to a distance of about 2ft, dropping blood leaves a circular spot with neat, crenated edges. As the dropping height increases the spot tends to throw out tiny droplets and spines which give an indication of distance. Similar examination of the shape of obliquely fall-

Changes in the shape of blood-splashes determined by dropping height

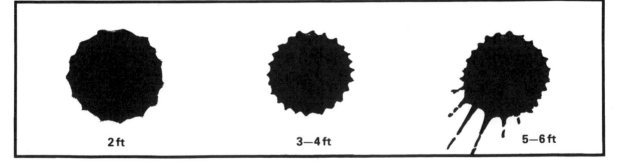

2 ft   3—4 ft   5—6 ft

ing blood-splashes yields information about the direction and speed of impact. Such evidence helps determine the positions of victim and murderer at the time of an assault, and may also indicate the manner of violence and type of weapon used.

A line of blood-spots on the ceiling of a room in which violent murder has been committed is likely to have been made by the killer wielding an axe or bludgeon in an arc over his head. Smears and trails on the floor may be produced by a wounded person

Shape of blood-splashes approximately related to angle of fall

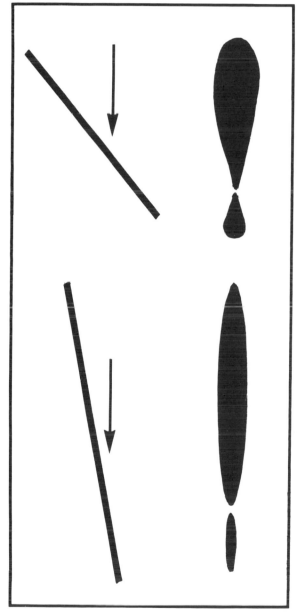

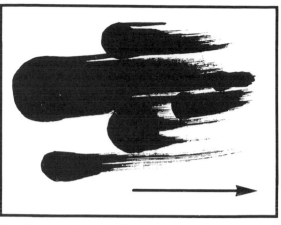

Blood-smears showing direction of travel

crawling about or by an assailant dragging the body of his injured victim. Smudges and smears on furniture and doorposts leaving bloody finger-prints or palm-prints may result from similar activities. Blood-smears tend to start as drops which become ragged at one edge, indicating the direction of travel.

One of the classic murder cases in which blood evidence played an important, if controversial, part was the trial of Dr Sam Sheppard. The doctor's wife was found dead in their Cleveland, Ohio, home in July 1954. Her body, with the head brutally battered by over thirty blows from a heavy bludgeon, lay on one of twin beds in the first-floor bedroom. The room, which had been ransacked, was heavily spattered with blood, and a trail of stains led down the stairs and out on to a terrace.

Dr Sheppard, who had been awakened from sleep on the living-room sofa by his wife's screams, claimed to have been knocked unconscious by an intruder as he rushed upstairs. His behaviour was judged to have been suspicious, and there was considerable prejudice against him, not least on account of his alleged infidelity. He was sent for trial and found guilty of second-degree murder, for which he was sentenced to life imprisonment. The coroner had made much of bloodstains on the pillow in the murder room, and a bloody imprint which he suggested had been caused by a surgical instrument which had served as the murder weapon. This instrument was never specified, but the imputation was plain that Sheppard, himself a doctor, had used it to murder his wife.

The murder room abounded in blood evidence which if properly examined would have led to other conclusions. It was left to Dr Paul Leland Kirk, Professor of Criminalistics at Berkeley, to make a thorough assessment of this evidence several months later in order to reconstruct the murder. As the bedroom ceiling showed no traces of blood, Kirk reasoned that the murder weapon had been wielded in a more or less horizontal fashion. This was borne out by the state of blood-splashes on the walls, some of which had been flung from the murder weapon as it was swung backward and forward to make contact with the victim's head. Other blood-spatters had come directly from the battered head. The Professor carried out experiments which suggested the most likely weapon to have caused the pattern of blood-splashes was a heavy flashlight. He also judged that the murderer stood between the twin beds, having noted blood-drops which had been smeared into streaks on the right side of the victim's bed. This interpretation was supported by blood-free areas on two of the walls behind the murderer which had been protected from flying blood-spatters by his body. A killer standing in that position must have swung the murder weapon with his left hand — Dr Sheppard was neither left-handed nor ambidextrous.

By implication, the murderer must have been thoroughly spattered with blood. Yet apart from a bloodstain on the knee of Sheppard's trousers, which got there when he stood close to the bed to take his wife's pulse, there was no evidence of other bloodstaining on his clothes. A number of factors similarly pointed away from Dr Sheppard as the murderer — it was certainly the case that the examination of the blood evidence had been bungled in the first instance. There was no better illustration of this than the admission during a second trial that the trail of stains leading from the bedroom through the living-room and out on to the terrace had not even been properly tested for human origin, nor was blood-grouping attempted. Professor Kirk's interpretation of the blood evidence went a long way towards securing Dr Sheppard's eventual freedom.

Blood continues to play an important part in forensic investigations, and the discovery of new antibodies has enabled blood-grouping techniques to be further refined. The Kell antigen, for example, is virtually confined to the white population, whereas the Duffy antigen is completely absent. Thus, blood-grouping characteristics can be used to give an indication of race, and help to pinpoint the origin of bloodstains.

Forensic laboratories have researched sophisticated techniques for analysing protein in blood, and have been able to produce blood profiles with the prospect of establishing unique blood 'finger-prints'. While this remains for the moment a serologist's dream, blood continues to give up its secrets, and a Home Office scientist has described it as 'a treasure trove of hidden clues'.
*26, 175, 180, 277, 342, 348, **399**, 401, 415, 462, **474**, 516, 552, **571**, 584, 617, 631, **671**, **691**, 721.*

BLUNT INSTRUMENT

The poker or ornament seized from the fireside, the hammer or wrench grabbed at the work-place and the stone or bough snatched up from the ground, form a category of weapons for dealing out murder with a blunt instrument. They are the natural successors to the club, man's first tool of aggression, and constitute one of the most commonly used group of murder weapons.

The blunt instrument, often the nearest article to hand, is the choice of the person in whom the killer instinct is suddenly roused. Unlike the gun, which permits distance between killer and victim, the blunt instrument is the weapon of close contact, of primitive fury and naked anger. The head is the natural target for the club, and as it takes a physical act of considerable strength to kill with a single blow, multiple blows are usually needed to finish off the victim after the first stunning hit. Consequently, such murders are rarely clean and neat — the scene is usually gory, with BLOOD spattered about the immediate surroundings and transferred to the murderer's clothing and to the murder weapon. Attacks with blunt instruments are characterized by their fury; the violence of the assault can often be seen on the victim's hands and arms in the form of defensive wounds sustained in the effort to ward off the assailant's blows.

A *cause célèbre* involving murder with a blunt instrument was the Cohen case, which occurred in South Africa in 1970. Ronald and Susan Cohen lived in a stylish house in Constantia, a fashionable district of Cape Town. Cohen, aged forty-one, was a successful business-man and Susan, a beautiful woman half his age, was his second wife. On the night of 5 April 1970 the couple were sitting reading in the library of their house. Ronald said he left for a few minutes, and when he returned he found an intruder struggling with his wife. He said later that he seized a bronze ram's-head ornament from a table intending to fight the attacker. Then he blacked out and remembered little until he came to and found his wife's body sprawled on the floor. He

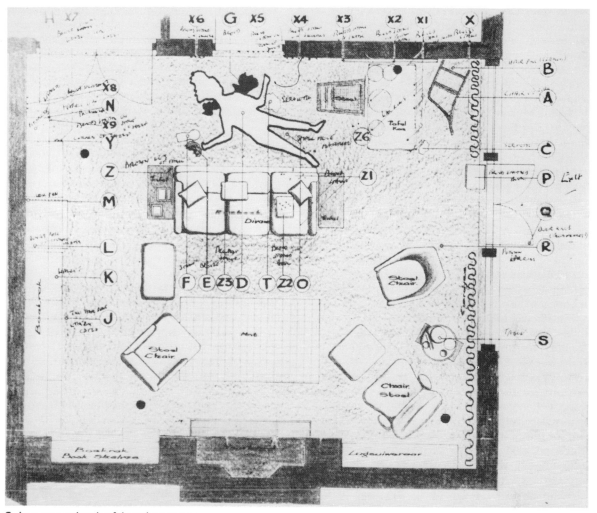

Cohen case: sketch of the crime scene

roused his housekeeper and told her someone had broken into the house. When police arrived they found Mrs Cohen lying dead in the library — her head was shattered, and there was a massive wound over the right ear and temple through which broken pieces of bone protruded. RIGOR MORTIS had not yet set in. Close by the body lay a bronze ram's head ornament, weighing eight pounds, and a stone statuette weighing twenty pounds. Both articles, which had been wedding presents, were bloodstained.

Ronald Cohen was near to hysteria. He had blood on his shirt, and there were bruises and scratches on his arms. There was no disorder in the library, and no signs of forced entry to the house. He said that when he saw his wife struggling with an unknown assailant he noticed out of the corner of his eye the ram's head ornament and 'lifted it up

with the intention of hitting the man with it. . . .' From that moment he had only flashes of recollection. He was not sure whether the man hit him or knocked him out, but he was able to give the police a detailed description of the intruder. He also remembered that the man was wearing gloves, and he recalled seeing him holding the statuette above his head — his next recollection was of seeing his wife injured on the floor.

These 'islands of memory' were a controversial aspect of Cohen's trial for murder. He had told the police that he distinctly remembered the impact of the blow he received on the back of his head before he blacked out. But, as a doctor pointed out in court, this went against medical experience in these matters. Any head injury severe enough to cause loss of consciousness results in retrograde AMNESIA, which blots out memory of the traumatic occurrence. This is a type of built-in protection which prevents repeated recollection of a painful event. There is a delay before sense impressions reach the memory, and when the brain activity is temporarily disturbed sensory input is not imprinted in the memory cells. Thus the victim's brain does not allow him to re-experience the pain of a stunning blow to the head. Dr Milton Helpern, who advised the Cape Town medico-legal authorities in this case, said that Cohen 'unwittingly denied this attribute that would otherwise have made his story credible. . . .' The defence presented evidence showing that Cohen was an obsessional, perfectionist personality who had reacted to a catastrophic stimulus. Extenuating circumstances were admitted, and the defendant was judged to have killed in a moment of insanity, not in a legal sense, but in 'another sense'. He was found guilty of a crime committed in a period of DIMINISHED RESPONSIBILITY, and sentenced to twelve years' imprisonment. Dr Milton Helpern, who advised the prosecution, stated he was later told by them that while in gaol Cohen confessed that he had killed his wife following a quarrel during which he accused her of unnatural relations with their children.

Wounds caused by blunt instruments are common on the head and face, where bone lies close under the surface of the skin — the knees and elbows also suffer in this respect. The skin and subcutaneous tissues are crushed against the underlying bone, causing lacerated wounds. These are characterized by rough and uneven edges and surrounding bruising. Strands of tissue, mangled blood-vessels and hairs lie in the base of the wound. The nature of the weapon may be discerned from the appearance of lacerations. Blunt, round-ended instruments tend to cause star-shaped wounds, whereas a hammer with a blunt-edged pein will give a characteristic crescent-shaped impression.

Where blows are delivered with great force the bone lying beneath lacerated wounds will be damaged, causing a variety of fractures ranging from cracks in the bone to complicated, depressed and comminuted fractures. The nature of such a fracture depends on the strength of the blow, the area of impact and the type of instrument used. The direction of a blow can often be ascertained from the position of a fracture and its secondary, radiating fissures which run away from the direction of the force. Fracture damage to the head is less when it is free to move with the blow than when it is supported — for example, against the ground.

Injury can occur to the brain without the skull being fractured, but brain-injury is inevitable when fracturing occurs. Apart from the gross case of bone-splinters being driven into the soft tissues, or the tissues themselves being pulped by repeated blows, there is the danger of haemorrhage as blood-vessels rupture under cracked bone and bleed into the space between the skull and brain membrane. The tough outer covering of the brain is the dura, and internal bleeding tends to collect between the dura and the inner surface of the skull. Subdural haemorrhages commonly result from severe head injuries, and if undetected can cause death from otherwise non-fatal injuries. Where head injuries are not fatal, but cause unconsciousness, a degree of amnesia may follow. The memory of the actual event is eradicated, and the moments associated with it are lost completely. AUTOMATISM may also result when a person appears to behave normally, carrying out complex activities of which there is no subsequent recollection.

The catalogue of murder by blunt instrument is vast, and most cases, though terrible enough, are unremarkable. Some are nevertheless distinguished by novel choice of instrument — for example, the two New Zealand teenagers Pauline Parker and Juliet Hulme, who killed Mrs Parker in 1954 with a half-brick in a stocking. (This case is described under FOLIE À DEUX.) Michael Queripel, another teenager, used a golf tee to murder a woman exercising her dog on Potter's Bar golf course in 1955, and Ruth Snyder and Henry Judd Gray, New York's 'Granite Woman' and 'Lover Boy', included a heavy sash-weight in their repertoire of instruments for murdering Albert Snyder in 1927. Mystery attached to the weapons used to kill Sir Harry Oakes in the Bahamas in 1943 and Marilyn Sheppard in Cleveland, Ohio in 1954. Both were UNSOLVED MURDERS and in the former four separate triangular-shaped wounds had been made in the head near the left ear by an unidentified four-pronged weapon. In the Sheppard case (both cases are described under BLOOD), a bloody imprint on the pillow beside the victim's shattered head was the subject of much speculation — a surgical instrument of unspecified origin was suggested.

Occasionally the gross circumstances of murder by bludgeoning are alleviated by a touch of innovation, as in the Podmore case. In January 1929 the body of an oil-company agent was found in a locked garage in Southampton. He had been battered to death, sustaining a puncture wound over the left eye and multiple fractures of the skull.

Sir Bernard Spilsbury examined the wounds, and judged that they had been caused by a hammer.

An advertisement was found in the dead man's lodgings which led the police to William Henry Podmore, who was wanted for robbery. He was located in London and questioned about his relationship with the dead man. Podmore, who said he had merely worked as his assistant, was imprisoned for fraud. In the meantime further searches brought to light an oil-sales receipt book which recorded fictitious entries assigning commissions to a W. F. Thomas, alias Podmore. Although the top copies had been torn out, the pencil used to write the entries had left indentations on the pages beneath. These were given substance by means of special photography, and it was proved that Podmore had been operating a swindle against the dead man's company. (See under QUESTIONED DOCUMENTS.)

As soon as he had completed his prison sentence for fraud Podmore was rearrested and charged with murder. The murder weapon had been retrieved from its hiding-place behind some boxes at the scene of the crime. That it was the implement used in the killing was put beyond doubt by Spilsbury, who found on it two HAIRS which were matched to the victim's head. No doubt Podmore had been confronted in the garage with evidence of his fraud, and roused to anger, picked up the hammer and struck down his accuser. The jury at Winchester Assizes found him guilty, and he was hanged in April 1930. Newspapers of the day declared, 'Two hairs hanged this man!', a statement which was certainly sensational but hardly accurate.

2, 56, 97, 324, 367, **625**, **635**.

BODY-SNATCHING

> **Don't go to weep upon my grave,**
> **And think that there I be.**
> **They haven't left an atom there**
> **Of my anatomie.**
>
> Thomas Hood

The growth of medical learning at the beginning of the nineteenth century brought with it a great demand for bodies to aid the study of human anatomy. Whereas in Europe the authorities permitted the corpses of suicides and unclaimed hospital deaths to be sent to the teaching hospitals, until 1726 Britain allowed only the bodies of executed murderers to be used for this purpose. It was believed that the threat of HANGING followed by dissection would act as a deterrent against crime, and to the extent that the number of public executions produced too few bodies for the medical schools, it might be said to have worked.

The shortage of bodies led to unedifying scenes at the scaffold when porters and students from rival hospitals fought over possession of a murderer's corpse. In order to meet the demands of teaching, surgeons resorted to buying corpses from an entrepreneurial band of grave-robbers who became known as 'resurrection men'. John Hunter, the famous English surgeon of the eighteenth century, set an example of the limits to which scientific curiosity might be pursued when he bribed the undertaker to release into his custody the body of the spectacular Irish giant, Charles Byrne. Instead of having the decent burial he had hoped for, Byrne ended up on the dissection table, and thence to the Royal College of Surgeons as a skeleton on display.

By the middle of the eighteenth century the resurrection men were well established in London and Edinburgh, and cemeteries were protected from their depredations by high railings, watchtowers and vigilant relatives of the deceased. The body-snatchers (or 'sack-'em-up men') became adept at their trade, exhuming their sought-after cadavers between night patrols and neatly restoring the graves. As the law stood at the time, there was no property in a dead body. Therefore, providing only the body was taken and its shroud and any other funerary items were left behind, the act of body-snatching was not in itself a crime.

The nineteenth century saw public opinion turn against the resurrectionists, and prison sentences were introduced for grave-theft. The trade nevertheless continued, and with corpses fetching between three and five guineas each, many resurrectionists were prepared to risk imprisonment for quick profits. It was alleged that as many as sixteen corpses were removed from a St Pancras graveyard in one night.

The most infamous body-snatchers were Burke and Hare, who provided corpses for Dr Robert Knox, the Edinburgh anatomist. In 1827 William Burke and William Hare lived in the sleazy West Port area of the city with their paramours, Maggie Laird and Nell Macdougal. Maggie let rooms, and when one of her lodgers died Burke and Hare took the body to Dr Knox, for whose medical work the supply of corpses rarely met the demand. In less than a year Burke and Hare delivered sixteen

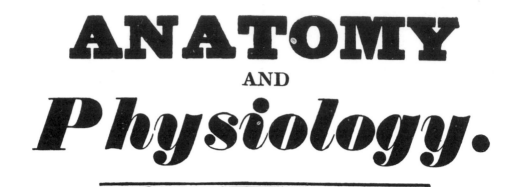

ANATOMY
AND
Physiology.

DR KNOX, F. R. S. E. *(Successor to* **DR BARCLAY,** *Fellow of the Royal College of Surgeons and Conservator of its Museum,)* will commence his ANNUAL COURSE OF LECTURES ON THE **ANATOMY** AND **PHYSIOLOGY** of the Human Body, on Tuesday, the 4th November, at Eleven A. M. His Evening COURSE of LECTURES, on the same Subject, will commence on the 11th November, at Six P. M.

Each of these Courses will as usual comprise a full Demonstration on fresh Anatomical Subjects, of the Structure of the Human Body, and a History of the Uses of its various Parts; and the Organs and Structures generally, will be described with a constant reference to Practical Medicine and Surgery.

FEE for the First Course, £ 3, 5s.; Second Course, £ 2, 4s.; Perpetual, £ 5, 9s.

N. B.—*These Courses of Lectures qualify for Examination before the various Colleges and Boards.*

Dr Knox advertises his courses in human dissection

cadavers to the anatomist's dissecting rooms.

At least two bodies turned up on the dissection tables whose identity was known to the students, and it soon became apparent that Burke and Hare's trade was not in grave-robbing. Their greed was such that for £10 a body they were prepared to murder to keep the surgeons' dissecting knives busy. Burke and Hare, together with their female companions, were arrested, and feelings against them in Edinburgh ran very high. Hare and Maggie Laird turned King's Evidence,

which resulted in Burke and Nell Macdougal being charged with MURDER. At their trial the case against Macdougal was judged NOT PROVEN, but Burke was found guilty. He was sentenced to hang and — ironically, for a body-snatcher — his corpse was to be handed over to the College of Surgeons for dissection. It was perhaps poetic justice that his skeleton should end up on display in the Edinburgh University Medical School.

Burke made a CONFESSION in the condemned cell prior to his EXECUTION before a large crowd in January 1829. His murder method involved getting his quarry into a drunken state and then, while Hare covered the struggling victim's nose and mouth, sitting on the man's chest. This crushed his ribs and forced the air out of his lungs. Death was thus caused by ASPHYXIA.

By 1830 surgeons were being arrested and fined for receiving exhumed bodies with the intention of dissecting them. The public outcry against body-snatching reached such heights that Parliament set up a Select Committee to consider the whole question of supplying the needs of the medical schools. As a result the Anatomy Act was passed in 1832, which made it an offence to rob a grave, and laid down that the only corpses which could be used for dissection were those of persons who died in hospitals and workhouses which were not claimed within seventy-two hours. The body-snatching trade dwindled after this, and the medical world regained that part of its reputation which had been lost during the scandals created by dissection-room practices.

Another kind of body-snatching also features in the annals of murder, albeit rarely. That is the securing of corpses for the purpose of NECRO-PHILIA or other perverted sexual practices. Ed Gein, an American farmer, developed such a morbid interest in female anatomy that he resorted to grave-robbing in order to obtain specimens. (See under CANNIBALISM.)

1, 11, 30, 40, 78, 144, 190, 191, 302, 463, 581, 688.

BURNING

Murder by burning is unusual, but the use of fire to destroy a victim's corpse after death has been procured by drugs or more violent means is well known. Burns are generally taken to refer to those injuries resulting from dry heat or from hot liquid (sometimes called scalds).

There are several classification methods for burns, including that of Dupuytren, a French surgeon, whose system included six degrees of burns according to the apparent severity of tissue damage. Modern medicine accepts the depth of a burn as the critical factor which determines treatment. A general rule is that burning which destroys more than 70 per cent of the skin is likely to be fatal, and in elderly people this can be reduced to 20 per cent. Calculation of burned area is based on the so-called 'rule of nine', in which the head and neck represent 9 per cent of the total body area and other parts of the body in proportion.

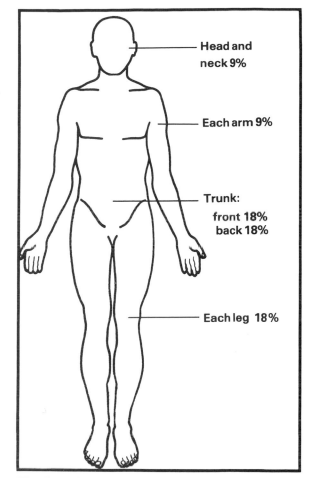

The 'Rule of Nine' applied in burn cases

Several factors are important in POST-MORTEM examination of victims in suspicious cases of burning; in particular, evidence which enables an assessment to be made whether the person was alive or not at the time the burns were sustained. The presence in the air passages of inhaled carbon particles is proof that the victim was alive at the time of the fire. Proof of even brief survival is also indicated by finding carbon monoxide in the blood. The demonstration of VITAL REACTION in burn blisters is of value in some cases of burning in showing that the injuries were caused during life. The presence of bone marrow or fat embolism in the lungs may indicate violent injury such as bone fracture inflicted before death. It is important that splitting and rupture of tissues due to intense heat is not confused with ante-mortem injuries inflicted by knife or gun. A characteristic of badly burned bodies is their aggressive appearance — known as

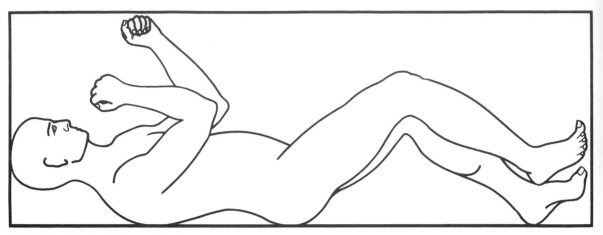

Pugilistic attitude of a burned body

'pugilistic attitude' — caused by contraction and stiffening of the muscles.

Suicide by burning is not common, although self-immolation for religious or political reasons is well known. IDENTIFICATION may be difficult in badly charred corpses, when examination of the TEETH can be especially helpful.

Burning after murder to conceal the crime is well recorded, and one of the most celebrated cases is that of the Blazing Car Murder of 1930. Alfred Arthur Rouse, a London-based commercial traveller, absconded from the scene of his burning car in a Northamptonshire lane. By the time passers-by reached the blaze the heat was so intense that the car could only be approached from a distance. The following day the smouldering wreck was found to contain an unrecognizably burned corpse.

Sir Bernard Spilsbury examined the remains, and noted that fine particles of soot were present in the lungs. There was no indication of poison or injury, but a scrap of cloth trapped by a fold in the body smelled of petrol. An expert fire-assessor suggested that the petrol union joint of the carburettor was deliberately loosened and petrol splashed from a can to make a trail to the roadside. This was then ignited, consuming the car and its occupant, who was presumed to be slumped unconscious across the front seats.

When Rouse was arrested he told a story of picking up a man who requested a lift and leaving him to replenish the car's fuel-tank from a can of petrol while he relieved himself at a discreet distance down the lane. While adjusting his trousers Rouse claimed to see a light followed by a mass of flame which enveloped his car and passenger. In his panic he ran away.

The identity of the fire victim was never established. Rouse was brought to trial and convicted of murder. The day after he was executed in March 1931 his CONFESSION was published, and his account corresponded in its essential details with that given by the fire-assessor.

The year before the Rouse case a blazing-car mystery had captured the headlines in German newspapers. In November 1929 police were called to the scene of a motor accident near Regensburg. A green Opel had crashed and caught fire, trapping the driver, who burned to death. The dead man was thought to be Erich Tetzner, a Leipzig businessman, whose wife immediately made an insurance claim against a large accident policy which her husband had taken out only a few weeks previously.

No other vehicle was involved in the accident, and it was thought that the driver might have suffered a heart-attack, or even committed suicide. The remains of the fire victim gave little to aid identification — the top part of the head was missing, together with the lower parts of the legs, and the rest of the body was badly charred. A careful post-mortem showed no trace of soot particles in the larynx or windpipe, and an analysis of the heart blood for carbon monoxide was negative. Thus the dead man could not have been alive at the time of the fire. Suspicion that the dead man might not be Tetzner began to harden. An examination of cartilages in the burned corpse enabled pathologists to arrive at an age for the victim which was several years younger than Tetzner. The discovery of microscopic fatty EMBOLISMS blocking the blood-vessels in the lungs — a phenomenon which may occur in a person subjected to violent injury — suggested the possibility that the fire victim might first have been murdered.

With suspicions thoroughly aroused, the police carried out surveillance on Frau Tetzner, whom they discovered was in telephone contact with her husband in Strasbourg. Erich Tetzner was arrested, and immediately confessed to picking up a hitch-hiker whom he doused with petrol while the man sat sleeping in his car. He then put a match to the vehicle, which he ran off the road to simulate an accident. This story, of course, did not conform with the absence of combustion products in the dead man's body, which would have been present had he been alive when consumed by the fire. Tetzner now changed his story to fit the facts, saying that he had run over the hitch-hiker, whose dead body he used as his fire victim. There seemed little doubt that Tetzner had first killed and mutilated his victim before incinerating his body in order to defraud the insurance company. He was tried for murder, found guilty and was executed at Regensburg in May 1931.

1, 2, 9, 34, 35, 81, 97, 118, 119, 318, 337, 359, 483, 523, 534, 564, 586, 672, 726.

C

CADAVERIC SPASM

The 'death grasp' is an uncommon condition in which a person at the moment of death clasps some near-by object in a dead man's grip. Cadaveric spasm, or instantaneous rigor, is usually associated with violent death. One of G. J. Smith's 'Brides in the Bath' victims was found firmly clutching a piece of soap after she had died by DROWNING.

The cause of cadaveric spasm is not fully understood, but it is known not to be a form of RIGOR MORTIS. It is a unique phenomenon which can neither be simulated nor produced by any means after death. Consequently, its presence is of great importance to the crime investigator — a weapon, or objects such as buttons, HAIR or a piece of cloth held in a dead man's grip, can afford vital clues. Similarly, stones or weeds clenched in the fist of a drowned person may help pin-point the place where drowning occurred.

Detective Chief Superintendent William Muncie reported an example of cadaveric spasm in a man who had been found battered to death in a wooded area near a mental hospital in Scotland. Gripped in the right hand of the corpse was a collection of leaves and vegetation which showed beyond doubt that he had been murdered where he was found. Both victim and killer proved to be patients at a near-by mental hospital — the significance of the cadaveric spasm was that detectives

Death grasp

were able to concentrate their efforts in the immediate locale, knowing that the man had not been murdered elsewhere.

1, 511, **625**.

CANNIBALISM

'Grace sat in my lap and kissed me. I made up my mind to eat her. . . . How she did kick, bite and scratch! I choked her to death, then cut her in small pieces so I could take my meat to my rooms, cook it and eat it.' Thus did Albert Fish write to the mother of his ten-year-old victim, admitting to the appalling combined crime of murder and cannibalism.

Grace Budd disappeared from her New York home on 3 June 1928, taken away by an elderly man known to the family as Frank Howard. Ostensibly he was taking her to a party. In reality Albert Fish, then aged fifty-eight and the father of six children, abducted the girl to an empty house in Westchester County, where he conducted his perverted rites. After strangling the girl he dismembered her body, and over a period of nine days ate strips of her flesh which he cooked with vegetables. Later he confessed that this activity kept him in a continuous state of sexual fervour.

Nearly six years after this horrific incident took place Mrs Budd received an unsigned letter from her daughter's murderer informing her of the manner of the child's death. When Fish was arrested in December 1934 he was eager to answer questions, and his CONFESSION came pouring out. He took police officers to the house in Westchester County where he had murdered the girl, and told them about his 'implements of hell' — a knife, cleaver and saw — which he used for his diabolical work. He also told them in a matter-of-fact way how he killed the girl, cut her throat and tried to drink her blood. He said in mitigation of what he had done, 'It was a kind of blood lust.'

A suitcase retrieved from the rooming-house in which Fish lived contained newspaper cuttings referring to the German murderer and cannibal Fritz Haarmann, who preyed on young boys and disposed of their bodies for meat. Fish admitted at least a hundred incidents involving sexually perverted acts with children. He carried out these activities through twenty-three states, and had been arrested eight times on various charges, including sending obscene letters.

Fish was indicted with first-degree MURDER and not surprisingly became the subject of intense psychiatric observation. He himself said, 'I am not insane, I am just queer,' and he spoke of his interest in religion and belief in the need for purging and physical suffering. He tortured himself, but when he tried to stick needles under his fingernails he could not stand the agony. 'If only pain were not so painful,' he said. The question of sanity was a key issue at his trial. Dr Frederic Wertham, the distinguished psychiatrist who appeared for the defence, declared him insane. Fish had told him of his fascination with accounts he had read of cannibalism, and that he was 'consumed with the desire to eat human flesh'. Fish's confession, read out in court, and the detailed revelations of the intense sexual excitement he gained out of the acts of cannibalism, brought gasps of horror.

The defence suggested Fish was infantile and had a childish ignorance of right and wrong. His sex life and general judgment were unbalanced, but, like many insane persons, his thinking was not affected. He was diagnosed as having paranoid psychosis, characterized by delusions and hallucinations, and to be insane under the law. The prosecution agreed that he was a sexual PSYCHOPATH, but denied evidence of any mental disease. The jury pronounced Fish guilty — which he accepted with a polite 'Thank you' — and the Press had a heyday with such headlines as 'Thrill Vulture' and 'Sinister Ghoul'.

Albert Fish, a mild-looking grandfather, was sent to the ELECTRIC CHAIR at Sing Sing in January 1936. The first electrical charge allegedly failed on account of being short-circuited by the presence of needles in the old man's body. Doctors had earlier found twenty-nine needles in his genitals which he had inserted over the years in his search for thrills.

There is ample evidence of cannibalism, the eating of human flesh, in prehistoric times. The practice was usually associated with magical rites, and in historic times some of the Oceanic and African tribes devoured their enemies. Sir James Frazer, author of *The Golden Bough*, noted that the 'flesh and blood of dead men are eaten and drunk to inspire bravery, wisdom or other qualities'. The heart was often eaten to acquire valour, and the male organs to gain strength. Part of the reason for eating the flesh of an enemy was to quench his spirit and prevent him taking vengeance. Homicidal cannibalism might serve a similar symbolic purpose in diposing of the murder victim. JACK THE RIPPER was perhaps a trend-setter when he removed a kidney from one of his victims and sent part of it to the chairman of the Whitechapel Vigilance Committee. The note which accompanied it declared, 't'other piece I fried and ate it was very nice'.

Cannibalism has been reported in modern times when groups of people have been subjected to intense hardship and starvation. A party of gold prospectors stranded in winter conditions in the San Juan mountains in America's West in 1873 was reduced to five members. Alfred Packer, with his admission that he killed and ate four of his companions, became a notorious modern cannibal. Similar stories emerged from the ordeals suffered by the pioneers who opened up America's West in the 1850s. The pressures which starvation can exert on civilized people were demonstrated by the Andes air-crash in 1972. A Uruguayan plane on a flight to Chile crashed in the mountains, and its passengers were marooned for ten weeks. Of the forty-five passengers on the plane only sixteen were recovered alive, and they had survived by eating the flesh of their dead companions.

Homicidal cannibalism is not rare, and Albert Fish appeared to have been impressed by Fritz Haarmann, an unsavoury dealer in meat in Germany after the First World War. Discharged from the armed forces, Haarmann settled down to the life of a petty criminal in his native Hanover. He was said to have suffered from EPILEPSY, which was put forward as an explanation for his crimes. His practice was to lie in wait for young refugees at the railway station and to offer them food and shelter. By this method, and aided by his accomplice, Hans Grans, the perverted Haarmann lured numbers of teenage boys to his den. There, under the guise of homosexual advances, he killed his victims, stripped the clothes from their dead bodies and sold their flesh for meat, apart from that which he ate himself.

It was estimated that for over a year this murderous pair averaged two victims a week, selling their clothes and flesh and storing their bones in a cupboard. When the fit took him Haarmann would throw a collection of human bones and skulls into the river Leine. An accusation of indecency against Haarmann put an end to this traffic, and when apprehended in July 1924 he made a ready CONFESSION to murder and other practices. He was charged with twenty-seven murders, although other estimates put it at nearer fifty. The knowledge that over six hundred youths disappeared in Hanover in one year alone suggests the higher figure might be more accurate. Haarmann, aged forty-five, was convicted, and suffered death by beheading. Grans was given a prison sentence.

18, 71, 78, 178, 191, 302, 323, 459, 475, 551, 661, 714.

CHILD-MURDER

About three-quarters of the child-murders which occur in Britain are committed by parents or close relatives. Children become the unhappy victims of family tensions, and make all too easy targets for the sexually motivated murderer. The advice to children not to take sweets from strangers remains ever true. New-born babies become victims of INFANTICIDE for reasons associated with the trauma of childbirth, but infants also become murder victims at their parents' hands for other reasons.

Terence Armstrong, a 5½-month-old son of a young couple living at Gosport, was murdered by his father, probably because he was unwanted. The child died at home in July 1955 as the result of eating poisonous berries — or so it was thought. The discovery at POST-MORTEM of red skins in the stomach supported this idea, but the child was duly buried. Subsequent examination of the STOMACH CONTENTS proved that the skins were not from berries, but were the soft capsules of the drug Seconal. An EXHUMATION followed, and the presence of Seconal in the child's body was confirmed.

The parents, John and Janet Armstrong, denied having any Seconal in the house, although it was noted that Armstrong had access to drugs in the course of his duties as a naval sick-bay attendant. An open verdict was recorded at the Coroner's inquest on the child's death, and there the matter rested for a year. Then in 1956, after she had been granted a legal separation from her husband on the grounds of cruelty, Janet Armstrong made a statement to the police. She admitted what had previously been denied, and now said that there had been Seconal in the house. Her husband had brought some capsules home from the naval hospital where he worked, and after their son's death had told her to get rid of them, which she did.

The Armstrongs were arrested and charged with murder. John denied all knowledge of how the baby was poisoned, but his wife confirmed in court the damning evidence of Seconal in the house, and let it be known that he had had the opportunity to be alone with the child when he came home to lunch. Something of the tension that existed between husband and wife was drawn out in Mrs Armstrong's admission that her husband had been violent towards her. He had also told her when she was pregnant that they could not afford another child. Baby Terence thus became the innocent victim of parental tensions. John Armstrong was found guilty of murder (though reprieved), and his wife was acquitted.

The very innocence and defencelessness of children makes them prey to the friendly stranger who entices or snatches them away from their normal surroundings. They may be seen as targets for KIDNAPPING like the Lindbergh baby, or more usually as subjects for sexual abuse which may lead to murder. The ease with which elderly, harmless-looking Albert Fish walked off with his young victim under the unsuspecting gaze of her parents demonstrates the dangers. (See under CANNIBALISM.) Frederick Nodder, known as 'Uncle Fred' to the children, Albert Arthur Jones who kept peppermints at the ready, and Raymond Morris who offered rides in his car, exemplified some of the techniques of the child-murderer. It is scant comfort to either victims or their parents to know that child-murderers when convicted and gaoled are treated as outcasts by their fellow-prisoners. Reduction in the numbers of child-murders, like most aspects of crime-prevention, requires a high degree of public awareness.

The murder of one child by another is not a common occurrence, but it is a phenomenon which makes sensational news. Sexual experimentation led to the death of twelve-year-old Lorna Max in California in 1959. Her body, stabbed and beaten, was found in a secret hideaway in some woods near her home, where it was alleged she ran a 'sex club' for the initiation of local boys. She had not been raped, but subjected to 'sexual mistreatment'. Police inquiries led them to fifteen-year-old Clifford Fortner, who admitted having been intimate with the girl, and later confessed to killing her. He had become jealous when he discovered she had been entertaining other boys, and his sexual exploration turned into violence. The youth was not sent for trial, as he was under age in the eyes of Californian law, but was sentenced to indefinite detention in a reformatory. Under English law any child over the age of ten years may be tried on a criminal charge.

Probably the most news-catching child-murders of recent years have been the twenty-eight killings committed in Atlanta, Georgia, between July 1979 and May 1981. Public fears rose as the death-toll mounted in the face of the failure of the police to apprehend the killer. The children, both boys and girls mostly in their early teens, died from ASPHYXIA. Some of the bodies were found lying on their backs with the arms outstretched above the head in some kind of ritualistic pose, and others were found floating in the Chattahoochee river. Police found substantial links between only seven of the killings, and only one showed signs of sexual assault.

The killings of the coloured children attracted intense publicity, and the police included PSYCHIC DETECTION and HYPNOSIS among the exhaustive methods used to examine the mass of information collected. There was a fear that the publicity itself might have triggered off 'copy-cat' murders so that more than one killer was at work.

On 22 May 1981 a police surveillance team patrolling near the Chattahoochee river heard a loud splash in the early hours of the morning and apprehended a man driving away from the area. Wayne B. Williams, a 23-year-old freelance photographer and music-talent scout, was kept under police surveillance for two weeks, in which time the corpse of the twenty-eighth murder victim was recovered from the river. Williams was charged with the murder of Nathaniel Cater and with that of Jimmy Ray Payne, the twenty-sixth victim.

From the time he was arrested until he appeared on trial in Atlanta, no murders occurred in the area, and this fact alone weighed heavily against Williams in the public view. The prosecution produced five hundred witnesses and a mass of scientific evidence. HAIRS and FIBRES found on two of the victims were matched to Williams's German Shepherd dog and to carpets in his home. Describing himself as 'a carefree, happy-go-lucky person', Williams denied knowing either of the murdered youths, and protested his innocence.

In February 1982 the trial jury convicted him, and he was given two life sentences. During the investigation it was stated that CONTACT TRACES had been found linking Williams to eight of the other victims, and there were suggestions of homosexual motives. Officially, only two of the Atlanta murders were solved — the other twenty-six remain open to speculation.

1, 27, 105, 223, 239, 322, 367, 385, 448, 579, 628.

CHLOROFORM

When Adelaide Bartlett was acquitted of the charge of murdering her husband by giving him chloroform Sir James Paget, a distinguished Victorian surgeon, was said to have remarked, 'Now she's acquitted, she should tell us in the interests of science how she did it.' The Bartlett case with its heavy sexual overtones caused a sensation in 1886.

Nineteen-year-old Adelaide married Edwin Bartlett, a man eleven years older than herself and a prosperous grocer, apparently on the understanding that their relationship would be on a platonic basis and would not involve sexual intercourse. Soon after her marriage Adelaide had an affair with her brother-in-law and a bitter row with Edwin's father. Bored and dissatisfied, she became friendly with the Rev. George Dyson, a young Wesleyan minister. Edwin approved of this liaison, even to the point of encouraging the couple to kiss in his presence. He also made a will leaving everything to Adelaide and naming Dyson as executor. When the Bartletts moved to fresh lodgings in London's Pimlico district Adelaide's relationship with Dyson flourished still further, and he tutored her in Latin and history. By discouraging her father-in-law's visits she succeeded in cutting some of her husband's close family links.

Shortly after this, in December 1885, Edwin was taken seriously ill for the first time in his life. He received some dental treatment, and recovered sufficiently to celebrate Christmas. At about this time Adelaide asked Dyson to buy some chloroform, which she explained was used by Edwin as a treatment for an internal complaint. Dyson complied with this request, making three separate purchases of the drug which he poured into one bottle — amounting to some four ounces of liquid — and gave to Adelaide on 29 December.

On the last day of the year Edwin visited his dentist, and appeared to be in good form and on amiable terms with his wife. About 4.0 a.m. on New Year's Day Adelaide roused her landlord, Mr Doggett, and asked him to 'Come down; I think Mr Bartlett is dead.' She told him she had awakened to find her husband lying face down, and attempted to revive him with brandy. Doggett noticed a strong smell in the room, like ether. There was a wine-glass on the mantelshelf near the bed — it was a quarter empty and the contents also smelled of ether. And on a near-by table stood a tumbler containing Condy's Fluid (a proprietary disinfectant solution) with an unlabelled one-ounce bottle inverted in it.

A POST-MORTEM examination showed that the dead man's stomach was inflamed, and smelled strongly of chloroform, the presence of which was confirmed by analysis. Doctors found about 1/16th ounce, from which they judged that a large dose of chloroform had been swallowed. Intriguingly, there was no trace of burning in the mouth or windpipe. Dyson, who was charged with murder along with Adelaide, related how she had asked him to buy chloroform. He told the chemist that he wanted it for removing grease-stains, and subsequently threw the bottles away on Wandsworth Common. He was discharged when no evidence was offered at their trial for murder at the Old Bailey.

Sir Charles Russell, the Attorney-General, told the JURY that chloroform was definitely found in the dead man's stomach — the question was, how did it get there? Dr Thomas Leach, Edwin Bartlett's physician, spoke of the dead man's eccentric views on marriage and of his belief in mesmerism and the vital force. Adelaide had confided in him, and mentioned her acquaintance with Dyson, which her husband condoned. Later, he declared his intention to resume conjugal rights and she had sought to quieten his new-found passion by getting him to inhale chloroform to make him drowsy. On New Year's Eve she gave him chloroform and he drifted off to sleep while she dozed in a chair by his side. She was awakened once by the sound of his snoring, and when she woke up again he was dead.

Defence counsel gave the court his version of events in the Bartlett home on New Year's Eve, which involved Edwin drinking chloroform from the wineglass while in a suicidal frame of mind. The Attorney-General's view was that there were only two ways in which the chloroform could have been swallowed by the dead man — while he was in an insensible state as a result of inhaling the drug, or by being given a draught containing chloroform which he swallowed quickly in innocence of its contents. He asked the jury if they could accept that Adelaide's reason for buying chloroform was solely to repulse her husband's advances.

The medical men called to give expert evidence agreed that less was known about death caused by swallowing chloroform than by inhaling it. Swallowed chloroform was usually associated with suicide, but Dr Thomas Stevenson, Professor of Jurisprudence at Guy's Hospital, said it was possible to put liquid down the throat of a person who was insensible from inhaling chloroform. Liquid put at the back of the throat would be swallowed by the reflex act of swallowing. This would not be so if the person were fully conscious. He also said it would be possible to put liquid down the throat of a sleeping person, although there was the danger of fluid getting into the windpipe. Dr Charles Tidy, Professor of Chemistry and Forensic Medicine at the London Hospital, gave it as his opinion that if a person had been rendered partially unconscious by inhaling chloroform the drug could be administered in stages as a liquid.

Mr Justice Wills told the jury that there was no escape from the dilemma arising from the fact that liquid chloroform had been given to the dead man, either criminally or not criminally. 'If you take the evidence on either hand alone,' he said, 'you would say the thing could not be done. Yet it had been done, and one of the two impossible theories must be right.' The jury concluded that although grave suspicion attached to the defendant, there was insufficient evidence to show how or by whom the chloroform had been administered. Adelaide Bartlett was therefore acquitted, and the first recorded charge of murdering a person with liquid chloroform left all the vital questions unanswered.

Chloroform was discovered in 1831 by the German chemist Baron von Liebig and others. This colourless, volatile liquid with its characteristic odour was widely used as a solvent. In 1847 Sir James Simpson, Professor of Obstetrics at Glasgow University, published his use of chloroform as an anaesthetic. He had been searching for a compound which would be superior to ether for easing the pains of childbirth, and he found chloroform to be a convenient substitute, with fewer unwanted side-effects. He was bitterly opposed by the medical fraternity, and the use of chloroform was denounced from the pulpit. But after Queen Victoria received it for the delivery of her eighth child in 1853 the drug was widely accepted.

Chloroform vapour in a concentration of 1 to 2 per cent is used for anaesthetic purposes, and is given by controlled inhalation. Small doses may be given by mouth to relieve vomiting, and chloroform is a constituent in some medicines used to ease coughs by soothing the bronchial passages. The drug is a powerful narcotic, initially causing feelings of stimulation when inhaled, and then producing unconsciousness. Chloroform has been used criminally to assist robbery and rape, when the usual method is to apply a soaked pad over the mouth and nostrils. Murder has been committed by forced inhalation of the drug, causing a poisonous build-up and paralysing the heart. Accidental deaths have occurred through swallowing chloroform, but the charge of murder by this method is rare, save for the Bartlett case. Ingestion causes burning of the mouth and oesophagus, with death resulting in hours due to heart-failure and liver-damage. The estimated lethal dose of chloroform by ingestion is 10 to 15 ml, although recovery has been recorded following doses as high as 120 and 150 ml. Post-mortem examination will disclose the characteristic smell of chloroform in the lungs, and the drug may be detected in all the body fluids. Addiction may occur through the habit of regularly inhaling chloroform to experience a sense of stimulation — ether and chloroform have long been used for drug 'sniffing'.

Ruth Snyder and Henry Judd Gray, the pair of murderous lovers electrocuted at Sing Sing in 1928 for killing Albert Snyder in New York, included chloroform in their murder plan. So too did Charles Jones and Albert Patrick in disposing of Texas oil millionaire William Marsh Rice in 1900. Dr Etienne Deschamps, the New Orleans dentist, used chloroform to assist his sexual lusts, but over-did the anaesthetic, killing a twelve-year-old girl. Dot King, the New York model, submitted to a similarly fatal dose when she was chloroformed in her apartment in the course of a robbery in 1923. Deschamps was hanged in 1892, but Dot King's murder was never solved.

1, 14, 42, 62, 89, 107, 121, 135, **148***, 156, 196, 235, 256, 300, 315, 337, 408, 424, 453, 455, 464, 500, 503, 538, 582, 589, 624, 656, 660, 666, 678, 696, 700.*

CIRCUMSTANTIAL EVIDENCE

The classic example of circumstantial evidence is the footprint in the sand seen by Robinson Crusoe, from which he inferred there was a stranger on the island. In law, circumstantial evidence is derived from facts not in dispute from which can be inferred a fact that is at issue.

Evidence of this type has acquired a bad name and is popularly regarded as unreliable, and inferior to direct evidence or eye-witness testimony. Tennyson Jesse, the distinguished crime writer, remarked that for obvious reasons murders are not performed in front of eye-witnesses. This is particularly true of poisoners, and circumstantial evidence played a major role in convicting Major Herbert Rowse Armstrong, the ARSENIC poisoner, in 1922. Tennyson Jesse argued that while they may be misinterpreted, 'circumstances themselves do not lie'. Certainly many murderers have been convicted on the strength of circumstantial evidence, and the value of this type of evidence has been upheld by numerous judges.

Chief Justice Lemuel Shaw defined the subject in his charge to the JURY at the trial of Professor John White Webster in 1850. The Professor was tried at Boston for the murder of fellow-academic Dr George Parkman, who disappeared following a disagreement about a loan. Parts of a human body were found in the assay oven in Webster's laboratory, including TEETH identified as those of

Parkman. The case against Webster was largely circumstantial, but none the less convincing. Chief Justice Shaw posed the question 'But suppose no person was present on the occasion of the death . . . is it wholly unsusceptible of legal proof?' He answered the question thus: 'Experience has shown that circumstantial evidence may be offered in such a case; that is a body of facts may be proved of so conclusive a character as to warrant a firm belief of the fact quite as strong and certain as that on which discreet men are accustomed to act in relation to their most important concerns. . . .'

Professor Webster's lawyer made loud protestations about the evils of circumstantial evidence, despite which the jury found his client guilty. The Professor himself showed the value of such evidence in his own case by confessing his crime — no doubt to the chagrin of his lawyer.

Judge Frederick Smyth was equally unequivocal at the trial of Carlyle Harris, the MORPHINE poisoner, in New York in 1892. He told the jury that circumstantial evidence is legal evidence, remarking that if all the circumstances point towards guilt, the jury would be bound to regard such evidence in the same way they would consider direct or positive evidence.

The history of criminal trials shows that direct evidence is by no means infallible. It is widely held, for example, that Timothy John Evans, hanged in March 1950, was erroneously convicted, and Oscar Slater, sentenced to death for murder in 1909 but later reprieved, was certainly convicted on mistaken eye-witness evidence.
2, 45, 92, 167, 201, 363, 509, 533, 535, 539, 655, 669, 690.

COMMON LAW

Common law denotes the law which is the same for all members of society, and is based on custom and usage as distinct from legislation. The term arose in England during the Middle Ages, and the system became a powerful force in that it freed the common man from the tyranny of the nobles. One of its maxims was that the king must recognize the law that made him king.

Although unwritten, common law embodies the customs and practices of precedent, and represents the common sense of the community. Cases decided in court thus have regard to earlier decisions, and the historical independence of the judges is to balance the rights of the citizen against the king. Common law is distinguished from statute law, which is enacted by Parliament, and from civil law, which emphasizes the power of the State.

Common law operates in England (though not in Scotland), in parts of the British Commonwealth and in the USA. It differs from the law in most European countries (including Scotland) in that it was not influenced by the spread of Roman law in the sixteenth century, which rests on statutes enacted by the State rather than on the custom and usage of the people.
348, **658**.

CONFESSION

When a person confesses to a murder the reason may derive from a straightforward acceptance of the hopelessness of denying guilt any longer in the face of strong evidence. But there are many other possible reasons too; a reduction in punishment may be sought, or an attempt be made to throw suspicion on to another person. Confessions are often made to gain time by directing investigators along a false trail, or to deceive by accepting guilt for a small offence in order to create an ALIBI for a greater crime. There are also individuals of a particular type who make a false confession to a murder in order to achieve notoriety. The Black Dahlia murder in Los Angeles in 1947 produced a rash of false confessions but no convicted murderer.

It is important to check a confession, to corroborate its details and thereby ensure its accuracy. For example, if a confessing murderer states that he hid the murder weapon in a particular place he will be asked 'to make indications' so that it can be retrieved and taken into account as supporting EVIDENCE. It is equally important to demonstrate that a confession has not been obtained by forceful means. If it is to be admissible in court it must be shown that it is both voluntary and trustworthy. Police interrogators therefore work to rules which ensure that any statement made by a suspect is not subsequently invalidated by accusations that pressure or inducement were used. An accused person must be informed of the nature of the offence with which he is charged, and be advised of his rights — to remain silent, and to request that a lawyer be made available. He is also warned that information gained from him may be used in evidence. He may knowingly choose to waive these rights before making a statement, in which case it is customary for the police to make sure that the procedure is properly witnessed and recorded.

Use of torture and the THIRD DEGREE to obtain admissions of guilt are largely a thing of the past, at least in countries where democracy prevails. Until the end of the eighteenth century confession was regarded as the best form of evidence, and not too many questions were asked about how it was obtained. Lord Crambo, Lord Chief Justice of Malta, provided a classic example of this in 1720 when he witnessed a street fight. He clearly saw a man stabbed to death, and observed the attacker escape. He also witnessed an innocent passer-by arrive at the scene and be seized by a mob. When the man was accused of murder and found guilty by a trial JURY, Judge Crambo, in full knowledge of the man's innocence, ordered him to be tortured in order to extract a confession. The real murderer was caught later, and stated that he saw the judge at a window overlooking the scene. He called on him to testify that the killing resulted from a fair fight. Lord Crambo admitted being a witness, but declared that he could not use private knowledge to settle a case in court.

The history of murder cases is littered with dramatic confessions, perhaps the most unusual ones being those made by an accused after he has been found not guilty. Brian Hume was tried in 1950 for the murder of Stanley Setty and the jury disagreed, but he was sentenced to twelve years' imprisonment when he confessed to being an accessory. On his release in 1958, he let it be known through the pages of the *Sunday Pictorial* that he had committed the murder.

Unusual confessions include that made by 21-year-old Constance Kent. Following her release from arrest and a charge of murdering her young half-brother at Road in Wiltshire, she entered a French convent. After two and a half years there she returned to England and joined a convent at Brighton. There, during Easter 1865, she confessed to the murder. She was sent for trial, and pleaded guilty. After a brief hearing she was found guilty and received sentence of death. This was commuted to life imprisonment, and she was released after serving twenty years. Another unusual confession was the written statement claimed to have been left by Henri Landru, the notorious French murderer. Prior to facing the GUILLOTINE in 1922 he scribbled the words, 'I did it. I burned their bodies in my kitchen oven,' on the back of a framed drawing which he had given to one of his lawyers. This confession only came to

Dr Ruxton's confession to murder

Lancaster.
14. 10. 35.

I killed Mrs Ruxton in a fit of temper because I thought she had been with a man. I was Mad at the time. Mary Rogerson was present at the time. I had to kill her.

B Ruxton.

light forty-six years later, when it appeared in a newspaper.

Some confessions appear more quickly, such as that of Dr Buck Ruxton, which was published on the Sunday following his execution in May 1936, (see under SKULLS for an account of the case). The night before his arrest, he handed the *News of the World* crime reporter a sealed envelope. It was to be opened only if he was hanged; otherwise it was to be returned to him.

TRUTH DRUGS and LIE-DETECTORS have become part of the modern interrogator's stock-in-trade. While they each have their applications — especially in eliminating suspects from an investigation there is still nothing to beat the straight forward admission of guilt in a voluntary confession.

21, 25, 62, 86, 90, 93, 103, 136, 283, 315, 380, 459, 480, 539, 562, 573, 581, 624, 645, 662, 667, **673***, 685, 690, 736.*

CONSPIRACY TO MURDER

The idea of criminal conspiracy — of persons joining forces in secret for some evil purpose such as murder — became fashionable in the wake of the ASSASSINATIONS of President John F. Kennedy and Dr Martin Luther King. Theses were made out involving government agencies in plots to further political ambitions by removing important national figures from the arena of power.

A conspiracy is an agreement between two or more persons to commit an unlawful act. Any individual who conspires to commit murder, or who solicits, proposes, encourages or persuades another to carry out murder, is subject to the rigour of the law. The English are perhaps particularly touchy on this point as a result of the Gunpowder Plot of 1605, when a Roman Catholic attempt to destroy the Protestant government of James I by blowing up the Houses of Parliament and their sitting Members was dramatically foiled.

Conspiracy to murder has also played a part on the domestic front, usually in attempts to solve love triangles. Fourteen hundred dollars was the price fixed for the CONTRACT MURDER of Barbara Finch, the wife of a Californian doctor. Bernard Finch ran a medical centre in Los Angeles, where he and his wife were popular on the social scene. In 1957 the couple decided to part company, and Finch rented an apartment where he could meet his new love, an ex-model named Carole Tregoff.

Finch wanted a divorce, but his wife refused in the knowledge that under Californian law the innocent party in a case where the grounds were adultery, cruelty or desertion might be awarded a major share of the property. If she claimed the whole of her husband's financial interest in the medical centre, together with heavy alimony payments, he would be left with virtually nothing.

Faced with this ruinous prospect, Finch and Tregoff decided to find a contract killer to eliminate Mrs Finch. They chose ex-marine John Patrick Cody, and after some bargaining the deal was settled for 1,400 dollars with 350 dollars as a down payment, and the date of completion as 4 July 1959. The choice of Cody was disappointing, for despite assuring Carole Tregoff that he had made the hit 'with a shotgun' he never so much as harmed a hair of the head of his intended victim. That was left to Finch and Tregoff, and as a result of their visit to Barbara Finch on 18 July their victim was shot dead on the driveway of her house. After two trial juries failed to reach a verdict, Finch and Tregoff were finally convicted of murder and of conspiracy, and sentenced to life imprisonment.

A lovers' conspiracy in another place and in another era similarly ended in disaster. In 1911 Henry Lovell William Clark, a doctor in the Indian Subordinate Medical Service at Agra and a married man with four children, took Augusta Fairfield Fullam, another man's wife, as his mistress. Finding themselves burdened with the time-honoured frustrations of such a situation, the lovers conspired to murder. First they poisoned Edward Fullam with ARSENIC, and then they hired four assassins to attack and murder Mrs Clark.

Following the double murder, police officers interviewed Mrs Fullam and searched her bungalow. Under the bed was a tin box containing neat bundles of love-letters amounting to some 400 epistles mostly written by her to Clark, and bearing his initials. The contents of this correspondence provided the main planks of their prosecution for murder; in one letter Mrs Fullam asks Clark to send her 'the powder', and in another wrote, 'How God has worked out all things so beautifully and brought us two most devoted and loving sweethearts closer together and given us freely to each other.'

An EXHUMATION order was granted on Fullam's body, and nearly fourteen months after his death arsenic was found in his corpse. The murderous conspirators were tried twice, on the first occasion for poisoning Fullam and on the

second for hiring killers to eliminate Mrs Clark. Mrs Fullam turned King's Evidence, and Clark made a CONFESSION in court. Both were convicted, and Clark was executed in March 1913; only her pregnant condition saved Mrs Fullam from the same fate, although she died of heatstroke the following year.
16, 195, 288, 421, 505, 543, 704.

CONTACT TRACES

When Edmond Locard, the pioneering French criminologist, remarked that 'every contact leaves a trace' he established one of the basic precepts of FORENSIC SCIENCE. John Glaister, for many years Professor of Forensic Medicine at Glasgow University, enlarged on the idea in his autobiography in a chapter entitled 'The Key of Interchange'. He explained that 'it is almost impossible for anyone to go to the scene of a crime without either leaving some trace of his visit behind him or carrying away, all unsuspectingly, some trace which links him with the place'.

This phenomenon provides the crime laboratory with its richest harvest of clues. Where the lawyer deals with the intangibles of motive, REASONABLE DOUBT and intent, the forensic scientist's stock-in-trade is physical evidence, the tell-tale contact trace which can link criminal and crime. FINGERPRINTS are an obvious example of this interchange, but the range of possibilities is vast — indeed, Harry Söderman, a distinguished Swedish criminologist, wrote that 'everything imaginable may constitute a clue'. Everything, that is, from earwax to ski tracks. Earwax traps dust particles from the environment, and may yield information about a person's occupation, while looking at ski tracks will tell the experienced observer the direction in which a traveller was moving. The list of contact traces includes BLOOD, glass particles, dust, FIBRES, HAIR, body-fluid stains, oil, paint, fragments of vegetation and a great many more substances, restricted only by the limits of scientific detection methods.

Contact trace EVIDENCE falls into a number of broad categories:

- Fingerprints and marks left on smooth surfaces by fabrics, footwear or tyres.
- Impressions left by tyres or feet in soft ground or by tools in materials such as wood or plastic.

Comparison of marks made on wood surfaces by an axe-blade

- Friction marks made by hard edges scratching over soft material.
- Traces of material carried from the crime scene on a criminal's person and on tools, weapons or vehicles used by him.
- Materials such as ink, paint and oil which are transferred to the criminal's clothing.
- Fibres or fragments detached from the criminal's clothing and left at the crime scene and similar materials carried from the scene by the criminal.
- Stains left by blood and other body fluids such as sweat, semen, saliva or urine.
- Biological material such as hair, vegetation and pollen.

The scene of the crime is meticulously examined for trace evidence, as is the body and clothing of both murder victim and suspect. Vital linking evidence may be found in unusual places, such as under the fingernails. The value of fingernail debris was demonstrated with great effectiveness by Locard in 1912, when he investigated a case in which a bank clerk in Lyons was suspected of murdering his girl-friend in a jealous rage. Emile Gourbin appeared to have proved a satisfactory ALIBI by establishing that he was playing cards with some friends at the time of the murder.

Faced with a lack of evidence, the police sent for Locard. He first examined the dead girl, and observed the marks of STRANGULATION around her throat. Then he went to the prison where the suspect was being held, and took samples of finger-nail debris which he examined in his laboratory. Under the microscope he saw numerous epithelial cells which could as easily have come from the man's own skin as from the dead girl's, but what caught the scientist's attention was that the flakes of epithelium were coated with pink dust. He identified this as face powder, and by comparing it with the cosmetics used by the girl he established that Gourbin, at the very least, had touched her face. Confronted with this evidence of contact with the murder victim, Gourbin made a full CONFES-SION, admitting that he had indeed strangled the girl and given a false alibi.

Much of the work of the police laboratories is painstakingly routine, involving chemical analysis to identify and compare samples of trace evidence. This helps to corroborate other pieces of evidence, and is an essential part of the jigsaw of crime investigation. Another type of forensic clue is inceptive evidence, whereby the scientist provides the first piece of the jigsaw which guides the police and enables an investigation to begin.

To the microscope used by Locard and his fellow-pioneers of forensic science has been added an arsenal of sophisticated laboratory equipment which enables minute traces of a wide range of materials to be identified and measured with speed. Spectographic analysis, X-ray diffraction, electron microscopy and neutron activation analysis are powerful tools used to examine contact traces in the search for links between criminal and crime. However, it should not be forgotten, as H. J. Walls, the British forensic scientist, has pointed out, that 'complexity and sophistication of equipment are useless unless the contact trace has first been found'. Thus the experience and trained eye of the on-the-spot investigator is all-important. So vital is this initial part of a murder inquiry that many American police forces have established crime-scene investigation as a field of study in its own right.

Every aspect of crime has its associated sphere of contact evidence, with particular demands on scientific skills. HIT-AND-RUN incidents, for example, tend to provide glass and paint fragments as clues; shooting involves specialized FIRE-ARMS evidence; murder by any violent means, such as strangulation, knife or BLUNT INSTRU-MENT, is likely to result in the transfer of blood, hairs and fibres; and RAPE involves specialized examinations for semen, saliva, hairs, fibres and TEETH-marks. Examination of QUESTIONED DOCUMENTS is a special study which may be called for in many types of crime.
67, 192, 255, **259**, *502, 532, 667, 671,* **703**.

CONTRACT MURDER

'It's real business all the way,' said Abe (Kid Twist) Reles in explanation of his career as a hired killer. He worked for Louis Lepke Buchalter, who became head of Murder Incorporated in 1933 and coined the term 'contract' to denote an assignment given to a hired killer to commit murder. Contract murders are usually associated with gangland crime, and in particular with the activities of Murder Inc. For as little as a thousand dollars — or more, depending on the importance of the victim and the degree of risk involved — killers hired by the moguls of gangland murdered thousands in cities throughout the USA during the thirties. The victims were usually rivals, informers or simply business-men who refused to pay protection money to the organized crime syndicates. The identity of the victim or 'hit' was often not known to the contract murderer until he read about the killing in the newspapers.

Reles, a professional racketeer during the prohibition era, confessed to eighteen murders, mostly committed with an ice-pick, as one of Buchalter's 'hit men'. When he was arrested he attempted to save his own skin by telling all he knew about Buchalter. Despite the protection of a heavy police guard at his Coney Island hideaway, Reles fell prey to his chief's revenge, who arranged for him to 'fall' to his death through a window. Buchalter was eventually convicted on murder charges, and despite a three-year battle to stave off execution went to the ELECTRIC CHAIR in 1944.

The idea of hiring a person to carry out a contract murder — or murder by proxy — also has its appeal outside gangland. Elizabeth Duncan, a seemingly respectable citizen of Santa Barbara, California, made an arrangement in 1958 for the contract killing of her daughter-in-law. Behind the harmless façade of a doting mother Mrs Duncan harboured a sinister mentality. Some of her nine or more marriages had been bigamous, but apart from this she had lied, committed fraud, threatened violence and connived at murder.

The object of Mrs Duncan's devotion was her son Frank, a 29-year-old lawyer. In 1957 he met a young nurse, Olga Kupczyk, to whom — against his mother's wishes — he proposed marriage. Mrs Duncan embarked on a vicious campaign against the girl, accusing her of promiscuity and failure to pay bills; she told her, 'I will kill you before you ever marry my son.' Nevertheless, the couple married in 1958. More accusations followed, and a plan was worked out to kidnap Olga and attack her with ACID. Frank had a furious row with his mother, who unmoved by his appeals began to lay murder plans in earnest by seeking a contract killer.

Mrs Duncan approached a Mexican café-owner whose help she sought to get rid of her daughter-in-law, who she claimed was blackmailing her. The Mexican woman, an illegal immigrant, offered the services of two unemployed 'boys' who did odd jobs in her café. Luis Moya and Augustine Baldonado, both in their twenties, were hired for 6,000 dollars to kill Olga. 'You better watch out,' warned Mrs Duncan, 'she's a pretty strong girl.'

On 17 November 1958 the contract murderers drove to Olga's apartment, where they struck down the seven-months-pregnant nurse and took her out to the mountains some thirty miles from Santa Barbara. They battered her about the head with a rock and strangled her, finally burying their victim — perhaps still living — in a sandy grave.

The contractors now demanded payment, only to be told by Mrs Duncan that she had no funds. After pressing their demands, Moya and Baldonado were given payments totalling 335 dollars, with promises of more to come. In the meantime Olga was reported missing, and the police learned of the girl's unhappy relationship with her mother-in-law. When she was questioned Mrs Duncan said she was being blackmailed by two Mexicans who had threatened to kill her. She refused to name them, but by now the police were on the trail of Moya and Baldonado, who were quickly arrested. Baldonado made a CONFESSION, and told the police where to find Olga's body.

Fifty-four-year-old Mrs Duncan and her two contract killers were convicted of murder and sentenced to death. Appeals to the US Supreme Court were rejected, and in August 1962 all three

The beach cottage from which Judge Chillingworth and his wife were abducted

died in the GAS CHAMBER.

Another contract murderer who made his 'hit' but failed to receive payment was Floyd Holzapfel. He was hired by Joe Peel, a West Palm Beach municipal judge, to murder fellow-judge Curtis E. Chillingworth. Peel — who had twice been guilty of professional negligence, and who had a liking for racketeering — aspired to be state governor. Fearing that Judge Chillingworth might reveal his shady enterprises, he recruited Holzapfel — an ex-convict who operated some of his get-rich-quick schemes — to murder him.

On a June night in 1955, while Peel secured an ALIBI watching TV, Holzapfel, aided by another thug, Bobby Lincoln, went out to the Chillingworths' beach cottage at Manalapan. They abducted the elderly judge and his wife at gunpoint and took them out to sea in a motor-boat. Their bound and weighted bodies were then thrown overboard. These were never found, and it was two years before the Florida authorities declared them dead, and five years before the police investigation achieved any firm results.

Holzapfel, who later claimed he was promised 2,000 dollars for killing the judge, received no payment from Peel. After a period of further racketeering involving hijack and murder, he injudiciously mentioned to a companion during a drinking bout that he had been hired to kill Chillingworth. This information reached the ears of the police, and also Peel, who reacted by trying to take out a contract to silence Holzapfel. Following further wrangles with Peel over money, and a spell of lying low in Brazil, Holzapfel returned to Florida, where he was enticed by the police into a drinking-bout during which he confessed to murdering Judge and Mrs Chillingworth. He subsequently made a formal confession which was corroborated by Bobby Lincoln.

Peel and Holzapfel were tried in 1961. 'I did it for Joe,' admitted the hired murderer, but while Joe was sentenced to life imprisonment and Lincoln was released from police custody, Holzapfel received sentence of death by electrocution but was later reprieved.

Outside of the organized crime syndicates, contract murderers have tended to bungle their assignments. The Finch-Tregoff eternal-triangle affair in Los Angeles in 1959 (see under CONSPIRACY) was a further example. In this case the hired killer failed to go through with his 'hit', and the hirers were obliged to carry out their own evil work.
65, 78, 749.

CORONER

A public office dating back to twelfth-century England and derived from *coronae custodium regis* — keeper of the royal pleas. Coroners were appointed in each county to protect the rights of the Crown and to collect the sovereign's dues. From the earliest times, the coroner's duties included the investigation of violent and unexplained deaths, since revenue was due to the Crown from fines and forfeiture of goods.

With the passage of time many of the historic duties of the coroner have disappeared, leaving the modern coroner system which is based on the investigation of violent and suspicious death, and includes one or two other lesser responsibilities. Coroners in England must be barristers, solicitors or doctors, and their appointment is for life. Their duty is to ascertain how, where and when a deceased person died. In cases of SUDDEN DEATH of unknown cause the coroner need not hold an inquest, but may order a POST-MORTEM to establish cause of death. Where there is reason to suspect foul play the coroner must hold an inquest with a jury. EVIDENCE is given on oath, and witnesses may be called. In cases where crime is suspected after a body has been buried the coroner may order an EXHUMATION in order that cause of death may be determined.

The coroner system has been criticized, particularly in regard to the so-called 'trial by coroner'. In 1929 Philip Yale Drew, an American actor performing in Reading, was a witness at a coroner's inquest called to investigate the brutal murder of a tobacconist in the town. Despite the fact that he was never charged, Drew was virtually tried for murder by the coroner. However, the jury returned a verdict of wilful murder against some person or persons unknown, and Drew was released from his undoubted ordeal.

The Reading coroner was heavily criticized for submitting Drew to his ordeal, while a fellow-coroner in Croydon attracted unwelcome attention for his handling of the Croydon poisonings case. Three members of the same family died of arsenical poisoning within a year, and despite advice from the Director of Public Prosecutions the coroner decided to hold all three inquests together. Considerable confusion resulted. Such incidents — and the Drew case in particular — caused questions to be raised in Parliament about the conduct of coroner's inquests. Numerous recommendations for revision were made, but it was not until

1953 that the Coroners' Rules were revised. They were again revised in 1981.
74, 368, 520, 531, 723, 724.

CORPUS DELICTI

The essential elements of a crime and the circumstances in which it was committed are known as the *corpus delicti* — literally, the body of the crime. In the case of murder it must be shown that a death has occurred, that the dead person is the person alleged to have been killed, and that the killing was the result of unlawful violence. The corpus delicti of murder, therefore, consists of more than just a corpse.

A number of murderers have believed that the corpus delicti is the body of the victim, and that without it a conviction for murder cannot be obtained. John George Haigh, who thought he had successfully obliterated his victim in an ACID bath, found to his cost that this was not so. In the first place, the victim was not totally destroyed, and identification was possible by means of the TEETH. Secondly, traces of BLOOD, recovery of a recently fired revolver, and other evidence provided a more than adequate corpus delicti to send Haigh to the gallows.

Perhaps James Camb believed that a murder charge could not be brought against him when he pushed his victim's body through a ship's porthole into the depth of the ocean off the coast of West Africa. In October 1947 the actress Gay Gibson was returning home from South Africa aboard the *Durban Castle*. When she was reported missing on 18 October the captain put his vessel about and made a search. This proved unsuccessful, and the ship resumed its passage to England.

Inquiries on board threw suspicion on to James Camb, one of the deck stewards. A ship's watchman reported that he answered a summons made on the bell-push in Miss Gibson's cabin at about 3.0 a.m. in the morning. When he reached her cabin he saw Camb in the doorway, who called out to him, 'All right.' Camb was arrested when the ship docked. He admitted being in Miss Gibson's cabin, claiming it was at her invitation. They had sexual intercourse, during which she had a fit and became unconscious. He tried artificial respiration, but realized she was dead, and in a state of panic pushed her body through the porthole.

James Camb was tried for murder, and the prosecution argued that in the course of his attempting RAPE the struggling girl scratched his arms and managed to ring the bell. Camb strangled her, and diverted the night watchman, who responded to the summons of the bell. When Camb was examined the following day by the ship's surgeon fresh scratches were noticed on his back and shoulders. Traces of blood-streaked saliva on the

Scratch marks on Camb's arm

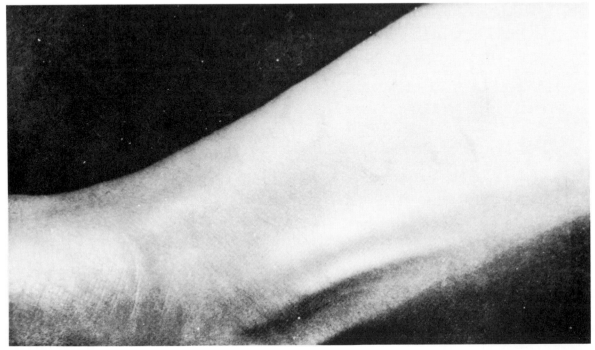

bed-sheets tended to support the idea of death by STRANGULATION. There were also urine stains in the bed which a pathologist said were likely to have been caused by a terminal act — in other words, the bladder emptied as the life was squeezed out of the victim.

Camb's defence was that the girl died of natural causes, such as a heart-attack or a fit. He said that during sexual intercourse her body stiffened and she clutched at him — he noticed that she had foam at her mouth. He attempted artificial respiration, and when he realized that she was dead he was overcome by 'complete panic'. He told the court, 'I hoped to give the impression that she had fallen overboard, and deny all knowledge of having been to that cabin.' He lifted her up and pushed her through the porthole.

What told heavily against Camb was his unsatisfactory explanation for not seeking help if the girl had suffered a seizure or fit as he had stated. His mere statement that he panicked and disposed of her body as an act of self-preservation did not impress the court. Despite the lack of a body, sufficient of a *corpus delicti* existed for the jury to bring in a verdict of guilty. Camb was sentenced to death, but did not hang because Parliament was discussing the abolition of capital punishment.

Other murder cases where the body was missing appear under CONTRACT MURDER and DISPOSAL OF THE BODY.
1, 48, 127, 197, 229, 282, 313, 351, 372, 574, 642, 659, 721, 747.

CRIME PASSIONEL

The 'crime of passion' is a defence plea recognized in France, where the law takes a more tolerant view than in other countries of husbands or wives who kill in the moment of passion when they find their partner has betrayed them for another. If the JURY accepts a defence pleading *crime passionel* in a murder case, this constitutes mitigating circumstances, and the punishment is usually less harsh. The death sentence has traditionally been avoided in such cases, and the *crime passionel* commands sufficient sympathy to be classed as second-degree MURDER and even win acquittal.

These considerations are peculiar to France, and most other countries take the view that crimes motivated by passion or jealousy do not merit special treatment. The *crime passionel* has introduced drama to many French murder trials, and none more so than that of Yvonne Chevallier in

1952. This was the classic case of the wife betrayed by her husband because of his love for another woman. Dr Pierre Chevallier had a distinguished career in the Second World War, and was made Mayor of Orleans. He entered national politics, and was elected a Deputy with aspirations to high office. His country-born wife tried hard, but could not adapt to her husband's fast-moving social life.

In due course Dr Chevallier took a mistress who understood him, while his wife was driven to chain-smoking and drugs. In 1952 Chevallier was given ministerial office, but at this moment of triumph his wife, despairing of losing him altogether, shot him. She put four bullets into him, stopped to attend one of her children, and then returned to fire a fifth shot at him. Public opinion was at first against Yvonne Chevallier for killing her husband, but as news of his infidelity became apparent attitudes softened. Her trial at Rheims was accompanied by a blaze of publicity, and all the ingredients of a *crime passionel* were assembled. She strongly impressed the court with her love for her husband and children, and with her thoughts of ending her own life because of his disregard for her. The jury's 'not guilty' verdict brought spontaneous applause from the court for Yvonne Chevallier.

France, with its reputation for hot-blooded attitudes to love but with their unfortunate by-products of jealousy and hate, is the home of the true *crime passionel*. The one case in English murder trial records which was treated as a *crime passionel* — even though the concept does not exist in English law — was that of Madame Fahmy, a Frenchwoman wronged in love. Marguérite Fahmy, a beautiful woman in her early twenties, was staying at the Savoy Hotel, London in the summer of 1923 with her husband. Prince Ali Fahmy was a wealthy Egyptian with a taste for luxurious living and exotic, if not perverted, sex. On the night of 10 July, after the couple had quarrelled, Madame Fahmy fired three shots at her husband from a .25 Browning pistol, causing wounds from which he died later.

Madame Fahmy's trial was a public sensation. There was no disputing that she had shot her husband, but in a brilliant defence her counsel, Sir Edward Marshall Hall, won the court's sympathy by drawing out the humiliation and terror she had suffered at the hands of her husband. The acquittal verdict was a popular outcome, showing perhaps that an English jury was capable of considering the spirit at least of the *crime passionel*.
23, 81, 215, 249, 263, 286, 327, 170, 523, 705.

CRIMINAL LAW

As distinct from the law which deals with the private wrongs of individuals (civil law), criminal law is concerned with acts which are contrary to peace, order and the well-being of society. It is an attempt by the State to preserve public order by making guilty persons liable to punishment in order to curb any tendency to private vengeance.

Criminal law recognizes blameworthy intention as a necessary component of a criminal offence. Before a person can be convicted of a crime, two things have to be proved: 1) that an act forbidden by criminal law has resulted from an individual's conduct; and 2) that this conduct was accompanied by blameworthy intention. The former element is called the ACTUS REUS and the second MENS REA. Criminal law requires that both of these must be proved beyond REASONABLE DOUBT.

The origins of English criminal law lie in the Saxon concept of offences committed against the King's Peace which included MURDER, arson and RAPE. In the USA each state has its own body of criminal law sharing a common origin with English legal practice.
332, **658**.

CRIMINALISTICS

Term used in the USA and some European countries to denote the application of science to the detection of crime. In other countries this field of study is known as police science and in Britain as FORENSIC SCIENCE. The origins of the scientific approach to crime investigation lie in the pioneering work of the Austrian lawyer Professor Hans Gross, whose *System der Kriminalistik* stressed the ways in which the criminal investigator could be aided by scientific method. His classic work *Criminal Investigation* was first published in English in 1906, and his methods have been adopted internationally.

Another founding father of forensic science was Edmond Locard, whose Institute of Criminalistics was established at Lyons in 1910, where advances were made in techniques for examining trace evidence. One of the first universities to offer courses in criminalistics was the University of Lausanne in Switzerland. The department set up by Professor A. R. Reis in 1902 developed into the Lausanne Institute of Police Science.

Modern police science has grown into a complex study combining such traditional methods as understanding a criminal's MODUS OPERANDI with the latest developments in FORENSIC MEDICINE and a highly sophisticated approach to crime-scene investigation. The great police institutions of the world — INTERPOL, SCOTLAND YARD, THE FEDERAL BUREAU OF INVESTIGATION, the SÛRETÉ NATIONALE and others — command impressive scientific resources. Many American police forces employ technically qualified staff whom they term criminalists. They are forensic scientists whose job is to analyse and interpret crime material as a support to law-enforcement. Kenneth W. Goddard in his book *Crime Scene Investigation* refers to the criminalist as representing 'the primary link between the world of science and the judicial system'.
259, **366**, **528**, *634*, **703**.

CRIMINOLOGY

Criminology is the study of causes of criminal behaviour, the dispensation of criminal justice, prevention and control of crime and the punishment and rehabilitation of the offender. The word is taken from Greek and Latin roots meaning 'study of the substance of crime'. The first serious studies began in Europe in the eighteenth century, and Cesare Beccaria (1738–94), a young Italian thinker, published an essay entitled 'On Crimes and Punishments', in which he put forward a critical view of the savage application of law as then practised.

Beccaria's ideas were taken up by later social reformers who represented the so-called classical school of criminology, which argued in favour of a humane legal system based on man's reasoning intellect. With the systematic collection of criminal statistics — which began in France in 1803 and in England two years later — it became possible to support theories with facts. An immediate result was the correlation between crime rates, especially for stealing, and degrees of poverty. During the next few decades some of the more brutal treatment of offenders was modified, and methods of EXECUTION were made less barbaric.

Other criminological studies began to focus on the criminal as a person, with a view to explaining his behaviour. Phrenology — reading the personality from the shape of the head — had its vogue, and serious questions were posed about criminal insanity. Anthropological explanations of criminal behaviour followed close on the heels of Charles

One of Lombroso's 'criminal types'

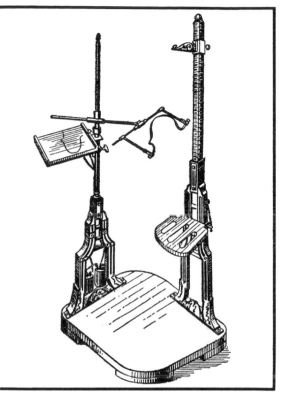

Craniograph for taking head measurements

Darwin's publication of his theory of evolution. Cesare Lombroso (1836–1909), an Italian ex-army surgeon, gained rapid fame as a criminologist with the publication in 1876 of his book *L'Uomo Delinquente* ('Criminal Man'). He wrote of the criminal that he 'reproduces in his person the ferocious instincts of primitive humanity and the inferior animals'.

Lombroso believed that the born criminal was characterized by such physical features as a heavy jaw, excessively long arms and an asymmetrical face with jug EARS. He also maintained that the type had extremely acute eyesight and a craving for evil. These claims were based on his examination of 7,000 criminals. In collaboration with Enrico Ferri, Lombroso founded the 'positive school' of criminology. He held professorships in psychiatry and criminal anthropology at Turin University, and came to be fêted as the 'Father of Criminology'. The idea of a physical criminal type is no longer discussed, and Lombroso's theories have been completely discredited by modern studies.

Subsequent developments in criminological studies have been largely in the fields of sociology and psychology. Attempts were made in the early 1900s to equate low mental ratings with a predisposition to criminal behaviour, but these failed with the growing influence of psychology. The two main emphases of modern criminology developed up to the present time have been based on the individual's release of aggression as the result of inner tension and on the rôle played by poor social environment. Some critics condemn the influence of sociology, which they argue is not a wholly scientific discipline. It has also been said that criminology is still at a fact-finding stage, and while the accuracy of the statistics and trends is indisputable, it is not feasible to adduce theories as to the deep-lying causes.

Criminology also embraces the study of penal systems, the application of CRIMINAL LAW and the development of scientific methods to control crime. Perhaps the greatest criminological advances have been made in FORENSIC SCIENCE, which helps the law-enforcement agencies in the detection of crime, and serves society in the prosecution of the offender. In this respect Dr Hans Gross (1847–1915), the Austrian lawyer who published the *Handbuch für Untersuchungsrichter* (Criminal Investigation) in 1893, might more properly be considered a founding father of modern criminology. (See also under CRIMINALISTICS.)
82, *443*, **502**, **658**, **691**.

CUT-THROAT

'He's got a luvely throat for a razor. Ho! Ho! Ho! I'll polish him off.'

Thus ran one of the many refrains about the fictional Sweeney Todd, the Demon Barber of Fleet Street, who shares pre-eminence with JACK THE RIPPER in the art of throat-cutting. Dr Bagster Phillips, who examined the body of Annie Chapman, one of the Ripper's victims, described her injuries in *The Lancet*. The wound in her throat consisted of two distinct cuts, parallel to each other and about half an inch apart. He added that it appeared as if the murderer had tried to cut through the spine to sever the head.

Homicidal KNIFE-WOUNDS are usually of the stabbing variety, for unless the intended victim is asleep or otherwise unprepared, throat-cutting is a difficult method. The word 'cut-throat' has traditionally been associated with the worst kind of villainy — pirates and bandits so immersed in pillage and murder that this kind of swift killing is second nature. Going for the throat with a knife is not a form of assault that normally occurs in domestic murders. It is much more common in SEX MURDERS, as demonstrated by William Heirens, Edmund Kemper, California's Co-ed killer of the 1970s, Heinrich Pommerencke, 'The Beast of the Black Forest', who committed ten RAPE murders in Germany in the 1950s, and Peter Kürten.

Throat-cutting is also a common method of committing suicide. The fatal incision is usually preceded by one or more trial cuts or hesitation wounds which result from the victim feeling for the right position for the knife. There may be as many as twelve of these practice strokes before the final determined cut is made, and these are a feature which distinguish suicide from murder. Other distinguishing characteristics are the absence of signs of a struggle in suicides, who also tend to tilt the head back, with the result that the carotid arteries slide away from the knife, thus creating less bleeding. Classic signs of homicidal throat-cutting are copious bleeding due to the victim's struggles and the presence of defensive wounds in the palm of the hand and between the fingers, resulting from attempts to fight off the assailant's knife. The classic 'ear to ear' cut severs the neck muscles, blood-vessels and windpipe down to the spine, leaving a wound up to eight inches long and three inches deep.

The annals of murder can always be relied on to produce exceptions, and the crimes of Mary Eleanor Pearcey fall into this class. She murdered her lover's wife by cutting her throat, and followed this up by mutilating her body and suffocating her child. Pearcey's MOTIVE was born out of jealousy, but her choice of throat-cutting, carried out with demonic violence, was unusual for a female murderer. (See under VICTIMOLOGY for a full account.)
58, 249, 260, 447, 522.

CYANIDE

During Hallowe'en 1974 Ronald O'Bryan, an optical technician working for a company in Houston, Texas, decided to give his children a treat. He handed out 'Pixy Stix' candy straws to his own children, and also to some of their friends. The 'treat' rapidly turned into a 'trick' when eight-year-old Timmy O'Bryan was rushed to hospital with convulsions and breathing difficulties. He died shortly after admission, and a POST-MORTEM examination showed possible toxic effects in the lungs and brain. Analysis of the STOMACH CONTENTS revealed the presence of cyanide.

Examination of 'Pixy Stix' belonging to the dead boy showed it had been doctored with enough cyanide to kill two people. Candy straws rounded up from the neighbourhood children by the police produced a lethal collection of confectionery. Six 'Pixy Stix' contained cyanide, a number of other candy straws had been filled with needles, and one contained a razor blade. Fortunately, no other children had been taken ill.

Ronald O'Bryan appeared grief-stricken by his son's death, although some of his friends thought his remarks somewhat strange. Suspicion began to focus on him, especially when it was learned that he had insured the lives of his children for large sums. He was paying out large premiums which he could ill afford at a time when he was in debt. Articles taken from his home were tested for cyanide, but wth negative results. On the basis of largely CIRCUMSTANTIAL EVIDENCE, O'Bryan was charged with the murder of his son, and of the ATTEMPTED MURDER of four other children.

He denied everything at his trial, but a witness who worked for a scientific supplies firm testified that O'Bryan had made inquiries about cyanide. The prosecution was unable to prove that the accused had either bought cyanide or put it in the candy straws. He was nevertheless found guilty and sentenced to death.

Cyanide is one of the most rapidly fatal poisons known, which made it a favourite agent for suicidal poisoning with many Nazi war criminals. Heinrich Himmler killed himself by biting into a glass capsule and swallowing the contents. Hermann Goering similarly cheated the hangman by smuggling a capsule of potassium cyanide into his cell by means of his tobacco pipe. Cyanide is also one of the fabled deadly poisons of crime fiction, sharing its distinction with ARSENIC, but few real murderers use it. Hydrogen cyanide (cyanide gas) is used as the killing agent in the GAS CHAMBER by those American states which adopted that method of execution.

Cyanide is found as a natural vegetable acid in many fruits and leaves, especially those of the cherry, peach and almond, and also in their stone kernels. It is harmless in its isolated natural form, but is usually found in association with a substance which reacts with it in the presence of water to release deadly hydrocyanic or prussic acid. Eating bitter almonds has been known to cause toxic effects, and it is the almond which gives hydrocyanic acid its characteristic odour. It is estimated that at least 20 per cent of individuals do not register the smell of bitter almonds, which accounts for some of the accidental deaths due to cyanide poisoning. The toxic action of cyanide is very rapid, and the fastest death on record from prussic acid is ten seconds. The acid acts virtually instantaneously, whereas the cyanide salts take longer, and depend on the gastric juices in the stomach breaking down the salt to release hydrocyanic acid.

Cyanide acts by interfering with the oxygen-carrying capacity of the blood and paralysing the respiratory centre of the brain. The pulse weakens, and there is rapid loss of consciousness. Other symptoms include convulsions, coldness of the extremities, and pupils dilated and non-reactive to light. There may be a fine froth at the mouth. Death occurs quickly, and usually within five minutes. Survival for four hours or more is an indication of non-lethal poisoning, and recovery is probable. The estimated lethal dose for prussic acid is between 50 and 100 mg.

There are few visible signs of cyanide poisoning at post-mortem, although the skin of the face and body may show irregular pink patches reminiscent of carbon monoxide poisoning (see under GASSING). The characteristic odour of bitter almonds may be detected at the mouth, and be evident in the chest and abdominal cavities. Cyanides are quickly altered by metabolic activity once they enter the body, and are converted into sulphocyanides which are normally present. This can present a problem if analysis in cases of suspected cyanide poisoning is not quickly carried out.

One of the most extraordinary cases of homicidal cyanide poisoning was that involving a Japanese bank-robber who killed twelve bank employees. Sadamichi Hirasawa arrived at a bank in the Teikoku suburb of Tokyo in January 1948 just before closing-time. He passed himself off as a doctor with orders to inoculate the bank staff against dysentery. The sixteen bank employees dutifully lined up and drank a concoction given them by the 'doctor'. Ten died immediately and two more died in hospital as the result of cyanide poisoning. Having immobilized the bank staff, Hirasawa stole all the money he could lay his hands on, which amounted to the equivalent of a mere 720 US dollars.

Hirasawa was eventually arrested, having been identified by a scar under his chin, and he made a CONFESSION to the murders. In 1948 Japan was under military occupation, and a court sentenced Hirasawa to death by HANGING. A legal row ensued, with Japanese lawyers claiming that the sentence violated the Japanese constitution which protected citizens from self-destruction. It was argued that hanging was self-strangulation. As a result Hirasawa remained in prison for over thirty years until, at the age of eighty-eight, he was granted amnesty by the Emperor. The cyanide poisoner had spent his time in prison painting and writing his autobiography, *My Will: the Teikoku Bank Case*.

A bizarre case of cyanide poisoning occurred in New York in 1953 when a doctor and his wife were found in their apartment in what the newspapers described as a suicide pact. The couple had died by drinking champagne laced with potassium cyanide. In due course suspicion focused on the dead couple's son, Harlow Fraden, and his friend, Dennis Wepman. These two young men in their early twenties enjoyed a platonic relationship full of literary and Bohemian pursuits. They indulged in flights of fancy, and developed a FOLIE À DEUX resulting in the murder of Fraden's parents, to which they made a full confession. Fraden observed that 'it was a delightful game', and his companion described himself as 'enthralled' by his friend's desire to destroy his parents, 'by observing it I might further my literary ambitions'. Fraden was found to be suffering from serious mental disorder, but Wepman was tried for murder and received a life sentence.

A case which demonstrated the dangers of cyanide was that involving Richard Brinkley in 1907. He made the acquaintance of Mrs Blume, an elderly widow living in Fulham, and formed a plan to acquire her property. He drew up a will for the old lady in which all her savings and property went to him on her death. He secured her signature on this document by disguising its real nature and telling her he was collecting names for a trip to the seaside. Two men, Henry Heard and Reginald Parker, were similarly duped to sign as witnesses.

When Mrs Blume died two days later (apparently from natural causes) Brinkley claimed ownership of her property. What he had not bargained for in his scheme was that the old lady's relatives would contest the validity of the will. When it became obvious that the witnesses would be questioned, Brinkley decided to murder them. He began with Parker, whom he visited at his lodgings on the pretext of wanting to buy a dog. Full of bonhomie, Brinkley produced a bottle of stout to help negotiations along and left this on the table when he went off with Parker to inspect the dog. While the two men were away Parker's landlord, Mr Beck, returned to the house with his wife and daughter. Seeing a bottle on the table, Beck decided to have a drink. Barely had he swallowed

it than he collapsed, foaming at the mouth and experiencing breathing difficulties. He died within minutes, followed by his wife, who had also drunk some of the stout. The stout (which had been heavily spiked with cyanide) was intended for Parker, who owed his escape to the unwitting intervention of his landlord.

It was discovered that Brinkley had bought cyanide from a chemist's shop for the alleged purpose of putting down a dog. Mrs Blume's body was exhumed, and although it was strongly suspected that Brinkley had poisoned her, no trace of cyanide was found in the corpse, which had been buried for five months. Richard Brinkley was tried for murder at Guildford in proceedings notable for the scientific evidence regarding the will (see under QUESTIONED DOCUMENTS). He was found guilty and later executed, illustrating the principle operating at the time whereby a person who intends to murder someone, but fails and unintentionally kills another, is no less guilty of murder. MENS REA, or guilty intent, still applied, and the murderer's MALICE AFORETHOUGHT was regarded as having been transferred. The concept of transferred malice no longer carries weight in English courts.

72, 126, 252, 520, **571**, *634.*

D

DEATH CERTIFICATE

When Dr Charles Friedgood was taken off a London-bound aircraft at New York's Kennedy Airport in August 1975 he precipitated a tightening of the law governing certification of death. Two months earlier he had signed a certificate declaring that his wife had died of a stroke, and her body had been released for burial.

While it was not illegal for a doctor to write a death certificate for a relative, it was not regarded as good practice, and the police became suspicious of Friedgood's intentions. The funeral was interrupted so that a POST-MORTEM examination could be carried out. Injection marks were found on the body, and toxicological tests proved positive for synthetic opiates. A lethal amount of such a drug was found in the liver.

A search of Friedgood's house was thwarted by attempts to hide vital evidence, but the police were later informed that a hypodermic syringe and drug-containers had been concealed. Meanwhile the doctor authorized the sale of his late wife's securities by forging her signature, and prepared to fly to London. The aircraft was dramatically halted on the runway, and the fugitive taken into custody. Friedgood was convicted of murder by a New York court, and sentenced to twenty-five years' imprisonment. In 1978 the state legislature enacted a law (popularly known as the 'Friedgood Bill' which prohibited doctors signing death certificates for relatives.

The practice of registering births and deaths in England began in 1538, when these events were recorded in the parish registers. The procedure was in the hands of the clergymen who presided over burials, and no detailed inquiries were made into causes of death. A Registration Act was passed in 1836, but it was not until 1874 that the registration of every death was made compulsory (1855 in Scotland). Subsequent legislation introduced more formality with a view to preventing the concealment of crime, and providing the authorities with statistical information on causes of death. The Births and Deaths Registration Act of 1926 related to medical certification of death and the disposal of the dead. Its provisions, amended in 1953, represent today's law, and require that a death certificate be issued by a qualified medical practitioner within five days.

The doctor — who must have attended the deceased within fourteen days of death — is obliged to state the cause of death in precise terms. The use of general descriptions such as 'heart failure' is not permitted, and where death arises from pre-existing conditions these must be noted in sequence. The completed certificate is a legal document required by the Registrar of Deaths, whose authority is needed before the body can be buried.

If the doctor believes death to have resulted from violence, from unknown causes or in suspi-

Certification of Mrs Armstrong's death from natural causes

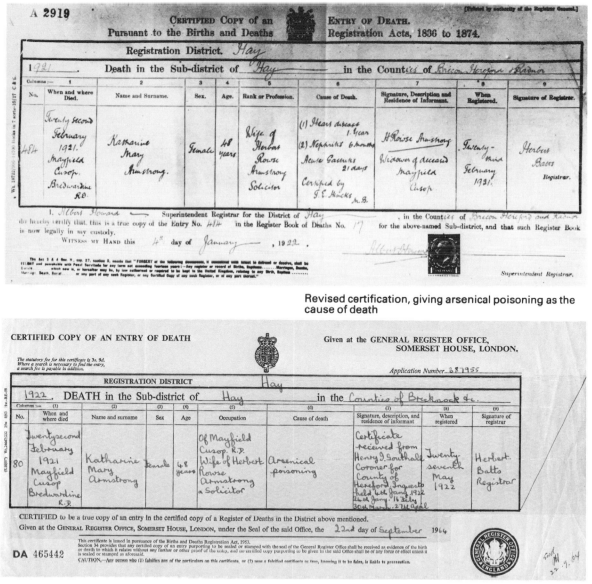

Revised certification, giving arsenical poisoning as the cause of death

cious circumstances, he is bound to report his findings to the CORONER. This action is noted in the Death Certificate, and the death will not be registered until an inquiry had been made. About one-fifth of all deaths in England and Wales are reported to a coroner, and most of these are satisfactorily attributed to natural causes following post-mortem examination. In the remainder, where suspicious circumstances are indicated, cause of death is ascertained by a coroner's inquest, and a police investigation may be involved.

Where cremation is the chosen method of disposal, death is certified in the normal way but additional precautions are taken. A buried corpse may be subject to EXHUMATION in the event of any suspicion as to the cause of death, but a body consigned to incineration is past recall. Consequently, a second confirmatory medical certificate signed by another doctor is required before authority to cremate can be issued.

Death certificates have been most frequently called into question in cases where death is subsequently suspected to have been caused by POISONING. The symptoms of many poisons are virtually indistinguishable from those of ordinary ailments, as external marks of violence are absent. The effects of ARSENIC, for example, are similar to those of gastro-enteritis, and have been so recorded in a number of instances. It has been said on numerous occasions that the family doctor rarely suspects poison, and where no suspicious circumstances are evident a normal death certificate is invariably issued. The doctor's mistake is only discovered by toxicological examination of the exhumed body, a fact which prompted Lord Russell of Liverpool to express surprise that more poisoners did not arrange for their victims to be cremated. No doubt the stringent regulations which have to be met in order to obtain authority to cremate a body were drawn up for this very reason.

Not surprisingly, there have been numerous attempts to mislead, and Dr Friedgood had his professional predecessors: Edward Pritchard, for example, the Glasgow doctor who poisoned his wife and mother-in-law with ANTIMONY in 1865 and issued a death certificate in each case. 'Nurse' Dorothea Waddingham, who ran an unregistered nursing-home in Nottingham, drew suspicion to herself when she sent an unusual note to the home's physician. This had the appearance of being written by a recently deceased patient, Ada Baguley: 'I desire to be cremated at my death, for

health's sake and it is my wish to remain with Nurse and my last wish is my Relatives shall not know of my Death. Signed Ada Baguley. Witness Name R. J. Sullivan.' On top of the note was the request 'Please return this letter.' This extraordinary application for cremation accompanied a normal death certificate signed by the attending doctor, in which cause of death was given as cerebral haemorrhage. These documents eventually reached the coroner, and in no time at all police officers were knocking on the door of Nurse Waddingham's establishment. A post-mortem examination showed that the body of the dead woman contained MORPHINE, a drug which had not been prescribed by her doctor.

Inquiries disclosed that Ada Baguley, who was bedridden, had made her will in favour of Nurse Waddingham in return for nursing care for herself and her mother for the rest of their lives. Old Mrs Baguley died in May 1935, to be followed by Ada four months later. Waddingham and Joseph Sullivan (who assisted her in running the nursing-home and was a co-beneficiary) were tried for the murder of Mrs Baguley. As there was no direct evidence against him, Sullivan was released. Waddingham said she had administered morphine to her patient on the doctor's instructions, but the doctor was adamant that he had given no such orders. Like others before her, Nurse Waddingham had committed a perfect murder, and had she been content to allow the body to be buried in the normal way there would have been no suspicion. But her blunder in sending the crudely conceived request for cremation in the belief that it was necessary for the dead person to have requested that form of disposal was her undoing. She was convicted of murder, and despite a recommendation to mercy was hanged in April 1936.
83, 256, 289, 349, 429, 524, 589, 740.

DECOMPOSITION

The putrefaction or breakdown of the human body after death is not a pleasant topic, least of all for the forensic pathologist who has to deal with such matters. Nevertheless, the state of decomposition of a corpse can provide useful evidence in the detection of crime, as was proved in the case of the Lydney murder. On 28 June 1964 two boys found a maggot-infested body in woods near Bracknell in Berkshire. Professor Keith Simpson was called to the scene, and he found a male corpse, fully clothed and extensively decomposed. His estimate of TIME OF DEATH was nine to ten days, but not more than twelve days.

In the POST-MORTEM room the pathologist found that the bones of the larynx were crushed, and death had resulted from bleeding into the windpipe. It was thought that the injury might have been caused by a karate-type blow to the throat. The estimated age and height of the dead man, together with evidence of a healed fracture of the forearm, led police to believe he might be Peter Thomas, who had been reported missing from his home in Lydney, Gloucestershire. FINGERPRINTS taken from the decaying corpse were found to match those of Thomas, whose prints were on file. Letters found at Thomas's home showed he had loaned £2,000 to a man called William Brittle, who lived at Hook in Hampshire.

Questioned by police, Brittle admitted visiting Thomas at Lydney on 16 June, the day he was reported missing. He said he had gone there to repay his debt, and on the return journey gave a lift to a hitch-hiker. Brittle's car was subjected to minute examination, but appeared quite 'clean'.

The decomposed body in the Lydney murder

Traces of Group O BLOOD found on the sleeve of his jacket raised hopes of linking evidence, for this was the same as Thomas's blood-group — but it also turned out to be Brittle's. The police learned that their suspect had trained for unarmed combat in the Army, and they strongly believed he had killed Thomas at Lydney with a blow to the throat and then carried the body in the boot of his car to Bracknell for disposal in a shallow grave.

Many weeks after the investigation had begun a man told the police that he had seen Peter Thomas in Gloucester on 20 June. If this were so it undermined the suggestion that Brittle killed Thomas on 16 June, and went against the evidence provided by the state of decomposition of the corpse which Professor Simpson was adamant put death a minimum of nine or ten days prior to discovery. After considering the circumstances and evidence in the case the Director of Public Prosecutions declined to proceed against Brittle, who was, however, subsequently committed for trial for murder from the Coroner's Court.

Professor Simpson testified that maggots of the bluebottle fly, *Calliphora erythrocephalus*, were found on the corpse, and the fact that they had not

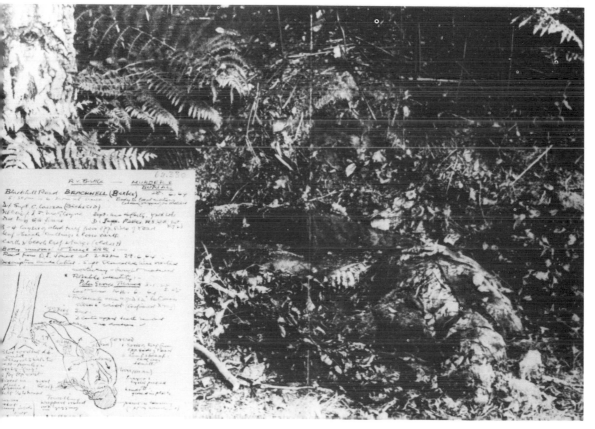

pupated indicated a minimum time since death of nine or ten days. Professor McKenny-Hughes, an entomologist, had the court ringing with laughter when in answer to counsel's question regarding bluebottle eggs he said that 'No self-respecting bluebottle lays eggs at midnight.' The Professor agreed with Simpson regarding the evidence of time of death represented by the maggots on the corpse. The jury was inclined to believe the experts and to discount the accused man's ALIBI. Brittle was found guilty of murder, and sentenced to life imprisonment.

Decomposition of the body usually sets in about forty-eight hours after death and following the disappearance of RIGOR MORTIS. Putrefaction is caused by bacteria which migrate from the intestines and spread throughout the body by way of the blood-vessels. The first visible indication of decomposition is a greenish discoloration of the abdomen which appears after two to three days. Marked reddish discoloration of the veins of the neck, shoulders and thighs quickly follows, and the network of veins beneath the skin becomes prominent, giving rise to an effect known as 'marbling'. Gross disfiguration of the corpse is usually evident after three weeks, when the features are swollen and unrecognizable and the whole is bloated. Partial liquefaction may be evident after four weeks.

The internal organs also deteriorate, but at different rates. The brain, stomach and intestines putrefy quickly, whereas the heart, lungs, kidneys, uterus and prostate are more resistant. For this reason post-mortem examination of even a badly decomposed body may yield useful information on, for example, the sex of the victim. Ultimately all the soft tissues decompose, the tendons and fibrous tissues being the last to go before the body is reduced to its SKELETON. The time required to reduce a corpse to bare bones varies, but usually takes a year in outdoor conditions. The process may be hastened if insects or animals attack the body.

Decomposition depends on a number of factors, of which temperature and moisture are the most important. Putrefaction begins at about 50°F, and is most active between 70 and 100°F. Cold delays the growth of bacteria, and at 30°F or less decomposition stops altogether. Moisture and air are essential for putrefaction, but conditions of extreme damp or dryness can modify the process, causing alternatively ADIPOCERE or MUMMIFICATION. Circumstances which delay decomposition are where the body is immersed in water or where it is clothed in tight-fitting garments. Bodies of old persons tend to decompose slowly, and fat persons decompose more rapidly than thin ones. Bodies of diseased persons also break down quickly, as do those which have been subjected to mutilation. A general rule set out by Professor John Glaister is that a body decomposes in air twice as quickly as in water, and eight times as rapidly as in earth.

Corpses buried in air-tight coffins remain intact for a long time, and trunk-murder victims have often revealed interesting secrets. Another mistake which is frequently made by murderers in DISPOSAL OF THE BODY is to subject it to the effects of QUICKLIME. Far from speeding the process of decomposition, this method has often tended to preserve the victim. A side-effect of poisoning with ARSENIC in some cases has been to slow down decomposition, as was discovered at the EXHUMATION of Major Armstrong's murdered wife. She had been buried for ten months in an airtight coffin, and the exclusion of air — added to the tendency of arsenic to preserve the tissues — resulted in a partially mummified body in which most of the internal organs were relatively intact.

An interesting footnote to an unpleasant subject is the curious phenomenon of cadaveric alkaloids. It was known in the 1860s that alkaloid poisons could form in bodies of persons who had died from natural causes. These poisons, similar to coniine, the active agent of hemlock, arose as part of the chemical breakdown of the body caused by putrefaction. In Italy, before a satisfactory test was established in 1878 to distinguish cadaveric alkaloids from vegetable alkaloids, murder charges had been brought following the discovery of poison in the bodies of two persons who had died suddenly. The subject of cadaveric alkaloids was brought into the defence of Dr George Lamson in 1882 when he was charged with murder by ACONITINE, although it failed to prevent his conviction.
571, *626*, **675**.

DIGITALIS

Doctors called to treat a sick woman in Paris in November 1863 were puzzled by her erratic heartbeat, which raced and slowed by turns. Madame de Pawr, a young widow, declined treatment insisting that she wanted to be seen only by Dr Couty ('Count') de la Pommerais. This 28-year-old homeopathic physician who had treated her late husband was her lover. Madame de Pawr told friends that she had a 'light case of cholera', but after a short illness dominated by stomach pains and vomiting she died. De la Pommerais issued a DEATH CERTIFICATE giving cholera as cause of death, and his mistress was duly buried.

The matter might have rested there but for an anonymous letter sent to M. Claude, head of the SÛRETÉ, suggesting that de la Pommerais had a financial interest in the widow's death. Inquiries revealed that the dead woman had taken out a large life insurance, and that the young doctor had already presented himself as the beneficiary. De la Pommerais — who was known to be a big spender and a gambler — dropped the impecunious Madame de Pawr when she was widowed and married another woman, although he later returned to his mistress. His wife was the daughter of the wealthy Dubiczy family, but his new mother-in-law was sufficiently wary to retain control of her married daughter's inheritance. Two months after the wedding, Madame Dubiczy senior was taken ill following dinner with her son-in-law, and she died soon afterwards. De la Pommerais thus gained access to his wife's newly acquired wealth, and used it to bail himself out of debt.

Claude decided to take personal charge of the inquiry into Madame de Pawr's death. After speaking to the dead woman's sister he learned of a plan which de la Pommerais had hatched with the professed intention of easing her financial worries. This required her to take out a large life policy, then to feign an incurable illness as a means of persuading the insurance company to change her policy for the seemingly lesser commitment of an annuity payable on a shortened life expectancy. Completely under de la Pommerais's domination, she also made a will in his favour, and thus placed herself in great jeopardy. The policy was taken out, but she had no time to put the rest of the plan into operation.

It was decided that EXHUMATION of the dead woman's body was necessary to determine if she had died from POISONING. The corpse showed no trace of the cholera which was supposed to have caused death, and tests were made for the usual poisons — ARSENIC and ANTIMONY. The analyses were carried out by Professor Ambroise Tardieu, Professor of Forensic Medicine at Paris University. No trace of poison was found, and the investigators were not encouraged by the knowledge that de la Pommerais used a wide range of homeopathic medicines, including numerous vegetable alkaloid poisons. Their work was made more difficult by not having a sample of the dead woman's vomit —

such material is naturally likely to contain heavy traces of any poison taken by mouth.

After all else had failed, Tardieu decided to inject a quantity of the extract he had made from the dead woman's organs into the blood-stream of a dog. His intention, like that of the toxicologist Jean Stas in a famous case of nicotine poisoning a few years earlier (see under TOBACCO), was to see if there was any toxic effect. The animal's reactions were dramatic — the dog vomited, and its heart-beat raced and then slowed in a replica of Madame de Pawr's symptoms. It was clear that the widow had been poisoned, but with which poison? Looking through de la Pommerais's collection of drugs, Tardieu noticed a bottle of digitalis, which he knew was used to regulate the heart-beat. By a stroke of good fortune he was able to prove his theory of digitalis poisoning when the police provided him with a sample of dried vomit which had been scraped from the floor-boards in the sick-room. Extracts were injected into frogs in a controlled series of physiological experiments which showed that digitalis present in the vomit extract regulated their heart-beats. New ground was thereby broken in the science of toxicology, and the evidence was sufficient to trap de la Pommerais, who was convicted of murder and executed in 1864.

The medicinal properties of digitalis extracted from the leaves of the purple foxglove (*Digitalis purpurea*) were discovered by Dr Withering, an English physician, in 1775. In minute doses the drug regulates the rhythm of the heart, but high regular doses have a cumulative effect, slowing the heart down to the point of death. Digitalis is the principal poisonous element of the foxglove, and all parts of the plant are poisonous. The fatal dose of digitalis (dry leaf extract) is 2g. Toxic effects occur within two or three hours of taking the poison, and symptoms include nausea, vomiting, diarrhoea, disturbed vision, delirium, irregular pulse and convulsions. Death occurs as the result of cardiac arrest.

72, 161, 545, **675**.

DIMINISHED RESPONSIBILITY

Under the Homicide Act of 1957, a defence to a charge of MURDER can be argued on the grounds that the accused was suffering from abnormality of the mind such as to impair his responsibility. The defence of diminished responsibility only applies in the case of murder, and is decided by the JURY with regard for the balance of probabilities rather than beyond a REASONABLE DOUBT. If pleaded successfully, the charge of murder is reduced to one of MANSLAUGHTER.

It must be shown that on balance the accused was suffering from such 'abnormality of mind (whether from a condition of arrested or retarded development of mind or any inherent causes or induced by disease or injury) as substantially impaired his mental responsibility for his acts and omissions in doing or being party to the killing'. Provision for diminished responsibility has long existed in Scotland, and it is the only recognition by the criminal law of England that mental abnormality may take the form of loss of control rather than loss of understanding (see M'NAGHTEN RULES).

The change in law came too late to save Ruth Ellis, the last woman to be hanged in Britain, whose counsel was denied permission to put to the trial jury a defence of provocation by jealousy.

Notice recording judicial death of Ruth Ellis

CERTIFICATE OF SURGEON

Having been directed by the judge that a verdict of manslaughter was not possible, the jury found the accused guilty, and she was executed in 1955. The case caused great consternation, and it was widely felt that the circumstances which led to Ruth Ellis fatally shooting her lover would have counted as a CRIME PASSIONEL in a number of other European countries.

Diminished responsibility has been successfully pleaded in many cases since 1957, including that of Mary Bell, an eleven-year-old who killed two small boys. In May 1968 a four-year-old boy was found dead in a derelict house at Scotswood in Newcastle. Two days later teachers investigating vandalism at a near-by school came across some childish scribblings which included a reference to the boy's death. Eight weeks later a second child, three-year-old Brian Howe, was found dead on a piece of waste ground in the same district — he had been strangled, and there were cuts on his body.

A massive police inquiry was begun, and as the result of questioning 1,200 children, attention focused on two girls whose behaviour was evasive. Mary Flora Bell and her thirteen-year-old companion, Norma Joyce Bell (no relation), were questioned several times, and after changing their statements twice were charged with the murder of Brian Howe. 'That's all right by me,' said Mary. The girls accused each other of 'squeezing' the boy's throat, but admitted breaking into the school and writing the notes which were found there. It also transpired that on the same day Mary Bell contributed a picture to her own school's 'News book'. She had drawn the outstretched body of a child lying on the floor near a window — the position in which the first dead boy was found.

The two girls were tried at Newcastle, and the difference in their demeanour soon became apparent. Norma was bewildered and child-like, while Mary remained calm and showed a grasp of what was happening far in advance of her years. Expert testimony was given concerning Mary's mental state, to the effect that she was regarded as suffering from 'psychopathic personality'. This was defined as a persistent disorder or disability of the mind resulting in abnormally aggressive behaviour. It was stressed that there was no evidence of mental illness, but that she had a lack of feeling for other humans with a tendency to act on impulse. The conclusion was that Mary Bell 'was and is suffering from such abnormality of mind . . . such as substantially impaired her mental responsibility for her acts and omissions in doing or being a party to this killing'.

Mr Justice Cusack made it clear to the jury in his summing-up that there was an alternative to murder in this case. He laid it out succinctly: 'Murder requires an intent to kill or to do serious bodily injury knowing that death may result. Manslaughter does not require that intent at all. It is sufficient if there is a voluntary, unlawful and dangerous act which results in death. . . .' He also pointed out that the law presumed a child under the age of ten to be incapable of discerning between right and wrong and incapable of committing a criminal offence. The jury found Norma Bell not guilty, and she was acquitted, but found Mary Bell guilty of manslaughter on account of diminished responsibility on both charges. She was sentenced to detention for life, but has since been released. *238, 307, 448, 472,* **510***, 613, 712, 739.*

DISPOSAL OF THE BODY

Apart from ensuring his escape from the scene of the crime, the murderer's greatest challenge is to avoid subsequent detection by disposing of his victim's body. The short-term aim may simply be to conceal the crime long enough to guarantee a comfortable getaway, but in the long term the objective is to prevent the body ever being found or identified. That way the chances of the murderer being linked with his criminal act are reduced, although many would-be perpetrators of the perfect murder have been made painfully aware that a missing body is not an obstacle to pursuing a charge of murder.

Few acts of the murderer show such dedication and ingenuity as the disposal of the victim, and few tasks are so awesome. The human body is surprisingly durable, and its destruction without trace is difficult. The most powerful agents, such as ACID and fire, are not infallible. Acid will reduce the flesh, and in time attack the bones, but as John George Haigh discovered, identifiable parts such as teeth and gall-stones can survive even this treatment. BURNING also destroys the flesh, but even the use of petrol does not necessarily generate sufficient heat to ensure that some charred but recognizable parts will not remain.

Secret burial is perhaps the disposal method which most readily commends itself to the murderer, but it too presents a few difficulties. Merely putting a body into the ground is no assurance that the grave will not be found, and that EXHUMATION will not reveal evidence of foul play. One of the drawbacks is that it is never possible to return all the soil to the original hole, with the result that there is usually ample evidence of disturbance. Also, vegetation is disturbed when burial is attempted on open land, and differently coloured sub-soil is brought to the surface, leaving a visible scar in the ground.

Furthermore, it is not always easy to find a piece of ground that offers the possibility of secret burial. This is especially the case in built-up areas, which probably accounts for city murderers resorting to methods such as making up parcels of human remains or putting bodies into trunks. Faced with such a disposal problem, Edgar Edwards — who murdered a family for gain in London in 1902 — bought a house with a garden large enough to accommodate a common grave for his two adult victims and their infant child. His mistake was to be seen digging a deep hole by his neighbours. Ronald Harries, who murdered his adopted uncle and aunt in Wales in 1953, buried the bodies in a farm field. Detectives tied cotton across gaps in the hedges and Harries broke the threads when checking that the graves had not been disturbed, and so led the police to the spot.

The shallow grave, dug in haste or in ignorance of how deep a grave should be, has set many investigations onto the trail of the murderer. The inadequately buried corpse is soon exposed by the effects of weather and the activities of animals. But for the workings of nature which unearthed part of his victim's body, August Sangret might have eluded justice. Sangret, a French-Canadian soldier stationed in Britain, murdered a young woman who, because she had left home and lived out of doors in a crude shelter, was known as the 'Wigwam Girl'. After he had stabbed and bludgeoned her in the Surrey woods near his Army camp, Sangret dragged the body to a near-by ridge, where he covered it in a shallow grave. Five or six weeks later, in October 1942, the corpse was uncovered by an Army vehicle and was sufficiently intact for identification to be made. It was soon learned that the dead girl had befriended Sangret, and suspicion fell on the soldier. Had he made a more efficient job of burying his victim it is possible that he might have escaped trial and execution.

Burial frequently necessitates transportation of the corpse, with all its attendant hazards of discovery. Edgar Edwards put the dismembered corpses of his victims in packing-cases and had them moved six miles across London in order to carry out a garden burial. Henry Wainwright courted disaster by carrying his mistress's dismembered body in several stinking parcels through London's East End. He was caught in the act of transferring this wretched cargo from a cab to his brother's house. The dangers of being thus caught red-handed have perhaps weighed heavily with those murderers who have elected for on-the-spot disposal. John Christie, the sex murderer who turned 10 Rillington Place into a murder house, put three of his victims into a cupboard which he then wall-papered over. Two more bodies were buried in the garden and another was interred under the kitchen floor. Frederick and Maria Manning put their victim's QUICKLIME-covered corpse into a grave under the flagstones of their kitchen floor, and Frederick Deeming acquired the odious distinction of adopting a similar procedure in two continents. (See under SKULLS.) Dr Marcel Petiot, the French wartime mass murderer, and H. H. Holmes, the notorious Chicago killer of twenty-seven in the 1880s, both operated murder houses fitted out to meet their needs for wholesale disposal of their victims.

Disposing of human remains poses two important problems of which the murderer often takes too little account. Firstly, dead bodies decompose and give rise to a frightful stench, and, secondly, the sheer bulk of the human frame makes dismemberment a daunting task. The unattractive smell of DECOMPOSITION has made the trunk murder, once so popularly combined with freightage by railway, rather unfashionable.

Dismemberment as an aid to disposal is usually ill-considered — it is the enormity of the task which mainly defeats the murderer unless he has some medical or butchery skills. Dr Buck Ruxton showed some skill in the disarticulation of his two victims in 1935 (see under SKELETON) but being faced with a welter of BLOOD, a mass of viscera and the problems of detaching limbs or sawing them up is a prospect which has defeated many a murderer lacking proper implements and a knowledge of dissection. Patrick Mahon bought a saw and a knife in April 1924 when he travelled to East-bourne to meet Emily Kaye with her murder carefully planned. They met at their 'love bungalow', where he killed her and set about destroying the corpse. When the police searched the bungalow they found pieces of boiled flesh in a saucepan, sawn-up pieces of the body in a hat-box, a trunk and a biscuit tin, and some charred bones in the fireplace. Sir Bernard Spilsbury had the grisly task of reassembling the body, but the head, so distinctive for IDENTIFICATION and notoriously difficult to destroy, was never found. Like Dr Crippen, Mahon had found a secret resting-place for this.

Kate Webster, who destroyed her mistress and disposed of some of the boiled remains in the river Thames in 1879, was also concerned about disposing of the head. She carried it around in a black bag for a while until she finally got rid of it. She tried to sell some jars of human dripping to a publican, but the head remained missing.

Dismemberment is a means of reducing a murder victim's corpse to manageable proportions to assist disposal, often by fiery and watery means. Professor John White Webster (see under CIRCUMSTANTIAL EVIDENCE) killed fellow-academic Dr George Parkman in 1849 following a row over money. In the privacy of his laboratory Webster cut up his victim's body into pieces suitable for burning in his assay oven. His plan was foiled by an inquisitive laboratory assistant and by the indestructibility of Dr Parkman's TEETH. In 1949 Brian Donald Hume, the post-war racketeer, dismembered his victim's body and made up the pieces into two parcels, He then set out in a hired light aircraft, flying over the Essex Marshes, into which he jettisoned his cargo. Unfortunately, the sea has a habit of giving up the unwanted dead, and a headless torso from one of Hume's packages was washed up about a fortnight later on an Essex mud flat. Disposal by immersion — throwing human remains into sea or river — has its possibilities, but even when it succeeds it does not necessarily confer protection on the murderer, as James Camb discovered. (See under CORPUS DELICTI.)

Apart from these commonplace but none the less horrifying methods of disposal, there have been a number of particularly macabre methods of destruction. The Hosein brothers, who each received life imprisonment for the KIDNAPPING and murder of Mrs Muriel McKay, were thought to have fed their victim's body to the pigs at Rook's Farm in Hertfordshire in 1968. No trace of the body was ever found in what was otherwise an amateurish crime. Even more grisly was the disposal technique used by Adolph Luetgert, the obese and over-sexed proprietor of a Chicago sausage factory. He kept a string of mistresses, and had a bed installed at the factory so that he could take his pleasures more easily. When his wife disappeared in 1897 a search of the factory turned up some pieces of bone, a few teeth and two gold rings in an emptied steam-vat. Perhaps the most bizarre prelude to disposal was adopted by two teenage murderers in New York in 1954. Their victim's body was found in the bath — it had been completely cocooned in plaster of Paris in an attempt to seal off the smell of decomposition while its ultimate disposal was being considered (see under MATRICIDE for an account of this case).

1, 2, 27, 149, 170, 172, 177, 183, 206, 249, **257***, 305, 309, 377, 426, 439, 446, 480, 527, 603, 604, 626, 667.*

DOMINANCE THEORY

'To succeed in life, one must have a fortune or a powerful position. One must want to dominate those who might cause one problems and impose one's will on them.' These are the words of Dr Marcel Petiot, who was sent to the GUILLOTINE in May 1946 after being convicted of murdering twenty-seven people at his house in Paris. They hardly justify even his alleged killing of traitorous Nazi collaborators in wartime France, but they speak eloquently of the philosophy of the criminal type who aims to dominate.

The German philosophers Arthur Schopenhauer (1788–1860) and Friedrich Nietzsche (1844–1900) recognized the will to power as a

fundamental drive in all living creatures, and Nietzsche expressed the idea of the individual who is too strong for his particular environment. His concept of 'superman', the ultimate goal of human existence, has been assimilated by various groups and individuals, including the Nazi movement and individual murderers such as Charles Manson (see under RITUAL MURDER).

The will to succeed and to dominate within his group is strong in most human beings. In ordinary life this is acceptable drive to reach the top of a profession or job, and 5 per cent of individuals in any group are likely to succeed. It is suggested that there is also a criminal 5 per cent in the ordinary population, consisting of individuals who may have been thwarted in their ambitions — perhaps for environmental or social reasons — and who are motivated by an urge for novel experience. Charles Manson belonged to this group, and so too did Nathan Leopold and Richard Loeb, the Chicago youths who murdered a fourteen-year-old boy in 1924 for excitement and experiment. All three of these murderers subscribed to Nietzsche's philosophy of 'superman'.

Studies of animals have shown that every group

Chapman (*left*), compulsive poisoner (*see under* Antimony), and Nietzsche, apostle of dominance

has a number of highly dominant individuals — usually about one in twenty. This is evident in pecking orders and recognition of status. Robert Ardrey in his book *African Genesis* stimulated thinking about dominance in animal communities, and related it to human behaviour. The theme was taken up and developed by American psychologist Abraham Maslow (1908–70), who expounded a thesis which he called 'a hierarchy of needs'. He contended that in man and other animals the most important priorities after food and security were sex and self-esteem. Beyond these are the intellectual needs of culture, self-fulfilment and exercise of the will. These ideas have been discussed at length by the novelist and crime writer Colin Wilson in his studies of the origins of violence and the psychology of murder. (See also entry under MACHISMO.)
738.

DROWNING

Murder by drowning is unusual, although disposal of already dead murder victims by throwing them into water is commonplace. The most celebrated exponent of drowning as a murder method was George Joseph Smith, the 'Brides in the Bath' murderer. Between 1912 and 1914 three of Smith's bigamous wives died in their baths while he collected the insurance money. He was arrested in 1915 after the father of one of his earlier victims read a newspaper account of the death by misadventure of Smith's latest wife. A 'Bride's Tragic Fate' bore too many similarities to the death of his

daughter not to arouse his suspicions, and the authorities were alerted.

At Smith's trial for murder his defence counsel, Sir Edward Marshall Hall, tried unsuccessfully to have EVIDENCE of the other two deaths excluded. The judge ruled the evidence admissible, and in consequence the prosecution was able to show that Smith had carried out SYSTEM MURDER. In each case he had gone through a form of marriage, insured his victims, bought a bath or went to considerable lengths to ensure one was available, and drowned them. Sir Bernard Spilsbury showed that the size of the bath in which the last victim died would not have permitted accidental drowning. He suggested that Smith lifted up his victim's legs while at the same time pressing on the head so that the body slid down into the water, submerging the mouth and nostrils. Smith was found guilty, and was hanged at Maidstone in August 1915.

Drowning is one of the deaths by ASPHYXIA in which air is prevented from reaching the lungs, and the vital oxygen supply to the brain is cut off. A person can also die of cardiac arrest or laryngeal spasm by the shock of falling into water — so-called 'dry' drownings. When a person drowns there is an initial struggle during which the body alternately submerges and comes to the surface. During this process water is gulped into the lungs, which eventually become waterlogged, and weights the body sufficiently to sink it. Struggling may continue for two to five minutes, and death ensues with 'going down for the third time'.

The classic sign of drowning is a fine froth at the mouth and nostrils. The main internal indication is a 'ballooning' of the lungs as a result of their distension with water. Drowning occurs more rapidly in fresh water than in the sea, and biochemical tests can be used to determine the type of water in which a victim drowned. This may prove important, for bodies often float long distances before they are recovered. When a person drowns in the sea, salt water taken into the lungs has a higher osmotic pressure than the blood. Consequently the water is not drawn through the breathing membrane and there is no dilution of the blood, although its chloride concentration is increased. In fresh-water drowning, water taken into the lungs is quickly drawn through the breathing membrane into the blood by osmotic pressure. The blood is thus quickly diluted, and its chloride concentration reduced. These changes can be determined by

Smith's murder apparatus

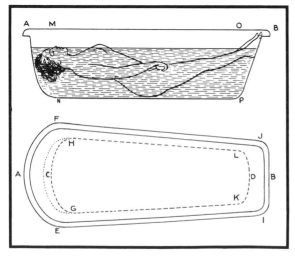

Letter setting out the similarity of the 'Brides in the Bath' deaths which drew attention of police to G. J. Smith

c/o Mrs Crossley
3 Clifton St
Blackpool.

Jany 3. 15

Dear Sir

I have been v. much struck
with the enclosed account and
its striking similarity to
a case which happened here
just 12 months previously
bath - pain in head - doctor
& inquest. I thought this might possibly
be of some use. I shall be v
pleased to answer any questions
you like . Yrs truly.

Joseph Crossley

analysing the heart blood soon after death.

The presence of foreign matter such as weed, silt and algae, swallowed while struggling in the water, also helps to establish the place of drowning. CADAVERIC SPASM, in which some weed or similar material is grasped by the drowning person, may also help to identify the place. The question of whether the body was dead or alive when it entered the water can be settled by means of diatom tests. Diatoms are microscopic algae with hard silicon shells which are widely found in both sea and fresh water. In the course of drowning, water containing diatoms is sucked into the lungs, and during the moments of struggling the diatoms enter the bloodstream and are pumped around the body to the heart. Extracts are taken of body tissues during the POST-MORTEM examination, and these are treated to destroy all but the tough diatoms. The presence of diatoms is clear proof that the victim was alive when entering the water. While an already dead body disposed of in water may have diatoms in the air-passages, none will have entered the bloodstream and been carried to other organs. Over 15,000 species of diatoms are known, and identification of the type can help locate the point of drowning. The hardy nature of diatoms makes this test particularly useful when other features have been destroyed by DECOMPOSITION.

Some types of freshwater diatom

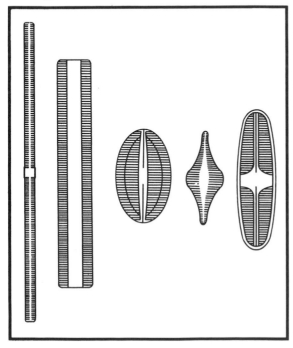

Within a few hours of immersion in water the skin on the hands and feet of a dead body wrinkles in a fashion known as 'washerwoman's hands'. The thickened skin on the palms of the hands and soles of the feet becomes sodden, and takes on this characteristic bleached and wrinkled appearance. It does not necessarily follow from the evidence of 'washerwoman's hands' that drowning was the cause of death, but only indicates the length of time the body has been immersed. The condition is well developed within 24 to 36 hours of immersion. The skin may become loose and detached from the body, especially in summer weather. In a remarkable Australian murder (known as the 'Hand in Glove Case') FINGERPRINT identification of the victim was made from a detached skin 'glove'. A body was found in the river near Wagga Wagga in December 1933 — its features were unrecognizable due to decomposition, and the skin was missing from both hands. The water-bloated skin from a man's hand and wrist was found on the river-bank, enabling the dead man to be identified, and leading to the conviction of the murderer, Edward Morey.

Denise Labbé's RITUAL MURDER of her young daughter in 1954, and Chester Gillette's murder of his girl-friend in 1906, were much-publicized drownings. Gillette took his pregnant girl-friend out in a boat on Big Moose Lake in New York County. He returned alone from what was supposed to have been a picnic, and the following day his companion's body, beaten about the face, was washed up. Gillette said the girl had committed suicide, then he said that the boat had capsized and she drowned accidentally. He was tried for murder amid glaring publicity, and was found guilty. EXECUTION of the death sentence was delayed for a year while appeals were heard, but he finally went to the electric chair in March 1908. Theodore Dreiser's novel *An American Tragedy* was based on this case.

1, 22, 29, 37, 71, 79, 95, 152, 170, 178, 191, 250, 270, 278, 321, 337, 394, 400, 413, 458, 470, 500, 517, **548**, 564, 594, 601, **625**, 677, 686, 705, 713, 743.

DYING DECLARATION

Statements made by a dying person may be acceptable as evidence in court, and be of great importance in a murder trial. The imminent prospect of death is held to be sufficiently awesome for declarations made by the dying to be equivalent to statements made under oath. Like RES

GESTAE statements, they are judged to be given at a time of crisis which precludes falsehood, and consequently are exempt from the rules governing hearsay EVIDENCE.

An unusual incident in which a dying woman made a declaration concerning the circumstances of her wounding featured in the Knowles case. Dr Benjamin Knowles, a medical officer serving in the Gold Coast territory of Ashanti, held a lunch party at his bungalow on 20 October 1928. He and his wife, Harriet, entertained a number of guests, including the District Commissioner. About two hours after the party dispersed, the Knowles's houseboy ran to the Commissioner's house to tell him that he had heard a shot. The District Commissioner went to the bungalow and spoke to Dr Knowles, who assured him that everything was all right.

The following day, not being satisfied that all was well, the District Commissioner returned to the bungalow accompanied by Dr Howard Gush. Knowles admitted that he and his wife had quarrelled, and claimed she had beaten him with an Indian club. Gush asked to see Mrs Knowles, and on examining her found that she had a large firearm wound in the buttocks. Her condition was serious, and the doctor made arrangements for her to be admitted to the Colonial Hospital at Kumasi. Having asked Knowles about the weapon which fired the shot, Dr Gush took away with him a .45 Webley revolver with five live rounds in the chamber and one spent cartridge case.

Knowles was arrested, and informed that as his wife's life was in danger she was to be asked to make a declaration, and he was advised to be present. On 22 October, having sworn an oath on the Bible, Harriet Knowles made the following declaration:

> There was a revolver standing or lying on a bookcase. It had been cleaned. I took it up and put it on the table near the bed. The boy came with the afternoon tea. I put the revolver carelessly on the chair, near the bed. I took a cup of tea, sitting on the chair. I sat on the gun. As I got up it caught in my dress with a lace frill. I tried to take it away from the lace, and suddenly it went off, the bullet passing through my leg. I did not realise I was shot until I saw blood running from my leg. I am not in fear of death.

Mrs Knowles made this statement and signed it in the presence of her husband, the Acting Commissioner of Police and the District Commissioner. The latter added for the record that he had taken the statement as 'I have reason to believe that H. L. Knowles is a dying woman, from wounds received.' Harriet Knowles died the following day.

Dr Knowles's trial for murder at Kumasi in November 1928 was an extraordinary affair. Acting Circuit Judge Frank McDowell, who presided, had it in his power to decide whether a jury should sit or not, and he decided against it. The Commissioner of Police conducted the prosecution, and the defendant, being allowed neither solicitor nor counsel, was obliged to conduct his own defence. He told the court that he and his wife quarrelled occasionally, and they had done so on the day of the lunch party. After their guests had left he retired to bed, and was awakened by the noise of a gun and his wife exclaiming, 'My God, I am shot.' He saw that she had a wound in the leg, and attempted to staunch the bleeding. She said, 'People will think I have done this myself purposely.'

The police produced some dubious FIREARMS evidence which purported to show how Knowles shot his wife. With the aid of a length of string to connect up various bullet-holes they tried to show that he shot his wife as she lay in bed, the bullet passing out of her body, through a fold in the mosquito netting, grooving the bedside table and finishing up in the back of the wardrobe. It was pointed out that this reconstruction was improbable, for the human body has great stopping power, and the bullet would have lost its impetus very quickly. Despite witnesses' testimony that only one shot was heard, the police now changed their story, arguing in favour of two bullets having been fired.

Having found the evidence 'very confusing', the judge nevertheless found Knowles guilty of murder, and sentenced him to death. This was commuted to life imprisonment, following which an appeal was made to the Privy Council in London. In November 1929 a Judicial Committee of five judges considered the appeal. Knowles, who had been returned to England, was too ill to appear, but on this occasion he was properly represented. Reference was made to the victim's dying declaration, and her account of how the gun discharged accidentally was tested in reconstruction by one of the judges. There was REASONABLE DOUBT about Knowles's guilt, and the trial judge was criticized for not considering the possibility of MANSLAUGHTER. Judgment was given in favour of the accused, and it was recommended that his conviction be quashed. Ultimately Dr Knowles was saved as much by his wife's dying declaration as by the shortcomings of judicial procedure in a far-flung British outpost.

Dying declarations are allowed in modern criminal procedure, being admissible only in relation to the circumstances immediately relating to an act of murder — this includes a victim identifying the person who caused the injury. It is up to the judge to advise the jury of any deficiencies in such statements, bearing in mind that they cannot be put to the test of cross-examination. The statement should be written down and signed by the person making it. It is also necessary that the person must be in a rational state of mind at the time, and believe that he is indeed dying.

An extraordinary dying statement which led to the conviction of a murderer was that made by Police Constable Nathaniel Edgar. He was found dying from gunshot-wounds in a London street in February 1948. He told a brother officer who arrived at the scene, 'The man was by the door. I got his identity card and name. He shot me in the legs with three shots. The pocket-book is in my inside pocket.' The entry in the policeman's notebook gave the name, Thomas, Donald, and an Enfield address. Edgar died while police hunted for his suspected killer in London's suburbs. Donald George Thomas, an Army deserter, was traced to Camberwell, where he was arrested at his lodging after trying to resist capture. He told the police, 'I might just as well be hung for a sheep as a lamb.' A gun found in his possession was proved by ballistics tests to have fired the fatal shots. Thomas was convicted and sentenced to death, but he was not hanged because the death penalty had been suspended in Britain for an experimental period of five years.
1, 9, 245, 287, 611.

E

EARS

Under the heading 'Training Recruits', Detective Inspector Kenneth Ferrier of Scotland Yard urged the aspiring detective of the 1920s to appreciate 'the value of the accuracy of description'. Among the features he noted as important in making a mental photograph were 'types of ears'. Ears are a highly characteristic feature of a person's appearance, as the American murderer Charles Henry Schwartz was unwittingly to demonstrate.

Schwartz lived in Berkeley, California, with his wife and children and enjoyed the kind of social life which befitted a successful manufacturing chemist. He had perfected a method of making artificial silk, and had set himself up in a new laboratory out of town at Walnut Creek. On the night of 30 July 1925 the premises were wrecked by a tremendous explosion, and a charred corpse, thought to be that of Schwartz, was found in the smouldering ruins.

Suspicion over the incident arose immediately the fire chief made it known that he had found evidence of arson. This was linked to other phenomena, the most important of which was a mysterious break-in at Schwartz's house, when several photographs showing his portrait were stolen. At this point Dr Edward Heinrich, the Californian criminologist, was called in, and further revelations followed. Examination of the burned corpse revealed that it had been subjected to various processes to remove its identifying features. The fingertips had been destroyed with ACID, the eyes gouged out and two TEETH had recently been removed from the upper jaw. Moreover, the victim of this violence had died, not in the fire, but as a result of a crushing blow to the back of the head. Despite the severity of the charring, sufficient of the dead man's right ear remained to enable a comparison to be made with a photograph of Schwartz.

The difficulty lay in finding a photograph, for owing to the burglary which had stripped the house of every likeness of her husband, Mrs Schwartz was unable to help the police. Fortunately, a friend came up with a photograph of Schwartz, and it was immediately apparent to Heinrich that the chemist was not the dead man. The shape of the fire victim's ear had a distinctive feature known as a Darwinian tubercle which was entirely lacking in the photograph of Schwartz. Two questions now arose. Who was the dead man? And where was Schwartz? The first was answered by public response to police appeals for information, and the charred corpse was identified as an itinerant preacher known to have befriended

Bertillon's collection of ear-shapes as used in *portrait parlé*

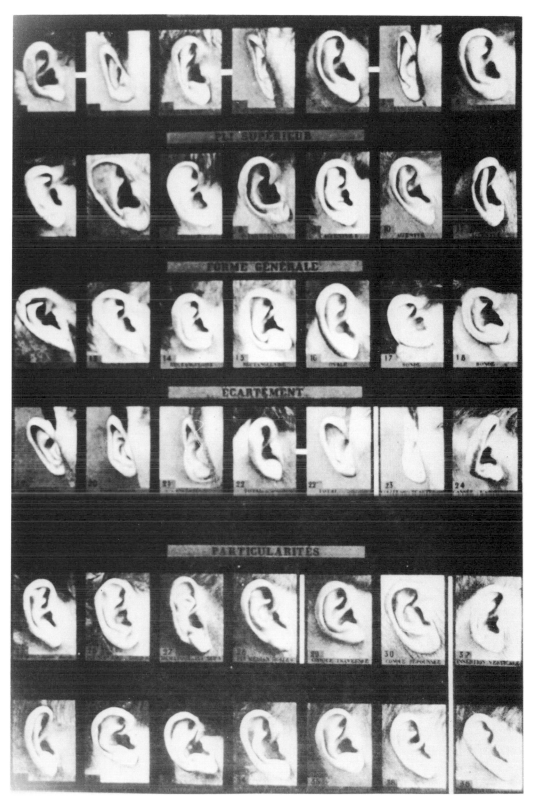

Schwartz. The second was answered following one of Heinrich's inspired descriptions which he based on an examination of the missing man's clothing and known habits. He told the police, 'Look for Schwartz where there are women. Look for a nervous man who jingles coins in his pocket, smokes numerous small cigars and walks with excessive military erectness.' The suspected murderer was eventually tracked to an apartment house in Oakland, where he was found dead in his room. He had shot himself after leaving a note to his wife in which he confessed to killing the preacher and burning his body.

Alphonse Bertillon recognized the significance of the ear in criminal IDENTIFICATION, especially as ear-shape remains unaltered from birth. He included ear description in his development of the *portrait parlé* system. The descriptive importance of the ear has not diminished with the advent of new identification techniques. Jacques Penry, inventor of Photofit, has said, 'Although as unique to every face as a FINGERPRINT is unique to each person, the ears have been almost entirely ignored as a means of identification.' The ear has its own terminology, the principal parts being the helix, lobule, tragus, antitragus, antihelix and concha. It is the prominence, shape and convolutions of these parts which give individuality to the structure. The profile gives the full shape of the ear, but equally important is the front view showing the ear in relationship to the head. The 'jug-ear', for example, is a most distinctive feature, and one which a witness is likely to remember.

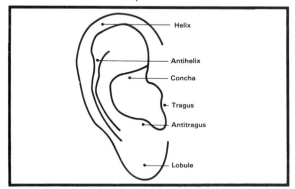

Helix

Antihelix

Concha

Tragus

Antitragus

Lobule

External characteristics of the ear

One of the most celebrated ears in crime cases belonged to the victim of a fatal shooting, when John Donald Merrett was freed of murdering his mother. In March 1926 Mrs Merrett was found lying on the floor of a room in her Edinburgh flat bleeding from a head-wound. Her son raised the alarm, shouting, 'My mother has shot herself.' The injured woman lingered for two weeks before dying in hospital. Merrett, suspected of forging his mother's cheques, was charged with murder and sent for trial.

The prosecution maintained that the nature of the victim's wounds ruled out suicide, while the powerful combination of Sir Bernard Spilsbury and Robert Churchill took the opposing view. The poor lady's right ear featured as an exhibit at the trial. The bullet, fired from a .25 automatic pistol, travelled in an upward direction, grooving the neck below and in front of the right ear. The bone of contention between the experts was the lack of powder tattooing around the wound which is invariably produced when a FIREARM is discharged at close range, as in suicide. The prosecution argued therefore that the pistol could not have been held close to the head, but was fired from a distance. Spilsbury contended that any powder residues on the skin could have been washed away by the bleeding, and he held the view that suicide was a possible explanation of the shooting. Merrett was given the benefit of a NOT PROVEN verdict on the murder charge, although he was convicted of forgery.

Merrett subsequently achieved notoriety as Ronald Chesney, murdering his wife and mother-in-law before taking his own life in woods near Cologne in 1954. As Sir Sydney Smith put it rather acidly, 'The slackness of the police and the credit given to the misleading evidence of Spilsbury and Churchill . . . allowed Merrett to live — and to kill again.'

1, 10, 21, 67, 217, 236, 245, 255, 277, 316, 320, **544,** *546,* **572,** *581, 632, 659,* **673,** *685, 711, 741.*

ELECTRIC CHAIR

'The mounting whine and snarl of the generator. The man's lips peel back, the throat strains for a last desperate cry, the body arches against the restraining straps as the generator whines and snarls again, the features purple, steam and smoke arise from the bald spots on head and leg while the sick-sweet smell of burned flesh permeates the little room.' Thus did Don Reid, a newspaperman, describe an electrocution at Huntsville Prison in Texas.

Electricity was first harnessed to judicial death in 1890 in the belief that it offered a more humane way of killing. The first victim was William

'Old Sparky'

Kemmler, a convicted murderer, who was electrocuted at Auburn State Prison, New York, on 6 August 1890. He took eleven minutes to die, and the opinion of the New York *Globe* was that 'Manufactured lightning to take the place of the hangman's rope for dispatching of condemned murderers cannot be said to be satisfactory.' Dr E. A. Spitzka, who attended as a witness, pronounced the EXECUTION a failure, and said that no more experiments should be made. Nicola Tesla, an electrical expert, added to this chorus of criticism by pointing out that electrocution was not necessarily instantaneous. Alternating current may pass through the body in such a way that the functions of vital organs are momentarily preserved, with the result that the victim may retain consciousness and experience great pain.

Despite the criticism, electrocution was adopted by fifteen states as their official method of carrying out the death penalty, but the electric chair has not been adopted outside the United States. The chair itself — often nicknamed 'Old Sparky' or 'Thunderbolt' — is usually stoutly built of wood, with strong leather straps to restrain the victim. The prisoner is strapped into the chair, and the 'death cap', containing one of the electrodes, is placed on his shaven head and fastened with a strap under the chin. The cap contains a sponge soaked with salt solution to improve contact and to prevent burning. The other electrode is secured to the ankle, and the executioner pulls a switch to send 2,250 volts through the body via the head cap and earthed through the leg. The charge is held for three seconds, and is repeated four times in the space of two minutes. Death usually occurs within that time from stoppage of the heart and respiration.

Robert G. Elliott, New York's official executioner who carried out over three hundred death sentences, believed that the initial charge of electricity 'shatters the person's nervous system instantaneously and beyond recall', a view also shared by prison doctors. Dr Amos O. Squire, who attended many electrocutions at Sing Sing, believed that the electric chair was more humane and less painful than HANGING. Thousands of condemned men and women have been taken from Death Row and 'burned', as the prison fraternity call electrocution, but controversy over the use of the electric chair has continued despite a US Supreme Court ruling that the method was not inhumane. The death penalty was suspended in the USA in 1972, and the sentences of many condemned prisoners were commuted to life imprison-

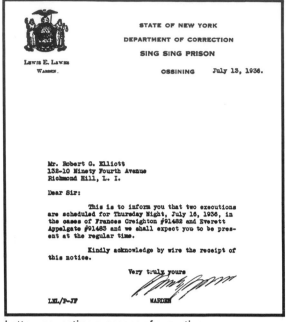

Letter requesting presence of executioner

ment. The moratorium was lifted in 1976, and John Spenkelink, the first man to be executed in the USA for twelve years, was electrocuted in Florida in 1979.

Frank Joseph Coppola, a former policeman under sentence of death for murder since 1978, went to the electric chair in Virginia in August 1982. He was executed at his own request to spare his sons from ridicule at school, the fifth person to be executed in the USA since the US Supreme Court lifted its ban.

Many dramas have been associated with the electric chair, including a photograph taken of the dying moments of Ruth Snyder at Sing Sing in 1928. A Press photographer who attended the execution as witness obtained a photograph, using a small camera strapped to his ankle. The five electrical charges needed to dispatch Ethel Rosenberg in 1953 no doubt gave the executioner some anxious moments, as did the failure of the first charge on Albert Fish. This elderly, frail man convicted of murder and CANNIBALISM had a number of needles in his body near the genitals which he had inserted at various times as part of his sado-MASOCHISM. It was these which allegedly short-circuited the first attempt to electrocute him at Sing Sing in 1936.
165, 205, 252, 492, 568, 619.

Ruth Snyder at the moment of death

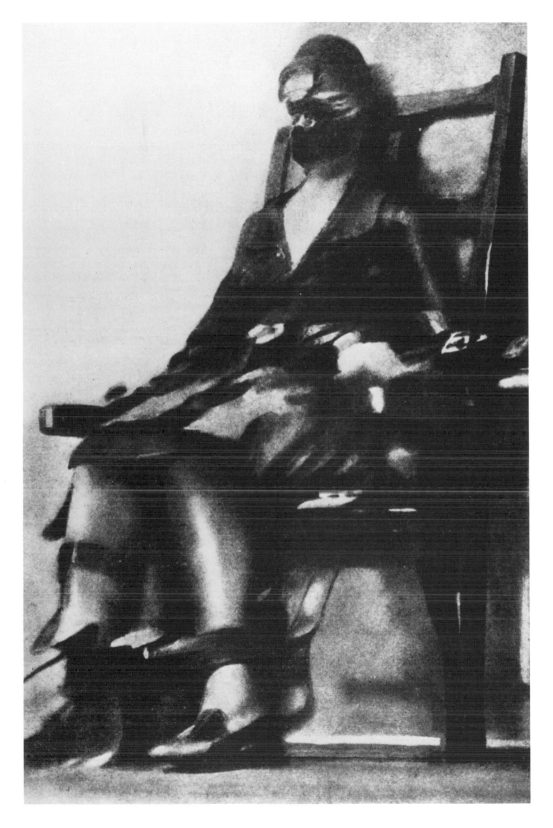

EMBOLISM

It is commonly believed that a tiny bubble of air injected into a vein will cause death due to air embolism. The amount of air needed to stop the heart depends on the health of the individual, but the 5 or 10cc delivered by an ordinary hypodermic syringe into the vein of a healthy person would simply cause annoyance and local pain. 'There is no doubt that it takes a lot of air to kill a person,' remarked Dr John Thompson in his book *Crime Scientist*, adding that best results might be obtained by using a bicycle pump. Opinions as to what constitutes a lethal quantity of air vary from 50 to 300cc. This discussion has made headlines in a number of cases alleging mercy killing.

In December 1949 Dr Hermann Sander attended one of his patients, Mrs Abbie Borroto, who was dying of cancer in a New Hampshire hospital. In the presence of a nurse he took a hypodermic syringe and injected 40cc of air into a vein in the woman's arm. A DEATH CERTIFICATE was made out giving carcinoma of the large bowel as the cause of death, and the body was duly buried. Some days after the funeral Dr Sander completed the dead woman's medical record by making a detailed entry of her final treatment, including the injection of air. This virtual CONFESSION to mercy killing was spotted by a hospital records clerk who reported it. In due course the newspapers learned of the story, and a great controversy blew up, with the doctor being applauded for an act of mercy killing. Dr Sander, having refused to reconsider the statement made on his patient's record, was brought to trial in what became known world-wide as 'The Mercy Killing Trial'.

Medical experts testified on the subject of air embolism, and Dr Milton Helpern pointed out that as the POST-MORTEM examination of the dead woman showed no competing cause of death, embolism resulting from the injection of air which Dr Sander admitted giving was the likely cause. Tension in this already highly charged case was further increased when Dr Sander changed his story, saying that his patient was dead when he put the hypodermic needle in her vein, and he injected the air simply to make sure. If this was so, then there was no case of murder. Arguments continued to rage over the amount of air needed to cause a fatal embolism, and some doctors thought that 40cc was too little, believing that 200–300cc was nearer the mark. But, as Dr Helpern pointed out, it depended on the condition of the recipient, and in the case of Dr Sander's heavily sedated, terminal patient, 40cc proved sufficient — that is, if she was not already dead. Dr Sander was found not guilty.

Air introduced into a vein in the arm travels through the bloodstream until it reaches the right side of the heart, where the mass of bubbles or froth can result in a blockage. The air may also be pumped through the lungs, whence bubbles can travel to the brain and block its blood-supply. Embolism is a pathological condition usually caused by pieces of a blood clot or diseased tissue finding their way into the large vessels of the bloodstream, and thence to the smaller vessels where a blockage is created. Air embolism can result from wounds in the neck or during surgical operations on that region of the body when air is pulled into the veins, and sudden death results owing to the mass of air stopping the blood-flow. Deaths from air embolism following criminal abortion procured by means of a Higginson syringe were common. This method involved introducing fluid, usually soapy water, into the womb in order to dilate it to such an extent that the blood-vessels connecting the foetus to the mother are broken and the foetus breaks away. If the nozzle of the syringe emerges above the level of the fluid reservoir air under pressure is pumped into the womb. A mass of air bubbles enters the woman's bloodstream and makes its way to the heart and brain, resulting in death.

Fatal embolism can also be caused by fat particles released into the bloodstream following bone fracture which impede the passage of blood through the vital organs. An important medical discovery which helped forensic pathologists determine whether injuries had been inflicted during life was that fat can be driven into the bloodstream from tissues as the result of external violence to the body. A German pathologist used this knowledge to good effect in 1929 in helping to secure a murder charge against Erich Tetzner in a blazing car case (see under BURNING for an account).

117, *324, 667*.

EPILEPSY

History's most widely witnessed murder occurred on 24 November 1963 in Dallas, Texas. An estimated eighty million people watched on US television as Lee Harvey Oswald, the man charged with the ASSASSINATION of President John F. Kennedy, was transferred from Dallas Police

Headquarters en route for the county jail. It was a journey Oswald was never to complete, for as he emerged from the police building flanked by detectives, and walking towards a waiting vehicle, John Leon Ruby stepped forward. Shouting, 'You son of a bitch,' he levelled a .38 revolver at Oswald and fired the single shot from which Oswald later died.

Ruby, a 52-year-old Dallas night-club owner, told the police officers who arrested him, 'You all know me. I'm Jack Ruby.' Within hours he was charged that he did unlawfully, voluntarily and with MALICE AFORETHOUGHT kill Oswald. Ruby's trial began on 4 March 1964. He pleaded not guilty by reason of insanity. His defence was that he had killed while undergoing a psychomotor epileptic seizure. A great deal of medical, psychological and psychiatric testimony was presented to the JURY.

Dr Roy Schafer, a clinical psychologist at Yale University, testified that Ruby was suffering from an organic brain disorder which he termed psychomotor epilepsy. Sufferers from this disorder are prone to uncontrollable and explosive behaviour if emotionally upset. It was suggested that emotional stress over the President's assassination built up in Ruby's organically impaired brain to the point where he exploded with rage and shot Oswald, the alleged assassin. This surge of hate was all part of a pattern in which consciousness is impaired and aggressive acts are committed automatically. Dr Schafer described psychological tests which he had carried out on Ruby in support of his opinion. The judge, Joe E. Brown, wanted defence attorney Melvin Belli to put the M'NAGHTEN RULES to his witness, but when counsel declined on the grounds that they were 'not the domain of the psychologist' the judge ordered the expert's testimony to be excluded. This decision was later reversed, but it formed part of a complicated argument between lawyers and doctors over interpretation of what constituted insanity.

Further experts were called, and Dr Martin Towler, Professor of Neurology and Psychiatry at the University of Texas, gave evidence regarding Ruby's epilepsy. The accused, it appeared, had a history of being involved in fights and incidents in which he sustained head injuries, the latest being early in 1963 when he had fallen while ice-skating and 'stunned' himself. Electroencephalogram (EEG) recordings of fluctuations in the electrical potential of the brain had been taken from Ruby, and were produced in court in a shoe-box. These brain-waves traced on strips of paper showed abnormal activity which indicated mild seizures.

A succession of distinguished experts appeared in court to give their interpretation of the evidence and then to have it challenged. Dr Robert Schwab, for example, a neurologist and EEG specialist, maintained that Ruby's EEGs did not support a diagnosis of psychomotor epilepsy, although he agreed they were 'mildly abnormal'. Dr Frederic A. Gibbs, the foremost American authority on electroencephalography, gave it as his opinion that Ruby had a 'particular, very rare type of epilepsy' which occurred in only 0·5 per cent of epileptics. He called this psychomotor variant seizure discharge, the characteristics of which were personality instability and lack of emotional control. Dr Manfred S. Guttmacher, a Baltimore psychiatrist, testified that in interviews he had conducted with Ruby the accused said he shot Oswald on impulse. The concept of irresistible impulse had been introduced in the USA in an attempt to soften the right and wrong effect of applying the M'Naghten Rules. Indeed, in his final speech Melvin Belli criticized the unembellished use of the M'Naghten Rules in Texas which prevented him arguing a case for irresistible impulse to explain Ruby's conduct.

Dr Guttmacher's conclusion that Ruby had psychomotor epilepsy, a condition also occurring in persons who were non-epileptics but had weak egos, did not help the defence. Ruby was seen as a man who simply cracked momentarily under an insufferable emotional burden, and the jury found him guilty of murder with malice. He was condemned to death, but in 1967 died of cancer in prison. Thus the most widely publicized murder of modern times ended in a classic courtroom struggle between medical and legal experts. All the familiar legal arguments about insanity were aired, and the latest scientific methods for probing the causes of mental illness were presented. Yet ultimately the century-old test — the 'right' and 'wrong' test as the M'Naghten Rules are sometimes called — proved a resilient standard.

Epilepsy has often been pleaded as a defence to a murder on the grounds that the crime was committed during a state of epileptic automatism. This plea has been used particularly in cases where there is no doubt about the accused's guilt. Epilepsy, or falling sickness, has been known since ancient times, and famous epileptics include Socrates, Alexander the Great, Julius Caesar, Byron and Dostoevsky. True epilepsy has no organic cause, being a functional disorder of the brain in which the steady and controlled discharge

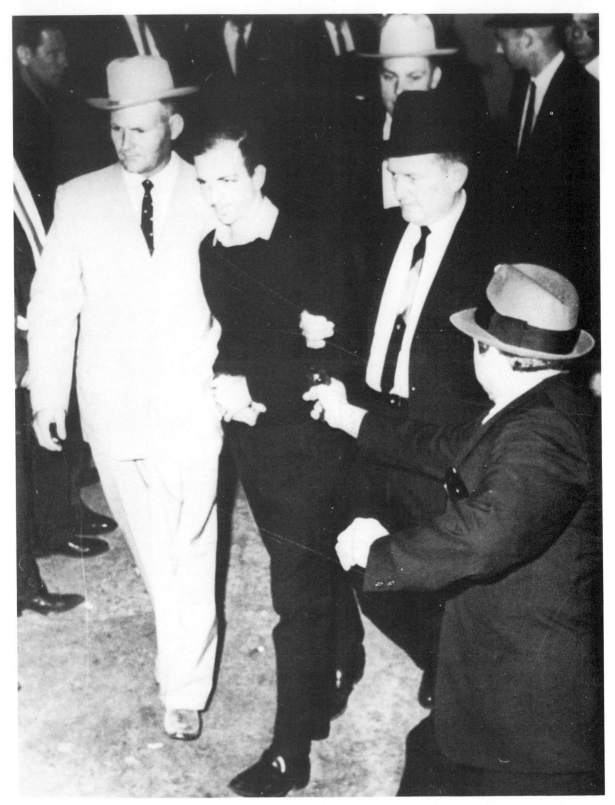

of electrical energy gives way to spasmodic, uncontrolled releases which cause the characteristic 'fits'. Disease or damage to the brain may also cause similar symptoms. Factors which can precipitate epilepsy include sudden fright, prolonged anxiety, overwork, and alcoholism.

Manifestations of epilepsy fall into three types, grand mal, petit mal and psychomotor epilepsy. Grand mal produces the characteristic 'fit' — the patient falls unconscious, and all the body's muscles go into spasm. This may last about half a minute, after which the contractions subside, breathing becomes less heavy and there is a return to consciousness. The recovery phase may take several hours, during which consciousness may be impaired and acts committed of which there is no subsequent recollection. This is known as post-epileptic AUTOMATISM, when in a confused state a person may carry out a complicated but routine procedure although with some aberration, such as driving a car but to a purposeless destination. Death rarely occurs as the result of such an epileptic fit.

Petit mal is a momentary loss of consciousness, perhaps for a few seconds when behaviour is slightly erratic — an unexpected and disjointed break in concentration while speaking conversationally, for example. There are no 'fits' or convulsions with petit mal. Psychomotor epilepsy is characterized by a type of seizure in which a person may appear to be fully aware and purposeful, yet acts aggressively with subsequent AMNESIA regarding his abnormal behaviour.

It is these states of altered consciousness produced by epilepsy, and which give rise to automatic behaviour, that are particularly significant in the medico-legal sense. If it can be shown that a murder was committed by a person while in this condition, with subsequent loss of memory, he is regarded in law as not being responsible, and not being able to form the necessary MENS REA or guilty intent.

It is estimated that in England and Wales one person in twenty has an epileptic fit of some type during their lifetime. This suggests that the link between epilepsy and crime is likely to be close. Indeed, a survey conducted by specialists at the Maudsley Hospital in 1952 reported that 18 out of 105 murderers examined showed symptoms of epilepsy, which is more than thirty times greater than the incidence of the disorder among the general population. In practice, it has proved

Assassin versus assassin: Jack Ruby shoots Lee Harvey Oswald

difficult to establish epilepsy as an explanation for murder. Dr Frederic Gibb, who testified in the Ruby trial, had examined ten murder suspects in cases where epileptic behaviour was suggested, but his findings were entirely negative. The advent of the EEG to record electrical discharge patterns in the brain has assisted the clinical study of epilepsy and other disorders, but it seems not to have helped the lawyers. The Maudsley Hospital survey showed a correlation between abnormal EEG and apparently motiveless crime, but in the cases of straightforward murder there was no greater abnormality in the EEGs than in normal individuals.

A case in which murder was committed during a psychomotor seizure was tried in America in 1950. In May of that year a nineteen-year-old boy named Elwell was seen late one evening carrying a body wrapped in a sheet from his aunt's house in Melrose, Massachusetts. Neighbours who thought they had heard a scream called the police — the occupant, Mrs Tully, was missing but there was BLOOD on the kitchen floor. Elwell was stopped in his car at a police road-block — there was blood in the car's trunk, but no body. The youth's response to being questioned was to ask, 'What body?' He then gave an account of two men who had murdered his aunt and forced him to drive with her body out into the countryside where he was ordered to dump it. Mrs Tully's corpse was duly recovered; the skull had been crushed, and there were also stab wounds in the back.

Elwell eventually broke down and admitted killing his aunt because she declined his request to borrow her car. He had struck her over the head with a steel implement and choked her when she started to recover consciousness. Having dumped her body, he ran over it several times with the car — he did not know why he did it. He was tried for murder, and although he said he wished to plead guilty, a defence was made out that he was guilty but insane. This was supported by the evidence of Dr Leo Alexander, Director of Neuropathology at Boston City Hospital, who gave it as his opinion that Elwell had committed the murder while undergoing a psychomotor epileptic seizure, and consequently did not know what he was doing. Elwell said that on the day of the murder he felt 'nervous and on edge'. He remembered giving his aunt the first blow, but then recollected nothing until he found himself miles away in Portland. Despite this evidence, the jury found the accused guilty and he was sentenced to death.

Disquiet over the verdict led to a re-examination

of the medical evidence by two doctors appointed by the Governor of Massachusetts. Dr William G. Lennox and Dr Douglas T. Davidson reported that Elwell had sustained a head injury when he was eleven years old, after which he had difficulty with his personal relationships. During his service with the US Marines he suffered several bouts of amnesia, one lasting for two weeks, and was always in some kind of disciplinary trouble. He was discharged on medical grounds in 1949, and prior to murdering his aunt had shown aggressive behaviour on at least four occasions. His mother recalled her son suffering fits at the ages of two and eleven. Elwell's EEG showed abnormal activity indicating damage in the left temporal region of the brain. Lennox and Davidson concluded that 'the murder . . . was committed during a period of temporary brain illness in which Elwell was not capable of judging right from wrong'. Following this report the Governor commuted Elwell's sentence to one of life imprisonment.

As a result of this case, epileptic automatism has perhaps been too readily suggested as a defence to murder, especially where there is no doubt about guilt. But in any given case an argument for loss of control as against knowing the difference between right and wrong has proved difficult to win. *388, 459,* **518**, *576.*

EVIDENCE

Evidence consists of statements made by witnesses in court about criminal matters, and includes relevant documents and exhibits. The purpose of evidence is to prove or disprove particular matters relating to a crime to the satisfaction of the JURY. The weight of evidence refers to its credibility in the eyes of the jury.

Evidence falls into two classes — direct and circumstantial. Direct evidence is provided by an eye-witness who has seen a crime committed, whereas CIRCUMSTANTIAL EVIDENCE involves relevant facts from which inferences may be drawn that a crime was committed. The presentation of evidence in English and American courts is governed by elaborate laws designed to exclude rumour, gossip and hearsay. This is to concentrate the minds of the jury on relevant issues and to protect the interests of accused persons. Consequently, certain forms of testimony are regarded as inadmissible. The main exceptions are hearsay evidence, other than a CONFESSION made by the prisoner or a DYING DECLARATION; opinion, other

than testimony provided by an expert witness; and evidence of an accused's criminal record or bad character which implies predisposition to guilt.

Under English law, a husband and wife may not be compelled to give evidence one against the other except when violence is alleged. The Criminal Evidence Act of 1898 made it possible for the first time for an accused person to give evidence on his own behalf. Prior to this he was permitted only to make an unsworn statement from the dock. Confession is admissible as evidence on the grounds that an accused person is unlikely to acknowledge incriminating facts against himself unless they are true. In the United States the fifth Amendment of the Constitution allows that a person is not compelled to be a witness against himself.

In court the examination and cross-examination of witnesses forms the heart of the criminal trial. The witness relates strictly what he saw or heard directly with his own senses. The skill of the great criminal advocate lies in drawing out this testimony in the clearest possible way for the jury. The judge ensures that the rules of evidence are maintained, and directs the court as to the admissibility of any contentious testimony.

There have been many dramas in murder trials over the presentation of evidence and the interpretation of admissibility. At the trial of George Joseph Smith in 1915, for example, evidence regarding the deaths by DROWNING of two of his previous brides was admitted with devastating effect. While the evidence on the death which formed the trial charge was circumstantial, the evidence of all three deaths showed SYSTEM MURDER in operation. As a consequence, the Brides in the Bath murderer was convicted, and the admissibility of damning evidence was upheld in the appeal court.

Equally dramatic was the handling of evidence at Steinie Morrison's trial in 1911 for murder. Leon Beron, an East End property-owner, had been found beaten and stabbed on Clapham Common. A crude letter 'S' had been slashed on both cheeks, and his murder occurred two weeks after three police officers had been killed in London by anarchists. Morrison was arrested following IDENTIFICATION provided by three cab-drivers. During the trial Morrison's counsel attempted to discredit two prosecution witnesses by attacking their characters. He was warned by the judge that under the Criminal Evidence Act, such an attack on the prosecution's witnesses paved the way for the defendant's character to be severely probed under cross-examination. Counsel persisted in his action, with the result that when Morrison appeared in the witness-box highly damaging evidence was brought out on his criminal background. In his summing-up the judge indicated that there was insufficient evidence to convict, but the jury — perhaps swayed by the details of Morrison's criminal past — found him guilty. He was reprieved, so that, unlike George Joseph Smith, he escaped EXECUTION, only to die in prison some years later.

*1, 6, 7, **28**, 85, 120, 343, 426, 435, 437, 483, 621, 702.*

EXECUTION

An American judge is said to have remarked, 'Some like chocolate, some like vanilla; I believe in the death penalty.' This trivial remark illustrates one extreme view of the merits of capital punishment. An opposing view has been expressed by Albert Pierrepoint, Britain's last official executioner, who wrote in his autobiography: 'I do not now believe that any one of the hundreds of executions I carried out has in any way acted as a deterrent against future murder. Capital punishment, in my view, achieved nothing except revenge.' But later, in a letter to one of the authors of this book, as the number of murders in Britain increased after the death penalty was abolished, he was inclined to modify these views.

Historically, taking the life of violators against the prevailing social code served the dual purpose of meting out retribution and deterring others from similar crimes. Other benefits were to ensure respect for authority and to promote the subjection through fear of the mass of the population. This was instanced by the practice of feudal barons in England of erecting gallows in a prominent place on their estates.

Execution has long been accepted as the punishment befitting the crime of MURDER. The earliest records show that the Chinese prescribed beheading for this purpose, while the Egyptians and Greeks favoured self-execution by commanding the condemned person to take poison. The development and widespread use of execution was fostered by the idea that the criminal was entitled to no consideration of mercy on the grounds that he deliberately chose to commit acts of wrongdoing. Executions, often accompanied by torture, were therefore conducted in public to achieve the maximum sense of society's retribution.

Capital punishment was first recorded in England about 450 B.C. when it was the practice to

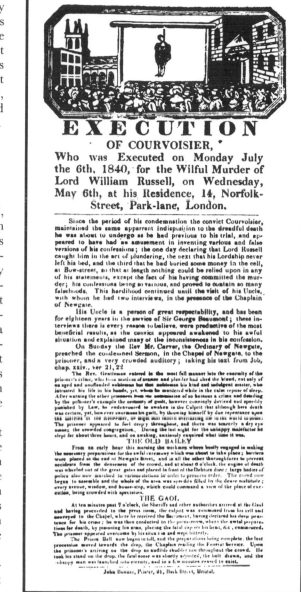

Nineteenth-century execution broadsheet

throw condemned persons into a quagmire, thus effecting their execution by drowning. The Anglo-Saxons favoured hanging, but also resorted to beheading, burning and stoning. By the Middle Ages the number of capital crimes had increased to include, in addition to murder, manslaughter, arson, highway robbery, burglary and larceny. The value of life continued to go down so much that during the reign of Henry VIII, 72,000 of his subjects were executed. The King also passed an

Act making it legal to punish felons by boiling them to death.

In the eighteenth century life was so cheap that individuals were executed for such trivial reasons as stealing turnips. The trend continued into the next century, to the point where over 200 offences, ranging from murder to picking pockets, were punishable by death. Few felons were spared, although women were occasionally burned in preference to hanging for the sake of decency! Even children as young as eight were strung up for stealing, and hanging days were turned into public holidays.

The cruelty and barbaric behaviour which governed executions gradually abated, so that in 1823 a statute was passed reducing the number of capital offences to a hundred. The first resolution to abolish capital punishment was raised in Parliament in 1840, and public execution was legislated against in 1868. At the same time, fresh codes of practice were drawn up governing the administration of capital punishment in Britain. These included the hoisting of a black flag above the prison wall after sentence had been carried out, and the tolling of the prison bell fifteen minutes before and fifteen minutes after the execution.

Even as late as 1831 a boy aged nine years was hanged at Chelmsford for arson, and it was not until 1908 that Parliament passed an Act defining a child as a person under fourteen years of age. A child under seven years was considered incapable of committing any crime. From the mid-nineteenth century there was an upsurge of humane feeling which led to the abolition of capital punishment in many European countries. Some rejected it only to reintroduce it later, and this pattern was repeated in the USA, where each state had jurisdiction over its use of capital punishment. Some states abolished the death sentence, others retained it for certain crimes, such as first-degree murder, RAPE or KIDNAPPING.

Methods of execution used in the twentieth century by those countries retaining capital punishment have odd national characteristics. The English have long preferred HANGING, the French are always associated with the GUILLOTINE, the Spanish with garotting (see under STRANGULATION) and the Americans with such innovations as the ELECTRIC CHAIR and GAS CHAMBER.

Today most European countries have abolished capital punishment save for treason in time of war, and in the USA the Supreme Court pronounced a moratorium on executions in 1967. This closely followed the public outcry at the long-delayed carrying out of the sentence on Caryl Chessman, who waited for twelve years before finally being executed with lethal gas. The US Supreme Court ruling was lifted in 1976, and the first man to test his freedom to be executed was Gary Gilmore, who demanded that the sentence of death passed on him in Utah be carried out. His death before a firing squad (Utah permits the choice of hanging or shooting) in January 1977 was attended by unprecedented interest from the news media. After Gilmore's execution the Utah Attorney-General told the Press, 'Capital punishment is symbolic of society's determination to enforce all of its laws.'

In 1979 John Spenkelink was the first murderer to be executed in the USA against his wishes for twelve years. He was electrocuted in Florida, and five months later Jesse Bishop, another condemned murderer, was sent to the gas chamber at Nevada State Prison. In Britain the last executions took place in 1964, when two men in their twenties convicted of murdering a workmate were hanged. Peter Allen was hanged at Liverpool, and Gwynne Evans at Manchester. The last woman to be hanged in Britain, Ruth Ellis, went to the scaffold in 1955.

The debate on capital punishment continues, and the upsurge of violent crime and terrorism has heightened demands for the retention or reintroduction of the death penalty. It is argued that society must protect itself against those who menace life and property, and some suggest that death is more humane than keeping a man locked up in prison for life. There is also the danger that an imprisoned murderer will escape to kill again. The contrary view is that capital punishment lowers respect for life, and by lending itself to sensationalism may even be an incentive to murder. There is too the grave danger that an innocent person will be executed, as for example Timothy Evans, hanged in 1950 for the murder of his daughter. Although Christie later confessed to the murder of Evans's wife, it is almost certain that he killed them both.

The argument moves backward and forward, but in any event the number of murderers executed is only a small fraction of the total number condemned to death — about 2 per cent in the USA prior to 1967. It is believed that more murderers die by their own hands than at those of the executioner, and what is clearly established is the abhorrence of capital punishment held by many of those uniquely placed to pass judgment. Albert Pierrepoint (former public executioner), Clinton Duffy

Scene outside Pentonville Prison following an execution

(former Warden of San Quentin Prison) and Robert G. Elliott (former New York official executioner) all come out against it. In face of this, the argument that it is not fair for society to ask any man to perform the role of executioner appears to carry some weight. However, the *New York Times* reported no shortage of volunteers for Gary Gilmore's firing-squad. One local resident suggested that the parents of the killer's victims be offered the chance to shoot him. The debate will no doubt continue, and the battle lines of deterrence and retribution will remain as marking posts.
4, 57, 60, 147, 205, 383, 420, 466, 549, 610, 616, 619.

EXHUMATION

The digging up, or exhumation, of a buried corpse is a rather ghoulish but often necessary procedure in the course of a murder investigation. Exhumations have frequently been carried out at night to defeat public curiosity, with the subsequent POST-

MORTEM examination being performed in primitive conditions. On many occasions in the 1920s and 30s this was the lot of Sir Bernard Spilsbury, whose expertise was called for to unravel the nature of death in corpses long dead and sometimes forgotten. One of the classic murder cases of that era which was revealed through exhumation was the poisoning of his wife by Major Herbert Rowse Armstrong. (See under ARSENIC for a full description.)

Murder is not the only suspected crime that may lead to disinterment — civil actions for damages, life insurance cases and instances of disputed death or identity may also constitute cause for exhumation. Suspected POISONING is probably one of the main reasons for seeking exhumation orders, and many murderers who thought they had committed the perfect crime have thereby been caught. With this in mind, Lord Russell of Liverpool remarked that 'it may seem strange that more poisoners have not arranged for their victims to be cremated'. That the exhumation procedure is necessary was borne out in a United States survey which revealed that forty-five exhumations out of a

Mrs Evans's exhumed coffin in the Christie case

hundred showed death to have been attributed to the wrong cause in the first instance.

In England a CORONER may grant an order for a body to be exhumed, or a licence may be obtained from the Home Office. In the United States authority is given by the coroner or medical examiner according to state legislation. It is customary for the exhumed coffin to be identified by the undertaker after the grave-digger has identified the grave itself. Where poisoning is suspected the pathologist takes samples of soil from immediately above and below the coffin for laboratory analysis. It may be necessary in court to prove that any poisonous substance found in the body did not originate from the soil surrounding the coffin.

The exhumation procedure is not particularly pleasant, especially when the body has only recently been buried. Sir Sydney Smith advocated speedy IDENTIFICATION of the corpse and then removing it to a table 'preferably in the open air'.

Certainly the pathologist who wrote, 'it is as well to take a dram, and also to stand on the windward side of the corpse' offered sound advice.

The coffin and its contents are usually taken to a properly equipped mortuary, although temporary post-mortem facilities may have to be used. The body is examined according to regular autopsy procedure, and an X-ray survey is often made as a matter of routine. Autopsies following exhumation are made because of doubt regarding the original findings of cause of death. This places a special onus on the pathologist to produce a report that cannot be undermined on grounds of inadequate procedure.

The conditions of burial and the cunning of a suspected murderer combined to defeat the experts in an unusual exhumation in 1934. Two years previously Mrs Edith Rosse had died at the house near Hyde Park in London which she shared with Maundy Gregory, the so-called 'Great Swindler' who offered titles for sale to would-be members of the nobility. Edith Rosse had twice been taken ill with violent vomiting and diarrhoea, and on the second occasion before she died she scribbled out a new will on the back of a restaurant menu-card leaving £18,000 to Gregory. Her DEATH CERTIFICATE gave kidney disease and brain haemorrhage as the causes of death.

Gregory took charge of the burial arrangements, and insisted that his late companion be buried in a riverside graveyard at Bisham in Buckinghamshire. He directed that the body be put in an unsealed shell placed in an ordinary wooden coffin and interred in a shallow grave, eighteen inches beneath the ground surface. The result was that when the graveyard flooded during the winter water entered the grave and the open coffin became a water-tank in which the body decomposed rapidly, with the products of putrefaction being continually washed away.

In the meantime Gregory had been reported to SCOTLAND YARD by a naval officer to whom he tried to sell a knighthood, and in February 1934 he was brought before the magistrates for this offence.

Edith Rosse's will

He pleaded guilty, and was fined £20 and sentenced to two months' imprisonment. On his release he was declared bankrupt, and he fled to France.

Suspicion aroused over Mrs Rosse's death led to the exhumation of her body. Spilsbury conducted the post-mortem, and could find no evidence to substantiate the causes of death given in the death certificate. Dr Gerald Roche Lynch, the Home Office Analyst, was called in to analyse the remains for possible traces of poison. As he watched the water pouring out of the disinterred coffin he is said to have remarked, 'Not a bloody chance!' He could find no traces of poison in the body, and the coroner, S. Ingleby Oddie, reported disappointingly that he had 'no option but to return an open verdict to the effect that cause of death was unascertainable'.

Maundy Gregory never returned to England, and died in 1941 in German-occupied France. He left behind the suspicion that he had murdered not only Edith Rosse but also Victor Grayson, the socialist politician. Grayson joined the ranks of MISSING PERSONS in 1920 after he had threatened to expose Gregory's swindling activities. He was never seen again, and it was widely believed that the 'Great Swindler' had arranged his elimination. *97, 159, 486, 520, 521.*

EXPLOSIVES

The bomb has long been the weapon of terrorism and ASSASSINATION. Several attempts were made to murder Tsar Alexander II before revolutionaries finally succeeded on 1 March 1881. A bomb was thrown under his carriage while he was driving in St Petersburg, and the vehicle was completely shattered. The Tsar stepped out unhurt, only to be the target of a second bomb which was thrown at his feet. It exploded in a sheet of flame, tearing off his legs and ripping open his abdomen. The mortally wounded Tsar was rushed back to his palace, but he was beyond medical help. He died from his massive injuries and great loss of blood.

The anarchists who terrorized European capitals for years at the end of the nineteenth century also favoured bomb-throwing. Several attempts were made on the lives of various crowned heads, and Paris became a centre for anarchist activities. Thefts of dynamite from French quarries fuelled a bombing campaign against public figures in the 1890s. A man known as Ravachol — whose real name was François Koenigstein — was associated with many of these incidents, which caused destruction of property and injury to life. Ravachol was to gain a place in criminal history less for being an anarchist than for vindicating Alphonse Bertillon's system of criminal IDENTIFICATION. Koenigstein had been arrested in 1889 for theft, when his anthropometric measurements were taken and routinely filed. Following an explosion at the house of the State Prosecutor in March 1892, a man believed to be an anarchist was located in a Paris restaurant. The place was ringed by police, and when Ravachol emerged he was overpowered and arrested. At the SÛRETÉ Bertillon soon established from his records that Ravachol and Koenigstein were one and the same person. Thus the bomb-thrower was caught, and also a man wanted for murder — he finished up on the GUILLOTINE.

Explosives are the stock-in-trade of terrorist groups around the world — the IRA, Red Brigade, Black September — and campaigns have been waged against both people and property in the furtherance of political aims. Government offices, public buildings and shops have been blown up and fire-bombed, aircraft hijacked and blown up, all with attendant deaths and injuries. London has been a focus for many of these campaigns of violence, which has had the effect of building up British experience in security matters, in bomb-disposal and in medical procedures to deal with the human aftermath.

Between 1968 and 1971 the Angry Brigade caused numerous bombings in London, and in 1972 eight of their members were charged with conspiracy to cause explosions. It was also alleged that they had an assassination list of a hundred and seventy names of public figures. Four of the accused were convicted and given prison sentences. During 1972–73 a letter-bomb campaign was directed against prominent Jewish figures living in London. These devices proved that with modern technology it was no longer necessary for the terrorist to stand and throw his bomb — he could discharge it with a variety of timers and detonators. The letter-bombs used two ounces of commercially available explosive detonated by a spring-loaded device when the letter was opened. Dr Ami Shachori, Cultural Attaché at the Israeli Embassy, was killed at his office desk in this manner.

Books with the centre hollowed out and filled with gelignite packed with nails have also been sent through the mail to public figures. Incendiary bombs made up in cigarette packets formed part of the campaign of public terror waged by the IRA in 1973. These and other bombs were left in a number of department stores in London's West End. Bombs were also concealed in innocent-looking shopping-bags and left in shops and public buildings. Their customary three pounds of explosive caused considerable damage.

In 1974 there were two major bomb explosions in Birmingham which resulted in extensive loss of life and the apprehension of the bombers. On 21 November a bomb exploded in a public house, killing ten and injuring thirty-six people. A second bomb exploded in another public house on the same night, killing eleven and injuring a hundred and twenty-six people. Six men who had met in Birmingham during the afternoon of that fateful day were arrested before they could make their escape by boat to Belfast. Two of the Birmingham Pub Bombers, as they became known, had traces of nitroglycerine on their hands when arrested. At their trial for murder the six were found guilty on all twenty-one charges of murder and were given life sentences.

The activities of terrorism have been equalled only by international co-operation to defeat politically motivated violence. This has been particularly evident in measures to thwart aircraft hijacking and the strengthening of airport security. Those who have to deal with the technical aspects of explosives have been aided by scientific and other measures. The 1970s and 80s have seen the use of sniffer dogs, bomb-handling robots, portable X-ray equipment and electronic stethoscopes. Much of the current knowledge about explosion injuries has come from wartime experience. Events in Northern Ireland have made possible advances in emergency surgery for survivors, but for the dead it is a matter of identification and picking up the pieces.

The majority of bombs fall into the four to ten pounds category, and while these cause mangling injuries, their fatal effects depend on proximity to the centre of the explosion. Anyone standing over such a bomb may be literally blown to pieces, but those not so close may suffer a variety of injuries caused by flash burns, air blast, flying fragments of glass, wood, metal and masonry, or crushing by heavy debris. In large detonations — which may involve hundreds of pounds of explosives — anyone near by may be subject to disintegrating forces which scatter body fragments over distances of 100 metres or more. Parts of the body are more or less recognizable, but the internal organs rarely survive. Identification of victims rests on the usual criteria.

The use of explosives for MOTIVES other than political ones is not common, but there have been a number of notable bomb murders, chiefly connected with air travel. One of the best known is that for which Albert Guay and his two accomplices were hanged in Canada in 1951. On 9 September 1949 a Quebec Airways DC-3 on a flight from Montreal to Seven Islands exploded in mid-air, killing all twenty-three passengers and crew. Among the victims was Rita Guay, whose husband had taken out not a return flight insurance on her life, but only a policy for a single journey. Investigators traced all but one consignee of freight on the fatal flight — the item unaccounted for was a 28 pound box allegedly containing a statuette but in reality holding dynamite. An airport freight-loader remembered being handed the box by a fat woman. She was eventually identified as Marguérite Pitre, Albert Guay's mistress. Guay was arrested along with Pitre and her brother, who had made the bomb's timing device. Guay made a full CONFESSION in which he implicated his accomplices in the plan to kill his wife and collect the insurance.

On 1 November 1955 a United Air Lines aircraft flying from Denver to Washington crashed in a field, killing all forty-four passengers on board. Two weeks later John Gilbert Graham confessed to the FBI that he had placed a bomb on the aircraft, which at the time it crashed was carrying his mother as a passenger. He had been with his mother when she checked in for the flight and in response to her request to take out modest flight insurance of 6,250 dollars he operated the machine incorrectly and took out a policy for 37,500.

Graham was an immature individual who liked to tell boastful stories about his achievements. He atttempted to commit suicide while awaiting trial, and later told psychiatrists about his love-hate relationship with his mother. His reason for planting the bomb was that his mother had refused all his pleas to remain with him during Thanksgiving. Insanity was not raised as an issue at his trial, and he was found guilty of murder. The plane bomber was executed in the GAS CHAMBER at the Colorado State Penitentiary in 1957.

An unusual case of parricide involving explosives occurred in 1942 at Rayleigh in Essex when teenage Eric Brown killed his father with an Army anti-tank mine. Mr Brown, a wheel-chair invalid, was blown to pieces as he was being taken for a regular outing by his nurse. His son, who had placed the mine under the seat of the wheel-chair, was tried for murder and found guilty but insane. The youth's motive appeared to be one of freeing his family from the bullying behaviour of his father.

New York's 'Mad Bomber', George Metesky, used explosives in his sixteen-year grudge campaign against his former employers. Between 1940 and 1956 he planted numerous devices, made in his home workshop, in theatres and other public places where their detonation caused many injuries but no deaths. With the help of James Brussel, a New York psychiatrist, the police drew up a remarkably accurate pen-picture of the 'Mad Bomber' which led to the identification of Metesky. He claimed he wanted justice for his compensation claim against the firm that dismissed him in 1931. Metesky was a paranoiac who acted as if he were God, punishing an unjust world that had caused him suffering.

100, 289, 355, 459, 525, 560, 628, 676.

EYES

When the body of a murdered policeman was found in an Essex lane on 27 September 1927 the discoverer recoiled in horror when he saw that both of the man's eyes had been shot out. PC George Gutteridge had the misfortune to question a motorist when the driver and his companion killed him with four revolver shots. The murderers were Frederick Guy Browne and William Kennedy, habitual criminals who were driving a stolen car. Their conviction for murder on the strength of FIREARMS evidence was a landmark for police science in Britain. Their callousness in shooting out the eyes of their victim was rooted in the superstition that the eyeballs of a dead man hold an image of the last things he sees. They therefore destroyed the impressions of their own faces which they believed were imprinted on his eyes at death.

This myth arose during the JACK THE RIPPER murders in London in 1888, when following the last killing in Millers Court a photographer was ordered to take pictures of the dead woman's eyes. This was probably a desperation measure by the police, but it brought them no closer to identifying the murderer. The idea had no basis in fact, anyway.

Eyes play an important part in scientific crime investigation in several ways. They are a major feature in facial IDENTIFICATION, as is demonstrated by the practice of blanking out the eyes in photographs of persons whose identity is not to be revealed. The eyes and eyebrows form a compelling focus when people meet face to face, and often lend significance to descriptions. Eye-colour is often noted, and intensely blue eyes have been associated with several murderers — James Hanratty, the A6 murderer, and Herbert Rowse Armstrong, the arsenic poisoner, both had noticeably blue eyes. Colour, together with other characteristics such as bulging, staring or close-set eyes, are included in the Identikit and Photofit identification systems. The importance of eyes in general descriptions was recognized by the French criminologist Alphonse Bertillon, who included their characteristics in the *portrait parlé* (speaking likeness), part of his criminal identification system in the 1870s.

The shape of the eye at death, particularly the pupil, is noted at POST-MORTEM, and may prove an indication of the cause of death. It is common procedure in the USA for pupil diameter to be recorded at autopsy. Widely dilated or pin-point pupils at death give cause for suspicion, and the possibility of drug use. Pin-pointing of the pupils is a feature of morphine poisoning, and was demonstrated during the sensational trial in New York of Dr Robert Buchanan in 1893 (see under MORPHINE for a full account). The opposite effect, dilation of the pupils, was a suspicious sign in the insulin murder committed by Kenneth Barlow (see under POST-MORTEM).

STRANGULATION is another mode of death which announces its presence in the eyes in the form of hundreds of tiny haemorrhages known as petechiae or Tardieu spots. These are caused by the rupture of small capillaries in the eye as a result of increased blood pressure, and are a classic

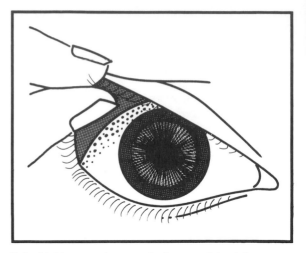

Petechial haemorrhages — indicators of death by asphyxia

feature of ASPHYXIA deaths such as HANGING, strangulation or SUFFOCATION. They also occur in large numbers in the scalp and face over the heart and lungs, where they were first described by the French surgeon who lent them his name — Ambroise Tardieu.

Discoloration of the eye after death as the result of drying of the cornea can be used as an indication of the time of death. If the eyelids remain open triangular patches of brownish colour — known as *tâches noirs* — form between the edges of the eyelids and the cornea. This condition, first described in 1833, denotes that at least three hours have elapsed since death, but applies only to *dry* eyes — it would not be seen, for instance, in a case of drowning. But in common with other indicators, such as LIVIDITY and RIGOR MORTIS it offers only an approximation of TIME OF DEATH.
1, **117**, *245*, *316*, *522*, **544**, **572**, *608*.

F

FEDERAL BUREAU OF INVESTIGATION (FBI)

The United States Congress established the Bureau of Investigation in 1908 to give the Department of Justice a permanent crime investigation agency. Its restricted powers hampered its early development, but the Bureau moved forward in

1924 when the Attorney General appointed J. Edgar Hoover to the position of Director. Hoover presided over the Bureau's affairs for forty-eight years, and turned it into a powerful and influential organization. He brought in a different type of recruit — men qualified as lawyers or accountants — who became the Bureau's agents, or G-men ('Government men').

Hoover set up an Identification Division with a

nucleus of 800,000 FINGERPRINTS which has grown into the world's greatest fingerprint collection of over 200 million records. Following the Lindbergh KIDNAPPING in 1932, the Bureau was given the responsibility for dealing with this type of crime — a task which it carried out with distinction. In 1935 the Bureau was given the name by which it is universally known today, the Federal Bureau of Investigation (FBI).

The FBI's powers grew and in 1939 the President entrusted it with responsibility for all security matters, including counter-espionage and anti-sabotage precautions. In the USA today police jurisdiction at a national level is carried out entirely by the FBI. It provides central services for all IDENTIFICATION, technical, forensic and statistical needs. The FBI's crime laboratory in Washington DC carries out forensic investigations for any state or local police force which requires assistance. In 1967, in order to speed up communications in the pursuit of crime, the Bureau set up its National Crime Information Center (NCIC) in the capital which for the first time linked together all law-enforcement agencies in the country. The NCIC computer can be directly reached from terminals situated in police departments in any state. Fingerprints and photographic identification of a crime suspect can thus be checked within minutes.

In recent years the FBI has been the subject of criticism over the question of political ASSASSINATION and the use of electronic surveillance. Increases in US crime figures, especially in narcotics offences and HOMICIDE, have heightened public concern. In the late seventies increases in the murder rate were as high as 70 and 80 per cent respectively in Miami and Washington DC. The attempted assassination of President Reagan, the stranger-to-stranger murders committed by the Son of Sam and the killing of pop musician John Lennon have renewed arguments about the right of Americans to bear firearms — a right insisted on by 50 million owners of handguns. *133, 141, 344, 390, 687, 720.*

FIBRES

When Leslie George Stone returned home from his posting in the armed forces in Hong Kong, he could not know that his demob. suit would incriminate him with murder. On 11 April 1937 he met his former girl friend, Ruby Annie Keen, in a public house at Leighton Buzzard. He had courted

this glamorous young woman six years previously, before the Army sent him abroad. They had corresponded for two years, and then their friendship petered out as Ruby, quite naturally, was courted by other men. By the time Stone returned Ruby was engaged to be married to a police officer. Nevertheless, she agreed to meet for old times' sake, and they were seen together in several public places, he dressed in his new grey worsted suit and she in a yellow dress with a black and white scarf around her neck.

The following morning Ruby's body was found in a coppice near her home. She had been raped, and strangled with her own scarf. There was evidence of a struggle; and footprints and knee impressions had been made in the soil around the body by the assailant. Stone was interviewed by the police when they learned that he had been seen in the company of the dead girl, and had been overheard pleading with her to forsake her fiancé and marry him instead. He admitted being with Ruby, but simply said that he had left her at 10.15 in the evening. He was asked to submit his shoes and suit for examination, and the findings of the forensic laboratory quickly focused on Stone as the chief suspect. His shoes matched the impressions left at the murder scene, and the weave of his suit was identical to the cloth pattern pressed into the knee-marks in the soil. Neither of these findings was conclusive, for both the shoes and the suit were of a popular ready-made type. But there were more detailed discoveries to come. Firstly the suit — which showed signs of having been thoroughly brushed — still had minute soil particles clinging to the weave, and analysis proved that these were identical to the clayey/sandy mixture at the murder scene. The clinching piece of evidence proved to be a tiny CONTACT TRACE — a thread of artificial silk found brushed into the cloth of the suit jacket. This matched the artificial silk of the slip worn by the dead girl, and the fragment even carried traces of the four dye colours used to print the floral design on the garment. This damning fibre clearly placed Stone at the crime scene, and he was eventually found guilty of murder and hanged.

Like HAIRS, fibres are commonly found as part of the transfer of materials which occurs when individuals brush against each other or make more violent contact. It is standard practice to examine carefully the clothing of a murder victim for fibres, hairs, dust and other debris to the extent of vacuuming out pockets and seams. The clothing of crime suspects is submitted to the same treatment in the search for contact traces. Methods of examining fibres are similar to those used for hair, with cross-sections and longitudinal views seen through a comparison microscope. Forensic laboratories keep reference sets of fibres for comparison so that quick identification can be made.

Natural fibres include wool, silk, mohair, cotton, hemp and lint; synthetics include nylon and a variety of man-made polymer fibres referred to by trade-names. The identification characteristics of these materials are similar to those of hair, and include size, shape, colour, firmness, coarseness and weave. Synthetic fibres can also be identified by their refractive index and by various staining tests. This is specialized work, particularly with the proliferation of man-made fibres used in modern clothing.

A case of murder in which the transfer of material went, not from victim to assailant as in the Stone case, but from murderer to victim, was that involving nineteen-year-old sensation-seeker Herbert Leonard Mills. He befriended middle-aged Mabel Tattershaw in August 1951 and took her to Sherwood Vale, near Nottingham, where he killed her by STRANGULATION. He then telephoned the London office of the *News of the World*, claiming to have discovered a murder and wishing to share the newspaper's glory in reporting it. Mills's call was reported to the police, who quickly traced him to a public telephone in Nottingham. He maintained the pretence of having stumbled across the body and hoping to make some money out of the newspaper for reporting a scoop, until evidence of contact began to emerge. Not only were some head-hairs identical with his own found on the victim, but under one of her fingernails was a small blue thread torn from Mills's suit during the violence of his assault.

Mills made a CONFESSION which he later withdrew. While his antics with the Press won him little sympathy with the jury, it was the damning forensic evidence which sealed his guilt. He was found guilty of murder, and was executed.

The records of routine forensic investigations are full of cases in which a murderer has been convicted by little more than a hair or a thread. A remarkably dogged investigation was that conducted by Dr J. B. Firth, Director of the North Western Forensic Science Laboratory of the Home

Cross-section of acetate rayon fibres

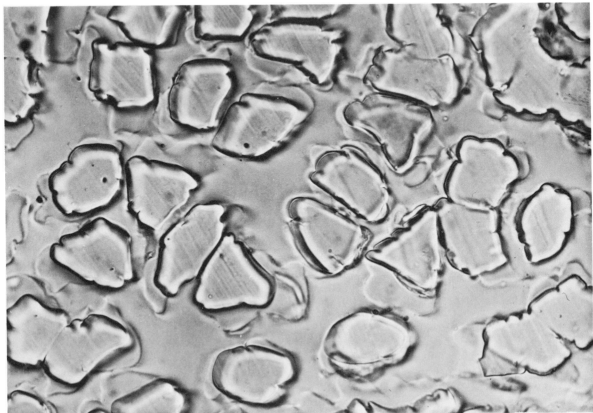

Torn piece of cloth matched to suspect's clothing

Office in 1940. The body of a fifteen-year-old girl, sexually assaulted and strangled, was found in a concrete blockhouse not far from her Liverpool home. Among the litter on the floor of the blockhouse was a small piece of fabric of the type used in bandages.

Within a few days, following intensive local inquiries, the police came up with a suspect. He was Samuel Morgan, a soldier in his late twenties, stationed at Seaforth Barracks. He had a cut on his thumb which his sister bandaged with his own Army field dressing. He told her that he had sustained the cut on some barbed wire, and when examined by a police surgeon was found to have a small healing wound on the right thumb. Dr Firth's examination of the piece of fabric found at the murder scene confirmed it to be part of a military field dressing treated with acriflavine. When Morgan's sister produced a discarded portion of the dressing with which she had bandaged her brother's thumb Dr Firth was able to make a detailed comparison. He found that the two pieces matched, even down to a corresponding double row of stitch holes. He also looked at samples of bandages issued to troops at Seaforth Barracks, and went to the factory at Preston where they were made. There he saw for himself that part of the manufacture involved a double row of stitches on the selvedge.

It was clear that the piece of bandage found in the blockhouse near the murdered girl's body had been wrenched from Samuel Morgan's thumb during the struggle. His presence at the scene was corroborated by contact traces of soil on his clothing, and he was found guilty of murder, a crime for which he was hanged.

220, 255, 282, 314, 449, 586, 667, **703**.

FINGERPRINTS

The unique character of an individual's fingerprints was touched on several times before their full significance was realized in 1880. For centuries the Chinese used thumb impressions to seal documents, and early scientists hinted at greater knowledge to come. The seventeenth-century anatomist Marcello Malpighi described the ridges of the fingertips. In the next century Thomas Bewick, the English naturalist, signed his books with 'his mark', and Johann Evangelist Purkinje, the Czech physiologist, published a description of fingerprints and their types. Then in 1880 Dr Henry Faulds, a Scottish physician working in Japan, suggested that fingerprints might offer a possible method of personal IDENTIFICATION.

Faulds's views published in *Nature*, the scientific journal, came to the notice of Sir William Herschel, who for several years as an administrator in India had used thumb impressions to identify illiterate prisoners. It fell to Sir Francis Galton, an influential English scientist, to verify the individuality and permanence of fingerprints. He laid the basis for a classification system which sorted the most commonly observed features of fingerprint impressions into three groups: arches, loops and whorls. He also established that identical fingerprints were not inherited, and that even identical twins had different ridge patterns. Galton's work was published in a book called simply *Fingerprints*, in 1892.

Another Englishman, Sir Edward Henry, who later became head of the CID at SCOTLAND YARD, completed the task of fingerprint classification. He established five groups of characteristics, adding tented arches to Galton's three groups and dividing loops into two types. Henry put fingerprinting to use in India in 1896, where he was serving as Inspector-General of Police in Bengal, but it was towards another continent that attention was directed for the first murderer to be convicted with the aid of fingerprint evidence. Juan Vucetich, an Argentine police officer, had adopted finger-printing in place of Bertillon's methods of identifi-cation. In 1892 a mother was found guilty of murdering her two young children on the strength of some bloody fingerprints found on a door-frame. The woman claimed a neighbour had attacked her and killed the children, but the fingerprints matched her own impressions, and in the face of such damning evidence she confessed to the crime.

In 1900 Sir Edward Henry published his account of fingerprint classification, and the following year he was appointed Acting Police Commissioner for the Metropolis of London. The Henry system was widely adopted by police forces around the world, and, excepting South America, remains the most commonly used system. In 1905 the use of fingerprints was demonstrated in Britain when Alfred and Albert Stratton were convicted of robbery and MURDER. An elderly man and his wife were beaten and robbed in their shop. The man died immediately, and his wife a few days later. One of the assailants left a clear thumbprint on a metal cash-box. This proved sufficient to convict the Stratton brothers, and convinced any lingering doubters as to the value of Henry's system.

Fingerprint classification is based on four groups of ridge patterns: arches, loops, whorls and composites. Arches are divided into two cate-gories, plain and tented, according to their shape, and whorls and composites are classed together. Loops are called ulnar when they slope towards the little finger and radial when they slope towards the thumb. Sixty-five per cent of all fingerprint patterns consist of loops; whorls make up about 30 per cent; and arches the remaining 5 per cent. As the proportion of loops far exceeds the others, they are further classified according to fixed character-istics called the core and delta. The core is approxi-mately the centre of the pattern, and a delta is formed by the division of a ridge. The number of ridges which lie between the core and delta of a loop represents an important classification feature.

Fingerprints are classified by the shape of their patterns, by the finger positions of the pattern types and by the detailed characteristics of the ridges. Henry's system of primary classification assigns a numerical value to each digit, starting with the right thumb (designated 1) through to the left little finger (designated 10). This standard notation is printed on all fingerprint record cards in those countries which use the system. The numbered digits are then considered in pairs, written in the form of a fraction, which is given an

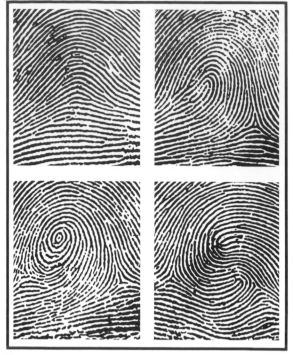

Four main fingerprint patterns

arbitrary numerical value. Wherever a whorl pattern appears in a set of fingerprints it assumes the value of the pair in which it is found.

Henry's primary classification system made possible 1,024 combinations of whorls, and the extension of the system to include other character-istics permits over a million groupings. A simple numerical formula is thus derived for every com-bination of fingerprint patterns, but while this ten-finger classification proved ideal for searching formal records, it is the single fingerprint which is most commonly found in crime. This was recog-nized at an early stage, and in 1930 a single-fingerprint system was devised by Chief Inspector Harry Battley of Scotland Yard. The single-fingerprint collection consists of ten numbered files each referring to individual digits as they appear on the ten-finger record card. Henry's classifi-cation is used, but greater attention is paid to the fine details of ridges, cores and deltas in the pattern.

While the formal fingerprint record contains carefully inked impressions set out in numbered boxes, fingerprints left at a scene of crime may be fragmentary and blurred. A refinement to identifi-cation in such instances is poroscopy, a method of examining sweat pores in the skin, developed by the French scientist Edmond Locard. He dis-

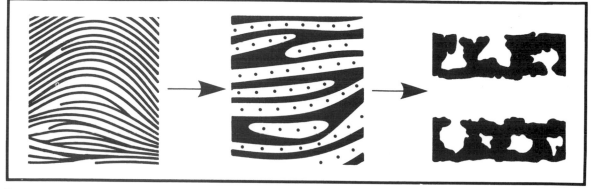

Poroscopy: progressive magnification of the sweat-pore openings

covered that the size, shape and position of the pore openings differ in each individual, and that in common with all fingerprint characteristics they are permanent and unaltered by age. Comparison of a crime fingerprint with impressions taken from a suspect is a highly skilled job, and the police forces in most countries use specially trained officers for the purpose. Identification depends on showing a minimum of sixteen matching characteristics in the ridge patterns (twelve in the USA). Where these points of comparison are shown, proof of identity is considered to have been established.

Crime-scene fingerprints fall into three types: visible impression left by a dirty or bloody hand; impressions made in soft materials such as putty, tar, soap or chocolate; and latent or hidden finger-prints. It is the latter which seize the imagination in detective fiction by requiring to be dusted. Latent fingerprints are impressions left on polished surfaces such as wood, metal or glass by the sweat-moistened ridges of the fingertips. Once such prints are located they are dusted with fine aluminium powder to make them visible. They can then be photographed or lifted off by means of transparent adhesive tape, and fixed on to a card for record purposes. Latent prints on porous surfaces such as paper, cloth and wood may be developed using iodine fumes or ninhydrin spray. Impressions on skin may also be 'visualized' using special X-ray techniques.

In theory, any ridged area of the hand or foot may be used as a means of identification, although systematic files are not kept. Palm-prints and foot-prints left at the crime scene have provided investigators with valuable evidence, as have toeprints and, moving to another area of the body, lip-prints. The lips have a distinctive pattern of lines

and grooves on them, and the value of these characteristics is to supplement other identification evidence. In a HIT-AND-RUN case reported in the USA lip-prints found on the front fender of a suspect vehicle were matched to the victim's.

Many improvements and refinements in the use of fingerprints have originated in the United States, which adopted systematic fingerprinting in the early 1900s. The basic Henry system was used by the FEDERAL BUREAU OF INVESTIGATION to build up its collection of 200 million records, and the system has been extended to include further classification features deriving from the ridge patterns. The FBI's Identification Bureau deals with over 30,000 fingerprints daily, using computerized procedures and machine searching. Laser equipment is in use which scans eighty fingerprints per second on microfilm and processes the data electronically. Advanced techniques are also being applied to the location of latent finger-prints at the crime scene, such as fluorescence under laser illumination. The Police National Computer installed at Hendon in 1976 has an index of two and a half million fingerprints, whose images are available on a storage and retrieval system, known as Videofile, which permits any set of prints to be displayed for comparison on a VDU. This greatly speeds up identification.

A preoccupation among criminals in the past has been to eradicate their own fingerprint impressions. The use of gloves and wiping objects they had touched at the crime scene were obvious precautions, but in two famous cases more drastic measures were taken. The American gangster John Dillinger had his fingertips treated with acid in the 1930s to remove the ridge patterns, and Robert Phillips, another American criminal, had the skin on the fingertips removed by plastic surgery and replaced with skin grafts taken from his chest. Both attempts failed miserably.

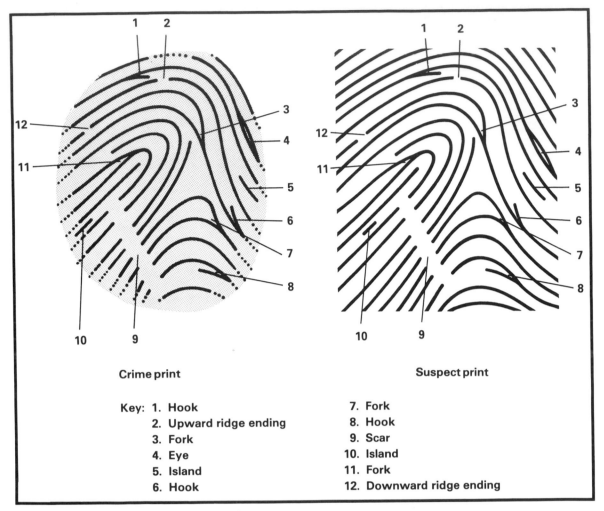

Crime print

Suspect print

Key: 1. Hook
2. Upward ridge ending
3. Fork
4. Eye
5. Island
6. Hook

7. Fork
8. Hook
9. Scar
10. Island
11. Fork
12. Downward ridge ending

Comparison of fingerprint impressions showing matching characteristics

Dillinger's ridge patterns reappeared, and Phillips was identified by impressions taken from the un-doctored second phalanges of his fingers. Such painful methods of eliminating fingerprints quickly went out of fashion, and criminals resorted to the use of gloves, although glove-prints, especially of leather or woven gloves, opened up new vistas for the detective. As Pudd'nhead Wilson remarked of his criminal adversary in Mark Twain's 1894 detective story, he could 'unerringly identify him by his hands'!

The record books of successful identification of murderers are full of outstanding cases. One which stands out as an example of police determination and public reassurance was that of Peter Griffiths in 1948. Officers investigating the brutal murder of four-year-old Anne Devaney discovered the likely murderer's fingerprints at the crime scene, but their problem was to identify their owner. The child's cot in the Children's Ward of the Queen's Park Hospital in Blackburn was found empty by the duty nurse when she did her morning rounds on 14 May. A search of the hospital grounds located the missing girl some three hundred yards from the ward. She had been sexually assaulted, and was dead from a brutal battering.

Detectives found that the murderer had moved a bottle when he approached the child's bed, and in so doing had left clear finger impressions on it. These prints were quickly isolated from those of the nursing staff, and the police decided to finger-print the entire male population of Blackburn in an attempt to find a matching set. This was a tre-mendous task, but on 12 August an officer examin-ing set number 46,253 found they matched the impressions on the bottle. Their owner, Peter

Griffiths, an ex-Serviceman working at a local flour-mill, was easily arrested. He told the arresting officers, 'I hope I get what I deserve.' He was tried for murder and found guilty, subsequently being hanged.

This historic murder inquiry established the credibility of fingerprinting in the eyes of the public, and was important because it showed that the ordinary, law-abiding person had nothing to fear from the procedure. In a dramatic sequel to this celebrated case, and to quell any anxieties over infringement of civil liberties, the entire fingerprint records so painstakingly gathered were publicly destroyed.

1, **41**, **68**, **96**, *130*, *131*, **160**, *313*, *320*, **326**, *490*, *495*, **674**, **727**.

FIREARMS

Several perceptive men of the nineteenth-century detective breed had looked at bullets recovered from victims' bodies and wondered about the individuality of the marks on them. In 1889 Professor Alexandre Lacassagne noticed grooves on a bullet extracted from a corpse, and thought the marks might be related to the gun which fired the projectile. There were seven grooves on the bullet, and a revolver recovered from the subject's apartment had seven grooves in the rifling of its barrel. The man who owned the revolver was convicted of murder.

This rather crude comparison helped to concentrate the minds of crime investigators on the relationship between guns and the bullets they fire. Thus began a period of development and innovation which led to the emergence of forensic ballistics — a scientific method for examining firearms evidence.

The significant achievements in this new field were made — appropriately, perhaps — in America, the home of modern firearms. Charles Waite laid the foundations of methods which were to be universally adopted. He established a reference collection of firearm specifications, and acquired the expertise whereby he could tell by looking at a bullet the make, model and calibre of the gun which fired it. With Philip Gravelle, he established the Bureau of Forensic Ballistics in New York in 1923. This was the first institute of its kind in the world, and in 1925 a third member joined the team. He was Calvin Goddard, an army doctor with an interest in firearms, and destined to become one of the foremost ballistics experts.

A major breakthrough in firearms examination came with the comparison microscope, invented by Philip Gravelle and developed by Goddard. This instrument enabled the marks on a crime bullet and a test bullet to be matched microscopically in a single image. This invention, coupled with microphotography, made forensic ballistics a powerful science, the merits of which were soon tested in a sensational murder case.

On 15 April 1920 a payroll robbery in Braintree, Massachusetts, ended in double murder. On 5 May two Italians, Nicola Sacco and Bartolomeo Vanzetti, were arrested and charged with carrying firearms without permission. They were questioned about various robberies, finally being charged with the Braintree murders. Sacco and Vanzetti, names that were to ring round the world, were tried in May 1921. Both men had radical leanings, and this, together with their immigrant status, earned them a great deal of public prejudice. Using dubious methods, the prosecution sought to prove that Sacco's .32 Colt pistol was the murder weapon. The experts were really amateurs, but the prosecution won the argument, with the two accused being found guilty of first-degree murder and sentenced to death.

The next six years were taken up with various legal appeals and stays of EXECUTION. Appeals and protests flooded in from all parts of the world, and in July 1927 a committee of three was appointed to re-examine the evidence. Among the new testimony heard was that given by Calvin Goddard, who demonstrated with the aid of the comparison microscope that the fatal bullets had unquestionably been fired by Sacco's pistol and by no other firearm. The hesitation over carrying out the sentence of death on Sacco and Vanzetti ceased, and the two men died in the ELECTRIC CHAIR on 23 August 1927.

Another champion of the comparison microscope was Sir Sydney Smith, whose ballistic evidence trapped the murderers of Sir Lee Stack, the British Sirdar who was shot in Cairo in 1924. Smith's work was instrumental in introducing the comparison microscope to Britain, where it was taken up by Robert Churchill, the firearms expert. Thus by 1930 forensic ballistics was an established and respected science. Crime investigators travelled to America to learn from Goddard, and in 1934 J. Edgar Hoover put the seal on the developers' work by setting up a department of forensic ballistics in the FEDERAL BUREAU OF INVESTIGATION.

The term 'forensic ballistics', strictly speaking,

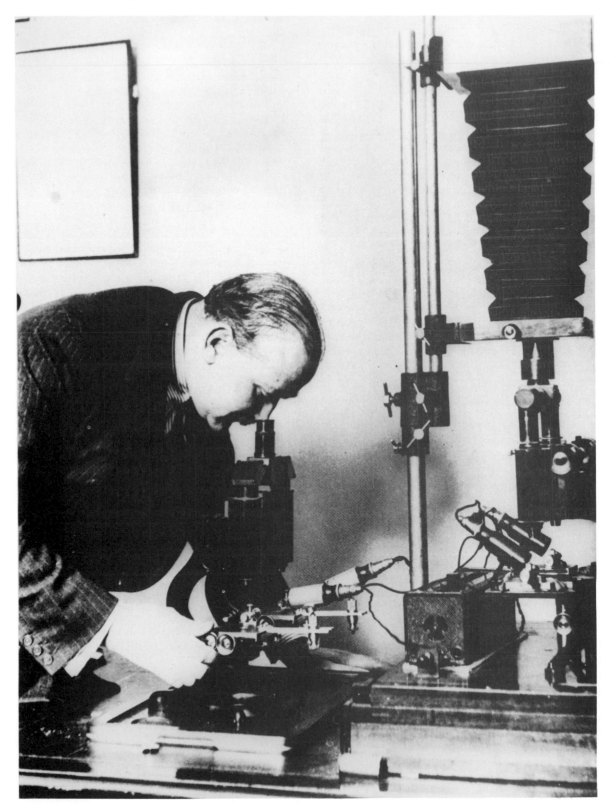

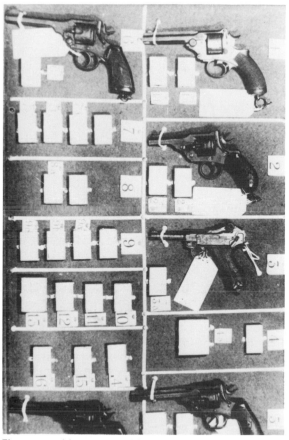

Firearms evidence assembled as murder-trial exhibits

refers to the study of projectiles related to legal questions. This concept has been broadened to take account of many related aspects of murder with guns, and 'firearms evidence' is today considered more appropriate. Except for the expert working in this specialized field, 'ballistics' remains the popularly used term. The concept is much as it was stated by Calvin Goddard in 1926 when he wrote about the irregularities of gun-barrels which leave their mark on every bullet fired — the 'fingerprint of that particular barrel' was how he put it.

In practice, the investigation of murder with firearms comes down to identifying the lethal weapon and tracing its user. A knowledge of firearms and how they work is essential to the crime investigator, although collecting and examining firearms evidence has become a task requiring special technical knowledge. In the USA, where gun-ownership runs to 55 million handguns

Robert Churchill at work with his comparison microscope

and 100 million shotguns and rifles, the task of record-keeping alone is monumental. But it is the detailed investigation of the 16,000 annual gun murders which is prodigious. Each incident represents a unique permutation of five essential elements: weapon, bullet, cartridge-case, bullet trajectory and wound.

Gunsmiths had known since the sixteenth century that the range and accuracy of firearms could be improved by cutting spiral grooves inside the barrel. These caused the bullet to spin when discharged from the barrel, but forcing bullets into muzzle-loaders proved too difficult. The development of breech-loading cartridges during the nineteenth century made rifled weapons viable. The explosive force of the cartridge's powder charge easily propelled the bullet down the rifled barrel, so that it emerged spinning on its axis and was driven to its target with greater accuracy and force.

In addition to improving performance, rifling became important in firearm evidence as gun-manufacturers cut the spiral grooves to different specifications. The raised parts of the rifling are called lands, and the lower parts grooves. The grooves may be machined to different depths and directions, rifling either to left or right, and the pitch may vary from one turn in eight inches to one in thirty-two.

Rifled weapons also vary in their bore, or calibre — that is, the internal diameter of the barrel measured between lands. Bullets are made slightly oversize for any particular weapon, although their normal calibre is matched to that of the gun. This

A rifled barrel

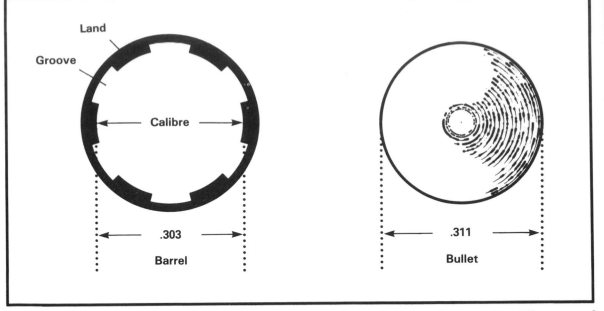

Calibre of gun-barrel and bullet

is to ensure a tight fit in the barrel, and to make full use of the power of the propellant in discharging the projectile. The rifling of the barrel grips the bullet and causes it to rotate. As it rotates the bullet expands into the grooves of the rifling, thus sealing the barrel and preventing leakage of propellant gas.

Thus a knowledge of firearm manufacturers' specifications enables an examiner to say from which type of gun a particular bullet was fired.

Calibre (mm)	Number of lands	Direction of grooves	Type	Maker
.38	5	right	revolver	Smith & Wesson
.32	6	right	automatic	Browning
.38	6	left	revolver	Colt
.45	6	left	automatic	Colt
.38	7	right	revolver	Webley & Scott

Rifled weapons may be long-barrelled rifles (2 to 3 ft), or short-barrelled pistols (1 to 12 inches). The long barrel of the rifle makes it accurate for ranges up to 3,000 yards, and the weapon has a muzzle velocity of 1,000 to 4,000 ft per second. Pistols, with their short barrels and low muzzle velocity (600 to 1,000 ft per second), are intended for use at close ranges (400 to 600 yards). Short-barrel rifled weapons form two classes — revolvers and pistols. These weapons are commonly regarded as the same, but there are fundamental differences, of importance to forensic investigations.

Revolvers are handguns in which the cartridges are placed in a five or six chambered cylinder. The cylinder revolves when the hammer is cocked, bringing each chamber successively in alignment with the barrel, and hence into firing position. Cartridges are hand-loaded, and the cylinder usually swings out from the frame of the gun for this purpose. This results in some loss of propellant gas between cylinder and barrel, and unlike the automatic pistol, there is no automatic ejection of cartridges. Extracting and reloading are hand operations, and unless the firer has been forced to reload, he leaves no spent cartridge cases at the crime scene. Revolver cartridges differ from those used in pistols by having a rimmed base and no ejector groove.

Pistols, like revolvers, are short-range handguns. The difference is that they have a sealed-in chamber which is an integral part of the barrel. There are one-shot pistols, but most are multiple-shot guns using automatic, magazine-fed cartridges. The spent case of a fired bullet is automatically ejected, a fresh round pushed into the breech from the magazine, and the firing mechanism recocked by the action of firing itself. The energy of the exploding gases which expel the bullet from the pistol can thus be harnessed to reload the weapon, and shots are fired in succession as long as the trigger is pressed, and until the magazine is exhausted.

Most automatics are designed for centre-fire ammunition, and the magazine containing seven or more rounds is housed in the butt. Jacketed bullets are normally used, as lead bullets may be damaged during automatic loading. The automatic pistol is one of the weapons most frequently encountered in crime cases on account of its ease of concealment and reloading.

Automatics are classified according to calibre and make. Many of the famous names in the manufacture of automatic pistols are European; Mauser, Walther, Beretta, for example. Calibre is designated in metric units in continental Europe, while the USA and Britain use inches.

Smooth-bore guns are characterized by the shotgun, and have barrels with smooth inside surfaces. Guns of this type are designed for sporting purposes, and fire a mass of small lead pellets or shot at a range of about fifty yards. Shotguns may have one or two long barrels which take hand-loaded cartridges. The empty cases are retained in the gun after the shot has been fired, and are removed by hand. In double-barrelled guns one barrel is usually 'choked' while the other is a cylinder barrel. 'Choking' holds the shot together over longer distances, unlike the sawn-off shotgun (much favoured in armed robberies) which allows the shot to spread too quickly for penetration at distance.

The calibre of shotguns is expressed as 'bore' — the term 'twelve-bore' being well known. The method of sizing the bore is ancient, and depends on the number of spherical balls of lead, each exactly fitting the inside of the bore, which make up a pound. It is common nowadays to give the calibre of all types of guns as the diameter of the barrel, expressed in inch or metric units. Hence the twelve-bore shotgun has a calibre of 0·729 inches.

It has been said that the bullet is really the weapon, and that cartridges and guns are simply means of getting it to the target. Ammunition has been subject to its own development process, from the days of muzzle-loaded shot to modern micro-calibre bullets. The aim has been to improve what is politely called 'stopping power'. Dum-dum bullets, first used in India around 1897, had a devastating effect. By cutting across the top of the lead bullet the moment of impact caused the bullet to 'mushroom', resulting in massive damage. Dum-dum bullets were outlawed by the Hague Convention in 1899, and since then all military bullets have been of the fully jacketed type which does not break up on impact. The Armalite rifle, developed in the USA in the 1950s, employed a different concept. The high muzzle-velocity (3,250 ft per second) discharges a small-calibre bullet which instead of piercing its target tumbles when it hits, and causes excessive tissue damage.

The first self-contained cartridge was produced in France in 1835, followed by the first metal-enclosed cartridge developed by Smith and Wesson in the USA in 1857. The modern cartridge is a complete round of ammunition consisting of a case, primer cap, propellant charge and bullet or projectile. The case is a metal cylinder designed to fit a particular gun chamber and method of extraction — i.e., rimmed (revolver) or rimless (automatic). In the centre of the base is a soft metal cap containing a primer charge. When this is crushed by the impact of the gun's firing-pin the percussion charge produces a rapid chemical reaction which sets off the main propellant charge.

The propellant charge or powder is a chemical mixture which generates gases by rapid combustion and expels the bullet from the gun, leaving the empty cartridge-case behind. Black powder, the traditional gunpowder mixture, is rarely found today except in old ammunition. Modern propellants are of the smokeless type based on nitro-cellulose and nitroglycerine. Both primer and main propellant are complex mixtures which leave detectable chemical traces on close-range targets, and may soil the hand of the firer.

Bullets are designed in a variety of shapes, weights and materials according to the ballistics performance required — i.e., military, target shooting, hunting or civilian. Lead was the traditional bullet fitted to the black powder cartridge and widely used in small arms and rifle ammunition up to the early 1900s. The introduction of smokeless powder with its greater propellant velocity meant that lead bullets were too soft to be gripped properly in gun-barrels. Consequently, the jacketed bullet was introduced, in which a lead core was strengthened by an outer jacket of cupronickel or other hard material. By completely enclosing the bullet it was protected from damage during loading, and did not strip as it travelled down the barrel. Moreover, the bullet usually hit its target cleanly, avoiding fragmentation or deformation on impact. Lead bullets toughened by the addition of tin are still used in revolver ammunition.

Bullets are either cemented into the top of the cartridge-case or crimped and held by means of a cannelure or circumferential groove. Additional cannelures in the bullet or cartridge-case are often used to carry small amounts of lubricant. Pistol

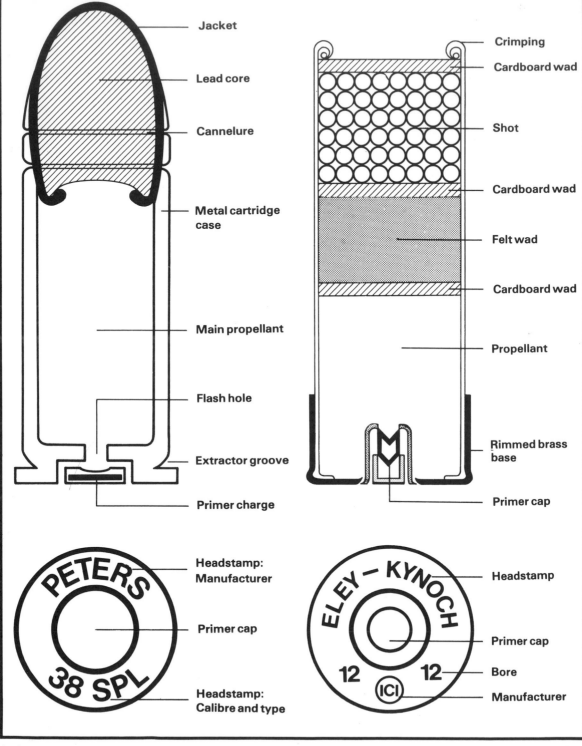

Jacketed automatic centre-fire ammunition

12-bore shotgun cartridge

and revolver bullets are intended to strike at short range, and for that reason are round-nosed and large in diameter to provide stopping power. Rifle bullets, by contrast, have pointed tips and longer bodies to obtain streamlined flight and long range. Manufacturers identify their ammunition by markings or 'headstamps' on the base of each cartridge. This usually includes the name of the maker, bore and chamber size.

Shotgun cartridges consist of a cardboard or plastic cylinder about 2½ inches long loaded with lead pellets or shot. The base of the cartridge is of rimmed brass, with a priming or detonating charge in its centre. The top of the cartridge is closed by crimping, and the shot is held above the propellant charge by cardboard, felt or plastic discs called wads.

The firing principle is the same as for other types of cartridge. The gun's firing pin activates the primer, which in turn ignites the main charge, and the shot is driven out of the cartridge and down the gun's barrel by the wads. The shot leaves the weapon as a solid mass at a velocity of up to 1,000 feet per second. Up to a range of three feet the effect is of a single shot, but beyond that the pellets spread and the effect is of multiple shots. The wads leave the gun with the shot and are projected several feet before falling to the ground. At close ranges wads are often driven into the target.

Shotgun pellets are made to specific sizes and weights according to the type of cartridge and its bore. Twelve-bore cartridges are most commonly used, and the shot they contain is 0·05 inches in diameter, with about 2,385 pellets making an ounce in weight.

The doctor called to the scene of a homicidal shooting examines the body and formally pronounces life extinct. He makes a note of the body's position and of its external wounds, but care is taken not to disturb the surroundings. The scene is photographed and the body removed to the mortuary, its position having been marked with the familiar chalk outline. Specialist crime-scene investigators then set to work. The essence of their craft is care — avoiding damage to vital evidence, being sure to record the position of every item and to mark it for future identification, and being meticulous about handling collected evidence. A discarded firearm may be evident at the scene, with empty cartridge-cases lying near by, and there may be bullets lodged in furniture or fittings, with bullet-holes in windows and fabrics. The relative position of each is measured and recorded.

This will provide information about bullet trajectories and help to reconstruct the crime.

The fictional portrayal of the detective carefully retrieving a firearm by lifting it with a pencil inserted in the barrel could not be further from reality. Such handling could destroy vital evidence — in a proper investigation, weapons are collected in gloved hands to avoid smudging FINGERPRINTS or other trace evidence and carefully placed in cotton-wool-lined boxes. The same applies to the idea that a penknife may be used to remove bullets lodged in walls or woodwork. All that would result is destruction of evidence. The collection of firearms, bullets and spent cartridge-cases is very much a 'kid glove' affair.

Once the victim's body reaches the mortuary for POST-MORTEM examination, the same careful attention is exercised to preserve vital evidence. The clothing is examined for bullet-holes and signs of scorching or powder traces caused by short-range or contact shooting. After the clothing is removed GUNSHOT-WOUNDS are examined, and their points of exit and entry determined. A wet 'blot' pattern is commonly taken in order to ascertain the powder pattern in close-discharge wounds. Probes may be passed to demonstrate bullet-tracks, and to provide information about the direction of the fatal shots.

The extraction of any bullets lodged in the body is a matter for skilful probing to avoid damaging the bullet. This procedure may be assisted by X-raying the body. Entry wounds — especially on normally exposed parts of the body, such as the head and face — are examined closely for signs of scorching or powder residues. Swabs may be taken for chemical testing, and the dermal nitrate test may be applied to the hands. This may be significant in the event that the victim struggled with his assailant and grabbed at the gun.

At the conclusion of these procedures the forensic laboratory will have a collection of crime-scene articles to work on. The firearm expert's report, coupled with that of the pathologist, will represent a reconstruction of the shooting and establish the cardinal features of the crime investigation. If a firearm is found at the scene, or has been discarded near by, it is relatively straightforward to establish whether it is the lethal weapon. This is done by comparing a bullet fired at the scene — as might be recovered from the victim's body — with a test bullet fired from the suspect gun. Crime bullet and test bullet are examined together under the comparison microscope. The working principle is that every gun

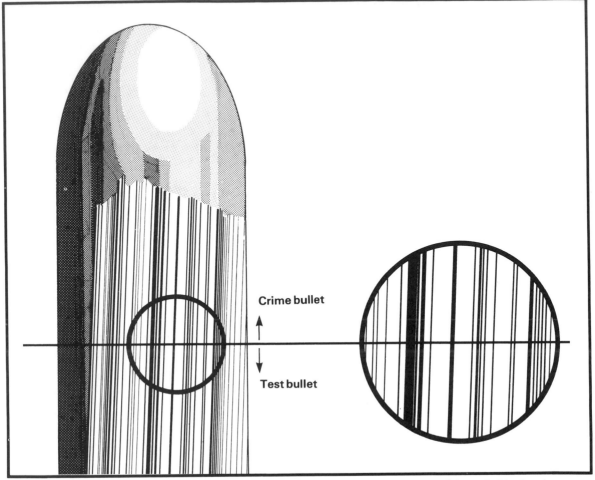

Striation marks on bullets matched under a comparison microscope

barrel leaves unique marks on each bullet fired from it. Therefore, if crime and test bullets match in terms of these markings, it is indisputable that they were fired from the same gun. Cartridge-cases also are indelibly stamped with a gun's individual pin and breech-face characteristics.

The number of grooves, their pitch and direction, are obvious points of correspondence, but there are additional features which help to confirm comparison. The cutting edges of the machinery used to make the rifling in gun-barrels is sharpened regularly, and the effect of this is to create microscopic imperfections which transfer their unique markings to the inside of the barrel. Consequently, each bullet which passes down the barrel will in turn receive an impression of these marks which are known as striations.

Other machined parts of the gun such as the firing-pin, extractor and breech blocks also carry individual characteristics which are transferred to the cartridge-case. Again, striations and machining marks are examined under the comparison microscope. Correspondence between such marks on crime and test bullets or cartridge-cases confirms a gun as a crime weapon.

Guns used for murder are not usually left at the crime scene, but they are often disposed of or hidden. They frequently come to light by accident or as the result of police searches when, provided they are not in too corroded a condition, test-firing a round of ammunition and comparison with crime-scene evidence will establish their standing as suspect weapons. As part of a murder inquiry, police may round up a number of guns of the suspected type and calibre and test fire them. As in all thoroughly proved crime-investigation procedures, a negative result will protect the innocent gun-holder and save the police a great deal of time by narrowing their list of suspects.

Suspect weapons are examined in the laboratory for any defects or mechanical peculiarities which would affect performance. The rifling characteristics are measured with instruments before test bullets are fired. At one time test bullets were fired into water or oiled sawdust, but the present-day method, which avoids the possibility of distortion, is to fire test bullets into a box filled with cotton wool.

Measuring trigger-pull is also standard investigation procedure in deaths involving firearms. This is especially important where murder is suspected, as defences are often based on arguments alleging accidental discharge of the weapon due to its having a hair-trigger. Trigger pull is measured by means of a calibrated spring gauge. All weapons maintained in good order have an average pull, and, allowing for some variation, pulls below this are considered potentially dangerous, and may be described as 'hair trigger'.

Average trigger-pulls for properly maintained weapons

.22 rifle	3–4 lb
Shotgun	4–5 lb
Revolver	4–5 lb
Automatic pistol	4–8 lb

A famous murder trial in which the question of trigger-pull played an important part was that of

Characteristic markings made on a spent cartridge case

Firing-pin depression

Breech-block markings

Elvira Barney in 1932. She was charged with murdering her lover with a .32 pistol. Firearms expert Robert Churchill contended that this pistol had a 14 lb trigger pull, and could only be fired deliberately. Sir Patrick Hastings, the defending counsel, maintained that the gun went off accidentally during a struggle. He illustrated his point by holding up the gun in court, and repeatedly pulled the trigger to show how easy it was. It was a brilliant piece of advocacy which won Mrs Barney an acquittal, although Sir Patrick admitted afterwards that the effort made his finger sore!

Forensic ballistics, or firearms evidence, is a complex field of study with many technical facets that can only be briefly touched on in a short article. It is the province of the expert whose skill and knowledge at every stage is of great importance. A successful prosecution in a murder case may depend on the thoroughness with which firearms evidence is prepared. This is illustrated by an early murder investigation which helped to establish the firearm specialist's professional standing in Britain.

On 27 September 1927 the body of a police constable was found in an Essex country lane. PC George Gutteridge had been shot four times, and his eyes had been shot out (see under EYES). It was assumed he had been gunned down while questioning a motorist, and a car belonging to a local doctor had been reported stolen. This was later found abandoned in London, and on its floor lay an empty cartridge-case.

The cartridge-case bore the headstamp R.L.IV, which identified it as Mark IV ammunition manufactured at the Royal Laboratory, Woolwich. It was special flat-nosed ammunition issued to British troops in 1914. Although badly misshapen, one of the bullets extracted from the dead policeman was shown to be a Mark IV, and rifling marks on it suggested the murder weapon was a Webley revolver. Most significantly, the cartridge-case showed a clear mark on its base imprinted by the breech of the gun that fired it. It was thought that the gun had been roughly cleaned at some stage with a metal rod which marked the breech face. It meant that the gun left a unique mark on every cartridge it fired.

SCOTLAND YARD detectives were convinced that the murderer knew the Essex countryside well, and their suspicions fell on Frederick Guy Browne, an ex-convict with a long record of violence. There was insufficient evidence to arrest Browne on a murder charge, but he was kept under surveillance. Four months after the murder he was picked up in Clapham and charged with car theft.

A loaded Webley revolver together with twelve Mark IV cartridges were found in his car, and there was an arsenal of weapons at his hideout. It was soon discovered that another man, William Henry Kennedy, had been associated with Browne. He was picked up in Liverpool, and the fact that his gun jammed probably saved the life of one of the arresting police officers. Kennedy proved the weaker of the pair, and he admitted being with Browne in the stolen car on the night of the murder, although he claimed that it was his companion who shot and killed the policeman.

Robert Churchill corroborated the earlier findings concerning the distinctive mark on the cartridge-case found in the abandoned car. That this matched a tiny flaw in the breech of Browne's Webley revolver was clearly demonstrated. Churchill tested fifty other Webleys to see if they made similar breech-marks on the cartridges fired in them. No comparable marks were made, and War Office experts tested over a thousand revolvers in the same way, and with the same result.

To clinch the firearms evidence, Churchill also demonstrated by test-firing a gun through pigskin that black powder deposits on the murdered man's skin came from the propellant used in Mark IV cartridges. Browne and Kennedy appeared at the Old Bailey on trial for murder. The combination of exhaustive police work and meticulous firearms evidence proved overwhelming. Both men were found guilty, and were hanged.

1, *4*, **104**, *164*, *204*, *213*, *226*, *245*, **259**, **316**, **338**, **339**, *365*, *393*, *422*, *485*, **512**, **528**, *553*, *595*, **627**, **633**, **635**, **657**, **674**, *692*.

FOLIE À DEUX

New Zealand teenagers Pauline Parker and Juliet Hulme developed a close relationship which Mrs Parker thought was unhealthy. When in 1954 it was decided that Juliet should go to South Africa with her father Pauline connived to travel with her friend. Both girls knew that Mrs Parker would oppose the plan, so they conspired to kill her. 'We decided to use a brick in a stocking,' wrote Pauline in her diary. When Mrs Parker's body was found it bore forty-five separate injuries inflicted with a BLUNT INSTRUMENT.

Pauline made a straightforward CONFESSION explaining how she had committed MATRICIDE, while Juliet said they merely wished to frighten Mrs Parker into consenting to their plan. The girls were tried for murder at Christchurch. It was shown in court that they were precocious and self-centred and that they had engaged in lesbian activities. The prosecution referred to them as 'dirty-minded little girls', and the defence pleaded paranoia and *folie à deux*. The JURY found them guilty, but since they were under eighteen years of age they were sentenced to be detained during Her Majesty's pleasure. They have since been released.

Folie à deux is a delusion or mental disorder shared by two persons. In the case of Parker and Hulme, the defence pleaded communicated insanity based on the undoubtedly strong bonds of homosexuality and mental fantasy which united the two girls. This closeness of relationship and purpose is more commonly shared by sisters or by husband and wife. Although many killings have been committed as CONSPIRACY to murder, the defence of communicated insanity is unusual. The notorious association between Raymond Fernandez and Martha Beck, America's 'Lonely Hearts Killers' of the 1940s, was a kind of *folie à deux*. Theirs was a relationship between two social misfits — she an overweight, oversexed person seeking lovers through the Lonely Hearts Clubs, and he a sexual entrepreneur who believed he could compel women to fall in love with him by HYPNOSIS.

Using his seductive abilities, they went into business wooing lonely women into their clutches for the purpose of robbery. Fernandez turned on the charm with Beck organizing the planning and making sure her partner's amorous inclinations did not get out of hand. In this way they tricked dozens of women out of their savings, and as their greed mounted, so they turned to murder. In 1948 they committed three murders, and when they were arrested were suspected of seventeen others.

The trial of Fernandez and Beck in New York allowed the newspapers to have a field day with stories of their weird sex life spliced with accounts of perversion and fetish. The couple pleaded not guilty by reason of insanity, and as if to emphasize the overriding nature of their relationship, Martha screamed out her emotions in court; 'I love him. I do love him and I always will', yet their exchange of letters while they were in custody was marked by alternating expressions of love and hate.

The 'Lonely Hearts Killers' were convicted of murder, and Fernandez made a confession in which he said, 'I'm not an average murderer.' They died in the ELECTRIC CHAIR at Sing Sing in 1951.

94, *237*, *281*, *297*, *584*, *587*, *602*, *739*.

FORENSIC MEDICINE

The word 'forensic' comes from the Latin *forensis*, meaning 'of the forum', and referring to the meeting-place in Rome where civic affairs and legal matters were considered and discussed by those with public responsibilities.

Forensic medicine, described by Professor Alfred Swaine Taylor as 'the application of every branch of medical knowledge to the purposes of the law', covers a wide field. Its origins lie in antiquity, but some of the first teachings in forensic medicine emerged from the German universities in the seventeenth century. The first chair in forensic medicine in the English-speaking world was established at Edinburgh University in 1807.

Historically, forensic medicine has also been known as MEDICAL JURISPRUDENCE, and in modern times by the more easily understood term legal medicine. Its subject matter has always been diverse, covering pathology, toxicology and medical ethics. Moreover, the medical profession, with its involvement in police matters and in determining cause of death in cases of violence, naturally took up the application of scientific methods of investigating crime.

The growth of specialization in modern times has led to many aspects of forensic medicine emerging as studies in their own right, such as forensic dentistry, FORENSIC PSYCHIATRY, forensic chemistry, forensic biology and, in a general sense, FORENSIC SCIENCE.

Alfred Swaine Taylor (1806–80) was Professor of Medical Jurisprudence at Guy's Hospital Medical School for forty-six years. During this period he wrote his *Principles and Practice of Medical Jurisprudence*, which became a bible of forensic medicine. He was one of several great figures who guided the development of the subject in Britain, but perhaps the most widely recognized personality was Sir Bernard Spilsbury (1877–1947). He is acknowledged as one of the most influential contributors whose emphasis on pathology as a means of inquiring into cause of death raised the status of murder investigation.

Spilsbury stamped his personality on most of the famous murder cases of his era, and helped to create the role of the expert as a public figure. One of his contemporaries was Sir Sydney Smith (1883–1969), a New Zealander who studied at Edinburgh, one of the homes of forensic medicine, and pioneered the scientific investigation of crime in Egypt. While Spilsbury had the public reputation, it was left to others to contribute to the written learning of the subject. Smith wrote his own text-book of forensic medicine, and edited Taylor's classic *Principles*, a task later inherited by Professor Keith Simpson, of whom it has been said that at least seven of his cases qualify him for the Guinness Book of Records! He too has published several books on forensic medicine and allied matters, and has made a number of important technical contributions to his subject.

Professor Francis Camps (1905–72) is another important name in forensic circles, and he was a leading member of the British Academy of Forensic Sciences, whose journal, *Medicine, Science and Law*, he edited. Although they would be the first to acknowledge the contributions made by their professional colleagues, these four men — Spilsbury, Smith, Simpson and Camps — between them accounted for most of the great murder cases which have occurred in Britain this century. In the USA the role of the medical examiner has perhaps offered less scope for public figures, but there is no doubting the recognition paid to Dr Milton Helpern (1902–77), who worked for fifty years in the Office of the Medical Examiner in New York City, being its Chief for twenty-five. He was an international figure at the forefront of developments in forensic medicine for most of his life. He participated in many of America's notable murder cases, and his country's first national medico-legal library, established in New York in 1962, was named after him.

97, 114, 115, 116, **117**, **299**, *324, 564,* **625**, *626,* **627**, *632.*

FORENSIC PSYCHIATRY

The application of psychiatry to legal problems has grown in recognition as the relevance of the criminal's mental state has increased. Not that mental illness is by any means a new field of study. Serious consideration of mental health in England began in 1780, and grew through a succession of Acts of Parliament. The concept of guilty intent (MENS REA) as a necessary component of a criminal act is deeply embedded in English law. So too is the humane idea that an insane person, not understanding his actions or being responsible for them, requires the protection of the law. This is only rendered possible by so defining legal insanity that courts may judge which mental states or disorder protect an individual from punishment.

The M'NAGHTEN RULES, formulated in 1843, attempted to provide a test for right and wrong which would stand in law. To establish a defence of insanity it had to be shown that at the time the accused person committed the crime he was suffering from a defect of reason which affected his ability to understand that what he was doing was wrong. The result has been more than a century of controversy, and it may be fairly said that at the time they were devised psychiatry did not even exist as an established discipline. With the benefits of modern thinking, the M'Naghten Rules are viewed as too rigid, and represent a purely fictional disorder of the mind which has no standing in the light of medical knowledge. Several attempts have been made to improve the tests for insanity, one of the earliest being the concept of irresistible impulse formulated in the USA in 1887. An important development — also in the USA — was the Durham Rule, brought in by the District of Columbia in 1954. This allowed that a person was not criminally responsible if his unlawful act was the product of mental disease or mental defect. Commenting on the Durham Rule, Justice William O. Douglas remarked that 'the psychiatrist . . . speaks to the Court and the Jury in the language of his discipline. He is at last free to advise the court and jury concerning the totality of the accused's personality and condition.' This was widely regarded as a breakthrough for forensic psychiatry, although it was only adopted by the District of Columbia.

In England the 1957 Homicide Act permitted pleas of DIMINISHED RESPONSIBILITY to the charge of murder, and represented a swing away from definitions of insanity, and placed an emphasis on criminal responsibility. In 1972 the Model Penal Code proposed by the American Law Institute replaced the Durham Rule. This interposed the term 'substantial capacity' between mental disease and its causation of crime. Thus criminal responsibility did not exist if as a result of mental disease or defect an individual 'lacks substantial capacity either to appreciate the criminality of his conduct or to conform his conduct to the requirements of law'. Like all previous tests of insanity, this rule leaves much open to interpretation, but it is in use in several states.

The debate continues, and there is some scepticism among the public who see murder trials becoming obsessed with arguments about the mental state of the accused. As the number of psychiatric experts representing defence and prosecution in court — often in studied disagreement — increase in number there is a feeling that criminal justice might be defaulting in its obligations to the victims of crime. Certainly a great deal depends on legal and medical interpretation. Some psychiatrists excuse criminal responsibility only on narrow grounds involving serious disorder such as SCHIZOPHRENIA, while others take a broader view and include less serious mental conditions which are also less well defined. An example of this approach was illustrated in a case in 1981 in which an English court accepted a defence plea based on pre-menstrual tension. A woman who admitted killing her lover was allowed to plead guilty of MANSLAUGHTER on grounds of diminished responsibility. Medical evidence was given that the accused had suffered from pre-menstrual tension for fifteen years, the effect of which was to build up adrenalin in the blood and cause changes in the body's hormones. This condition led to irritability, aggressiveness and loss of self-control.

100, **117***, 126, 389, 451,* **518***, 590.*

FORENSIC SCIENCE

The science which supports expert EVIDENCE in English law courts is called forensic science (see also FORENSIC MEDICINE). In other countries this technical expertise is known as CRIMINALISTICS and police science. It forms part of the inter-relationship between science, medicine and law, and covers a wide field, including physics, chemistry and biology.

Before 1900 the technical side of criminal investigation was provided by the detective and the doctor, who between them were judged to know sufficient science to aid their inquiries. The development of FINGERPRINT identification, FIREARMS examination, chemical analysis and microscopy inspired by the vision of a number of pioneers — notably Gross and Locard — provided the courts with a new breed of experts for the prosecution of crime.

Forensic science laboratories deal with the often minute debris of criminal activity — dust, HAIRS, FIBRES, drugs, stains and a host of CONTACT TRACES. Professor Paul Kirk, Head of the University of California Department of criminalistics, said of the criminal, 'wherever he steps, whatever he touches, whatever he leaves, even unconsciously, will serve as silent evidence against him'. This is what provides the forensic scientist with his work, and the scope is enormous, including everything from examining QUESTIONED DOCUMENTS to matching damaged paintwork in

HIT-AND-RUN cases, and involves every type of crime from arson to murder.

SCOTLAND YARD set up the Metropolitan Police Forensic Laboratory in 1934, and the Home Office operates eight other laboratories providing a regional service. The tradition became established that these laboratories dealt with all aspects of scientific evidence apart from fingerprints — which are handled by specialized departments — and the medical side of crime — which is attended to by the police surgeons, and Home Office pathologists.

The FEDERAL BUREAU OF INVESTIGATION operates a crime laboratory from its headquarters in Washington D.C. which carries out over 150,000 examinations annually on evidence material. The FBI's facilities are available to every police force in America, and many large police departments have their own laboratories.

Some technical experts believe that forensic science is under-exploited, and that it could play a much larger part in the solution of crime than is at present the case. In the United States it is thought that only a very small percentage — between 3 and 10 per cent — of potential evidence at a crime scene is actually collected and processed in serious crime investigation. It is widely recognized that the future development of forensic science lies in improving the means by which evidence samples are collected and brought into the laboratory. Dr Ray Williams, Director of the Metropolitan Police Forensic Laboratory, has written that the 'technical limitation in forensic science is the ability to pick out the vital piece of evidence in the initial search'. The weak link in the forensic chain is the man on the spot — the investigating officer who first reaches the undisturbed crime scene. In recognition of this deficiency, police forces around the world have introduced special training programmes for scenes-of-crime officers and evidence technicians. The Americans have led the way, and some of the larger police departments have long since discarded the 'murder bag' in favour of mobile police laboratories equipped to deal with every type of evidence collection.
67, **259**, **445**, **502**, **636**, *667*, **702**, **703**.

G

GAS CHAMBER

The State of Nevada proposed the use of lethal gas for EXECUTIONS in 1921. The method was suggested by Major D. A. Turner of the US Medical Corps as a more humane manner of meting out capital punishment than the ELECTRIC CHAIR or HANGING. The original idea was to pipe the gas into the condemned cell so that the prisoner died peacefully in his sleep.

The first gassing took place in 1924 in a chamber specially constructed for the purpose, and the ten states which adopted lethal gas used rooms set aside in their prisons for that purpose. The green-painted, octagonal room in California's San Quentin Prison became a symbol for execution by gas. The Warden of San Quentin from 1942 to 1954, Clinton Duffy, described the process thus: 'In a matter of seconds the prisoner is unconscious. At first there is extreme evidence of horror, pain, strangling. The eyes pop, they turn purple, they drool. It is a horrible sight, witnesses faint. It is finally as though he has gone to sleep. The body, however, is not disfigured or mutilated in any way.' The lethal gas is produced by pouring sulphuric acid on to pellets of sodium cyanide. Two minutes or less inhalation of the resulting hydrocyanic gas produces death. Underneath the chair in the gas chamber is a bowl connected by a tube to a container of acid outside the room. A pound of CYANIDE is measured into a gauze bag which is hung from a hook beneath the chair and poised over the bowl. The condemned man is brought into the chamber and put in the chair; his arms and legs are strapped, and a stethoscope attached to his chest and led through a seal to the doctor outside. After the chamber is sealed acid is released into the receiving bowl, and at the Warden's command the executioner pulls a lever which lowers the cyanide into the acid bowl. The gas fumes rise from beneath the chair, and death is quick if the condemned person takes deep breaths

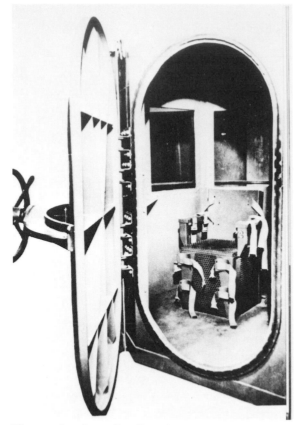

The gas chamber at San Quentin

men go to the gas chamber, and wrote three books. Finally, all appeals exhausted and after the eighth stay of execution, Caryl Chessman — whose plight had excited world-wide interest — was placed in the chair in the octagonal chamber and gassed to death on 2 May 1960. His end was described as dying hard, 'gasping, drooling, rolling his head — surviving the engulfing gas for several seconds'. Commenting on execution by lethal gas in his *Murder USA*, John Godwin wrote that every other method made it impossible for the victim to post-pone death, however briefly, by his own conscious actions. In the gas chamber the condemned man can hold out for as long as he can hold his breath. To the extent that the victim is advised to take deep breaths to pull the gas down into his lungs he had to aid in his own destruction, which, wrote Godwin, 'is a crime against human decency. . . .' *166, 193, 209, 252, 261.*

GASSING

Mike Malloy, an inveterate Irish drunk, appeared to a group of New York entrepreneurs to be the ideal victim for an insurance murder. Operating from a Third Avenue speak-easy, the 'Murder Trust', consisting of five men and including a bar-tender, a taxi-driver and an undertaker, insured Malloy for nearly 2,000 dollars and then set about murdering him. At New Year 1932 they treated their victim to all the drinks he could imbibe, including liquor spiked with anti-freeze, and at dawn left him for dead. While the irrepressible Irishman had drunk himself into a stupor, he was not ready to meet his Maker, for he popped up next day, 'dying for a drink'.

During the following week his erstwhile friends plied Malloy with turpentine, wood alcohol, sardines doctored with tin-tacks and horse lini-ment. Still he would not succumb, and his resilience won him the nickname 'Durable'. The 'Murder Trust' twice unsuccessfully tried to kill him with HIT-AND-RUN tactics, and even left him drunk and dowsed with water to freeze in New York's bitterly cold winter. But the irrepressible Malloy staggered back from the brink of oblivion, looking for his next drink. Finally, in desperation, the 'Trust' made him drunk once again and pushed a gas-pipe down his throat. At last, his resistance sapped, Malloy died of gas poisoning. One of the 'Trust' — perhaps as a boast, or possibly out of relief — spoke out of turn and the police took an interest in the Irishman's death.

as he is advised to do in order to hasten loss of consciousness. The doctor outside the chamber listens for the cessation of heart-beat through his remote-control stethoscope, and pronounces that death has occurred. Finally, the lethal gas is sucked out of the chamber by a fan and the corpse is sprayed with liquid ammonia to neutralize any lingering traces of hydrocyanic gas. The whole process is known to prison inmates as 'the big sleep' or 'the time machine'.

One of the most celebrated victims of the gas chamber was Caryl Chessman, who spent nearly twelve years on Death Row. He was the so-called 'Red Light Bandit' who was indicted in 1948 on eighteen charges, mostly for RAPE, but including one of KIDNAPPING with bodily harm and with intent to commit robbery, which in California was a capital charge. Chessman was found guilty and sentenced to death, but this was not carried out owing to faulty procedure in handling the trial transcript. This led to the first of many stays of execution and to a prolonged fight against sen-tence, during which Chessman saw over a hundred

Following EXHUMATION of his body, a POST-MORTEM examination soon took note of the cherry-red colour of his skin (one of the characteristics of carbon monoxide poisoning), and murder charges were not long delayed. The members of the 'Murder Trust' were eventually sentenced to death and met their end in the ELECTRIC CHAIR.

The use of gas alone as a method of murder is unusual — it is more commonly found as an accompaniment of death where murder is dressed up to look like suicide. A classic example of this ruse was provided by Reginald Ivor Hinks, who had designs on his father-in-law's property. In 1933, at his house in Bath, Hinks knocked his relative unconscious with a blow to the head, and then dragged the body to the gas cooker in the kitchen, put the old man's head in the oven and turned the gas on. What looked like suicide from gas poisoning rapidly turned into murder when the bruise on the back of the victim's head was shown to have been caused before death, and Hinks died on the gallows.

The coal gas which at one time was supplied for domestic use was a common cause of death by gassing and accounted for large numbers of accidents and suicides. The killing component of coal gas is carbon monoxide, which in effect is a blood poison. It works by displacing the vital oxygen normally carried to the body's tissues by the haemoglobin in the blood. Haemoglobin is the blood's colouring material, and oxygen, brought in through the lungs, combines with it to form oxy-haemoglobin. Carbon monoxide has three hundred times more affinity for haemoglobin than has oxygen, so that the latter life-giving substance is easily displaced. The effect is that less oxygen reaches the body tissues, and death results from oxygen starvation. Since nerve cells are especially prone to lack of oxygen — those of the brain begin to die after eight minutes — deterioration is rapid. Carbon monoxide is an insidious poison, for it is colourless and non-irritant. It is also readily absorbed by the body, and quickly accumulates its poisonous products in the bloodstream.

Symptoms of gas poisoning vary according to the amount of carbon monoxide accumulated in the blood. There are seldom any symptoms until saturation has reached 20 per cent, and then usually only when the victim is engaged in physical acts of exertion. The first signs are dizziness and difficulty in breathing, and the symptoms move progressively towards unconsciousness and death as the level of carbon monoxide builds up. Coal gas containing 5 to 10 per cent of carbon monoxide is likely to be lethal within two to five minutes. Even small proportions of carbon monoxide in inhaled air may prove fatal, due to the steady accumulation of the poison in the blood. A person at rest inhaling 0·1 per cent carbon monoxide from the atmosphere may have a blood saturation level of 50 per cent in just over two hours. With exercise this time would be halved, and in general conversion of more than 50 per cent of the blood's haemoglobin to carboxyhaemoglobin will cause death.

The indications of carbon monoxide poisoning after death are distinctive. The blood (which often fails to clot) has a bright cherry-pink colour which reddens the organs and muscles — the face usually has a high pink colour. Patches of post-mortem LIVIDITY are also bright pink. Diagnosis is not made solely on these appearances, for CYANIDE poisoning and other conditions can cause high colour. Confirmation of carbon monoxide poisoning is made by means of chemical and spectroscopic tests on the blood.

Suicide by gassing has been safeguarded against by the introduction of natural gas which contains little or no carbon monoxide, but the danger of accidental death lurks in various forms of incomplete combustion. Smouldering upholstery in burning buildings and paraffin heaters used in unventilated conditions are common causes of accidental death. The subtle nature of carbon monoxide poisoning produces weariness and lethargy, and the victims sleep on till death. Car-exhaust fumes are another potent source of carbon monoxide which result in both suicide and accidental death. Running a car engine in an unventilated garage quickly leads to a build-up of gas to the point where the unsuspecting victim collapses and, in the classic manner, sleeps away to death.

A number of murderers have flirted with gas. H. H. Holmes had gas piped to some of the rooms in his murder house; Sidney Fox, before he committed MATRICIDE, attempted to gas a lady-friend while she lay asleep; and John Christie, the infamous murderer of 10 Rillington Place, used gassing as part of his murder technique. Carbon monoxide was found in the blood of three of his victims, a phenomenon which he explained at his trial. After he had made his victims partially drunk, he persuaded them to sit in an old deck-chair of the type which had a sun canopy over the head. He then rendered the women fully unconscious with coal gas drawn from the house supply and led to the lethal deck-chair by means of a rubber tube. This procedure was his prelude to acts of STRANGULATION and RAPE.

Gassing also formed part of an unusual crime in 1953 which became known as the Ritual Burial Case. Michael Conroy, left alone in his house in a London suburb, was searching for some money which he had mislaid. While examining the divan bed he discovered the corpse of his thirteen-year-old son hidden in the torn mattress. Conroy believed that both his wife and son were staying with relatives, and at first Mrs Conroy denied knowing that her son was dead. Then she said he had suffered an epileptic fit during which he choked and died. She admitted 'burying' the boy in the bed, where he had been found with his hands crossed on his chest like an ancient warrior laid to rest.

Post-mortem examination revealed a 55 per cent saturation of carbon monoxide in the boy's blood. That alone added up to lethal gassing, but in addition massive doses of phenobarbitone were found in his body. Teresa Conroy was charged with murder, and she was found guilty but insane at her trial at the Old Bailey.
379, 523, **548***, 586, 626.*

GUILLOTINE

Contrary to popular belief, the instrument of EXECUTION used in France since 1792 was not designed by Dr Guillotin. A similar beheading device, nicknamed 'the Scottish maiden', was in use up to 1716 in Edinburgh. Dr Joseph-Ignace Guillotin, Professor of Anatomy and Physiology at Paris, proposed reforms regarding the punishment of criminals in his country, and campaigned for a 'simple mechanism of decapitation'. His advice that every person condemned to death should have his head severed was incorporated into the French Penal Code in 1792, and the apparatus used for this purpose came to be known as the guillotine.

Dr Guillotin was concerned that the instrument of execution should be infallible, and after consultation with Charles-Henri Sanson, the official executioner, the first guillotine was built. It was used in Paris in April 1792, when a highwayman was publicly put to death. The doctor was pleased with the result, and concluded that all the victim felt was 'a slight chill on the neck'! The following year Louis XVI experienced the same 'slight chill' and the guillotine became a symbol of the Reign of Terror which followed the French Revolution. The guillotine, judged to be faster and less humiliating than beheading with the sword, was nicknamed 'The People's Avenger'.

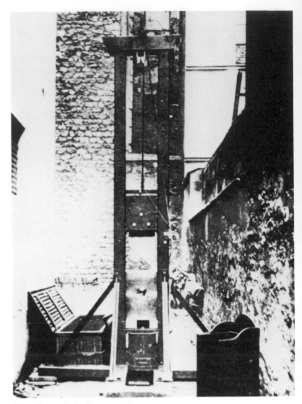

The 'People's Avenger'

In due course the guillotine was adopted as France's official mode of execution for all condemned criminals. The last public execution was at Versailles in 1939, when the murderer Eugen Weidmann was guillotined. On this occasion — which was attended by immense public interest — the executioner failed to align the tilting table carrying the condemned man's body with the notch into which his neck fitted. As a consequence Weidmann's head had to be pulled into position by the hair and ears before the knife could descend to do its work. When his head fell some members of the crowd were so exhilarated that they rushed forward to dip handkerchiefs in the blood. F. Tennyson Jesse, who witnessed the execution, described it graphically: 'The voice that had been so beautiful, so soft, so gentle in the courtroom, was stilled for ever. There only came as a last exclamation from Weidmann — and that was involuntary — the whistling that always sounds when a head is cut off. For the neck gives out a gasp as the last breath of air leaves the lungs, though the head be already in the basket. It is the man's windpipe and not his tongue that protests.'

After this spectacle the authorities decided that

future executions would be carried out privately within the prison precincts.

The guillotine is a simple apparatus consisting of fifteen-foot-high grooved uprights on a supporting base. A triangular steel blade — called a *couperet*, and weighing seven kilograms — is mounted on a 45-kilogram weight which travels in the grooved uprights. The condemned person is strapped to a tilting table which is so positioned that when it is turned horizontally the neck (previously shaven) fits into the notch, or *lunette*, ready to receive the knife.

Argument has existed since the inception of the guillotine as to whether it produced instant death. There were stories of the eyes of severed heads following the movements of the executioner, and a well-known French dramatist wrote that the victims 'twist their eyes and grind their teeth for a good five minutes after the execution'. There were also horror stories of a severed head which spoke, and it was alleged too that Charlotte Corday's face blushed after she had been guillotined. Substance was given to these ideas by Dr Sömmering, a distinguished German anatomist, who declared that it was by no means certain when a head is severed from the body 'that the feelings, personality and ego are instantly abolished, and that the unfortunate decapitated person does not feel the after-pain where the neck is affected. . . .' The librarian of the Paris School of Medicine lent his name to some of these ideas, and an uproar ensued in Parisian medical circles. The Establishment roundly denounced the suggestion that pain could subsist in either portion of a decapitated body, and one of the official executioners let it be known that 'There is no survival of consciousness, but only a non-coordinated nervous agitation'. The *British Medical Journal* pronounced its verdict on the

Heads severed by the guillotine's 'chill wind'

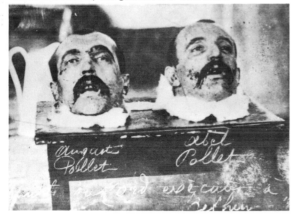

matter in 1879 in a report which stated that the head of a guillotine victim 'was perfectly dead to all intents and purposes'.

Attempts to abolish capital punishment in France, and with it the guillotine, have persisted down the years. The number of executions dropped during the 1970s, there being only seven sentences of death carried out in ten years. A concerted effort to abolish the guillotine was mounted in 1978, but a public opinion poll showed a majority in favour of its retention. In 1980 the European Parliament urged all countries still enforcing the death penalty to abandon it, and in 1981 the French Parliament conducted its first full debate on the subject for seventy years. As a result, and with four condemned persons under sentence of death, Parliament decided to abolish the guillotine. Thus 'the Avenger', which had a bloodier record than most methods of execution, was consigned to its place in history. No longer was it possible for a condemned murderer, as in the case of Pierre François Lacenaire, to feel 'the chill on his neck' twice on account of the guillotine's blade sticking in its grooves, or for the mob to sing its taunts to the condemned:

> **The guillotine awaits you,**
> **We'll cut you short**
> **Your heads shall fall.**

185, 364, 379, 402, 420, 428, 444, 606, 638, 647.

GUNSHOT-WOUNDS

Gunshot-wounds (or GSW) are not always as obvious as commonly believed. Penetrating wounds in the head may be overlooked altogether if the victim has a mass of hair, and non-penetrating injuries which gash the skin may have the appearance of KNIFE-WOUNDS. The experienced pathologist is on the alert for these misleading signs, and Professor Francis Camps warned of the dangers of preconceived ideas, it being 'only too easy to find what one expects'.

It is of prime importance to determine whether wounds are homicidal or self-inflicted. If homicidal, the investigator will want to know the distance from which the shots were fired, their direction and also the position of the body when struck. He will have some of this information from analysing the available FIREARMS evidence, and may already know the type of weapon involved. The appearance of the wounds on the body will tell

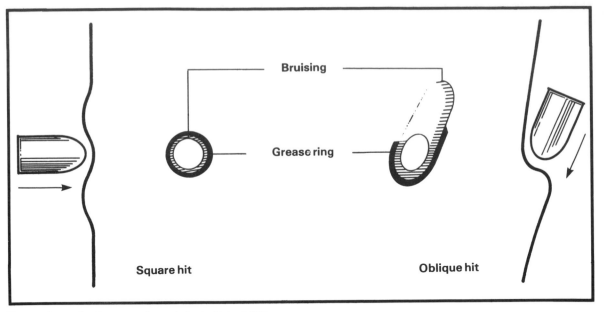

Comparison of entry wounds made by bullets striking the body squarely and obliquely

the skilled examiner a great deal more about the nature of the shooting, and his report will be added to the firearms evidence.

When a bullet penetrates and passes through the body it makes both entry and exit wounds. The appearance of these is especially valuable in deciding the distance and direction from which the shots were fired. The typical appearance of an entry wound is of a neat round hole slightly smaller than the diameter of the bullet. The natural elasticity of the skin closes it up slightly after it has been perforated, and in doing so wipes the bullet clean. Entry wounds therefore have a circular bruise at their margin, and also a grease ring. When the bullet strikes at an oblique angle the entry wound is more oval in shape, and there is an irregular area of bruising. The blood loss from entry wounds is usually slight.

Neat entry wounds of the type described result from shots fired at a distance of eighteen inches or more. Shots fired at closer ranges result in different wounds. Contact wounds — where the muzzle of the gun is placed directly against the skin — are more gross, and have distinctive characteristics. The hole is larger than the bullet, and its margins are bruised by the recoil of the gun. A clear imprint of the gun-muzzle is often found as a bruise. There may also be scorching around the wound caused by the force of the discharge.

Where bone underlies the point of entry, local destruction is more evident. Gases discharged from the gun-muzzle undermine the skin, causing it to split and tear. A characteristic star-shaped or cruciate wound is caused which may be mistaken for an exit wound. The presence of powder residues will help to ascertain the true nature of the wound, and this is one of the reasons why it is inadvisable to wash gunshot wounds at the crime scene.

Firearms discharged at close range, between two and eight inches, cause powder tattooing around the entry wound. Particles of burned and partially burned powder are forced out of the gun-muzzle along with the bullet. Together with other debris — grease particles and pieces of lead stripped from the bullet — these are deposited on the skin or clothing.

Black powder produces the heaviest deposits, while smokeless powder, which is more completely combusted, has less effect. In powder tattooing particles are driven under the skin, and may not be wiped away. Individual powder grains may be picked out of the tattooed skin and under the microscope yield information about the type and manufacture of the cartridge used in the shooting. A typical close-range wound in which the skin is tattooed also exhibits an area of burning known as a scorch zone, caused by the hot gases emitted from the gun-muzzle. Estimates of close-range shots are sometimes made by test-firing the crime weapon loaded with the same ammunition as that used in the fatal shooting. Shots are fired at various

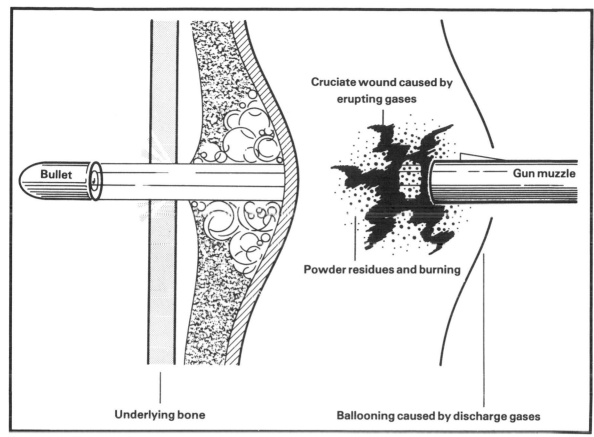

Cruciate wound caused by
erupting gases

Bullet

Gun muzzle

Powder residues and burning

Underlying bone

Ballooning caused by discharge gases

Contact gunshot wound

distances in order to match the tattoo pattern found on the victim.

Where a firearm is fired through clothing, either in contact or at very close range, the discharge products will be evident on the fabric. Close examination of the clothing is thus of great importance in the investigation of gunshot wounds. It is significant that when suicides elect to shoot themselves through the heart they usually open their

Near-contact gunshot wound

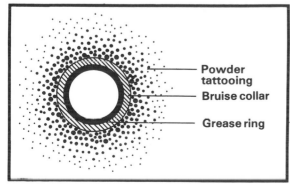

Powder
tattooing

Bruise collar

Grease ring

clothing to bring the gun in contact with the skin.

The relationship between entry and exit wounds will generally help determine the direction of shooting. The size of exit wounds varies according to the velocity of the bullet at the point of exit, whether the bullet strikes bone in the course of its passage through the body, and whether it breaks up.

Where a bullet passes only through soft tissue it exits leaving a small roundish hole with slightly torn edges. If the bullet has been deflected by hitting bone, splinters of bone and bullet fragments will lead to severe damage, causing gaping wounds as the debris is driven out of the body by the force of the shot. Such wounds often resemble lacerations caused by BLUNT INSTRUMENTS. Fragments may exit at different places, causing several wounds, and, to tax the medical examiner further, two bullets may enter at the same point but exit separately. It is the practice of pathologists examining the victims of fatal gunshot wounds to pass probes through the points of entry and exit to establish each bullet-track.

A phenomenon occurring with the use of high

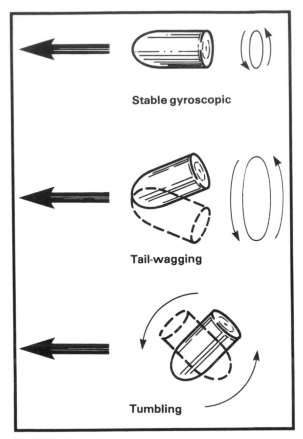

Stable gyroscopic

Tail-wagging

Tumbling

Characteristics of bullets in flight

velocity bullets is cavitation or soft-tissue track. This form of tissue damage is particularly severe in non-perforating wounds, where the total energy of the bullet is transferred to the tissues surrounding the bullet track. When a high-velocity bullet fired from a rifle penetrates the body the transfer of energy sets up high-pressure waves in the tissues, and creates a temporary cavitation track behind the bullet. Consequently, instead of a track approximating to the calibre of the bullet, the core of damage is much greater. Head wounds caused by modern high-velocity rifles exhibit severe cavitation in brain tissues, which are often pulped as a result of the high pressure set up in the skull.

The performance of bullets in flight has considerable bearing on the wounds they cause. For example, bullets fired from rifled weapons spin at 2,000 to 3,000 revolutions a second, but over the first few yards and at the end of their trajectory their path is unstable. The projectile wobbles before it picks up, or loses smooth gyroscopic flight in a condition known as 'tail-wagging'. A bullet with tail-wag does not strike cleanly but leaves a

ragged entry wound which makes estimation of firing distance difficult. Severe wounds are also caused by tumbling bullets, a flight pattern in which the projectile turns end over end. This is a design feature of micro-calibre ammunition. Both tail-wagging and tumbling bullets dissipate their energy on impact, causing wide cavitation tracks in soft tissues.

Unlike wounds inflicted by bullets fired from rifled weapons, shotguns rarely produce exit wounds in the body. Shot has little penetrating power, and is easily arrested by tough tissue or bone. Consequently, the shot and wads are often found in the wound.

Where a shotgun is discharged in contact with, or within a few inches of, the body the shot does not scatter but enters as a solid mass through a single hole. The hot gases and flame emitted from the gun's muzzle will tear the tissues and burn the skin. Powder particles are forced into the wound and around its perimeter, causing tattooing. At close range wads are also driven into the wound, and their recovery may prove useful in identifying the type of cartridge used. Contact wounds in the head or mouth, such as those met with in suicidal use of the shotgun, result in massive destruction.

At close range, from one to three feet, a more or less triangular wound about 1½ to 2 inches in diameter results. There is evidence of scorching and tattooing, also singeing of hair by flame unless the weapon was fired through clothing. Beyond a range of three feet the shot begins to spread out, and at four feet the wound appears as a central hole with small perforations around it. No powder deposits are visible to the naked eye, although a swab taken from around the wound may reveal traces.

At ranges over four feet the shot continues to spread out and produces a mass of small perforations with no central wound. Some say an approximation of the range can be obtained by measuring the diameter of the wound in inches (including the outermost perforations), subtracting one, and giving the range in yards. Thus with a wound measuring nine inches across, this rule-of-thumb method indicates a firing range of about eight yards. The exact range depends on the choke of the weapon, and only a test-firing will give an accurate answer. (See under FIREARMS.)

Accurate reconstruction of a fatal shooting can be critical in establishing criminal responsibility, as was shown in the Whistling Copse shotgun killing. On the night of 10 October 1927 Enoch Dix, a Somerset farm labourer, was poaching on

Lord Temple's estate at a place known as Whistling Copse. It was nearly midnight on a moonlit night when Dix began picking off a few roosting pheasants with his .410 shotgun.

The poacher's shots were heard by his lordship's gamekeepers, William Walker and George Rawlings, who were out on duty about a mile away. Loading their twelve-bores, they made for Whistling Copse. They found Dix, and challenged him. Shots were exchanged; Walker was left dying with a wound in the throat; and the poacher fled.

There was difficulty in identifying Dix, and Rawlings told police that the poacher had shot his companion at point-blank range. Dix at first denied all knowledge of the incident, but as Rawlings was insistent that he had hit the fleeing figure with a blast from his 12-bore, he was examined for wounds. Incredibly, his back, neck and thighs were peppered with shot-holes, which his wife had dressed so that he could maintain the pretence of not being hit. It was useless for him to deny any longer that he had been in the copse, but he said simply that his own gun discharged accidentally with the shock of being hit by Rawlings's shot.

There was no question as to whose gun had fired the fatal shot — it was a matter of deciding who fired first, and at what range. At this point firearms expert Robert Churchill was called in to help. He set about calculating the firing distance by shooting at a series of whitewashed metal plates with Rawlings's gun. He used identical cartridges to that discharged at the poacher, and produced the following results:

Range (yards)	Diameter of spread (inches)
15	27–30
20	36–38
30	40–42

After considering these test results, and having examined the spread of shot-wounds in Dix's back, Churchill concluded that the shot which hit the poacher had been fired at not less than fifteen feet. Therefore, if Dix's gun had discharged accidentally when he was hit, as he claimed, it must have gone off at a distance of fifteen yards from the two keepers. At that range tests showed Dix's shotgun to produce a spread of 27 to 30 inches, whereas the wound in the dead keeper's throat was only five inches in diameter. To cause such a wound, the poacher's gun must have been fired at less than five yards. Dix was eventually found guilty of MANSLAUGHTER, and was sentenced to fifteen years' penal servitude. Dix in evidence kept referring to the copse as 'the Whistling Corpse', which added levity to the otherwise sombre court proceedings. **214**, *316*, **548**, **625**, **627**, **633**.

HABEAS CORPUS

A legal writ issued by a judge requiring that an imprisoned person is brought before a court in order to test the legality of his detention. Habeas corpus, meaning literally, 'You must have the body', has its origins in English COMMON LAW and in the concept that the king is at all times entitled to be given an account of why 'the liberty of his subjects is restrained'.

The Habeas Corpus Act came into effect in England in 1697, while the procedure is also guaranteed under the Constitution of the United States of America. The provision of habeas corpus is regarded as vitally important in safeguarding the freedom of the individual citizen, to the extent that it may only be suspended at times of national emergency such as war. **28**, **658**.

HAIRS

In any struggle between victim and attacker hairs and FIBRES from one are inevitably transferred to the other. These CONTACT TRACES provide valuable linking clues, and, using a comparison microscope, the forensic scientist can make even a single hair yield information about its owner's race, sex and age. The importance of hair in criminal investigation was realized at an early stage in the development of FORENSIC SCIENCE, and one of the first scientific papers on the subject was published in France in 1857. By the early 1900s microscopic examination of hair was well established, and in 1931 Professor John Glaister published his *Hairs of Mammalia from the Medico-legal Aspect*, which became a standard reference work.

One of Glaister's cases illustrates the value of hair evidence. In September 1947 Mrs Catherine McIntyre was found dead in her bed by her son when he returned for lunch at their lonely house in Perthshire. She had been battered about the head, and various articles had been stolen. A police search of the ground near the house brought to light a hideout in the bracken where it appeared the murderer had lain in wait. Lying among the trampled-down bracken was a sawn-off shotgun with blood on the butt, a bloodstained handkerchief and a discarded razor-blade. A pair of bloody overalls and a railway ticket of a type issued only to uniformed soldiers were also discovered. Polish soldiers at a near-by camp were questioned, and appeals for information were broadcast on the radio. As a result a farmer came forward to report a missing shotgun, and to inform the police that a Pole called Stanislaw Myszka had worked on his farm for a while. Myszka — who turned out to be a deserter from the Polish Army in Exile — was arrested after a chase, and Mrs McIntyre's wedding ring was found hidden in his shoe.

Professor Glaister, who had carried out the POST-MORTEM on the murder victim, was intrigued by the razor-blade found near the scene of the crime. This article had some hairs attached to it, and it seemed that the blade had been used for a dry shave. Glaister asked the police to furnish him with a sample of beard shavings from Myszka for microscopic comparison. He concluded that the two samples of beard hair matched for colour and detailed structural characteristics, and in the cautious words of the scientist his report concluded that they were 'consistent with a common source'. This finding went some way towards placing Myszka at the hideout near the McIntyre house in which the murder weapon had been found. The Pole was tried for murder at Perth and convicted following presentation of scientific evidence at his trial.

Unless it is burnt, hair is extremely durable. It remains identifiable on bodies in an advanced state of DECOMPOSITION or attached to a murder weapon long after the crime is committed. Hair is composed of protein substances, chiefly keratin, and head hair grows at an average weekly rate of about 2·5mm, the beard growing faster and body hair more slowly. Growth ceases at death, but as the skin shrinks the hair, especially the beard, becomes more prominent, giving rise to the murder myth that hair grows after death. The absorbent property of hair makes its examination important in cases of ARSENIC poisoning. Hair picks up the poison from the bloodstream, and it is possible to work out the approximate strength and frequency of the dosage by analysis.

Microscopic examination of hair can determine the following information:

- Whether it is human or animal
- If human, which race
- Whether it fell out or was pulled
- If animal, which species
- The part of the body it came from
- How it was cut or dressed

Human hair is divided into six types according to site of origin — the head, eyebrow/eyelash, beard/moustache, body, pubic and axillary (underarm). These types are distinguished by their thickness, curl, colour, shape, softness, springiness and brittleness. Pubic hair, for example, is stiff and wiry, and beard hair is often angular in cross-section. Sex is not easily determined from head hair except by signs of dressing — i.e., whether it is bleached, dyed, lacquered, singed or waved, although modern fashions tend to reduce these possibilities. Pubic hair in women is generally shorter and coarser than in the male. It is possible to tell the age of hair only within wide limits, but chemical changes which occur with age can be determined by laboratory tests.

Viewed longitudinally, human hair consists of three parts: root, shaft and tip. There are also three parts in cross-section — the cuticle (outer sheath, formed of overlapping scales of epidermis), the cortex (contains pigment and gives hair its natural colour) and the medulla (central core which contains air). There are marked differences between the cuticle layers of human and animal hair, and different shapes are apparent for different animal species. Forensic laboratories keep recognition charts which enable an animal hair found on a suspect's clothing, for example, to be quickly identified. In the laboratory hair samples are dry-mounted for viewing under the

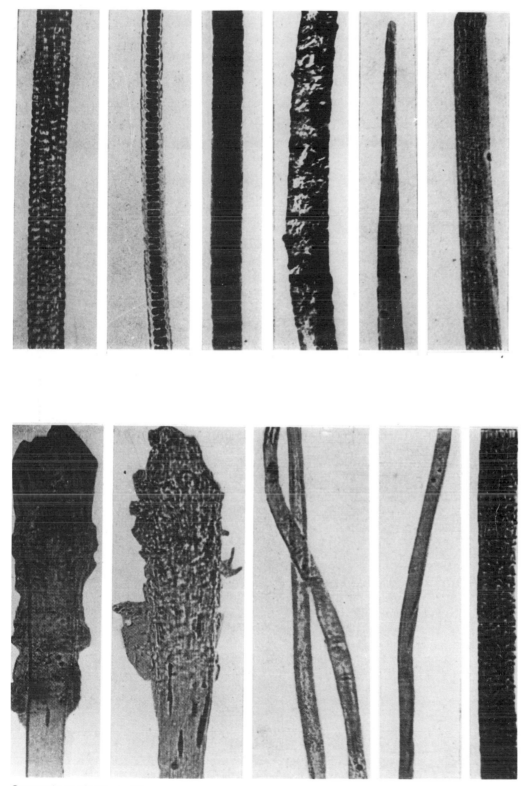

Comparison of hairs and fibres

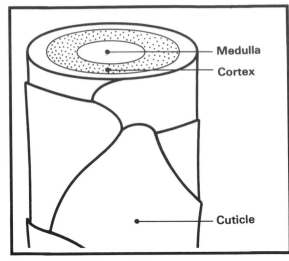

The structure of human hair

microscope. Alternatively they may be embedded in wax blocks and cut into thin slices for examination. Identification cannot be made with certainty on hair evidence alone. The best the scientist can do, as in the case of Stanislaw Myszka, is to say that a suspect's hair matches a crime sample. This can prove valuable corroborating evidence of guilt, as numerous murder cases have shown.

Hair evidence was a major feature of the trial of John Norman Collins, the so-called 'co-ed' killer, in Ann Arbor in 1970. Seven brutal murders occurred during the period August 1967 to July 1969 in the Ypsilanti area of Michigan. Sexual mutilation was a feature of the murders, and the police were sufficiently frustrated to call on the Dutchman Peter Hurkos to provide some PSYCHIC DETECTION. The seventh victim had been seen in the company of a young student identified as John Collins, who was questioned but released through lack of evidence.

Investigators made a breakthrough when bloodstains were found in the basement of the house belonging to Mrs Fran Loucks, Collins's aunt. Collins admitted using the house during his relatives' absence, and while the BLOOD found on the basement floor proved to be of the same group as the last co-ed victim, the real discovery lay in some hair clippings. These had escaped the sweeping up which followed the routine haircuts administered to her two sons by Mrs Loucks. Tiny hairclippings of male origin had been found on the underclothing of the last murdered girl. The two sets of hair matched, and it was apparent that the girl had been murdered in Mrs Loucks's basement. Subsequently her body, carrying with it telltale traces of hair, was removed and dumped in some shrubbery on the outskirts of Ypsilanti. Collins was charged with the murder of the last 'co-ed' victim, and was convicted mainly on scientific evidence. He was sentenced to confinement and hard labour for life.

One of the methods used to compare the hair samples in the Michigan investigation was neutron activation analysis. This is a highly sensitive method developed by Dr Robert J. Jervis of the University of Toronto in the 1950s to identify the chemical elements in hair and other crime materials. The method consists of bombarding the sample with high-density neutrons in a nuclear reactor which causes the material's chemical atoms to become radioactive. This irradiation is measured to identify the various elements and to determine the amounts present. Hair naturally contains minute amounts of a number of chemical elements, including antimony, arsenic, copper, iron and zinc. Where agreement can be found by neutron activation analysis between the types and amounts of trace elements found in two samples of hair, scientists are confident that the hair came from the same source.

Neutron activation analysis came into prominence in the 1960s when the method was used on a sample of Napoleon's head hair. The result showed that the hair of the ex-Emperor, dead for almost a hundred and fifty years, contained thirteen times more arsenic than is normal. This led to speculation that he had been poisoned during his last days on St Helena. If such sophisticated techniques of analysis represent one extreme of criminological interest in hair, the other extreme must be that demonstrated by John Christie, the sex murderer, who had a hair fetish and kept samples of female pubic hair in a tobacco tin. (See under GASSING for an account of the case.)
99, 255, 371, 397, 449, **528,** *667.*

HANGING

A remark made of an executed murderer by an eminent Scottish judge that he was 'none the waur o' a hangin'' was recalled by Sir Sydney Smith in summing up his feelings about Sidney Fox, who in 1929 murdered his mother (see under MATRICIDE). The belief that hanging was an appropriate mode of EXECUTION for convicted murderers is

The drop at Wandsworth Prison

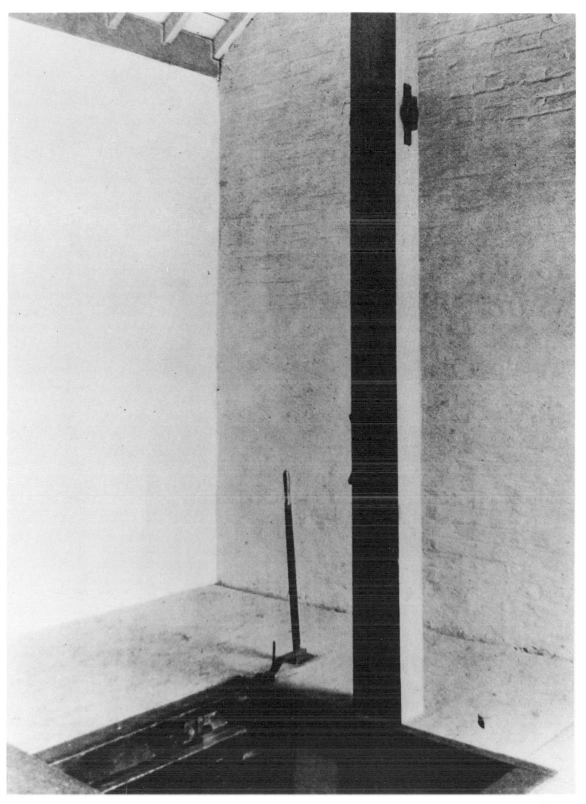

one that has echoed down the centuries and found a home in England: that this is the judicial means of carrying out the sentence of death.

Hanging is thought to have its origins in Persia, whence the method spread to Europe via the Huns, and to England by way of the Anglo-Saxons. It has been used in England since the twelfth century, and was introduced to America by the early settlers, where it persisted until the advent of new execution methods such as the ELECTRIC CHAIR and GAS CHAMBER. In ancient times felons were simply strung up from the branch of a tree, a process which continued well into the twentieth century in the form of LYNCH-ING. The first innovation was a gallows constructed of two legs supporting a cross-beam. The condemned person mounted a ladder placed against the beam, and after the noose had been placed around his neck the hangman pushed the ladder away, leaving the victim suspended. This procedure, in common with lynching, resulted in slow STRANGULATION rather than instantaneous death, and it was the custom for spectators to pull on the victim's legs to hasten his end.

The first significant improvement in technique came in 1760 with a gallows designed to fracture the neck and result in quick death. Dislocation of the cervical vertebrae was effected by means of a drop — a trap-door through which the victim plunged at the pull of a lever to be brought up violently by his own weight at the rope's end some distance beneath. In 1783 a gallows with a drop capable of hanging twelve people was erected outside London's Newgate Prison. Until 1834 it was common for the bodies of hanged criminals to be suspended from a gibbet until they rotted. Like the public hanging itself, this debasement of the body was supposed to be part of the deterrent value of execution.

Following a campaign led by the novelist Charles Dickens, who wrote of the sickening behaviour of the crowds attending hangings, public execution was abolished in 1868. With hanging confined to the relative privacy of prison precincts, attention focused on perfecting the technique to make the method as humane as possible. James Berry, the Yorkshire executioner who held office from 1884 to 1892, devised a system of drops based on the weight of the prisoner. This was designed to cause instantaneous death and leave as few marks as possible on the body. Experiments were also made with regard to the knot, and it was found that the location under the angle of the left jaw resulted in a tilting back of the chin and a rupturing of the spinal cord. It was well established in executioners' experience that incorrect placing of the knot resulted in strangulation, while too long a drop tore off the victim's head.

H. L. Mencken, the American journalist who

James Berry's 'Table of Drops'

SCALE SHOWING THE STRIKING FORCE OF FALLING BODIES AT DIFFERENT DISTANCES.												
Distance Falling in Feet from Zero	8 Stone	9 Stone	10 Stone	11 Stone	12 Stone	13 Stone	14 Stone	15 Stone	16 Stone	17 Stone	18 Stone	19 Stone
	Cw. Qr. lb.	Cw. Qr. lb.	Cw. Qr. lb.	Cw. Qr. lb.	Cw. Qr. lb.	Cw. Qr. lb.	Cw. Qr. lb.	Cw. Qr. lb.	Cw. Qr. lb.	Cw. Qr. lb.	Cw. Qr. lb.	Cw. Qr. lb.
1 Ft.	8 0 0	9 0 0	10 0 0	11 0 0	12 0 0	13 0 0	14 0 0	15 0 0	16 0 0	17 0 0	18 0 0	19 0 0
2 ,,	11 1 15	12 2 23	14 0 14	15 2 4	16 3 22	18 1 12	19 3 2	21 0 21	22 2 11	24 0 1	25 1 19	26 3 9
3 ,,	13 3 16	15 2 15	17 1 14	19 0 12	20 3 11	22 2 9	24 1 8	26 0 7	27 3 5	29 2 4	31 1 2	33 0 1
4 ,,	16 0 0	18 0 0	20 0 0	22 0 0	24 0 0	26 0 0	28 0 0	30 0 0	32 0 0	34 0 0	36 0 0	40 0 0
5 ,,	17 2 11	19 3 5	22 0 0	24 0 22	26 1 16	28 2 11	30 3 5	33 0 0	35 0 22	37 0 16	39 2 11	41 3 15
6 ,,	19 2 11	22 0 5	24 2 0	26 3 22	29 1 16	31 3 11	34 1 5	36 3 0	39 0 22	41 2 16	44 0 11	46 2 5
7 ,,	21 0 22	23 3 11	26 2 0	29 0 16	31 3 5	34 1 22	37 0 11	39 3 0	42 1 16	45 0 5	47 2 22	50 1 11
8 ,,	22 2 22	25 2 4	28 1 14	31 0 23	34 0 5	36 3 15	39 2 25	42 2 7	45 1 16	48 0 26	51 0 8	53 3 18
9 ,,	24 0 11	27 0 12	30 0 14	33 0 23	36 0 16	39 0 18	42 0 19	45 0 21	48 0 22	51 0 23	54 0 25	57 0 26
10 ,,	25 1 5	28 1 23	31 2 14	34 3 4	37 3 22	41 0 12	44 1 2	47 1 21	50 2 11	53 3 1	56 3 19	60 0 9

attended several executions as a witness, wrote:

> A criminal executed by a competent hangman shows no sign of suffering. He drops straight through the trap, and when he comes to rest remains hanging almost motionless. There is no struggle. After a while the legs draw up a bit, but not violently. The heart keeps up a gradually diminishing beating up to ten or twelve minutes, but all consciousness has departed and the criminal dies without apparent pain.

Mencken commented favourably on the English method of making the noose, which produced death more quickly than the traditional 'hangman's knot' which Pierrepoint disparagingly referred to as the 'cowboy's coil'. A metal ring woven into one end of the rope, with the other end passed through it to form the noose, resulted in a faster action when the drop was opened, and exerted greater pressure on the blood-vessels in the neck, and thereby speedier loss of consciousness. Stoppage of the blood-supply to the brain results in unconsciousness within several seconds. This fast noose combined with the effect of the drop to cause a fracture-dislocation of the cervical vertebrae (usually the second and third, or fourth and fifth) and ruptured the spinal cord. Thus death was virtually instantaneous, although heart and lung action might continue for up to fifteen minutes. But some prison warders did not approve, and when Clinton Duffy of San Quentin was asked by newspaper-men for his impressions of the execution of Robert James (also known as Raymond Lisemba) in 1942 — the last man to be hanged there — he answered bitterly: 'I wish everyone in California had seen it. I wish they had all seen the flesh torn from Lisemba's face by the rope and his half-severed neck and his popping eyes and his swollen tongue. I wish they had seen his legs swinging and smelt the odors of his urine and defecation and sweat and caking blood.' And he added, 'Every legislator who helped pass the law that made it necessary for us all to go through this ordeal should have been with us today.' James killed his wife by drowning, having first attempted to murder her by the unusual method of subjecting her to rattlesnake bites.

Albert Pierrepoint, public executioner in England from 1931 to 1956, paid great attention to

The 'tools of the trade'

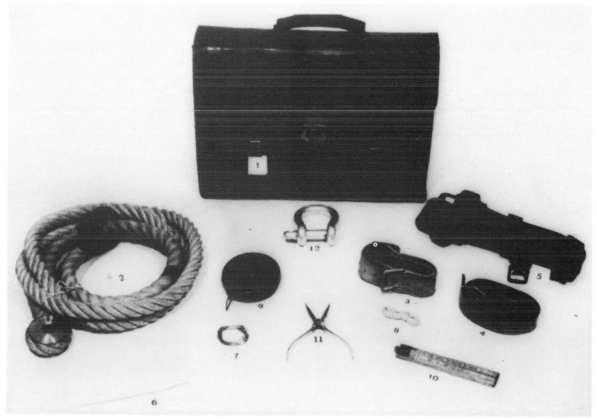

the humane side of his job, and prided himself on his speed and efficiency. Once he got his prisoner to the scaffold he quickly positioned him on the drop, put the cap over his head, adjusted the noose and operated the lever: 'Cap, noose, pin, lever, drop . . .' was the hangman's routine which took as little as fifteen seconds. The body used to be left suspended for an hour to ensure death and to avoid the horrendous consequences of burial alive, which had been known in earlier times when half-strangled victims were quicky interred. Following an inquest, the body was normally buried within the prison walls, a fate lamented by Oscar Wilde in his *The Ballad of Reading Gaol*:

> **For where a grave had opened wide,**
> **There was no grave at all:**
> **Only a stretch of mud and sand**
> **By the hideous prison-wall,**
> **And a little heap of burning lime,**
> **That the man should have his pall.**

Neither Berry nor Pierrepoint had any doubts as to the efficiency and humaneness of their methods. Berry described the 'English Method' as the 'best yet known, because it is absolutely certain, instantaneous and painless'. And Pierrepoint, giving evidence before a Royal Commission on capital punishment in 1949, reported that hanging was 'quick, certain and humane', adding, 'I think it is the fastest and quickest in the world bar nothing. It is quicker than shooting and cleaner'.

The history of judicial hanging is not without its share of stories and attendant phenomena, and there is no stranger tale than that of John Lee, who survived three attempts to hang him. He was convicted of murder in 1884 after the elderly lady whom he served as footman was found dead with CUT THROAT and bludgeoned to death. The young man was convicted largely on CIRCUMSTANTIAL EVIDENCE, and sentenced to death. Berry was the hangman and after he had made all the usual preparations at Exeter Gaol he pulled the lever, but nothing happened. He furiously worked the lever and stamped on the trap-doors, but the drop refused to work. Lee was removed, and the arrangements checked — a test drop with a weight worked perfectly. The condemned man was brought back, but a repeat performance resulted — the drop would not open. After further checks of the apparatus, Lee was placed on the scaffold a third time. In his memoirs Berry wrote, ' . . . I stood back and pulled the lever. The noise of the bolts sliding could be plainly heard, but the doors did not fall.' Lee, who had dreamed that he would not hang, was returned to his cell, and received an

Sir Bernard Spilsbury's record of a judicial hanging

official reprieve within hours. He said, 'It was the Lord's hand which would not let the Law take away my life', but his would-be executioner was of the opinion that 'the woodwork fitted too tightly in the centre of the doors'. John Lee, 'the man they could not hang', served twenty-two years in prison, and after his release in 1907 married and emigrated to the USA. This survivor of the scaffold died in 1933 at the age of sixty-eight.

In 1957 the law was changed in England with the passing of the Homicide Act, which made a distinction between capital and non-capital murder, with the result that the number of hangings decreased. Finally, what proved to be the last executions in Great Britain took place in August 1964, and in December Parliament passed the Abolition of the Death Penalty Act. Henceforth conviction for murder resulted in sentences of life imprisonment.

22, 24, 60, 84, 103, 107, 303, 417, 420, 440, 494, 504, 524, 549, 550, 593, 664, 737.

HEAD-WOUNDS

The correct interpretation of fatal injuries is important, and a category which presents special difficulties is head-wounds. When William Banton

Moore found his wife lying unconscious in the bathroom with a bloody head-injury he hardly imagined that he would be charged with murder.

On 4 December 1970 Moore, a young architect from a prominent Kentucky family, picked up his wife Louisa from the airport, following a trip to New York City. Louisa had a drinking problem, and their marriage was rocky. On the drive back to their Louisville home divorce was high on the list of conversation topics. When they reached home the couple decided that the night's rest would be taken in separate rooms. Moore put his wife's suitcases outside her bedroom, and went downstairs to watch television.

About midnight he decided to retire, and in the course of walking to his bedroom noticed that Louisa's bags were still unpacked. He went into the bathroom, where he found her inert body on the floor with BLOOD splashed about from a head-injury. He tried to revive her by artificial respiration, and then called a doctor, who pronounced her dead. The police were notified, and Moore was found in the incriminating position of appearing red-handed in the blood-smeared room containing his wife's body, which bore a severe head-wound. After he had told the officers quite emphatically that no one could have entered the house without his knowledge, he was arrested and charged with murder.

The prosecution at Moore's trial contended that he had struck his wife down in the bathroom and repeatedly bashed her head against the bath. Attention was thus focused on the head-wound, which consisted of a skull fracture under a cleanly torn flap of the scalp. Bleeding had been profuse, as is common in scalp wounds. Doctors for the prosecution maintained that this injury resulted from repeated blows delivered by a BLUNT INSTRUMENT. Dr Milton Helpern was called as a defence witness, and his findings and interpretation were rather different. For a start, the lack of laceration and bruising around the wound told against the idea of multiple blows from a blunt instrument. Such attacks invariably result in heavily bruised and mangled tissues with complicated, splintered fractures of the underlying bone. But his principal findings concerned the injuries to the brain itself.

A direct blow delivered to the head when it is in a stationary position typically results in a shattering fracture with pieces of bone being driven into the soft brain matter lying beneath the impact area. This is the classic 'coup' injury — a direct blow to the fixed head. But Mrs Moore had not sustained this type of injury — she had the opposite-side injury known as *contre-coup*, for which there is a completely different explanation. Helpern summed this up as 'a cardinal sign of damage to a moving head by impact against a hard, stationary surface'. Instead of injury to the brain being confined to the area under the site of impact, the damage occurs at a point on the opposite side of the brain. An illustration of contre-

coup is the drunk who pitches over backward and hits his head on the hard surface of a road. The skull is fractured at the rear, but the force of the impact damages the frontal lobes of the brain. An exceptionally heavy impact may even fracture the thin bone over the eye-sockets.

The mechanism of contre-coup injuries is not completely understood, but is believed to occur when the brain strikes the inside of the skull following the sudden arrest of the moving head against a hard object. Rotational forces also act on the brain, causing it to continue moving inside the skull, setting up shear stresses after the head has come to rest. The result is damage to membranes and blood vessels and compression of brain tissue.

Despite Helpern's telling interpretation of the dead woman's injuries which suggested an accidental fall, William Moore was convicted of murder and given a twenty-one years' prison sentence. Appeals were rejected, but as the result of continual pressure by his family the medical evidence was re-examined, and Moore's case was reviewed by the state governor.

In December 1974, having been convinced that the medical evidence which convicted Moore was incorrect, the state commuted sentence to time served, and he regained his freedom.
117, *324*.

HIT-AND-RUN

Charles Arthur Mortimer, a soldier in the Welch Regiment, took to murder and adopted an unusual weapon of destruction — his motor-car. On 7 August 1935 he stole a car and amused himself

Contre-coup injury

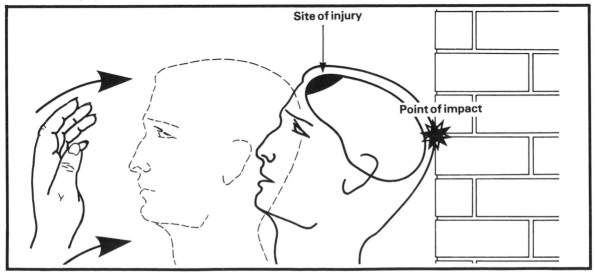

driving around Hampshire's country lanes. In separate incidents he ran down two girls who were riding their bicycles. He did not kill them but stopped long enough to attack one of his victims with his fists before driving on. These mad antics were reported to the police, and the car in question was later found abandoned.

The following day Mortimer resumed his violent activities in another stolen car. Near the village of Winchfield he came across two girls riding together on their bicycles. He drove into one of them, sweeping her up on to the front of his car and carrying her along until she slid off and disappeared over the parapet of a railway bridge. The girl sustained severe injuries from which she later died. Meanwhile Mortimer ran down another cyclist before being captured following a dramatic car-chase which ended when he crashed into a police road-block.

The hit-and-run driver was charged with murder, and to counter-claims that the fatality was an accident the prosecution at his trial introduced testimony regarding the other attacks. This amounted to evidence showing that Mortimer developed a SYSTEM OF MURDER. Despite a history of mental disturbance and EPILEPSY, he was convicted and sentenced to death. This was subsequently commuted to life imprisonment following a medical inquiry.

Hit and run deaths are usually accidents where the driver, in order to conceal his identity, fails to stop and assist the victim. While the driver's culpability may amount to a serious criminal charge, motor vehicles are seldom used as deliberate instruments of murder, save perhaps in gangland killings.

There are exceptions, as the Mortimer case shows, and among the charges levelled at Dr John Hill, the Texas plastic surgeon accused of murdering his wife in 1969, was an extraordinary allegation by his second wife. She claimed that Hill tried to kill her while she was travelling in his car by crashing the passenger side into a concrete bridge abutment. Despite extensive damage — the front wing and passenger door were torn off — the lady was only cut and bruised. In a further sensational development she claimed that Hill tried to inject her with procaine hydrochloride while she sat dazed in the wrecked car. She fended him off, but had he succeeded she would have died with every appearance of being killed by the shock of the crash. (See under BACTERIAL POISONING for an account of this case.)

The motor-car brought mobility and flexibility to crime in general and to murder in particular. The car has extended the murderer's horizons, taking him to out-of-the-way places to commit secret HOMICIDE, and affording him the means of removing his victim's body to a disposal site far from the scene of the crime. Cars have also provided possibilities for disposing of the victims by simulating a motor accident, as alleged in the case of Dr Hill, and certainly perfected by Tetzner and Rouse, who set their cars ablaze with the victim already dead or unconscious inside (see under BURNING).

Cars, like their drivers, both leave and collect trace material which indicates their presence at a particular place. This is part of the chain of evidence transfer by contact, which is such a boon to the crime investigator. Tyre impressions, for example, while not in the same class as FINGERPRINTS, do have their stamp of individuality. It is the routine investigation of hit-and-run incidents which has helped to develop the full diversity of the forensic scientist's skills. The usual problem in these cases is to find the offending vehicle. The invariable transfer of CONTACT TRACES, especially following the violent impact of a moving vehicle and the human frame, provides a wealth of clues.

Examination of the physical evidence at a hit-and-run scene is preceded by photography, and measurements are taken to record the relationship between the elements of the incident before the scene is disturbed. The position of the victim's body, the point of impact, skid marks and impact debris are all noted. Perishable evidence such as tyre tracks or foot impressions in tar or mud are dealt with first, and then a search pattern is started. This usually takes the point of impact as the centre, and the area is methodically combed for trace evidence which may be as minute as a pinhead chip of paint.

A variety of trace material may be found — typically, broken glass, paint-flakes and fragments of trim or ornamentation. Traces of BLOOD, human tissue, HAIRS or clothing FIBRES may also be evident. The victim's clothing and body are carefully examined for marks which may have been made by the vehicle. Smears of grease, dirt or paint may be found, and the body may bear tyre impressions or distinct patterns made by a radiator grille or a piece of car ornamentation.

Each type of trace material has a story to tell. A single paint-chip, for instance, may encapsulate the year, make and model of the vehicle in question. Paint detached from a car body by the force of impact with a heavy object usually comes away as a flake made up of all the layers of paint applied to the car in its lifetime. Microscopic examination of the edge of the flake, together with spectrographic analysis, yields detailed information about the pigments used in its manufacture. In this way a profile is built up which by reference to a standard collection of automobile paint-types will identify the origin of the sample. H. J. Walls, the distinguished British scientist, has said that it would be almost possible to claim that paint keeps the forensic scientist in business.

Pieces of broken glass found at the crime scene, especially from headlamps, can also tell more than the hit-and-run driver imagines. Sufficient fragments may be pieced together to identify a manufacturer's type of head glass, and thereby narrow the field of inquiry. Again, police investigators have access to reference collections of standard head glasses for speedy checking. Portions of broken trim, manufacturers' emblems and other ornaments also play their part in pinpointing the precise make and model of a hit-and-run vehicle.

The value of the wealth of trace evidence usually found at a hit-and-run scene is that while a single item may tell part of the story, taken together there may be sufficient material to complete the picture. Moreover, flakes of paint, pieces of glass and other debris shed by the missing vehicle can all be fitted back into place once it has been located. Thus irrefutable evidence may be assembled which relates that particular vehicle to a specific crime scene.

Similarly, tyre impressions recorded at the scene as photographs or plaster casts can be used to identify the manufacturer of the tyre and the size of the wheel. Defects and signs of wear are also important, for as surely as a fingerprint, they can unquestionably identify a vehicle. Dirt knocked from the underside of a car by the force of impact may contain materials such as chalk which is characteristic of a particular district. Depending on the circumstances, a cake of dirt may be found to fit precisely into a cavity beneath a suspect car, and provide corroborating evidence at the scene of the crime.

Analysis of such physical evidence may enable

The victim's face leaves an impression on the car windscreen

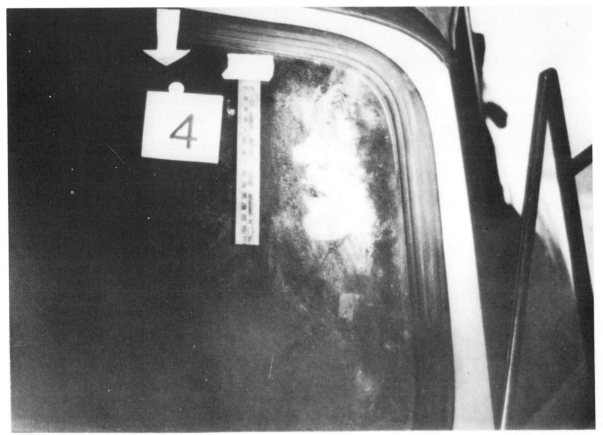

the police to issue a fairly full description of the vehicle they are looking for. Once located — hit-and-run vehicles are often abandoned — the suspect car is thoroughly examined for evidence which will link it to the crime incident. Many remarkable discoveries have been made in this type of investigation, and few more so than that of a Metropolitan Police fingerprint officer in 1959. During the routine dusting of a suspect car he found an almost photographic likeness of the hit-and-run victim on the unbroken windscreen. This image had been made by the impact of the woman's face leaving an unmistakable profile on the car which killed her.

Vehicle examination is painstaking. Every dent, blemish and stain is scrutinized. Broken glass, trim and other fittings and damaged paintwork are looked at carefully to see if any debris found at the scene makes a fit. Paint-flakes and broken head-lamp glass are especially significant in providing linking evidence. Clothing fibres may have been ground into the bodywork of the car by the force of impact, and an outline of clothing pattern may also be evident. Torn, identifiable fragments of cloth-ing may adhere to the underside of the car, and

organic traces such as blood, tissue and hair may be typed and related to the victim's characteristics. A single hair stuck in the grease of a back axle has proved sufficient to link vehicle and victim.

A good example of tracking a murderer down by a combination of forensic work and an eye-witness's observation was provided by a wartime case. In November 1941 two girls were found dead from KNIFE-WOUNDS in a Buckinghamshire wood. There were tyre impressions in the soil near by, and also a patch of oil. A twelve-year-old boy said he had seen the girls asking the driver of an Army truck for a lift. The boy even remembered the details of the vehicle's military markings. Armed with this information, the police quickly located the truck, which had a leaking back axle. Its tyre impressions matched those at the crime scene, and the leaking oil also matched. This and other cor-roborating evidence led to the conviction of Harold Hill, a serving soldier, for murder.

The forensic examiner's range of skills in dealing with crime vehicles is completed by his under-standing of evidence of mechanical failure and signs of deliberate tampering, calculation of speed at the time of impact, assessing the nature of 'blow-outs' and knowing whether the lights were on or off at the time of the collision.
251, *367*, **528**, **627**, *667*, **703**.

Imprint of victim's clothing left on a hit-and-run vehicle's bodywork

HOMICIDE

This is a general term denoting the killing of one human being by another. There are four types of homicide, of which MURDER is one. The basic divisions are criminal and non-criminal homicide.

Criminal homicide includes murder, which is unlawful killing with MALICE AFORETHOUGHT, and MANSLAUGHTER, which is killing without malice aforethought. In the United States murder may be classed as first or second degree according to the extent that the killing is premeditated. Murder in the first degree is punishable by death in many states, and in the second degree by imprisonment. Homicide committed in the course of RAPE, robbery and arson is usually rated as first-degree murder, sometimes referred to as 'felony murder'.

Manslaughter is classed as either voluntary or involuntary according to the circumstances of the homicide. Voluntary homicide includes the 'heat of passion' killing committed intentionally but under extreme provocation. Involuntary manslaughter has been the subject of much debate, as its definition poses problems. It covers the circumstances where a person is killed without intent during the course of an unlawful act, such as abortion, or where a lawful act is pursued in an unlawful manner, such as dangerous driving. Under COMMON LAW a killing resulting from the commission of an unlawful act was regarded as a criminal homicide; as murder if the offence was a felony, and as manslaughter if it was a misdemeanour. This was seen by some courts as unnecessarily severe, and attempts to soften the law have blurred its definition. Some American states, for instance, have the offence of 'negligent homicide' on the statute books, which attracts lesser penalties than manslaughter.

There are also two classes of non-criminal homicide — justifiable and excusable — where no blame attaches to the killer because he was acting with proper authority. Thus the public executioner who is instructed to carry out the sentence of the law commits justifiable homicide, as does the soldier who is commanded to kill his country's enemies. Similarly, the police officer who in the course of carrying out his law-enforcement duties kills a person resisting arrest acts within the law.

Excusable homicide results from misadventure or self-defence. Misadventure occurs where a person in course of a lawful act accidentally kills another — for example, the hunter who shoots and kills a concealed person. Homicide committed out of necessity by a person defending himself against attack in a fight or quarrel is also excusable, but the law must be satisfied the killing was unavoidable in order to protect the person's own life or the lives of those he was lawfully defending. The guilt of deliberate murder perpetrated under the cloak of self-defence is avoided by showing that an attempt was made to avert bloodshed.

The fate of a person charged with homicide will depend to a great extent on the influence his lawyer has over the jury when the charge is classified. There is a world of difference between murder and manslaughter and between first and second degree murder, although as Ambrose Bierce, the American journalist and author, commented, it makes no difference to the victim.
459, **510**, *620*, **635**.

HOMOSEXUAL MURDER

Murder committed by homosexuals tends to involve children and adolescents who become victims of sexual exploitation because of their innocence and accessibility. Violence with overtones of sado-MASOCHISM ending in murder is a common pattern in the aggressive homosexual. This is not a new phenomenon, as demonstrated by the activities of Fritz Haarmann in the 1920s (see under CANNIBALISM).

San Francisco, with its gay culture representing a seventh of the city's population, is a mecca for all the sexual diversions needed by homosexuals. Violence is no stranger to this world of drugs, blackmail and prostitution, and many homosexual murders are committed there. But it is Houston, Texas which spawned America's Fritz Haarmann in the person of the mass murderer Dean Corll. At the time of his death in 1973 his twenty-seven victims represented the record for mass murder in the USA (equal to H. H. Holmes's estimated total) until he was overtaken by Wayne Gacy, a fellow homosexual murderer with thirty-two killings to his name.

Corll, an electrician in his early thirties, was shot dead in his house at Pasadena by Wayne Henley. Corll used eighteen-year-old Henley as his accomplice to provide him with boys to torture and kill. After bouts of drinking moonshine, sniffing acrylic paint and smoking pot, Corll handcuffed his victims to a torture board and sodomized them. They were then killed by a variety of brutal methods and disposed of. Events came to a head when Henley came round from a drink session to find himself handcuffed to the torture board and held captive by the crazed Corll. He talked his way out of this predicament, and immediately shot and killed his tormentor.

Henley's CONFESSION led the police to a boat-yard near Houston. Buried under the floor of one of the sheds were the remains of twenty-seven bodies in plastic bags. Most had been brutally abused and mutilated. There may have been more recoverable bodies, but at twenty-seven the police decided to discontinue their gruesome labours. Henley was eventually found guilty of six murders and he was sentenced to a total of 594 years in prison. His killing of Dean Corll was judged to be justifiable HOMICIDE.

Similar youth murder was committed by John Wayne Gacy, whose conviction in 1980 showed him high indeed in the annals of MASS MURDER. Gacy, a homosexual who had served time in a reformatory for committing sodomy, developed a successful business as a building contractor, and nurtured ambitions to be a politician. He was regarded as a friendly man who loved children, and he staged huge parties at his ranch-style house in the Norwood township near Chicago. He also liked to dress up as a clown to entertain children at the local hospitals.

But Gacy's genial exterior masked perverted sexual urges. He committed his first murder in 1972 after abusing a youth he had picked up in Chicago. During the next six years he murdered thirty-one boys and youths after using them to satisfy his sexual needs. He killed them by STRANGULATION, and corpses of twenty-seven victims were found in shallow graves under his house. Gacy made three confessions, but declined to testify at his trial for murder. Defence psychiatrists pictured him as psychologically inadequate, but knowledge that he had posed as a police officer with a red light on his car during his prowling for victims suggested he well knew what he was doing. The JURY found him guilty, and he was sentenced to life imprisonment.

Jealousy is a strong MOTIVE for disagreement among homosexuals which may lead to violence and murder. It is unusual, however, for lesbians to kill one another, and when they do resort to murder the victims tend to be heterosexual. Margaret Allen — or 'Bill', as she preferred to be called — fell into this category. A wartime bus conductress in Manchester, she was a frustrated lesbian who withdrew into her own quiet world of chain-smoking and mental depression. In 1949, in a fit of violence, she murdered an elderly woman who appeared to have intruded into this lonely existence with friendly, or possibly busybody, intentions. 'I was in one of my funny moods,' 'Bill'

Dr. Robert J. Stein, identifying skeletons found under Gacy's home

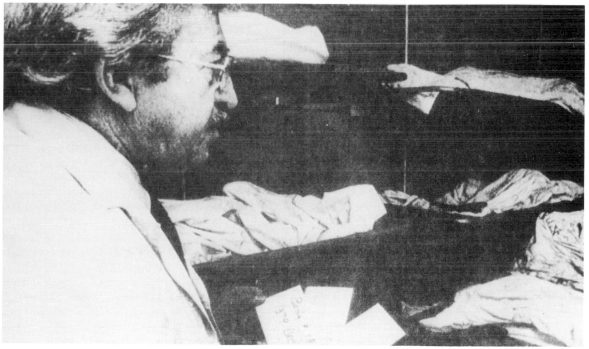

explained as the reason why she battered the woman to death with a hammer in the cellar of her home. She dumped the body near a main road in the hope that it would be mistaken for a HIT-AND-RUN victim. Strangely, she then went out of her way to create suspicion by talking to newspaper reporters about the crime, and eventually admitted her guilt to the police. She was hanged in Manchester's Strangeways Jail on 12 January 1949.

71, 171, 178, 191, 261, 298, 302, 349, 434, 451, 529, 576, 740.

HYOSCINE

Hawley Harvey Crippen, a 48-year-old mild-mannered doctor, unwittingly achieved the kind of notoriety for which many murderers crave. He did this by killing his wife Cora with hyoscine, dismembering her body and burying parts of it under the cellar at 39 Hilldrop Crescent, North London, and trying to abscond to America with his girl-friend, Ethel le Neve. He was the first criminal to be apprehended by means of transatlantic radio communication and returned to London to face trial for murder.

IDENTIFICATION of his wife's rotting viscera was made by means of a surgical scar, and attested to by Dr Bernard Spilsbury. Crippen was known to have bought hyoscine from a London chemist which, together with his pretences and precipitate flight, settled his guilt. He was convicted at his Old Bailey trial in October 1910, and was hanged. Since then his name has been taken into the language as an expletive, and his effigy has chilled the spines of countless visitors to Madame Tussaud's waxworks.

Hyoscine, or scopolamine, is found in the leaves and seeds of henbane (*Hyocyamus niger*), a botanical relative of the deadly nightshade. The drug acts as a depressant on the central nervous system, and is used medicinally in small doses of hundredths of a grain to relieve anxiety, soothe stomach ills and to treat travel sickness. In stronger doses it slows down the reflexes, causes hallucinations and impairs judgment, effects which have led to the use of scopolamine as a TRUTH DRUG. Hyoscine is rapidly absorbed through the mucous membranes, and also through the skin. Its metabolism in the body is not fully understood, and individual sensitivity to the drug makes medicinal dosing a skilful matter. A dose of a quarter to half a grain may prove fatal, producing convulsions, unconsciousness and death through respiratory failure.

Inspector Dew notifies the arrest of Dr Crippen and Ethel le Neve

Crippen bought 5 grains (325 mg) of hyoscine hydrobromide, allegedly for medicinal use, and the same drug was found in his wife's remains. Two-fifths of a grain showed up in the analysis, and the estimate for the whole body was half a grain. A great deal of discussion has ensued in criminological circles as to Crippen's MOTIVE. Sir Edward Marshall Hall, the great defence advocate (who did not defend Crippen at his trial) suggested that Crippen could not cope with Cora's sexual demands, and, having taken a lover, found himself in considerable difficulties. Knowing that hyoscine was sometimes used to depress the appetites of nymphomaniacs, he decided to administer the drug to his wife in order to keep her quiet. He did not intend to kill her, but overdid the dose. When he realized with horror that she was dead he panicked and set about disposing of the body. Another suggestion is that Crippen believed his wife's excessive drinking triggered off her outrageous and humiliating behaviour towards him. One of the treatments at that time for alcoholism was hyoscine, and Crippen bought some of the drug for that purpose. As in the other theory, he miscalculated the dose with fatal consequences.

> 117. AURAL REMEDIES CO., Craven-house, Kingsway, London, W.C.—A firm which runs a treatment for deafness on the lines of the late Drouet Institute. It has for '' consulting specialist '' one H. H. Crippen, M.D., a graduate of an American Homœopathic Hospital College, who was at one time connected with the Drouet Institute, and has also been interested in other quack remedies. (Vol. 66, pp. 1098, 1411.)

Dr Crippen — beware of quacks. (From *Truth Cautionary List* of 1910 before the murder.)

1, 63, 79, 97, 158, 176, 177, 207, 216, 250, 253, 309, 333, 351, 352, 470, **491,** *589.*

HYPNOSIS

Can a person be hypnotized and as a result commit murder? This question has often been debated, and hypnotists maintain that an individual will not carry out instructions for acts which would be contrary to his moral outlook. In 1951 a Danish bank-robber put this claim to the test by killing two people allegedly while under hypnosis. This man, 31-year-old Hardrup, a tool-maker, shot dead the manager and cashier of a Copenhagen bank when they refused to comply with his demands to hand over their takings. He was soon

No.

THE WESTERN UNION TELEGRAPH COMPANY.
THE LARGEST TELEGRAPHIC SYSTEM IN EXISTENCE.

DIRECT ROUTE *FOR ALL PARTS OF THE* **UNITED STATES.**
CANADA, CENTRAL AMERICA, WEST INDIES,
SOUTH AMERICA, & *VIA THE* **PACIFIC CABLE** *TO* **AUSTRALIA,**
NEW ZEALAND, FANNING, FIJI *AND* **NORFOLK ISLANDS.**

ATLANTIC CABLES direct to CANADA and to NEW YORK CITY.
DIRECT WIRES TO ALL THE PRINCIPAL CITIES.

No.	Service Instructions.	Time Received.	
1228	Col	8·46/	WESTERN UNION TELEGRAPH Co. 31 JUL 1910 EFFINGHAM HOUSE, ARUNDEL ST. STRAND, W.C.
Handed in at		**No. of Words.**	
Montrose Via Father point que		10	

CABLE OFFICE: EFFINGHAM HOUSE, ARUNDEL ST.,
STRAND, Telephone 1113 Gerrard.

To   Handcuffs Ldn Eng

Crippen and leneve
arrested wire later
Dew

The public are requested to hand in their replies at the Company's Stations, where free
receipts are given for the amounts charged.
CABLE ADDRESSES ARE REGISTERED FREE OF CHARGE.
No inquiry respecting this Message can be attended to without the production of this Paper.

arrested, and during interrogation told police that his MOTIVE was to obtain money to fight subversion. This was a cause which he put on a lofty platform, comparing himself to Joan of Arc.

Through other inquiries it was learned that while in prison after the war Hardrup had come under the influence of a man called Nielsen, a professional criminal and former Nazi sympathizer. Nielsen was arrested, but Hardrup went to some lengths to clear him of any involvement in the bank killings. Several months later Hardrup changed his story and told the authorities that Nielsen had hypnotized him and instructed him to carry out the bank robbery. He was also ordered not to mention Nielsen's name. Doctors who examined Hardrup thought he was suffering from SCHIZOPHRENIA, and believed that his change of heart may have resulted from the realization that his idealistic motive was not taken seriously, and that he was simply regarded as insane.

In 1954 both men were put on trial. The evidence was mainly psychiatric, and a picture emerged of Nielsen dominating his malleable partner by means of yoga, mysticism and hypnotism. The prosecution maintained that it was a straightforward matter of CONSPIRACY, while the defence argued that Hardrup was not responsible for his actions by reason of insanity. The police psychiatrist believed that Hardrup simulated hypnosis, an opinion countered by another doctor who said he had subjected the accused to hypnosis himself and questioned him about his relationship with Nielsen. From the response to these questions he concluded that Hardrup's behaviour could only be explained by accepting that he was controlled through hypnosis by Nielsen.

Finally, after claim and counter-claim regarding Hardrup's mental state, the JURY retired. Their verdict was that Hardrup was not responsible due to insanity, and that Nielsen, by exerting influence, including the use of hypnosis, manœuvred Hardrup into a state where he might kill. Nielsen was sentenced to life imprisonment, and Hardrup was sent to a psychiatric institution. The jury remained unconvinced that the robbery and murders had been activated by hypnotic influence. As Dr Lindesay Neustatter remarked in his book *The Mind of the Murderer*, the answer to the main question posed at this trial 'can a murder be committed either in a hypnotic state or as a result of post-hypnotic suggestion is unfortunately not supplied'.

Hypnotism has, however, proved its worth in assisting the investigation of crime, including murder, and has been used by the police of several countries. Its special relevance is in the examination of witnesses whose memory of an incident may be obscured by anxiety, or of RAPE victims who find it too painful to recall the details of an assault. The Los Angeles Police Department scored a success with hypnotism in a case of a school-bus hijacking in 1977. The driver was too shocked at first to give much assistance to the investigators, but following hypnosis he gave detailed descriptions of the hijackers, and remembered the registration number of their escape car.

SCOTLAND YARD has experimented successfully with hypnotism, and has been impressed by the amount of new information brought to light by examining witnesses in this way. While evidence gained by hypnotizing witnesses and victims of crime cannot legally be used in British courts, its value lies in reducing time which might otherwise be wasted chasing false leads or suspects. The dangers of the technique, as in the use of TRUTH DRUGS, are misleading or fantasizing statements by the subject.

The powers of hypnotism have been known for centuries, and the Greeks and Romans were well versed in their use for healing purposes. In modern times hypnotism has found a place in psychiatric treatment, and also in childbirth to relieve labour pains. Hypnotic therapy was widely used after the Second World War to treat combat neuroses. An Austrian physician, Franz Anton Mesmer (1734–1815), was one of the first to theorize about the power which one mind could exert over another. He supposed this to be due to magnetic forces, and his ideas became fashionable in Vienna and later in Paris, where he set up a clinic for medical treatment by hypnosis. Mesmerism (as his treatment became known) was popular in England during Queen Victoria's reign, but the scientific community regarded Mesmer's ideas with great scepticism.

Hypnosis is a temporary trance-like state in which the mind is open to greater suggestibility. There are various methods of inducing this condition. One involves the subject looking into the compelling gaze of the hypnotizer, coupled with verbal suggestion. Hypnotism may also be induced by the injection of scopolamine or other so-called truth drugs. There are various degrees of the hypnotic state, and some 10 per cent of people cannot be hypnotized at all.

Hypnotism is frequently used as a ploy by minor criminals in an attempt to escape punishment for their offences, and some mentally deranged persons, as in the case of Hardrup, will insist that they acted while hypnotized. The involvement of murder is unusual, but cases of rape followed by hypnotism of the victim with a command to forget the incident, and thereby protect the assailant, are known.

518, **693**.

IDENTIFICATION

One SCOTLAND YARD detective-inspector adjured recruits as follows: 'The value of the accuracy of description of details cannot be over-estimated, as it enables officers to narrow considerably their investigations. . . . Often when receiving an accurate description of a man who may have been seen loitering in the neighbourhood where a crime has been committed, the officer in charge of the case can visualise the appearance of the man as vividly as if he were present.' This passage, written in 1928, exemplifies the preoccupation of criminal investigators with identification.

The memory of the experienced detective became the method by which criminals were recognized, and there were few better exponents of this skill than Eugène François Vidocq (1775–1857), originator of the French criminal police and Chief of the SÛRETÉ. A similar sight recognition method was employed in London at the beginning of the nineteenth century, when it was the custom for detectives to review identification parades of men in custody to determine which felons they recognized.

The amazing variation of physical characteristics of the human body, especially those of the face, make sight recognition sufficiently reliable for most purposes. Descriptions of wanted criminals were recorded by the Ancient Egyptians, and Dr Robert Heindl, the German criminologist, likened their descriptions to the *portrait parlé* (speaking likeness) developed in France by the great Bertillon. The problem of identifying wrongdoers was solved in earlier times by branding and mutilating, practices which persisted in Russia until 1860. And in tribal Africa today the practice adopted by sexually assaulted women of biting a piece out of the lip of their attackers leaves such assailants branded for life as rapists. In 1876 the theory published by Cesare Lombroso, the Italian crimi

nologist, in which he expounded his concept of the born criminal with distinctive characteristics, was at first thought to offer an orderly system of identification. Lombroso's ideas were soon discredited, and it was discovered that the sought-after breakthrough had already occurred.

A Belgian statistician, Adolphe Quételet (1796–1874), put forward the proposition that no two human beings had exactly the same body measurements. This was taken up in 1861 by the Warden of Louvain Prison, who began to record the physical dimensions of his inmates. These ideas reached Alphonse Bertillon, who in 1879 was working as a clerk in the Prefecture of Police in Paris. He became convinced that no two individuals had the same body measurements in combination. He reasoned that the chances of two persons having the same height were four to one, and that the chances of two persons having the same combination of, say, height and length of arms was less. He listed fourteen measurements including length of head, circumference of head, length of fingers, length of foot and so on, which gave only a two hundred million to one chance of being duplicated in two individuals.

Bertillon's system of anthropometry, or 'man measurement', was widely adopted for criminal identification throughout Europe. Police kept card-index files in which they recorded the measurements of known criminals. Thus they had a sure method of identifying the habitual offender, for the measurements were based on unchanging parts of the SKELETON, and while a criminal could alter his appearance, he could not disguise his body dimensions. Bertillonage, as the system was known to the French, was extended to include various refinements, including photography for 'mug-shots' and a formalized *portrait parlé*. A new terminology was invented to assist police officers in making more exact descriptions. Series of words and phrases describing the visible characteristics of the human head were each given a code letter.

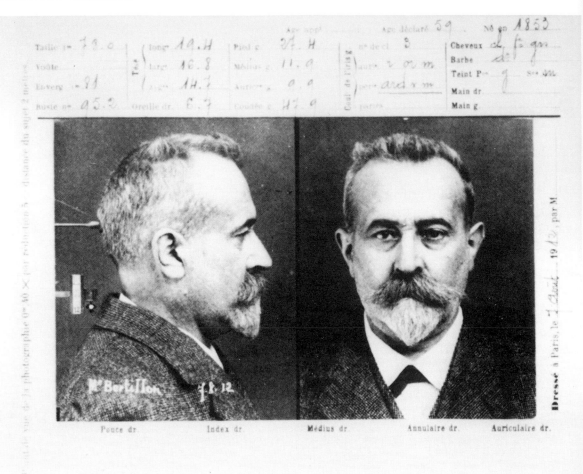

Bertillon photographed using his own methods

Thus a group of letters could be used as a shorthand formula to describe a particular set of features.

Portrait parlé was further developed in Italy to take account of additional human characteristics such as body movements and behaviour patterns. Although widely used in Europe during the latter half of the nineteenth century, especially in France, the system was regarded as cumbersome by the detectives who had to use it. The advent of FINGERPRINTING in the early 1890s sounded the death-knell for Bertillon's methods, and despite vigorous attempts to fight off the new system of absolute identification, anthropometry and *portrait parlé* faded.

Witnesses' descriptions of criminal suspects and verification of identification remain an important and often controversial aspect of investigation. New techniques such as 'Identikit' and 'Photofit'

evolved from the old *portrait parlé* concept, and the ultimate in criminal identification, the moving visual image, has been provided by closed-circuit television in crime-conscious environments such as banks. The Identikit system, devised in the 1940s by Hugh C. McDonald of the Los Angeles police, was based on face-types. From various line drawings of types of chins, pairs of lips, sets of eyes, noses and hair-styles, the inventor claimed it was possible to construct 62 thousand million different faces. To construct a face, a witness selected a set of features that most resembled his recollection of the suspect. Code numbers allotted to each feature made it possible to wire the Identikit formula from one country to another, and many of the world's police forces had the system in use by 1960.

The first time the Identikit system was used in Britain it brought instant results. An Identikit picture was published of a man suspected of murdering the woman assistant in a London curio shop in 1961. Within four days a policeman on

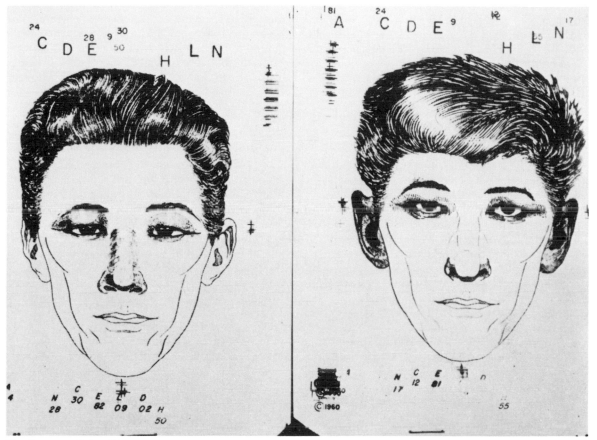

The first use of Identikit

patrol spotted the suspect, Edwin Bush, who was subsequently hanged for murder. The early success of Identikit was not sustained, and the method was criticized for its lack of facial details. Identification problems formed part of the controversy of the A6 murder investigation in 1961. James Hanratty was convicted of the murder, and subsequently hanged on identification evidence that has several times been challenged. A pair of lovers in a parked car were threatened by a gunman who shot the man dead and committed RAPE on the girl. The girl survived her GUNSHOT-WOUNDS and issued a description of the killer which was made up into an Identikit picture. A second picture was issued from a description given by a witness who saw a man near the scene of the crime.

This identification information was published, and the outcome was that the murder victim's widow saw a man in the street who she said was her husband's murderer. The man was James Hanratty, who resembled neither Identikit picture but had icy-blue eyes, a characteristic of her attacker which the rape victim vividly recalled. Hanratty was picked out in an identity parade and sent for trial. He claimed he was innocent, and pleaded an ALIBI which he could not substantiate and which he later changed. Despite the problems of identification, Hanratty was found guilty, and he was hanged in 1962.

In 1970 the Home Office adopted a new system of facial identification known as Photofit, invented by Jacques Penry. This system replaced the Identikit line drawings with photographs of five groups of facial characteristics — forehead/hair, eyes, nose/mouth and lower jaw/chin. There are five hundred such features coded in these groups, making possible five thousand million combinations of life-like faces. Like its forerunner, Photofit is used to build up a picture of a suspect as described by a witness. Penry's intention was to use the concept of three categories of basic facial features — rounded, angular and mixed — to train potential witnesses such as bank staff, Post Office employees, security workers and police officers to improve their powers of observation. Photofit has been successfully used in twenty countries, and its inventor believed his system offered as much individuality as the fingerprint.

The problems plaguing the identification of criminal suspects beyond REASONABLE DOUBT were highlighted by the Barn Murder case in 1972.

Photofit's five basic facial segments

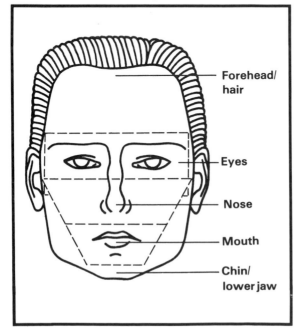

In the early hours of a November morning two men forced their way into the home of the Barn Restaurant owner at Braintree, Essex, where in the course of robbery one of them shot dead his wife. Photofit pictures of the gunman were prepared from witnesses' descriptions, and as a result George Ince was picked out of an identification parade and sent for trial. There was virtually no supporting forensic evidence, and the trial was conducted almost entirely on matters of identification. The jury failed to reach agreement, and a retrial was ordered. At the second trial Ince's alibi was confirmed, and he was found not guilty. Shortly afterwards an incident occurred which put the original identification into bad light. Two men were located at a Lake District hotel, and as a result of FIREARMS evidence a gun belonging to one of them proved to be the weapon used in the Barn Murder. They admitted taking part in the robbery at the restaurant, and at the third Barn Murder trial one was convicted of murder and the other of MANSLAUGHTER.

The identification of individuals in murder investigation is not confined to the living — there are always the remains of the victims' corpses to be considered. The murderer may leave his victim's body intact, or he may choose to mutilate it and disperse parts of it. Intact bodies offer the best chance of speedy identification from their physical characteristics, clothing, surroundings and personal belongings. Portions of bodies and corpses undergoing DECOMPOSITION make identification correspondingly more difficult.

Where a murder victim is not immediately recognizable from appearance or belongings, a full description is prepared taking account of such obvious physical characteristics as sex, age and stature. Social background and occupation may be apparent from an examination of the clothing and personal effects. Other evidence is adduced from fingerprints, scars, tattoos and BLOOD group, all of which help to build up a working description which can be publicized and checked with MISSING PERSONS information.

Where the body is incomplete, or has been reduced to a skeleton, the application of various forensic methods can produce vital identification information. Sex, age and stature, for example, are determined from measurements made of the long bones, pelvis and skull. Evidence of fractures or disease in the bones also helps to individualize the remains, but the best evidence lies in the TEETH. Forensic dentistry has made considerable progress over recent years, and dental characteristics have become a routine method for identifying disaster victims.

Efforts on the murderer's part to render identification of his victim impossible can also be defeated. Facial disfigurement of murder victims is quite common, and Dr Buck Ruxton, for example, went to considerable trouble to remove the teeth from one victim and the eyes from another. A portrait photograph of Mrs Ruxton was superimposed on an X-ray photograph of the skull thought to be hers. The match was uncanny, and reflects the close correspondence between facial features and the underlying bone structure of the skull (see under SKULLS for a full account).

Memory and description remain at the heart of modern identification procedures. The formal identification parade or line-up is used routinely by police forces as a method which allows an eye-witness to a crime to test his recollection of a suspect. In Britain the Home Office lays down strict rules for the conduct of ID parades, but mistakes are made, as demonstrated in the Barn murder case. Description is fallible, but the police must continue to tap the visual recollection of persons who have witnessed a crime and endeavour to recreate a visual image to assist their investigations. Eye-witness testimony may provide the first vital lead in a murder inquiry, but the danger, well recognized, lies in bringing in convictions on identification alone.

16, 67, 97, 143, 217, 222, 229, 242, **257,** *277, 387,* **544, 572,** *598, 633, 646,* **673, 727.**

INFANTICIDE

The destruction of weak or disfigured children has its origins in superstition and was practised by the Eskimos and Australian aborigines. Infanticide has also been widely practised as a form of population control and, in Europe, as a means of disposing of unwanted and illegitimate children. It has been said that during the seventeenth century the killing of bastard children was as common as abortion was rare. In England during the reign of James I it was found necessary to pass an Act making it MURDER for a mother to kill an illegitimate child.

Technically, until the Infanticide Act of 1938, a mother who killed her child was charged with murder, and judges were obliged to pass sentence of death. In practice, for many years leading up to the new Act, sentence was never carried out. The 1938 Act recognized that a mother who killed her newly born infant out of distress or inexperience lacked the MENS REA, or guilty intent, which applied to murder, and therefore required special consideration. As a result of this new law, a mother who killed her child under the age of twelve months was punished as if she were guilty of MANSLAUGHTER. Only the mother can be charged with infanticide — any other person assisting in the act of killing is liable to be charged with murder (see under CHILD-MURDER). The Act does not apply in Scotland, where the murder of a child by its mother is treated as culpable HOMICIDE.

The medical aspects of infanticide rest on whether the infant had a separate existence, and whether it died as a result of a wilful act or omission by the mother. In law a child is regarded as having an independent life when it has passed from its mother's body and breathed or shown some other indication of separate existence. The charge of infanticide cannot be made unless separate existence is shown, and there must also be visible evidence of the wilful omission of proper attention to the infant, or of deliberate harm done to it. Common injuries which cause death are due to SUFFOCATION, STRANGULATION and blows to the head. DROWNING is also encountered as a cause of death in cases of infanticide. (See also under ASPHYXIA.)

448, **625.**

INTERPOL

It was obvious at the turn of the century that the variety of crime and ease with which criminals could move between countries needed to be matched by international co-operation between the world's police organizations. As early as 1864 train murderer Franz Müller was brought back to England from New York after he had taken passage across the Atlantic. This was made possible by the investigating officers pursuing their quarry in a faster ship, a device repeated in 1910 when Dr Crippen was apprehended, his capture aided by the use of wireless.

The first international meeting of criminal police took place in Monaco in 1914, but the First World War prevented any progress. In 1923 the International Criminal Police Commission (ICPC) was created, following a conference in Vienna. World war again impeded progress, and it was not until 1946 that the ICPC — or Interpol as it was to be internationally known — really began to fulfil its originators' aims. In that year, under the presidency of F. E. Louwage, Inspector-General of the Belgian Police, Interpol became established with its headquarters in Paris in the SÛRETÉ building. In 1956 its name changed to International Criminal Police Organisation.

The objective of Interpol is to co-ordinate the fight against crime by encouraging assistance between the police forces of different countries. Interpol is not itself a world police force, and its consititution expressly excludes involvement in political, religious, military or racial activities. Its prime role is to act as a co-ordinating centre for information, enabling its member nations to track crime beyond their national borders. Its radio-communications centre in Paris is equipped with powerful transmitters which keep in touch with twenty regional centres in Europe, the Middle East, North Africa and South America. Interpol's criminal records office holds files on top criminals, and also records details of passports, car registrations, stolen property and MISSING PERSONS.

Each member country has a National Central Bureau which deals with Interpol affairs, exchanging information and undertaking such police operations on behalf of another country as its own laws will permit. SCOTLAND YARD is Britain's Bureau, but, strangely, the United States FEDERAL BUREAU OF INVESTIGATION is not a National Central Bureau, although the US Bureau of Narcotics works closely with Interpol on international drug-trafficking.

Interpol publishes an official journal *International Criminal Police Review*, to distribute information to over a hundred member countries. It is particularly active in the field of drug-control, and has gained agreement with the UN on extradition procedures in connection with trafficking offences. National bureaux in France, Italy and Turkey have successfully co-ordinated their efforts against the illicit drug trade, and millions of dollars' worth of hard drugs are confiscated annually as a result. *224, 367, 684.*

J

JACK THE RIPPER

Jack the Ripper is probably history's most talked about, and certainly its most written about, murderer. The Ripper's name, synonymous with horrific murder, has become part of the folk-lore of crime, and his exploits represent a kind of universal standard against which other murders are measured — the Yorkshire Ripper, for example.

From a criminological point of view, Jack the Ripper is important in that his butchery of five East End prostitutes in London in 1888 established SEX MURDER as a particularly brutal type of killing. It is one in which the normal sex drive goes into reverse and satisfaction is sought through mutilation and destruction. Had he been caught, the mental specialists of the time would have had a field day with one of crime's greatest PSYCHOPATHS. As it was, he defied capture, and his mental health, like his identity, remains a mystery.

Medically speaking Jack the Ripper is signi-

ficant as the prime exponent of the CUT-THROAT. He probably killed his victims as they lay on the ground, insensible from partial STRANGULATION. The Ripper was also adept with the knife as a tool of dissection. The debate continues on the question of whether or not he exhibited any medical skill in his mutilation. At least some of the doctors who examined his victims thought he did. The fact that he removed the uterus from one victim and the kidney from another has been widely commented on as an example of fetishism.

From the viewpoint of the document-examiner, the Ripper's letters (if indeed they were not hoaxes) offer intriguing material for analysis. The character of the sender of the famous letter sent 'From Hell' to Mr Lusk along with a piece of kidney and signed 'Catch me when you can' has been diagnosed from the spiky writing as aggressively psychopathic. As far as the police are concerned, the Ripper killings remain unsolved. The real detective talent of the day was hampered by

Ripper victim Catherine Eddowes, from sketch made on the scene

Ripper victim Marie Kelly

bungling superiors who lacked vision and strategy and had little expectation of finding the murderer. Beyond recognizing bloodstains for what they were, the police had no FORENSIC SCIENCE to turn to for assistance. Their sole source of technical advice was provided by the doctors who examined the victims, and their interpretations of the wounds were often conflicting.

For his part, the Ripper used all the cunning

Catherine Eddowes

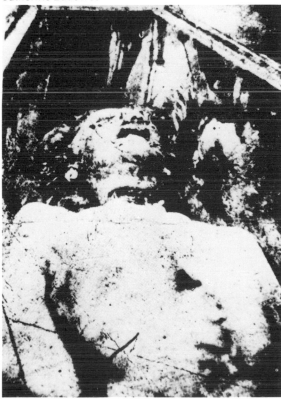

later associated with the sex-murderer. He knew his territory, lured his victims into quiet traps and quickly dispatched them — a pattern echoed over ninety years later by Peter Sutcliffe, the Yorkshire Ripper, who killed thirteen women. Not for these killers were there the complications of disposing of the bodies — they lay where they fell in dark, dingy alleys. London's East End was saturated with police and plain-clothes detectives after the earlier murders, but still the Ripper managed to repeat his horrors until, strangely, the killing stopped in November 1888. It has been suggested that some calamitous event, such as suicide, occurred to restrain his murder lust. Certainly he belonged to that band of killers who do not stop of their own choosing.

More ink has been used to expound theories on the Ripper's identity than on any other criminal matter, yet confirmation remains tantalizingly remote. Known murderers such as Neill Cream, George Chapman and Frederick Deeming have been suggested as candidates for the Ripper and, from the realms of speculation, further identities have included the Duke of Clarence, Dr Stanley, J. K. Stephen, M. J. Druitt, Sir William Gull and Dr Alexander Pedachenko. Unnamed identities and selected occupations have been drawn from among doctors, slaughtermen, midwives, Black Magicians and Freemasons.

Jack the Ripper has inspired a literature so vast that it has its own bibliography. Most is speculation, but the range is impressive in its artforms — plays, films, books and ballet — and also in its imaginative scope, which embraces everything from abortion to witchcraft. What is certain is that Jack the Ripper created a murder syndrome which in his day was judged to be without MOTIVE, but which today we know as sex murder. While other

murderers come and go, the Ripper, as criminologist Richard Whittington-Egan has aptly put it, 'remains, fresh as new-spilt blood, talked about, speculated upon and, every few months it seems, "finally" and "definitively" identified'.
38, 114, 116, 157, 176, 189, 212, 312, 384, 392, 406, 425, 475, 476, 488, 522, 592, 643, 650, 722, 742.

Jack the Ripper Murders: Doctors and victims

	Nicholls	Chapman	Stride	Eddowes	Kelly
Dr Llewellyn	★				
Dr Phillips		★	★	★	★
Dr Blackwell			★		
Dr Brown				★	
Dr Sequiera				★	
Dr Saunders				★	
Dr Bond					★

Victim	Throat Wound	Bruises	Circumstances of Death	Mutilations	Doctors' Comments on Injuries
Mary NICHOLLS 31 August 1888	Cut from left to right in two gashes.	Bruising along lower edge of right jaw; circular bruise, left side of face.	Killed where found. No cry or shout.	Abdomen slashed.	'Deftly and skilfully performed.' (Dr Llewellyn)
Annie CHAPMAN 8 September 1888	Cut from left to right back to spine.	Chin and sides of jaw bruised as result of brawl. Face and tongue swollen.	No signs of struggle.	Disembowelled; uterus missing.	'Obviously the work was that of an expert — or one, at least, who had such knowledge of anatomical or pathological examinations as to be enabled to secure the pelvic organs with one sweep of the knife.' (Dr Phillips)
Elizabeth STRIDE 30 September 1888	Cut from left to right.	Bruising over both shoulders. No marks of gagging, no facial bruises.	Throat cut when victim lying on ground. No signs of struggle, no shout or cry.	No mutilation.	—
Catherine EDDOWES 30 September 1888	Cut from left to right.	—	Throat cut when victim lying on ground. No cry.	Abdomen laid open. One kidney and uterus missing. Also facial cuts.	'A good deal of knowledge as to the position of the organs in the abdominal cavity.' (Dr Brown) 'No stranger to the knife.' (Dr Sequiera)
Marie KELLY 9 November 1888	Cut from left to right.	—	Killed while lying on bed. No evidence of struggle — clothing neatly piled on bed.	Extensive mutilation of body and facial disfigurement.	'No scientific or anatomical knowledge.' (Dr Bond)

JURY SYSTEM

Juries have been part of English legal procedure since the twelfth century. It was the custom of the King's Council (Curia Regis) to send for representatives of the local community to assist the judges by telling them what they knew of a particular local case, and informing them of any relevant customs. In due course the system was formalized with the election of sworn men or juries (from the French *juré*, meaning sworn) to meet the assize judges sent out into the country by the King's Council to try important cases. One of the main functions of the jury was to bring accused persons before the judges for proceedings which were often conducted on the trial by ordeal principle. (See under THIRD DEGREE.)

Initially, juries were used to assist the government, but by the fifteenth century their role had changed to one of independence of both the judiciary and the government. The system evolved into a method of safeguarding individual freedom, and the jury — usually a body of twelve persons — was sworn to decide questions of fact according to the evidence, while accepting the judge's direction

Jurymen resting at Palmer's trial in 1856

on questions of law. Thus the jury assumed responsibility for deciding the issue of guilt or innocence and the judge passed sentence according to their verdict. The jury retires alone to consider its verdict, and if it so decides may bring in a verdict contrary to the judge's summing-up.

The jury system is taken to represent the common-sense view of ordinary people in considering criminal accusations with the advantage that the public can see that justice is done. Until 1967 it was the case under English law that a jury verdict must be unanimous, but following the Criminal Justice Act of that year, majority verdicts were permitted. Qualification for serving on a jury is that of citizenship, denoted by inclusion in the Electoral Register within the age limits of 18 to 65. Exceptions include peers, judges, Members of Parliament, policemen, mentally ill persons, solicitors, medical practitioners and ex-prisoners.

The grand jury — so named to distinguish it from lesser juries — has its origins in the ancient concept of members of a community meeting together to consider the case against a suspected neighbour. The grand-jury system is practised in the United States, and is founded in the Fifth Amendment to the Constitution, whereby a person cannot be held to answer a capital crime unless indicted by a grand jury. Twelve, or sometimes twenty-three, persons are sworn to make inquiries about a crime, to keep the proceedings secret and to make no charges out of malice. The prosecution presents a bill or written accusation to the grand jury with supporting evidence. If a majority of the jurors consider the charge is supported by the evidence, and thus to warrant a trial, they will find a 'true bill', which in turn becomes an indictment. Alternatively, they may find 'no bill' or may decline to take any action at all.

The grand jury system was abolished in England in 1933 because it was thought to favour prosecution, and in the USA it has been argued that the powers of the grand jury have been abused for political ends. There, members of a jury are selected by a process known as *voir dire*. Prospective

jurors are questioned by the lawyers representing the defence and prosecution to determine if they will 'speak the truth', which is the meaning of *voir dire*. The term, which originates in French law, is also applied to the so-called 'trial within a trial' when a judge suspends the normal proceedings of the court in order to examine a procedural issue. A *voir dire* was called by the judge during the controversial trial of Steven Truscott, who was charged with RAPE murder in Canada in 1959. The argument, conducted in the absence of the jury, concerned the admissibility of EVIDENCE regarding the medical examination of the suspect. The judge ruled that statements made by the accused were inadmissible, but he allowed the doctors to present their testimony. (See under STOMACH CONTENTS for an account of this case.)
423, 472, 681.

KIDNAPPING

'Your boy has been kidnapped get $600,000 in $20s — $10s — Fed. Res. notes. . . .' This was part of the terse ransom note received by Robert Greenlease in September 1953. His six-year-old son Bobby had been abducted during the previous day from his school in Kansas City. The boy had been taken away by a woman claiming to be his aunt, and alleging that his mother had been rushed to hospital. This deception was uncovered when the school authorities telephoned the hospital and learned that Mrs Greenlease was not a patient.

The ransom demand was the highest in American history, but effective action by the FEDERAL BUREAU OF INVESTIGATION was delayed on account of the Lindbergh Law enacted in 1932, which required seven days to elapse before the FBI could act. Meanwhile the local police carried out their own inquiries, and the kidnappers played a cruel game of cat and mouse with the anxious parents. On 4 October, following the kidnappers' instructions, a duffel bag containing 600,000 dollars in notes was placed at a designated spot by a road bridge. The Greenlease family received a call telling them the money had been collected but not yet counted — the missing child was not returned.

Two days later a St Louis cab-driver reported to the police that he had carried a passenger who, in a state of drunkenness, had talked about the kidnapping. Following this lead, the police arrested Carl Austin Hall in a matter of hours, and also his companion, Bonnie B. Heady. Hall made a CONFESSION in which he admitted killing the child shortly after he was abducted from his school. At a deserted farm Hall attempted to strangle the boy, but when he struggled shot him to death. With Heady's help he buried the corpse, and the evil pair then set about torturing the Greenlease family with their ransom demands.

Having squandered a considerable inheritance, Hall had taken to drugs and alcohol and embarked on a criminal career. After his release from prison he met Bonnie Heady, a woman who shared his appetite for both crime and drink. They dreamed up the idea of kidnapping the son of a wealthy Kansas citizen in order to set them up with funds. They revelled in the commission of their crime, which was conducted with sadistic enjoyment. Heady claimed not to have been involved in the killing, but she and Hall were found guilty of kidnapping for ransom and were sentenced to death. They perished together in the GAS CHAMBER at the Jefferson City State Penitentiary in December 1953. Half of the ransom money was recovered but the remaining 300,000 dollars was never located. Following this case the Lindbergh Law of 1932 was changed, allowing the FBI to bring its full investigative resources to bear immediately in kidnap cases.

Kidnapping is a slang expression coined in England about 1860 to describe the practice of seizing children and sending them to serve as slaves on the British plantations in America. Another form of kidnapping was the practice of 'pressing' or 'shanghaiing' sailors which was well established throughout Europe and in seaports around the world. Kidnapping was thus an activity designed to force individuals into involuntary servitude, or, as later developments demonstrated, to hold hostages as a means of raising

To All Law Enforcement Officials, Wardens of Penal Institutions, Etc

Reproduced below will be found specimens of the handwriting represented by **two note** transmitted by the alleged kidnapers in the Lindbergh case:

The Lindbergh ransom note

ransom money. This latter form of kidnapping was prevalent in the Mediterranean countries where groups of bandits saw easy ways of making money. The Dilessi murders in Greece in 1870 caused a stir throughout Europe when Lord Muncaster and three tourist companions were murdered by brigands after the authorities refused to meet their ransom demands.

In America the growth of organized crime in the 1920s encouraged the practice of kidnapping, despite Pennsylvania's enactment of the first laws against the crime as early as 1875. The underworld saw easy pickings in abducting wealthy persons from their comfortable surroundings and charging high ransoms to their families. This was often found to produce better cash returns than robbing banks, and involved fewer risks. In 1931 kidnappings in the USA reached a total of 279, and the fashion for this crime reached its peak in 1932 with the abduction and murder of the infant son of Charles Lindbergh, the world-famous aviator. This crime was to prove a watershed in American criminal history.

On 1 March 1932 the Lindberghs' son was taken from his bed in their New Jersey home. The kidnapper had used a ladder to gain access through a second-floor window, taking the child and leaving a ransom note demanding 50,000 dollars. A second ransom note was received increasing the demand to 70,000, and Dr John F. Condon, a friend of the Lindberghs, announced in the newspaper columns

that he was willing to act as negotiator. A further note was sent to Condon by the kidnapper acknowledging his role as go-between. After weeks of anxious delays and the passing of more ransom notes, Condon met a man called 'John' in the Bronx to whom he gave 50,000 dollars in exchange for the information that the missing child would be found on board a boat called *Nellie* near Martha's Vineyard in Massachusetts. His heart full of hope, Colonel Lindbergh and his friend searched for the *Nellie*, only to return without his son and the bitter victim of a hoax. The body of the kidnapped child was found in an advanced stage of DECOMPOSITION at a spot about five miles from the Lindbergh home in May 1932. The boy had been killed by a blow to the head, and had been dead for about two months.

The ransom notes were examined by Albert Osborn, a well-known examiner of QUESTIONED DOCUMENTS, who concluded that the writer was a person of German origin. A truly remarkable piece of detective work arose from expert examination of the 'do-it-yourself' wooden ladder used by the kidnapper to gain access to the upper floor of his victim's house. Arthur Koehler of the US Forest Products Laboratory traced the preparation of the wood used to make the sectional ladder to a particular type of planing machine. He discovered that over 1,500 American timber-yards used this type of machine, but, undaunted, he asked each to produce a sample of wood prepared on this equipment. By comparing the samples microscopically

The ladder used to effect the kidnapping of the Lindbergh baby

with the wood used to make the ladder he traced the source of the timber to a New York retailer. The blade which machined the wood had in it imperfections which flawed the wood, leaving a unique set of markings.

This information pointed to New York as the likely home of the kidnapper, and when some of the ransom money turned up in Harlem the police began to close in on their quarry. The kidnapper then made his final mistake when he handed a filling-station attendant a ten-dollar gold certificate as payment for gasoline. Most of the Lindbergh ransom had been paid in notes which it was possible to convert to gold, but on 1 May 1934 President Roosevelt abandoned the gold standard and the gold certificates were called in. Thus the kidnapper gave himself away by using illegal currency. The filling-station attendant noted his vehicle licence number and reported the transaction to the bank. The note was quickly identified as part of the Lindbergh ransom, and on 19 September 1934, Bruno Richard Hauptmann, a former German soldier who had entered the country

illegally, was arrested outside his Bronx apartment.

Part of the ransom money was found in Hauptmann's apartment, and his handwriting was shown to match that on the ransom note. He was tried for murder in January 1935, and, strongly protesting his innocence, was pronounced guilty. He was sent to the ELECTRIC CHAIR on 3 April 1936 for a crime which changed the law. Following a public outcry at the abduction of the Lindbergh child, it was made a federal offence to transport a kidnapped person across a state line, and the death penalty was available to juries trying such cases. FBI involvement was thus permitted after seven days had elapsed and the so-called Lindbergh Law came into being which greatly curtailed the incidence of kidnapping in America.

In England kidnapping is an offence under COMMON LAW, and is committed where a person of any age is abducted against his or her will. Perhaps the most extraordinary case on record is that of the kidnapping of Mrs Muriel McKay by the Hosein brothers in 1969. Their MOTIVE was to obtain money and they set the ransom at one million pounds after kidnapping the wrong victim. By the time the Hoseins were arrested their victim's body had disappeared without trace, but they were nevertheless convicted. (See under QUESTIONED DOCUMENTS.)

Kidnapping is an international crime, and children are frequent victims. Eight-year-old Graeme Thorne was abducted in Sydney, Australia, in 1960 after an announcement that his parents had won a large sum of money on the football pools, and four-year-old Eric Peugeot, son of the French car millionaire, was kidnapped in Paris, also in 1960. The Thorne child was found murdered, but young Peugeot was returned to his parents unharmed. In both cases the kidnappers were convicted. The growth of terrorist activities around the world, and the desire to raise funds and pressurize governments, has led to a spate of kidnappings in Italy and elsewhere. A political twist has thereby been given to a criminal activity which had long been one of straightforward greed.
106, 145, 234, 266, 281, 362, 506, 514, 515, 587, 609, **671**, *701, 716, 717.*

KNIFE-WOUNDS

The Grand Master of the knife murder was JACK THE RIPPER. The body of Ann Nicholls, the first of his five victims, was found in the early hours of 31

August 1888 in Buck's Row in London's East End. Her injuries were reported in detail in the *Star*: 'The throat is cut in two gashes. . . . There is a gash under the left ear, reaching nearly to the centre of the throat. Along half its length, however, it is accompanied by another one which reaches around under the other ear, making a wide and horrible hole, and nearly severing the head from the body.'

In the hierarchy of murder weapons the knife superseded the axe and bludgeon, lending subtlety and concealment to the act of killing. Nevertheless, the use of the knife necessitates a willingness to be in contact with the victim — unlike the gun, which permits distance between the murderer and his target. The carrying of knives is part of the culture of gangland and of prison life, where concealment and the tigerish lunge are the essence of violence. Most knife-attacks involve stab-wounds — injuries resulting from cunning and passion — while the cut-throat is the savage, ritualistic blood-letting wound inflicted by the PSYCHOPATH.

Knives run a close second to guns as chosen murder weapons, especially in the closed environ-ments of the inner city and the prison. An insight into this type of violence has been provided by Jack Henry Abbott in his controversial book *In the Belly of the Beast*: 'You've pumped the knife in several times without even being aware of it. You go to the floor with him to finish him. It is like cutting into hot butter, no resistance at all.'

A curious knife murder with many unusual aspects was the killing in Cleveland, Ohio, of millionaire publisher Daniel Kaber. On the night of 18 July 1919 Kaber — who was bedridden following a stroke — was heard screaming in terror by several members of his family and household. By the time help arrived he lay in a pool of blood on the floor of his bedroom, the victim of a slashing knife attack. The bloodstained weapons lay near by — a razor and a nail-file sharpened to make a dagger. Kaber died in hospital, and in a DYING DECLARATION he referred to 'the man in the cap', and alleged, 'That woman had me killed.'

'That woman' was his wife Eva, or so it was suggested by his father, who accused her outright of murder. Eva Kaber denied the charge, and defended herself with an effective ALIBI. A CORONER's inquiry found that Kaber had been murdered by a 'person or persons unknown'. Eva

Common targets for stab-wounds

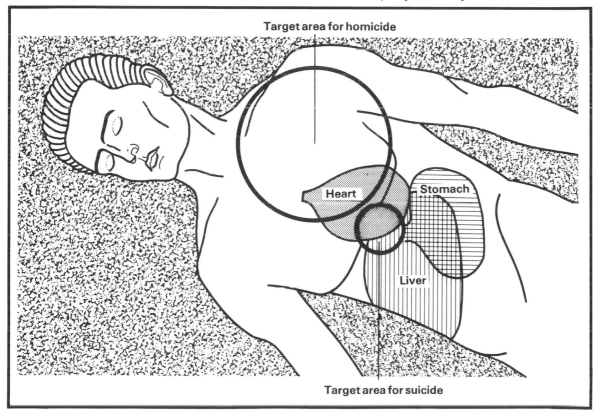

Target area for homicide

Heart

Stomach

Liver

Target area for suicide

moved to New York, but she was pursued by her father-in-law's accusations and shadowed by private detectives. Following the posting of a reward for information, two Cleveland ladies reported their willingness to act for Kaber senior.

One of these women worked her way into Eva's social circle and learned a great deal about that lady's intentions. It appeared that she had made threats against her husband and offered a 5,000-dollar contract for a HIT-AND-RUN murder. After several failed attempts to arrange a CONTRACT MURDER, she made the acquaintance of Erminia Colavito (also known as 'Big Emma'), who was a Mrs Fixit in crime circles.

An attempt was made on Daniel Kaber's life using poison, but when this subtle method failed extreme measures were decided on. Two contract killers were dispatched to the millionaire's house, where they brutally slashed him to death with knives. The police rounded up the murder gang, including Eva and 'Big Emma', and all were found guilty of murder and sentenced to life imprisonment.

Injuries made with a knife fall into two basic classes — incised wounds (cuts) and stab wounds. Because cuts are made with a sweeping movement, they are usually found on unprotected parts of the body such as the hands and face. The wound

Types of stab entry wounds

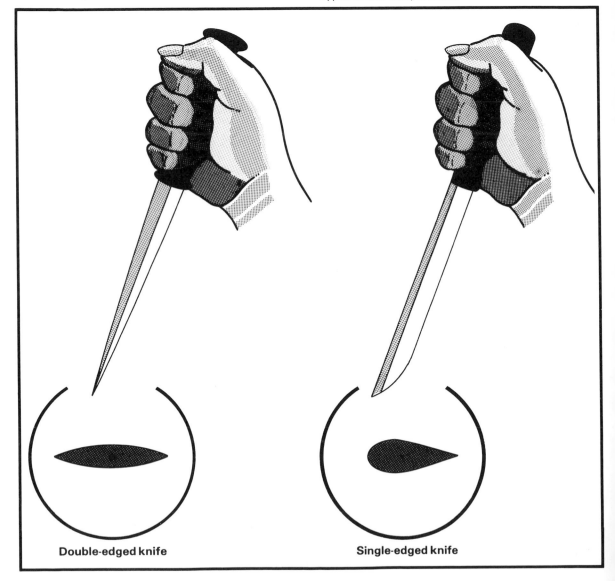

Double-edged knife

Single-edged knife

which most requires expert opinion as to whether it is self-inflicted or homicidal is the CUT-THROAT. In general, suicidal throat-cutting has a clean and deliberate appearance, whereas the homicidal cut-throat is normally crude and suggests a struggle. Since a suicide usually extends the neck before making the cut, the line of the wound is frequently transverse. This stretching action also causes the carotid arteries to slip back, thus escaping the knife and reducing the loss of BLOOD.

Stab wounds are characterized by their penetration into the body. Their points of entry are usually small slits which look relatively minor, and there is often little external bleeding. Consequently, the seriousness of such wounds can be under estimated, and in reality a single entry wound may effect great penetration and cause internal haemorrhage and death.

The weapon used in stabbing is most commonly the knife, but stab wounds can be caused by all manner of implements, including bayonets, scissors and even hat-pins. In cases of multiple stabbing it is likely that some of the entry wounds will be torn as the victim struggles under the assault, or as the knife is twisted in the body. The least torn wound will be the best indicator of the type of weapon used, and because the knife need not necessarily have penetrated to the hilt, the deepest wound will indicate only the minimum length of the knife.

The length of the entry wound is a guide to the width of the knife, but it is only an approximation, for allowance has to be made for the elasticity of the skin. Roughening or bruising around the edge of the entry wound indicates use of a relatively BLUNT INSTRUMENT such as a poker or pair of scissors. The sharper the weapon, the cleaner the wound will be.

Like cut-throats, stab-wounds may be either suicidal or homicidal, although self-inflicted stabbing is less common than throat-cutting. Homicidal stabbing, on the other hand, is a common occurrence, wounds usually being found on the neck, chest, abdomen and back. The chest is the area usually aimed for, presumably because it is the seat of the heart. Penetrating wounds of the chest frequently pierce the heart or large blood-vessels and lead to serious internal bleeding. Wounds in the neck often damage the carotid and jugular blood-vessels and cause extensive bleeding.

The distinction between suicide and HOMICIDE is usually clear. Persons bent on suicide select a 'target area' — usually over the heart — and

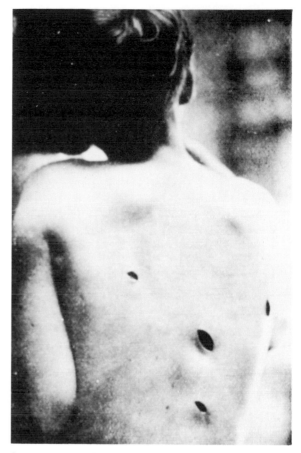

Stab-wounds inflicted on one of Peter Kürten's victims

because suicides are deliberate, the 'target area' is further narrowed down to the epigastric region. Here the heart is felt to beat strongly and there are no ribs to impede the knife. The clothing is sometimes lifted in order to make the fatal thrust easier. The wound is usually a single (or, at the most, a double) thrust with no hesitation cuts.

Stab wounds outside the general 'target area' of the heart are regarded with suspicion, especially if they have been made through the clothing. The suicidal wound must also be in an accessible part of the body. A further distinguishing feature is the likelihood of finding defensive wounds on the hands of the murder victim.

The angle of a knife-wound in the body is also important in helping to establish whether a fatal stabbing is murder or not. When Patrick Swift, an iron-worker, was found dead in the kitchen of his home at Stockton-on-Tees from a single stab-wound his wife told the police that he had stabbed himself following a drunken quarrel. There were no witnesses, and although the police were suspicious of Mrs Swift they had no evidence on which to act. However, when Sir Bernard Spilsbury, the great pathologist, made his assessment of the fatal injury it was seen in a different light. Patrick Swift was right-handed, and the angle of the stab-wound was such that he could not have stabbed himself with that hand, nor could he have mustered sufficient strength with his left hand. The knife which killed him struck him down with a piercing wound near the heart, and was forcefully wielded by a person standing facing him. In other words the death was murder, not suicide.

The knife is not only an instrument of death; it also serves the murderer intent on mutilation or dismemberment.

Dismembering a corpse is not an easy task even with the aid of a sharp knife. Cartilage and bone are tough materials, but the skilled dissector can disarticulate a corpse if he has enough time. Some even take pride in their work. Charles Avinmain, the so-called 'Butcher of the Seine', whose murder victims turned up in the river during 1867, told the police when he was caught, 'I do not wish it to be said that I dismembered my victims . . . I dissected them in a decent and proper manner. I am not a bungler.' Patrick Mahon, the Crumbles murderer, whose exploits shocked England in 1924, could not make the same boast. His attempts at dismembering his victim's body, even with the aid of a saw, were the work of desperation and brute force.

JACK THE RIPPER remains the most controversial murderer with the knife. About his perfection at cutting the throats of his victims there is no argument, but whether his mutilation and dissection demonstrated skill or not remains a subject for debate.
5, 97, 515, **625**, **627**.

L

LIE-DETECTOR

Practised liars well know that they must look their questioner straight in the eye when they tell their falsehoods. The averted eye, the slight tremor in the voice, a quickened pulse and faster breathing are all telltale signs of deception. These well-known, involuntary physiological reactions form the basis of modern lie-detection apparatus. The possibility of measuring these reactions began in 1896 with Dr Scipione Riva-Rocci's development of the pressure cuff as a means of measuring blood-pressure. In 1908 Professor Hugo Münsterberg of Harvard University made a scientific study of the correlation between deception and changes in pulse and respiration rates, and in the same year Sir James Mackenzie, the English heart specialist, invented the 'ink polarograph' heart recorder.

Since 1923 advocates of the lie-detector in the USA have campaigned to have information gained by its use accepted as evidence in court. Apart from modest success in minor cases, acceptance has not come, and controversy over the lie-detector continues. The procedure has been criticized for having insufficient scientific foundation, and also because it relies too heavily on the integrity and skill of examiners. The Chicago Bar Association, for example, took the view that over 90 per cent of lie-detector results were due less to the efficiency of the equipment than to the efficiency of examiners. Nevertheless, many government agencies and industrial corporations use lie-detectors as a standard procedure for screening job applicants.

The lie-detector, or polygraph, is a mechanical device which is attached to the subject to measure his blood-pressure and respiration. A pneumatic arm-cuff measures the former, and a flexible rubber tube fastened across the chest monitors respiration. These physiological actions are transferred by pens to moving graph paper, thus making a visible record. Increases in perspiration are also measured by means of electrodes attached to the hand. The examination is carried out in a private room free of noise and interruption. The only persons present are the subject and the examiner, who has been thoroughly briefed about the events which form the basis of the interrogation. Control questions establish the subject's normal physiological responses to giving truthful answers. Questions are then put relating to the crime under investigation, and these lead up to a peak-of-tension test. This is based on a vital aspect

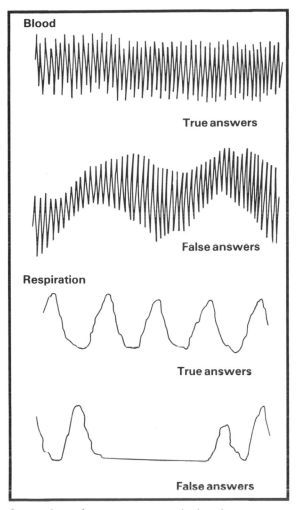

Blood

True answers

False answers

Respiration

True answers

False answers

Comparison of responses to questioning shown on blood-pressure and respiration recordings

of the crime, details of which have been withheld during the early part of the examination. A carefully structured sequence builds up to this question, which might, for example, concern the murder weapon. If the subject has guilty knowledge, his nervous tension reaches a peak when the crucial question is asked, and then subsides when the moment has passed. Interpretation of the results depends on the skill and experience of the examiner, aided by the visible evidence of any stress reaction seen in the pen-recorded traces. Three or four lie-detector tests are usually conducted, and evidence of deception in at least two is regarded as necessary for the procedure to carry any weight. That a great deal depends on the integrity and experience of the examiner has been acknowledged by the advocates of the lie-detector.

Many user agencies have been meticulous in devising codes of practice governing the conduct of tests.

Many American police departments ask suspects to submit to a voluntary lie-detector test, and the mere suggestion is often enough to produce an on-the-spot CONFESSION. Confessions obtained after a voluntary lie test (but not as part of it) have been admitted in American courts. A particular anxiety which weighs against the acceptance of the test is an individual's privilege against self-incrimination. Two murder cases demonstrate the hazards of the lie-detector. In September 1973 Barbara Gibbons was murdered at her home in Canaan, Connecticut. Her son, Peter Reilly, aged eighteen, arrived home late in the evening to find his mother lying brutally battered. She died later in hospital, and Reilly was taken into police custody under suspicion of murder. After six hours' interrogation he was given a lie-detector test, and made a confession to murder. On the basis of largely CIRCUMSTANTIAL EVIDENCE, Reilly was sent for trial at which he was found guilty of MANSLAUGHTER.

A campaign to prove Reilly's innocence was supported by playwright Arthur Miller, and Dr Milton Helpern reviewed the medical evidence. It was argued that there was no way Reilly could have carried out the act attributed to him and remain completely free of blood-traces. The value of the lie detector evidence was brought into question when Helpern pointed out that the nature of the fractures in the victim's thigh-bones was incompatible with Reilly's confession to the police. The feeling was that the youth had been confused by an authoritative examiner and admitted acts he had not committed. It was obvious that a miscarriage of justice had occurred, and Reilly was freed. The case remains an UNSOLVED MURDER.

A second celebrated American murder case featuring lie-detector evidence was that in which Dr Sam Sheppard was convicted on the basis of confusing scientific evidence (see under BLOOD for a full account).

In 1956 an attempt to stage a retrial was rejected by the US Supreme Court, but in the following year the whole affair was reawakened as a result of admissions made by a convict. Donald Wedler, serving a sentence in a Florida prison, told the authorities that he had murdered a woman in Cleveland in 1954. Wedler's confession, which referred to his attempt to burgle a lake-side house during the course of which he silenced a woman with an iron pipe, sparked off attempts to prove

Sheppard's innocence. Erle Stanley Gardner, a lawyer and crime writer, suggested Wedler be given a lie test. The examiner who conducted this was satisfied that he was telling the truth. Sheppard's brothers and their wives — who had been subjected to criticism early on in the affair — also took the tests. An impressive group of lie-detector experts concluded that they too were telling the truth, and had in no way attempted to conceal evidence. The next move was to submit Sheppard himself to the lie-detector, a procedure which his lawyer had earlier refused. Permission was granted for Sheppard to be given the lie test in the Ohio State Penitentiary, but mounting opposition led to permission being withdrawn. Disappointment was voiced by Sheppard's supporters, and also by advocates of the lie-detector, who believed, in the light of Wedler's confession, that the final step of examining Sheppard himself should have gone ahead. After ten years in prison and two years on bail, Sheppard was found not guilty.

Despite the continuing suspicion with which they are regarded in some American legal circles, lie-detection machines are being increasingly used by commercial companies around the world for security screening purposes. New techniques are also being developed, including psychological stress evaluation which monitors the slight change in voice which occurs when a person is lying. (See also under VOICEPRINTS.)

26, 39, 146, 324, 342, 552, 584, 617, 618, **635***.*

LIVIDITY

When he moved his mother's body from the bed where he strangled her to the kitchen stove where he pretended she had died of BURNING, Petrus Hauptfleisch did not bargain for the post-mortem action of the body which would give him away. In a rare case of MATRICIDE, Hauptfleisch, a slaughterer who lived in Cape Province, South Africa, killed his elderly mother and left her lying on her back. While he was deciding on DISPOSAL OF THE BODY, the blood in the corpse drained down to the lowest parts where it began to coagulate, making livid stains on the skin.

Having pondered the question of how to explain his mother's death, the murderer decided his story was that she accidentally burned to death while cleaning out the chimney of the kitchen stove with petrol. In accordance with this plan, he placed the body face down over the fireplace and doused it with petrol. He then set fire to the corpse and rushed out of the house screaming that his mother had been burned.

The dead woman was found with her face and chest badly burned and Hauptfleisch told his story to the doctor, adding that he had warned his mother against using petrol. The doctor was quick to notice post-mortem lividity on the back of the corpse which clearly indicated that death had not occurred where the body was found. The woman had died while lying face upward, and the blood had drained to the small of the back and the backs of the thighs, where it left the characteristic stains of lividity. By the time the murderer moved the body to the kitchen stove the staining was fixed, and showed that his story was false. Despite his protestations of innocence Hauptfleisch was tried for murder and found guilty. He was hanged in Cape Town in 1926.

Post-mortem lividity — also referred to as hypostasis and *livor mortis* — begins immediately after death, but is usually not apparent for three to four hours. It is fully evident after about twelve hours, when the blood coagulates in the vessels, giving rise to livid patches or staining on the skin. Lividity occurs in the underlying parts of the body which are not in contact with a hard surface or restricted by pressure from clothing, such as waistbands or collars. The characteristic sites for lividity are the back of the neck and thighs and the small of the back. The internal organs are also affected, and again the blood sinks by gravity to the lowest parts. (Shakespeare touches most aptly on the phenomenon in *Romeo and Juliet*, V, iii, 'Beauty's ensign yet/Is crimson on thy lips and in thy cheeks,/And death's pale flag is not advanced there.')

The onset of lividity is now very seldom taken into account in establishing TIME OF DEATH, for allowance has to be made for many factors which influence its appearance. For example, in cases where the corpse is obese, or where there has been great loss of BLOOD due to injury, lividity will be less apparent. It is important to distinguish between lividity and bruising, especially where violence is suspected, and this is done by cutting into the area of staining. Blood drains freely from the vessels in a livid stain, whereas in a bruise the blood is mixed with the surrounding tissues.

A murder case in which the appearance of lividity provided an early clue for the investigators occurred in 1946 when a woman's body was found by the side of the A20 Maidstone to London road

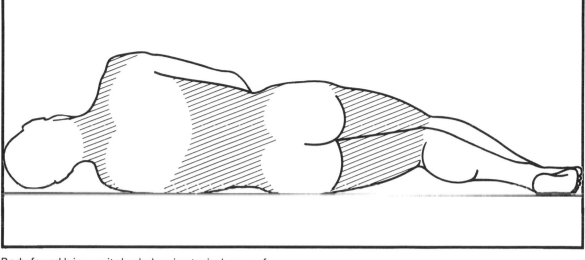

Body found lying on its back showing typical areas of lividity

at a spot in Kent called Wrotham Hill. The woman had died from STRANGULATION, and the police formed the opinion that she had been killed elsewhere and her body dumped near the roadside. The pathologist called to the scene was Dr Keith Simpson who estimated time of death at between 7 and 9 a.m. that morning. At the POST-MORTEM examination he concluded from the patches of lividity on the body that the woman had been in a sitting position when she met her death. He advised Detective Superintendent Robert Fabian of SCOTLAND YARD that the woman had been sitting on a 'fairly hard seat', or at least something less well upholstered than a car seat. This supported Fabian's hunch that the woman had hitched a lift, probably from a lorry-driver, and a police message was broadcast to trace any lorry travelling on the A20 at Wrotham Hill between 5 and 8 a.m. on the day of the murder.

Following intensive inquiries, the police were led to a brick lorry operated by a Cambridge firm and thence to its driver, Sydney Sinclair, who as Harold Hagger had several convictions to his name. Under questioning Hagger admitted giving the woman a lift and driving off the main road into a lane. He claimed that he strangled her in his cab with a scarf after she had tried to steal his wallet. Later, as the lividity on his victim's body showed, he moved the corpse and left it on Wrotham Hill. Hagger's CONFESSION combined with weighty forensic evidence at the crime scene convicted him of murder for which he was hanged.
48, 55, 210, 505, 506, **571**, *626.*

LSD

When he was arrested in British Columbia on suspicion of brutally murdering eight members of two families Dale Nelson told police, 'It must have been the LSD.' His victims included five children, one of whom, an eight-year-old girl, he took to a wood near West Creston where he carried out revolting mutilations on her body. Certainly the nature of the killings suggested the work of an unsound mind, and the murderer himself indicated the possible cause in his remark about LSD. A defence plea of insanity was nevertheless rejected at his trial in 1971, when he was found guilty of murder and sentenced to life imprisonment.

LSD, short for lysergic acid diethylamide, is a hallucinogenic drug which was discovered by a Swiss chemist in 1943. He also discovered, by accidentally breathing in some of the drug, that it caused him to hallucinate and experience unusual visual sensations. The drug, which is non-addictive, was quickly taken up by the American hippie communities, and its easy manufacture made widespread use inevitable.

LSD has a powerful effect on the nervous system, producing disorientation and feelings of euphoria. One of its characteristics is its unpredictability even in experienced users, and its ability to produce violent and psychotic behaviour. The so-called 'flash-back' is an effect in which the user experiences psychotic events two or three weeks after recovering from an LSD 'trip'.

During the flash-back the user relives the bad moments of the previous trip, experiencing anguish and depersonalization. The phenomenon of drug-induced murder has taxed the understanding of forensic psychiatrists, notably in the case of Herbert Mullin, the US mass murderer, who killed thirteen people in the early seventies. While he claimed to have been commanded to kill by voices which he heard, and was known to be a SCHIZO-PHRENIC, some of his murderous exploits were also probably fuelled by drug-taking.

A small dose of 25 micrograms of LSD is sufficient to interfere with the brain's reception of outside sensory stimulation and to produce hallucinations. As little as 1 mg of the drug results in severe toxic effects, interfering with vital functions and causing death.
452, **491**, *652*.

LYNCHING

'The executioners tied the knot around their prisoner's neck, flung the rope over a limb of the oak tree, placed Frank upon a table, and proceeded, after checking to see that everything had been done properly, to kick the table away from under the feet of the suspended figure.' Thus ran a newspaper report of the lynching of Leo Frank in Georgia in 1913. One of the lynch party said afterwards that the lynching was 'a duty of the state'. Crowds gathered around the dead man, pieces were torn from his shirt and strands of the rope which hanged him were taken as souvenirs. An attempt to mutilate the body was prevented, but one man managed to kick the head of the corpse when it was taken down by the undertakers. There

The body of Leo Frank on view after his lynching

were cries of 'Now we've got you! You won't murder any more little innocent girls. We've got you now!'

The unfortunate victim of this lynch party was Leo Frank, a 29-year-old American Jew, who was superintendent at a pencil factory in Atlanta. In April 1913 a fourteen-year-old white girl was found dead in the factory's basement — she had been strangled and beaten. A note supposed to have been written by the dead girl blamed her ill-treatment on the Negro nightwatchman who found the body. Frank, who had paid the staff, including the dead girl, was questioned by the police. Another Negro employee alleged that Frank had asked him to carry the body to the basement, and also accused him of perverted sexual practices.

Frank was put on trial for murder, but as the law of Georgia did not permit him to testify under oath the best he could do in his own defence was to refute the allegations in a statement. Contrary to expectation — no white man had previously been convicted on the testimony of a Negro — Frank was found guilty and sentenced to death. Despite threats to his life, the state governor reprieved the condemned man, and commuted his sentence to life imprisonment. This so incensed a group of fanatics pledged to the dead girl's memory that they abducted Frank from prison and drove him 175 miles to her birth-place, where they hanged him. Photographs of the body dangling at the end of the lynch mob's rope were displayed in many Georgia shops.

Lynching is mob MURDER, and not necessarily by HANGING, although that has been the most common method. The practice of lynching originated in the USA, and flourished in the southern and western states due to the primitive desire for revenge, the ineffectiveness of law enforcement in the frontier states, fear of Negro domination and the influence of evangelical religion. In the forty-six years between 1882 and 1927 nearly 5,000 persons were lynched in the USA, mostly in the ten southernmost states. The total included 3,500 coloured victims, some of whom were women.

The term 'lynching' arose from the actions of a Quaker named Charles Lynch, who was born in 1736 in the town now known as Lynchburg, Virginia. Lynch was a prominent figure in the community, and together with a number of fellow Virginians established an extra-legal court to deal with lawlessness in their state. The nearest court was 200 miles distant, and horse-stealing and other lesser crimes were rampant. The chief punishment meted out by 'Judge' Lynch was flogging, but his method of dispensing summary justice caught on in other states where the penalties were more severe. Summary courts spread, especially in the western states where law-enforcement was virtually non-existent. Thus, lynching was born, and what began as illegal but well-intended community justice deteriorated into mob violence. Alleged offenders were seized and often tortured and murdered without the benefit of any type of hearing or defence.

In the southern states the concept of lynching quickly took hold, and early ideas of vigilantism gave way to terrorism and the subjugation of the Negro population. Many of the victims were Negroes accused of RAPE but even as late as 1932 a coloured man was lynched in Louisiana for insulting two white women. While, as the case of Leo Frank demonstrates, whites also ended up as lynch victims if they fell foul of a prejudiced white community.

With the turn of the century and the growth of effective law-enforcement, the practice of lynching decreased, although a resurgence in the 1930s led to the setting up of the Southern Commission on the Study of Lynching. The commission confirmed the familiar root causes: 'sparsely settled portions of the South, where cultural and economic institutions are least stable and officers of the law are furthest apart, poorest paid and most dependent upon local sentiment'. The last reported instance of lynching in the USA was in 1954, which suggests the habit dies hard.
186, 262, 565, 719.

MACHISMO

A Spanish word denoting masculine assertion and achievement which has come into vogue in sports-writing and elsewhere. *Machismo* is demonstrated by feats of skill, strength and stamina which catch the headlines and win admiration. The prodigious feats of the record-breaking athlete or mountain climber are examples of socially acceptable assertion, but *machismo* is also talked of in relation to the tough, virile attitude of the criminal. In this sense it is public admiration at the spectacle of dominant behaviour, bravado and insolence of the kind shown by the dangerous criminal who breaks out of jail and thwarts the authorities by keeping on the run. (See also DOMINANCE THEORY.)

John McVicar, who successfully took a university course while serving a prison sentence for robbery with violence, wrote an account of his criminal background which was published in 1974. He likened the attitude of the professional criminal to playing blood sport for real and went on, 'Before anything, the professional criminal wants respect, prestige and recognition of those who subscribe to his own need of machismo.' In this way he gives vent to his aggressive instincts, and justifies them within his own social group. This is the so-called sub-culture of violence which criminologists have seen emerging, particularly in the larger American cities. It is here that the concept of machismo flourishes, and where physical violence, assault and MURDER are most evident. The roots of violence exist in social groups — usually male, middle-class and often non-white — who feel alienated from the rest of society. Feeling that they have been either deserted or victimized by the normal processes of law and order, they have developed a culture in which individuals depend on their own physical attributes for protection. Thus the individual's ability to assert himself, to be *macho*, is regarded as a virtue.
493, **658**.

MALICE AFORETHOUGHT

Part of the definition of MURDER which constitutes the guilty intent or MENS REA of the offence is malice aforethought. The term does not have the sense of the words when normally used to denote ill-will and premeditation, but implies the intention to kill or cause grievous bodily harm.

There are several types of malice, chief of which are express and implied malice. Express malice is the intention to kill or cause injury which results in death. Implied malice describes the situation in which there is no specific intention to kill but where there is a clear aim to inflict serious harm, knowing that death may result. Killing a person with malice aforethought is to commit murder, whereas the absence of malice reduces the charge

to MANSLAUGHTER.

Other classes of malice which have formed part of the definition of HOMICIDE but no longer have legal weight are transferred, universal and constructive. Transferred malice applied to the circumstances where the intention to kill one person ended up with the death of another, and universal malice was the random intention to kill. Constructive malice, whereby a killing committed in the course of robbery by a number of armed individuals resulted in a murder charge against each, was abolished under the 1957 Homicide Act. Hitherto it had been argued that as each individual in such circumstances set out with the intention of using violence if it were needed, each was guilty of murder even though only one of the number committed the act. The change in law meant that only the individual whose hand caused the killing was judged to be culpable of murder.

Thus under English law express and implied malice aforethought remain as part of the assessment of murder, although the whole concept of malice has been criticized as misleading. Death resulting from misadventure or in reasonable self-defence is judged to be without malice, and therefore not murder but EXCUSABLE HOMICIDE.
163, **510**.

MANSLAUGHTER

The killing of a person without MALICE AFORETHOUGHT is defined as manslaughter and not MURDER. Many kinds of unlawful HOMICIDE fall into this category in which death is caused unintentionally in the course of committing a crime, by culpable negligence or under strong provocation.

Manslaughter is divided into two classes, voluntary and involuntary. The first covers the situation in which, for example, passions are aroused during a quarrel and one of the participants is killed. The second can result from an unlawful act likely to cause bodily harm, an omission to perform a duty required by law or an act of criminal negligence. In each case the ACTUS REUS of homicide is lacking in malice aforethought.

The chief distinction between murder and manslaughter is the absence of malice. Manslaughter — known as culpable homicide in Scotland — is considered to be an ill-defined term, as it encompasses a variety of crimes, ranging from killings judged to be lacking in malice to those implying negligence. Mitigating circumstances which reduce murder committed with malice to a charge of manslaughter were defined under the 1957 Homicide Act as DIMINISHED RESPONSIBILITY. **510**.

MASOCHISM

Richard von Krafft-Ebing (1840–1902), Professor of Psychiatry at the University of Vienna, was a pioneering authority on the causes of mental illnesses, especially those concerning sexual deviation. His *Psychopathia Sexualis*, published in 1886, was the first scientific account to appear in this little understood field of sexual aberration.

He coined the word masochism to denote the type of perversion in which sexual gratification is obtained or increased by the suffering of pain and humiliation. The significance of masochism — which is the opposite of SADISM — is that invited cruelty can lead to death at the hands of another person. There are cases in which masochists have effectively committed self-murder, and Krafft-Ebing wrote that 'in its extreme consequences masochism must lead to the desire to be killed by a person of the opposite sex in the same way that sadism has its acme in lust murder'.

Masochism owes its name to Leopold von Sacher-Masoch (1836–95), an Austrian novelist who found that his literary efforts were enhanced by experiencing pain at the hands of his wife, whom he asked to whip him. His stories, not surprisingly, abound with sequences devoted to torture and subjugation. In his *Venus in Furs* the hero is beaten by his wife's lover and driven to perverted delights. 'The sensation of being whipped by a successful rival before the eyes of an adored woman cannot be described', he wrote.

Sacher-Masoch's pursuit of the erotic and perverted experience was insatiable, and he sought ever heightened pleasures by being flailed with hooked whips, cut with razor blades and spiked with sharp needles. He did not make old age, but died aged fifty-nine after a lifetime devoted to pain and punishment. His legacy was to give his name to a perverted practice which until his time had not been defined by medical science.
409.

MASS MURDER

Burke and Hare, Edinburgh's infamous body-snatchers of the nineteenth century, were

Some mass murderers who claimed ten or more victims with a note on their motives.

DATE	NAME	COUNTRY	MINIMUM NO. OF VICTIMS	MOTIVE
1829	Burke and Hare	Scotland	16	gain
1873	Mary Ann Cotton	England	15	gain/elimination
1895	H. H. Holmes	USA	27	gain/elimination
1908	Belle Gunness	USA	14	gain
1921	Henri Landru	France	11	gain
1924	Fritz Haarmann	Germany	27	gain
1927	Earle Nelson	USA	22	sex
1928	Carl Panzram	USA	21	revenge/elimination
1944	Marcel Petiot	France	27	gain
1948	Sadamichi Hirasawa	Japan	12	gain
1949	Howard Unruh	USA	13	psychopath
1958	Charles Starkweather	USA	11	psychopath
1964	Albert DeSalvo	USA	13	sex
1966	Charles Whitman	USA	16	deranged
1973	Dean Corll	USA	27	sex
1973	Edmund Kemper	USA	10	sex
1973	Herbert Mullin	USA	13	deranged
1979	John Wayne Gacy	USA	32	sex
1980	Peter Sutcliffe	England	13	sex

IN THIS TRUCK IS A MAN WHOSE LATENT GENIUS IF UNLEASHED WOULD ROCK THE NATION, WHOSE DYNAMIC ENERGY WOULD OVERPOWER THOSE AROUND HIM. BETTER LET HIM SLEEP?

Notice written by Peter Sutcliffe and displayed in the cab of his lorry

supposed to have murdered sixteen persons, delivering up the corpses for dissection at Dr Robert Knox's medical school for a ghoulish fee. They were trend-setters in the field of mass murder, not only in terms of the numbers of their victims but also in the pursuance of an undeniably base, yet understandable, MOTIVE — gain. The next hundred years saw the notorious mass murderers, Mary Ann Cotton, H. H. Holmes, Belle Gunness, and Henri Landru, who between them disposed of over seventy victims for reasons of gain or straightforward elimination. Since their day mass murder has become the business of the lone killer, striking with alarming frequency and for complex motives. L. C. Douthwaite in his book *Mass Murder* published in 1928, explained that once the barrier holding back the impulses of sex and acquisition is crossed, and murder is committed for the first time, compulsion to continue takes over. As he put it, 'murder grows by what it feeds upon'. This is certainly borne out by the increasing frequency of multiple killings over the last fifty years, which suggests that murderers are simply not satisfied with one victim.

The accompanying league table of mass murderers who claimed ten or more victims includes only two women, Cotton and Gunness, and shows, with the progression of years, that the simple murder for gain of Burke and Hare becomes murder for sexual motives with the Yorkshire Ripper. America dominates this catalogue, as does swift mass murder with FIREARMS — for example, Whitman's sixteen killings in a single day. Double and triple killings and other multiples are so common that even the Son of Sam with his six murders does not feature in the company of the major multicides.

Mass murder has become a phenomenon of twentieth-century crime and a new terminology has been developed to describe it. Murders are 'random', committed 'stranger to stranger' and motivated by 'manic sex impulses'. The killers have become drug-enhanced 'psycho' or 'whacko' personalities. The problem is highlighted in the USA, where gun ownership is increasing at the rate of three million weapons a year, where many city police forces are under strength and where the court system is criticized for being too weak.

1, 13, 20, 21, 44, 78, 129, 151, 155, 174, 191, 227, 228, 247, 261, 281, 288, 292, 298, 302, 403, 414, 434, 439, 451, 514, 515, 519, 529, **569***, 577, 648, 689.*

MATRICIDE

Killing of a mother by her son is among the least frequent types of murder. Criminological studies of matricide suggest that such killers are usually excessively attached to their mothers and that the act of murder is a demonstration of their independence. This hostile act, which has been likened to a cutting of the umbilical cord, has its origins in Greek tragedy, and for that reason has been called the Orestes complex. Orestes' father, Agamemnon, was murdered by his mother, Clytemnestra, and her lover. When he reached manhood Orestes consulted the Delphic Oracle as to whether he should avenge his father's death. Armed with the Oracle's justification and with a sword, he and his sister, Electra, set out on their mission of revenge. First Clytemnestra's lover was struck down and then Orestes beheaded his mother. Orestes was pursued by the Furies, but was eventually reprieved by judgment of the gods. No such luck befell teenagers Theresa Gresh and Billy Meyers, charged in 1954 with murdering Theresa's mother. Mrs Gresh's body was found in the bath of her Manhattan apartment. She had been bludgeoned and slashed twenty-one times, six thrusts penetrating the heart. When the smell of the decaying corpse became unbearable the body was put in the bath and sealed over with plaster of Paris.

Theresa and Billy were charged with first-degree MURDER and referred for psychiatric examination. The girl had led a lonely life following the break-up of her parents' marriage. She was immature and suggestible, and had established no close relationships until Billy came along. Seventeen-year-old Billy was a Marine who had a background of illegitimacy and over-compensation by his mother. Theresa gave herself to him completely, and she admitted that they engaged in daily bouts of sex. Billy wanted to marry, but Theresa's mother stood in the way by her refusal to entertain the prospect. According to him, Theresa murdered her mother, and his contribution was to seal the body in the bath. Theresa admitted complicity, but said that Billy did the killing. A great deal of the trial was taken up with psychiatric evidence, and both accused were called to testify. Each blamed the other for planning and carrying out the murder. For Theresa it was argued that she was in an excitable state due to EPILEPSY, and for Billy that he was suffering from SCHIZOPHRENIA. Theresa Gresh was convicted of second-degree murder and sentenced to 20 years'

imprisonment; Billy Beyers was sent to the ELECTRIC CHAIR.

Hatred of women and homosexuality are factors which often lurk in the background of the Orestes complex. Edmund Kemper, the co-ed killer, certainly harboured a hatred for women, and included in his trail of destruction was the murder of his mother followed by decapitation. In his case his mother recognized the sadist in her offspring, but Mrs Fox probably saw only the loving child in her son until he strangled her. Sidney Fox was a homosexual who travelled about England with his elderly mother, providing for their needs by fraud. In April 1929 Fox insured his mother's life against accidental death, and six months later murdered her in a Margate hotel room with only twenty minutes to run on the insurance policy. His attempt to create a diversion by starting a fire under the old lady's chair did not save him. (See under POST-MORTEM for a full account.)
*1, 12, 126, 129, 154, 219, 306, 346, 386, 407, 483, 515, **622**.*

MEDICAL JURISPRUDENCE

The application of every branch of medical knowledge to meet the needs of the law is known as medical jurisprudence, although the term FORENSIC MEDICINE is in more common use. The first professorship in medical jurisprudence in the English-speaking world was created by George III in 1807 at Edinburgh University. The appointment was filled by Andrew Duncan junior, whose father, Professor of Physiology at the same university, was one of the first doctors in Britain to turn his attention to the legal aspects of medicine.

The first book on the subject in English was written by Samuel Farr and published in 1788. The application of medical knowledge to both civil and criminal branches of the law and to the legal responsibilities and ethical conduct of doctors was the subject of numerous treatises published during the next seventy-five years. The first comprehensive book was written by Professor Alfred Swaine Taylor, and published as *Principles and Practice of Medical Jurisprudence* in 1865.

The Scottish universities at Edinburgh and Glasgow led the field in legal medicine in Britain and established famous father-and-son professorial successions — the Duncans and Littlejohns at Edinburgh, and at Glasgow John Glaister senior and junior, who between them held the chair for sixty-five years. A family tradition

also marked the beginnings of medical jurisprudence in America, where the brothers T. R. and J. B. Beck ushered in major advances in thinking. Their *Elements of Medical Jurisprudence*, which appeared in 1823, was the first major American work of its kind, and was the equal of most other works on forensic medicine published up to that time.
117, 571.

MENS REA

Literally translated, *mens rea* means 'guilty mind', and refers to the long-established concept that there cannot be a criminal act (ACTUS REUS) without criminal intent. This has been an important factor in discussions of criminal responsibility since the thirteenth century.

In MURDER guilty intention is described as MALICE AFORETHOUGHT, which distinguishes it from MANSLAUGHTER. There have been numerous attempts to define the nature of guilty intent, and the view held at one time that everyone except a madman was responsible for his actions has given way to definitions of mental states and degrees of responsibility.

The M'NAGHTEN RULES were drawn up in 1843 to define the grounds on which an accused could be judged not guilty of a crime by reason of insanity. Consequently, a person judged to be within these rules is held to be without criminal intent or *mens rea*. Criminal law puts considerable emphasis on *mens rea*, and the problem has lain in determining what mentally deranged states of mind absolve an accused from responsibility. It is a recognizable defence that a person can deny responsibility on the grounds of AUTOMATISM, and in England the Homicide Act of 1957 introduced the concept of DIMINISHED RESPONSIBILITY. When successfully pleaded this reduces the charge of murder to one of manslaughter. In the USA successive refinements made to the M'Naghten Rules have led to the idea of irresistible impulse, which also lessens the degree of criminal responsibility.
510.

MERCURY

On 23 December 1898 Harry Cornish, athletic director of the Knickerbocker Club in New York, received an unexpected gift. A small package arrived anonymously through the mail. It contained a bottle of Bromo-Seltzer, which he thought was a leg-pull in view of the imminent Christmas festivities.

He took the bottle home to his apartment, where he lodged with elderly Mrs Katherine Adams and her married daughter. A few days after Christmas Mrs Adams woke up with a severe headache, and, remembering the bottle of Bromo-Seltzer, asked Cornish to make her up a draught. She drank the mixture, remarking that it tasted bitter. Within minutes she was violently ill, and within half an hour she was dead. Analysis of the anonymous gift of Bromo-Seltzer showed that the innocuous salts contained mercuric CYANIDE.

In the ensuing discussion about Mrs Adams's sudden death it was recalled that six weeks previously a member of the Knickerbocker Club had also died in mysterious circumstances after receiving a bottle of medicine through the post. EXHUMATION of this man's body showed the validity of the comparison, for he too had been poisoned with mercuric cyanide. The handwriting on the package sent to Cornish came under close scrutiny, and some of the members of the Knickerbocker Club thought they recognized the style. Suspicion fell on Roland B. Molineux, a former member, who had left the club after an argument with Cornish. It was also known that he had quarrelled with the other member who died.

Molineux came from a good background — his father was an army general — and it was several weeks before the police arrested him. A grand jury declined to indict him, and it was not until July 1899 that he was eventually rearrested and put on trial for murder. The handwriting evidence linking him to the lethal package was strong, and fourteen experts testified that his writing matched that of the sender. It was also known that Molineux worked as superintendent at a dye factory where he had access to mercuric cyanide. Having established that there had been a quarrel with Cornish the prosecution believed they had effectively proved Molineux had motive, method and opportunity. The jury thought so too, and returned a guilty verdict.

Molineux spent eighteen months in Sing Sing prison before an appeal court reversed the trial verdict and set him free. A new trial was ordered and this took place in 1902. General Molineux was said to have ruined himself in paying for his son's defence, but his efforts paid off, for public opinion had turned in Roland's favour and he was acquitted. He subsequently became a minor celebrity, having written while in prison a book called

The Room with the Little Door. He died in 1917 in a hospital for the insane.

Mercury and its compounds are widely used in industry and agriculture, and they are extremely poisonous. The liquid metal gives off a poisonous vapour, and mercurial compounds may be absorbed through the skin. The most common salt is mercury bichloride (corrosive sublimate), used at one time as a disinfectant. Fatal accidental poisonings have resulted from the use of mercuric chloride as a vaginal douche. Mercury poisoning follows a similar pattern to that of ARSENIC and ANTIMONY, although its fatal use has been associated more with suicide than murder. When taken by mouth, as in the case of Mrs Adams, the immediate symptoms are burning and swelling in the mouth, followed by violent abdominal pains with vomiting and diarrhoea. A large dose may cause death through heart failure within an hour, although the victim of a fatal dose may linger for a week or so. A fatal dose may be as low as 3 to 5 grains. Both arsenic and mercury have featured in the treatment of venereal disease.

Chronic mercury poisoning leads to anaemia, gastric disorder and kidney failure. There is also inflammation of the gums, resulting in an ulcerated and foetid mouth. The teeth become loose as the gums shrink and a characteristic blue-black mercurial line may be seen on the gums. The victim may be subject to the 'shakes', or mercurial palsy. A historic case of chronic mercury poisoning was the death of Sir Thomas Overbury in the Tower of London in 1613. He was employed in an intrigue, and then slowly poisoned as an inconvenient witness while he lay confined in the Tower. *358, 404, 424, **571**, 630, 651, 656.*

MISSING PERSONS

It is still commonly supposed that a charge of MURDER cannot be brought when there is no victim's body. That this is a fallacy is borne out by the number of murderers who have been convicted without the aid of a corpse.

People disappear from their normal surroundings for a variety of reasons, most of them unconnected with any foul play. Loss of memory, mental illness, accident, desire for anonymity and simple truancy on the part of children are among the most frequent causes, but KIDNAPPING and UNDETECTED MURDER also feature. The total number of persons who disappear for all manner of reasons in the course of a year in Britain is difficult to ascertain, as there is no central co-ordination of records. Some estimates put the figures as high as 60,000 persons, of which some 6,000 cases a year are dealt with by the Salvation Army. In the USA the New York Police Department, for example, has a Missing Persons Bureau dealing with about 3,000 cases a year. A success rate of 98 per cent is claimed, which is a tribute to their well-organized methods. A large proportion of persons reported missing (about 85 per cent) eventually reappear of their own accord. Of the remainder some disappear for ever and a few turn up as unidentified victims of secret murder.

Missing persons have provided some abiding mysteries, as in the case of Ambrose J. Small, the Canadian millionaire who disappeared in Toronto in 1919 on the day he sold his theatrical empire for a down payment of a million dollars. A nationwide search and inquiries in the USA failed to locate the missing man. It was known that his wife had banked the cheque, and investigators came across an intriguing Oriental-style love nest which her husband had used secretly at his Grand Opera House.

Bodies found in various parts of North America were offered to the authorities as Ambrose Small, and there were numerous false sightings of the missing man as far south as Mexico. The floors of Small's house were taken up, the city refuse dump in Toronto was turned over, the ashes of the Grand Opera House boilers were sifted, and twenty-four years after his disappearance the debris of the opera house was examined when demolition teams tore the building down. Not a solitary trace of his remains was ever found, and he was officially declared dead in 1924. The strong presumption that he had been murdered was never substantiated.

Occasionally tantalizing pieces of a missing person turn up — for example, the human arm disgorged by a captive shark in 1935 before astonished visitors to an Australian aquarium. In cases of this type identification becomes a challenge, and the owner of the arm was named following FINGERPRINT examination and recognition of a tattoo. No further pieces of the body were found, but a sensational case developed which resulted in the killing of an important witness and an inconclusive murder trial. Sir Sydney Smith examined the arm and concluded that the body to which it had belonged had been dismembered and put in a trunk for disposal at sea. With the trunk filled with *disjecta membra*, the offending limb was left over — the solution to the problem was to rope this member to the outside of the trunk and consign the whole package to a watery grave. In time the arm worked loose and was eventually borne up from the sea by a shark, to present another murder mystery.

CIRCUMSTANTIAL EVIDENCE plays a great part in cases where the body of a presumed murder victim is missing. Edward Ball was tried for MATRICIDE in Ireland in 1936 in a remarkable case which provided ample evidence of violence but no body. Following the discovery of an abandoned car with a bloody interior, police traced the owner to a Dublin address. Mrs Vera Ball, a doctor's wife separated from her husband, was not at home; her nineteen-year-old son Edward supposed she was staying with friends.

A search of the house turned up a quantity of bloodstained clothing and bed-linen; it was also noted that the door to Mrs Ball's bedroom was locked. Once access had been gained to the room detectives discovered a large wet stain on the carpet which was being dried out with an electric fire. Adding to the suspicious circumstances was the revelation that a suitcase left with friends by young Edward contained bloody clothing.

Extensive searches failed to locate the missing woman. Edward Ball's story was that his mother, who was in a depressed state, had cut her throat in her bedroom. He found the body, and decided to dispose of it by throwing it into the sea. Despite the lack of a corpse, Ball was put on trial for murder. The argument against him was that throat-cutting as a method of committing suicide was a difficult proposition, and that the loss of blood on the carpet suggested the victim met her death there rather than on the bed. The likely murder weapon was a hatchet stained with BLOOD found in the garden. Ball's defence was that he was suffering from SCHIZOPHRENIA, a conclusion reflected in the jury's verdict of guilty but insane.

The mysteries of the missing have also provided some spectacularly successful conclusions. The chorus girl who went missing for forty-two years provided one of these. Mamie Stuart, an attractive 26-year-old, whose home was in Sunderland, married a marine engineer from Wales in 1918. The couple moved to Swansea the following year and took up residence in a furnished house. Mamie wrote to her parents, and the last they heard from her was just before Christmas 1919. Nothing more was heard of the girl, although a portmanteau containing some of her clothes was found in a

Swansea hotel where it had been left unclaimed for several months. Her husband, George Shotton, was interviewed and he stated quite simply that after a quarrel he and his wife had separated.

The police, who had discovered that Shotton was already married, were highly suspicious of him. They searched every inch of the Swansea house and dug the garden over several times — no trace whatsoever was to be found of Mamie. Shotton was charged with bigamy, for which he served an eighteen-month prison sentence, and that seemed to be the end of the affair.

But forty-two years later three young men potholing along the Gower coast found the whitened bones of a human SKELETON at the bottom of a fifty-foot air shaft — they had discovered Mamie Stuart's tomb. Forensic scientists set about identifying the remains, determining age and sex as a matter of routine, but aided by rotting remnants of clothing and by the wedding and engagement rings hanging from one bony finger. The body had been cut into three pieces for disposal by sawing through the spine, upper arms and the thighs. A coroner's inquest concluded that the remains were indeed those of Mamie Stuart, and named her husband as the murderer. A startling statement was made at the inquest by an ex-postman who recalled seeing Shotton all those years previously struggling with a heavy sack outside the Swansea house. He declined an offer of help, putting the sack into his van and driving off.

A nationwide search located Shotton, who with thirty-eight years of guilt on his conscience, had died in 1958 and lay buried in a Bristol cemetery. The identification of Mamie Stuart's remains was a text-book example of forensic procedure. This is always the hardest part of such inquiries — checking out recovered human remains with information of persons listed as missing. Discovered bodies bearing marks of violence often defeat the best efforts of investigators to identify them. They thereby continue to protect the murderer, whose act remains for him a perfect murder.

Norma Bell Carty Wilson, a wealthy 57-year-old lady with a background of business dealings in oil and real estate, was last seen alive in her native America on 8 November 1968. On that day she left Los Angeles bound for Montreal and a meeting with her financial adviser, Tom Devins, whose real name was Thomas Edward Utter.

Mrs Wilson's trip took her to Europe, and she sent postcards, dated 10 and 14 November, to her husband. After that nothing was heard from her, and Bill Wilson reported her to the Los Angeles

Norma Wilson's bloodstained clothing

authorities as a missing person.

An investigation by the District Attorney's department revealed that Norma Wilson met Devins in Montreal, where a bodyguard named Bob Forget was hired to protect her. Carrying 137,000 dollars in cash and wearing expensive jewellery, Norma was escorted to Europe. It was known that she left Italy in a hired car with Devins bound for Geneva, but he arrived at their destination without her. He said she planned to visit a health spa in Sweden.

In a statement to investigators, Forget alleged that Devins had asked him to kill Norma because she had become aware that he was defrauding her. Forget refused and beat a hasty retreat to the United States. Later he claimed Devins told him he had shot Norma in the head at a location in the Alps during the drive to Switzerland. He had dismembered her body, burying it in different places, and leaving her bloodstained clothes in a box at Geneva railway station.

This allegation was unsupported by any linking evidence with Norma Wilson, and there was no body. However, Forget mentioned that Devins had asked him to get rid of a large emerald which Norma had worn as a ring. Forget said he had tried to smash the stone by placing it on a metal wrench and hitting it with a hammer. When it would not splinter he threw it into a pond. As the emerald was harder than the metal, there was a chance that an imprint had been left on the steel of the wrench. Pictures taken on an electron scanning microscope at the Jet Propulsion Laboratory in Pasadena showed a pattern made by the gem in the metal which matched the geometric description provided by the insurance company. Thus part of Forget's story was borne out.

Investigators also recovered Devins's gun, a 9mm Browning pistol, which he had left with a relative for safe-keeping. It was known that he had bought the gun in Hollywood before going to Europe, and FIREARMS examination showed that it had subsequently been fitted with a new barrel. When INTERPOL announced that Norma Wilson's blood-stained clothes had been found at Geneva railway station the presumption that she had been murdered was considerably strengthened.

Forget's evidence was central to Devins's trial for murder, but the defence declined to put a case, declaring that the prosecution was based on CIRCUMSTANTIAL EVIDENCE. Devins was found guilty and given a life sentence, but in 1972 the California Court of Appeals reversed the murder conviction. In January 1974 a walker in the Swiss Alps found some human remains, among them a jawbone identified by the TEETH as belonging to Norma Wilson. Two months later Devins escaped from prison — where he was serving a sentence for theft — and fled to France and then to Australia. Plans to extradite him to Switzerland to stand trial for murder fell through, and in 1978 he became a free man.

The disappearance of Lord Lucan in 1974 created a sensation in the British Press, and the murder on which charge he was named in his absence remains unsolved. On the evening of 7 November 1974 a distraught woman bleeding from a head-wound burst into a public house in London's West End shouting for help. She claimed to have been attacked in her home, and was frightened for the safety of her children. Within minutes police were at the home of Lord and Lady Lucan in fashionable Belgravia.

A search of the house revealed the body of the

Lucan children's nanny, Sandra Rivett, in a canvas mail-bag in the basement. The woman had been killed by blows to the head delivered with a BLUNT INSTRUMENT — her body was still warm. A piece of bloodstained lead piping was also found in the house. Lady Lucan, who had separated from her husband, lived in the house with her three children and their nanny. She related how she went downstairs and was attacked by a man who suddenly leapt out on her. She identified the attacker as Lord Lucan, who said he had meant to murder her but had killed the nanny by mistake.

While Lady Lucan rushed off to fetch assistance her husband fled the house. Later that same night he telephoned his mother, telling her a 'terrible catastrophe' had taken place. He claimed to have intervened in a fight between his wife and an intruder. Later still Lord Lucan called on some friends in Sussex and he repeated this story, adding that someone had killed the nanny and he feared his wife would implicate him. After telephoning his mother once more Lucan left his friends' house and was never seen again.

Two days after the murder the car Lord Lucan had driven to Sussex was found abandoned in the Channel port of Newhaven. There were BLOODstains in the car which proved to be of Group A, matching Lady Lucan's type, and the rare Group B, matching Sandra Rivett's. These were the same groups as those found at the Lucan home.

Warrants were taken out for Lord Lucan's arrest on charges of MURDER and ATTEMPTED MURDER, and INTERPOL was alerted. It was significant that Lady Lucan's routine placed her in the downstairs part of the house at that particular time on that particular day, which was normally the nanny's day off. It was Sandra Rivett's great misfortune to have changed her day off, and since she was of the same height as Lady Lucan, she may have been killed by mistake.

The police spent several months trying to locate the missing murder suspect. He was reported as having been sighted in France, Belgium and Spain, but the feeling grew that he might have committed suicide on the gorse-covered Sussex Downs in the vicinity of his abandoned car. Aerial photographic surveys were made of the area using special filters and composite colour photographs to highlight the richer shades of undergrowth where a body might be lying. Despite these intensive searches no traces of the missing man came to light — possibly he drowned in the sea — and in June 1975 a coroner's inquest brought in a verdict of murder by Lord Lucan.

M'NAGHTEN RULES

Daniel M'Naghten

In all countries with a civilized legal system it is accepted that persons suffering from serious mental disorder are not responsible for any crime they may commit. It is assumed that every individual is sane and possesses sufficient reason to be responsible for his acts unless he proves otherwise. The problem has always been to decide what degree of mental disorder absolves a person from responsibility, the onus for proving exemption being placed on the offender.

The legal criteria applied where insanity is pleaded as a defence are the M'Naghten Rules. These constitute the present law on insanity in England, and the provisions apply in most of the English-speaking countries (Scotland excepted). The rules derive from the aftermath of the trial for MURDER of Daniel M'Naghten in 1843. In that year, this Scot from Glasgow shot Edward Drummond, private secretary to Sir Robert Peel, the Prime Minister, in a London street. Drummond died five days later, and it became apparent that he had been mistakenly killed by M'Naghten, whose intended victim was the Prime Minister whom he believed to be persecuting him.

M'Naghten was tried for murder at the Old Bailey, when evidence was given regarding his state of mind. The defence was brilliantly conducted by Alexander Cockburn (later Lord Chief Justice of England), who argued that the accused man had a background of morbid delusion, and that at the time he committed the murder he did not know that what he was doing was wrong. The jury acquitted M'Naghten on grounds of insanity, but immediately after the trial the House of Lords, in recognition of public concern, exercised their constitutional right to consult the judges on the law relating to insanity in criminal cases. The judges' answers became the M'Naghten Rules.

The main provisions of the rules are that the JURY should be told that every man is to be presumed sane until the contrary is proved to their satisfaction. To establish a defence on the grounds of insanity it must be shown that at the time of committing the offence the accused was labouring under such a defect of reason from disease of the mind as not to know the nature and quality of his act, or if he did know it, that he did not know that what he was doing was wrong.

The M'Naghten Rules have been applied in several notable murder trials up to the present time, often with controversial results. Ronald True, an ex-Royal Flying Corps officer, was tried in 1922 for the murder of a prostitute. Sir Henry Curtis-Bennett, his defence counsel, sought to establish a defence plea of insanity by showing that True was irresponsible, and, at the time the crime was committed, did not know the difference between right and wrong. This contention was backed by medical evidence of insanity, and a picture was drawn of an unstable personality who had a persecution complex and lived in a world of fantasy. Despite Curtis-Bennett's attack on the M'Naghten rules as being out of tune with medical knowledge, the jury nevertheless returned a guilty verdict following the judge's summing-up in which he said, 'You will probably feel that the prisoner did know at the time the physical nature and quality of the acts he had perpetrated.'

An appeal was lodged, and although this was dismissed the Home Secretary reprieved True after three doctors had examined him and declared him insane. He was committed to Broadmoor, where he died thirty years later. Following this case a committee was appointed to report on the insanity laws, but the M'Naghten Rules survived unchanged. Another ex-Air Force officer, Neville George Clevely Heath, found himself in the dock at the Old Bailey in 1946 charged with murder. His appetite for sadism in committing two brutal murders caused a post-war sensation in England.

He was charged with the particularly savage killing of a young woman in a London hotel in the course of which he mutilated the body. (See under SADISM for a description of the case.)

Heath's counsel entered a defence plea of insanity, and attempted to show that his lack of remorse and disregard for concealment were not the actions of a sane person. On the vital question of whether or not he fully understood the nature and quality of his act, medical witnesses for both defence and prosecution believed that he did know. The judge reminded the jury of the provisions of the M'Naghten Rules and directed them to apply the tests. He also pointed out that the 'plea of insanity cannot be permitted to become the easy or vague expression of some conduct which is shocking'. Heath was found guilty, and hanged in October 1946.

The M'Naghten Rules have been widely adopted in the British Commonwealth countries and in the USA, although not by the state of New Hampshire, which rejected them in 1869 in favour of its own rule. The New Hampshire Rule, as it became known, was an attempt to soften the M'Naghten approach and took the view that there could be no fixed rule governing criminal responsibility of a mentally ill defendant. If the jury believed as a matter of fact that a defendant was suffering from a mental disease or defect, and that a criminal act was the result of that condition, their decision should be one of not guilty by reason of insanity.

No other state accepted the New Hampshire Rule, but several adopted a supplementary rule of criminal responsibility based on the principle of irresistible impulse. The M'Naghten Rules have been criticized for omitting provision for any form of emotional insanity or impulse; this new approach put emphasis on lack of control rather than lack of understanding. Consequently, a person could be found not guilty by reason of insanity if he was unable to control his acts, even though he knew that what he was doing was wrong. The concept of irresistible impulse was not the breakthrough that was hoped for. While a few insane individuals clearly acted on sudden impulse, many, suffering from paranoia or SCHIZOPHRENIA, acted with careful premeditation. For example, it was held that the voices and commands heard by the schizophrenic did not qualify as irresistible. Son of Sam's plea of guilty on the basis that he was driven to commit murder by demons was not accepted by Judge John Sharkey in New York in 1977.

In 1954 the United States Court of Appeals in the District of Columbia renewed the debate on the relationship between insanity and criminal responsibility in a decision which became known as the Durham Rule. Monty Durham was a mentally ill burglar in whose defence the New Hampshire Rule was applied. He was held not criminally responsible 'if his unlawful act was the product of a mental disease or mental defect'. The question of insanity was thereby judged to be a matter of fact which the jury could decide, and which did not require to be defined in law. This approach was welcomed by the psychiatrists for its flexibility, but was criticized by the lawyers for its failure to provide a definition of insanity. In practice the Durham Rule has not met with success, and has been rejected by every court which has considered it. The fear has been that the rule puts too much responsibility on juries and allows psychiatrists to regard all criminals as mentally ill.

A further attempt was made in 1955 to draw up a test for insanity which would overcome previous difficulties. The American Law Institute framed a rule to determine criminal responsibility as part of its Model Penal Code, whereby 'A person is not responsible for his criminal conduct if at the time . . . as a result of mental disease or defect he lacks substantial capacity to appreciate the criminality of his conduct or to conform his conduct to the requirements of the law. This formulation was more acceptable to the lawyers but less so to the psychiatrists, who disliked its attempts to define 'mental disease or defects' in legal terms.

The 'right and wrong' test of the M'Naghten Rules still applies, but medical opinion plays an increasingly important role. The traditional emphasis on insanity is giving ground to refinements of criminal responsibility, such as DIMINISHED RESPONSIBILITY. (See under FORENSIC PSYCHIATRY.)
1, 54, 109, 127, 336, 346, 378, 389, 454, **518**.

MODUS OPERANDI

The criminal's *modus operandi* (MO) or method of operation is a much-loved component of crime novels, and is often the means by which the detective gets his man. In real crime investigation MO plays an important part, for, as Sir Harold Scott, a former Commissioner of the Metropolitan Police, has said, it 'is based on the fact that criminals are creatures of habit and are apt, once a particular method has proved successful, to go on repeating it'. Felons are also highly superstitious about changing their style.

All police forces keep informative MO files on

MODUS OPERANDI OF THE SON OF SAM

DATE	DAY	TIME	DISTRICT	VICTIMS	PLACE	METHOD	
29 July 1976	Thursday	1.10 a.m.	Bronx	Female, aged 18 — killed Female, aged 19 — wounded	Shot in stationary car	5 shots .44 Bulldog	
23 October 1976	Saturday	2.00 a.m.	Queens	Male, aged 20 — wounded Female, aged 18 — unwounded	Shot in stationary car	5 shots .44 Bulldog	
27 November 1976	Saturday	11.55 p.m.	Queens	Female, aged 16 — wounded Female, aged 18 — wounded	Shot in street	5 shots .44 Bulldog	
30 January 1977	Sunday	12.15 a.m.	Queens	Female, aged 26 — killed Male, aged 30 — unwounded	Shot in stationary car	3 shots .44 Bulldog	
8 March 1977	Tuesday	7.40 p.m.	Queens	Female, aged 19 — killed	Shot in street	1 shot .44 Bulldog	
17 April 1977	Sunday	3.00 a.m.	Bronx	Female, aged 18 — killed Male, aged 20 — killed	Shot in stationary car	4 shots .44 Bulldog	
26 June 1977	Sunday	3.00 a.m.	Queens	Female, aged 17 — wounded Male, aged 20 — wounded	Shot in stationary car	3 shots .44 Bulldog	
31 July 1977	Sunday	2.30 a.m.	Brooklyn	Female, aged 20 — killed Male, aged 20 — wounded	Shot in stationary car	3 shots .44 Bulldog	

which are recorded the characteristic features concerning the methods of known criminals — broad headings include method, MOTIVE, time and known individualistic traits, such as the trickster who likes to pose as a clergyman. The characteristics of new crime are checked against the MO files to see if there is a match which provides a short-list of likely offenders.

In the investigation of murder, especially in a series of killings, an MO is built up as the inquiry proceeds. Individualistic touches such as JACK THE RIPPER's left-to-right throat-cutting and the Boston Strangler's habit of tying a little bow in the ligature around his victims' throats, were part of those murderers' MO. The establishment of any pattern in a killer's activities will help to formulate investigative policy, and is part of the procedure whereby the detective tries to outguess the criminal.

David Berkowitz, the demented Son of Sam, who terrorized New York City with his apparently motiveless killings for twelve months, established a tantalizing *modus operandi*. He operated at the weekends, usually on Sundays, in the early hours of the morning, shooting young couples sitting in their cars with a .44 calibre Bulldog pistol. The murder investigation was the largest single operation ever mounted by the New York Police Department, costing some 90,000 dollars a day and involving 300 detectives, dealing with 215 calls a day on the police hot line. Over 3,000 suspects were questioned, and an attempt made to check out each of the 28,000 .44 calibre Bulldog revolvers manufactured up to that time.

Son of Sam was eventually traced to his Yonkers apartment because of a traffic violation. On the night of his final killing he left his car by a fire hydrant and received a parking ticket. Police officers found his Ford Galaxy with a loaded .44 calibre revolver on the seat outside his flat, and arrested him as he emerged from the apartment building. David Berkowitz, 24, a postal worker and former auxiliary policeman, pleaded guilty and was sentenced to 365 years imprisonment. He did not appeal.
405, 611.

MORPHINE

The ingenuity of the murderer's mind is such that no sooner has a potential weapon appeared than it is put to use. Thus the first known MURDER by morphine was committed in 1823 by a young Paris

doctor, Edme Castaing, seventeen years after the drug was discovered. But the heyday of the drug's criminal use was in the 1890s in New York City. If it can be said that murder begets murder, events in that city's medical circles certainly bear it out.

Carlyle Harris was a medical student whose grandfather was a respected professor of medicine in New York. Young Harris liked his sexual indulgences, and had designs on a teenage girl, Helen Potts, whom he secretly married. The girl's mother was horrified to discover that Helen, who was still at school, was married, and demanded that Harris make a public announcement. This did not fit in with the young student's plans, and he did not wish to rouse his grandfather's anger. He therefore decided to murder his wife.

Helen suffered from insomnia, a complaint which gave Harris the opportunity he was seeking. Although still a student, he prescribed drugs to enable his wife to sleep. The treatment was a routine mixture of quinine and morphine which a pharmacy made up in six capsules. Harris gave his wife four of these, instructing her to take one each night before retiring. On 31 January 1891 the girl complained of feeling ill, and she lapsed into unconsciousness. The doctor called to attend her noticed the pin-point contraction of the pupils of her EYES — a well-recognized indicator of morphine poisoning. Helen died the following day.

At the inquest the CORONER ruled that death was accidental, due to the girl taking more than one of the prescribed capsules. An alternative was that the pharmacy had made an error in dispensing the prescription. As Mrs Potts did not wish to make public her daughter's relationship with Harris, further inquiries were not pursued, and Helen Potts was buried.

Two months later, an investigative reporter of the *New York World*, intrigued by rumours about Harris's sexual behaviour, published the results of his probe into the case. He had discovered much of what the dead girl's mother wished to keep hidden, and his report led to an EXHUMATION of the body. Dr Rudolph Witthaus, the eminent toxicologist, found morphine in all the organs. Carlyle Harris was arrested and charged with murder.

Harris's method of murder was cunningly conceived. The six capsules had been properly dispensed by the pharmacy, but he had doctored one of them with a fatal dose of morphine. He included this with the four he gave Helen, retaining two in his possession. His thinking was that if his victim swallowed the doctored capsule before she had consumed all of the others, there would be a properly dispensed capsule remaining to indicate that she had probably taken an overdose. On the other hand, if she used the doctored capsule last he would come forward with the two he had retained, again to show that an overdose of properly dispensed drugs was the most likely cause of death.

Carlyle Harris was tried for murder in January 1892. Medical experts for defence and prosecution battled it out in court in New York's first murder-by-morphine case. Despite the fact that he did not testify, Harris expected to be acquitted. The JURY had other ideas, and, convinced that he had doctored the capsules, found him guilty. He went to the ELECTRIC CHAIR in May 1893.

At the very time that Harris was being found guilty of murder by morphine, a New York doctor, Dr Robert Buchanan, was hoping to profit from the student's mistakes. The doctor told a saloon audience that Harris was a fool, and that he believed it possible to get away with murder by morphine, declaring 'in chemistry every acid has its base and every agent its reagent'. This was a precept which he intended to put to the test.

Buchanan, a vain and boastful man, had established a wealthy practice in New York and was set for a comfortable career. But he grew tired of his wife and developed a taste for brothel-visiting, a diversion hardly in keeping with a doctor's professional standing. One of his particular haunts was an establishment run by an unattractive, obese madam called Anna Sutherland. For reasons probably connected with rumours that the brothel proprietress had made a fortune out of prostitution, Buchanan made a play for the lady's affections. In 1890 he divorced his wife and within three weeks married Anna Sutherland, a woman twice his age, and rapidly featured as chief beneficiary in her will.

The doctor installed his new wife as receptionist in his New York consulting rooms. Not surprisingly, the ex-brothel madam did not impress his patients, and his once profitable practice began to deteriorate. At about this time the Carlyle Harris murder trial was in all the news headlines, and the small print debated the phenomenon of pin-pointing in the pupils caused by morphine. Buchanan told his cronies that 'the preparation of an undetectable poison could easily be accomplished' — providing one was an expert, of course.

In 1892 Dr Buchanan announced that he was travelling to Europe in April to engage in further studies at Edinburgh. But a few days before he was due to sail, Anna Sutherland was taken ill. A doctor was called, but she died — ostensibly of a cerebral haemorrhage — on 23 April. Two days later Buchanan, richer to the tune of 50,000 dollars, sailed to Europe — or so he wished people to believe.

While he was away one of his late wife's friends voiced suspicion about the manner of Anna's death. This reached the alert ears of the same reporter who had investigated the Carlyle Harris case, and another probe was under way. The fact that Buchanan had remarried his first wife, and had cancelled his trip to Europe, added fuel to the flames of suspicion. The authorities were persuaded to exhume Anna's body, and once again Dr Witthaus found evidence of criminal poisoning by morphine. There was one mystifying feature, however — the cardinal sign of morphine poisoning, the pin-point pupils, was missing.

The reporter tracked down Buchanan in a saloon and questioned him over a few drinks. The wily doctor gave nothing away, but, while the reporter was looking his quarry straight in the eye he noted how the man's eyes were enlarged by the spectacles he was wearing. In a flash of memory he recalled how a school friend had drops of belladonna put into his eyes during an ophthalmic examination. Convinced that he had discovered Buchanan's secret, the reporter persuaded the authorities to make a further check on Anna's corpse — traces of belladonna were found in both eyes.

Dr Buchanan was tried for murder in March 1893. Strong CIRCUMSTANTIAL EVIDENCE weighed against him, notably his boastful statements referring to the Carlyle Harris case. Again the experts battled it out in court, and in a dramatic demonstration the prosecution proved that morphine pin-pointing of the pupils could be counteracted with belladonna. A cat was killed with morphine, and then belladonna dropped into its eyes, effectively masking the effects of the poison. Despite this unusual demonstration, informed opinion believed that Buchanan would be acquitted. But when the boastful doctor insisted on going into the witness-box against all advice he was condemned by masterly cross-examination. The jury found him guilty of first-degree murder, and he went to the electric chair in July 1895.

The new agent of death which caused so much excitement in New York had been discovered in 1806 by Friedrich Sertürner, a German chemist. The parent substance of morphine is opium, the narcotic drug derived from the Indian poppy and used for centuries. Opium contains a number of narcotic substances known as alkaloids, of which morphine is the most powerful. Sertürner discovered that morphine reacts with acids to form salts, including morphine hydrochloride, or what is commonly called morphia. This is more powerful than opium, and its solubility in water makes it easy to administer. The introduction of the hypodermic syringe by a French doctor in 1853 opened up new doors for medical treatment with drugs by injection, but also provided fresh pathways for murder.

The great benefits of morphine were apparent during the First World War, when it was widely used for treating battle casualties. The drug kills pain because it is a powerful depressant, but it is also poisonous and addictive. Its danger lies in the human body's easy tolerance of morphine. Patients treated for painful illnesses require ever-increasing doses to maintain relief, and morphine addicts often take up to ten times the normal therapeutic dose. Difficulty in controlling morphine dosage led to the maxim that it is better to have a little pain with too little of the drug rather than no pain at all with too much. Individual susceptibility to morphine varies widely, as does the fatal dose, which for the average adult is usually in excess of 200 mg.

Morphine poisoning produces narcosis and then deep coma. This is accompanied by slow respiration, sweating and reduced reflexes. The pulse slows down and the temperature drops. Convulsions reminiscent of STRYCHNINE poisoning may occur, and death results from respiratory failure. A lethal dose may cause death within an hour. The tell-tale sign of morphine poisoning is the pin-point contraction of the pupils of the eyes. Opium may be smelled on the breath, and also in the stomach at POST-MORTEM examination.

Criminal use of morphine has tended to be confined to the medical profession for the simple reason that medical attendants have easy accesss to drugs. Nurse Dorothea Waddingham was hanged in 1936 for killing two elderly patients in her nursing-home with morphine, and Dr Robert Clements found the drug convenient for disposing of at least one of his wives.

On 26 May 1947 Clements called a doctor to his Southport home to attend his wife. The fourth Mrs Clements was found unconscious, and she died the next day. A death certificate was issued stating that cause of death was myeloid leukaemia, a conclusion confirmed by the doctor who carried out the post-mortem. However, Mrs Clements's pin-pointed pupils had not been overlooked, and other doctors involved in the case reported suspicions of a morphine overdose to the CORONER.

Inquiries revealed that Dr Clements had prescribed large doses of morphine for a patient who had never received them. Mrs Clements's funeral was stopped, and a second post-mortem ordered. This examination clearly showed that cause of death was morphine poisoning. When police officers called on Dr Clements they found him dead from a suicidal dose of morphine. Sadly, the doctor who had performed the first erroneous post-mortem examination also committed suicide — he chose CYANIDE as his poison.

A coroner's court judged that Dr Clements had murdered his wife. Suspicion was voiced regarding the deaths of his other wives; the first had died in 1920, ostensibly of sleeping sickness, the second in 1925 of endocarditis and the third in 1939 of cancer. It was a remarkable sequence of tragedies unless Clements had a hand in their deaths. He signed the DEATH CERTIFICATE in each case, and in every instance he gained financially. No further investigations were made, owing to the lapse of time.

An unusual case of morphine poisoning which did not involve a doctor as one of the main participants occurred in Surrey in 1926. In the summer of that year Hilary Rougier, an elderly retired farmer, went to live with William Lerwill and his wife, friends of several years standing, at their house in Lower Knaphill. A doctor was called to the old man in July, when he seemed to be suffering from a respiratory ailment. His condition worsened, and he died the following month, ostensibly from cerebral haemorrhage. To the surprise of his relatives, who thought he was worth about £6,000, Rougier left only £50.

In 1928, as the result of strong rumours about the suspicious circumstances of his death, Rougier's body was exhumed. Sir Bernard Spilsbury found no signs of cerebral haemorrhage, but traces of morphine were detected. It was also discovered that the dead man's assets had been whittled down to £50 as a result of cheques paid to Lerwill during a two-year period. The largest cheque, for £1,850, had been written out by Lerwill, and there was no doubt as to the validity of Rougier's signature. Lerwill claimed that Rougier was a paying guest who also helped him with business commitments.

Evidence was given at the coroner's inquest regarding a number of morphine preparations found in the Lerwills' house. The jury concluded that their paying guest had died of morphine poisoning — not self-administered. No charges were pressed against the Lerwills, but they split up after suing two newspapers for libel and William went to Canada. In 1933 he returned to England, and his movements were followed by a trail of worthless cheques. While visiting the Devonshire village of Combe Martin, he took his own life by swallowing CYANIDE.

9, 72, 76, 97, 112, 208, 220, 243, 258, 292, **491**, *515, 630,* **675**.

MOTIVE

Motivation is one of the three essential components of a criminal act — the others are method (see MODUS OPERANDI) and opportunity. Establishing the motive of a crime is one of the traditional ways in which the investigator begins to build up a picture of the likely suspect. In the case of domestic murder, which at one time constituted the largest class of all homicides, the question is always asked: 'Who stands to benefit from the victim's death?' ARSENIC, for example, was known in seventeenth-century Europe as 'inheritance powder' because of its widespread use to eliminate family competition.

Elimination, gain, revenge, jealousy, lust and conviction are the six classes of motive into which F. Tennyson Jesse, in *Murder and its Motives*, believed all murders could be classified. She did not include a separate category for CRIME PASSIONEL, as that type of killing easily fits into one of the six motives.

Criminologists today ascribe motive to a crime as a convenient way of indicating the apparent cause, believing that the real motive lies in realms which are the territory of FORENSIC PSYCHIATRY. Increasingly murder is committed by the PSYCHO-PATH for reasons which the popular press like to describe as 'mindless'. When obvious motive is missing murder may appear to be motiveless, and, until they were better understood, sexual killings were described in this way. The aggressive psychopath may unleash a series of murders accompanied by sexual mutilation, as in the case of Peter Sutcliffe, or SCHIZOPHRENIA may give rise to an outburst of rage and violence as in the Son of Sam killings.

Murders of strangers by lone killers are always the most difficult to solve — the outstanding example being JACK THE RIPPER — whereas domestic murders lend themselves to easier detec-

tion. In these cases the killer often does not attempt to escape and there is usually a large amount of evidence and corroboration testimony available to the investigators. Recent murder records are distinguished by an increase in stranger-to-stranger killings — for example, the murder of pop star John Lennon in New York in December 1980. In this killing, as in many of its predecessors, the motive was rooted in the depths of a deranged mind.

One of the strongest motives for murder is jealousy, and when this emotion comes to the boil it easily overrides normal restraints, as demonstrated by Jean Harris's shooting of her lover, Dr Herman Tarnower. On 10 March 1980 Harris, the 57-year-old headmistress of a private school for girls in Virginia, set out on the five-hour drive to his house in Purchase, New York. She was suicidally depressed because he had spurned her love for the attentions of another woman, and also because her teaching career was going downhill. She had made her will and put a .32 revolver in her handbag.

Herman Tarnower, aged sixty-nine, a successful cardiologist and internationally renowned author of *The Scarsdale Diet*, had been Harris's lover for fourteen years. He had grown tired of their relationship, and pushed her aside in favour of a younger woman who worked in the medical group he had founded. Thus Jean Harris became the jealous partner in a lover's triangle. When she arrived at the house late in the evening Tarnower was asleep. She claimed later that she awakened him, they talked and she invited him to kill her. Four shots were fired, and when the housekeeper rushed to the bedroom he found Tarnower lying injured from GUNSHOT-WOUNDS on the floor with Harris caressing him. The doctor died later, and Jean Harris was arrested as she was about to drive away. 'I did it', she told the police.

Jean Harris did not deny shooting Tarnower, and her defence was that the killing was accidental. The prosecution maintained that she had killed her former lover in a fit of jealous rage. The flavour of the strong emotions involved in the lover's triangle came out during the murder trial, and it was evident that Tarnower had controlled her disturbed mental state by prescribing amphetamines and barbiturates. For her part, Harris had written him a long letter containing her feelings of wretchedness, referring to his humiliation of her and pouring out hatred for the other woman.

After a trial lasting nearly four months the JURY

took eight days to reach its decision. They found Jean Harris guilty of second-degree MURDER. Her sentence was life, with a specified minimum of fifteen years.
380, 381, 642, 682.

MUMMIFICATION

Leslie Harvey, a taxi-driver who lived at Rhyl in North Wales, decided to redecorate his mother's house while she was away in hospital. On 5 May 1960 he called at the empty house to size up the job, when his gaze fell on the cupboard at the top of the stairs which was locked as it always had been since his boyhood. Curious, he forced the door with a screwdriver, and to his horror was confronted with a human mummy covered in dust and cobwebs, with its clothing hanging in mouldering rags. The police were called, and the pathologist who examined the body described it as rock-hard — it was so firmly fixed to the floor of the cupboard that a garden spade had to be used to prise it loose.

X-ray examination of the mummy showed a SKELETON with a female pelvis and closure of the epiphyses. Osteoarthritic changes indicated an age between fifty and sixty and showed that the person had a limp, with a tendency to favour the right leg. Meanwhile Mrs Sarah Harvey was questioned about the mummy in the cupboard at her house. She told police officers that Mrs Frances Knight, a semi-invalid, had boarded with her during the early months of 1939. Mrs Harvey said that one day she heard her boarder screaming and found her lying on the floor of her room in great pain. Shortly afterwards the woman died, and Mrs Harvey, not knowing what to do, hid the body in the cupboard where it was found twenty years later.

Scientists concluded that the mummification was a natural process caused by gradual drying out of the body in the cupboard, which had doors permitting a free circulation of air currents. Descriptions of Mrs Knight fitted the general characteristics of the mummy, and in view of Mrs Harvey's admissions, identity was not seriously doubted. POST-MORTEM examination of the body, however, showed no obvious cause of death, and suspicion focused on a groove on the left side of the neck which was associated with a disintegrating vestige of a knotted stocking. It was concluded that the woman had died of strangulation, and Mrs Harvey was charged with murder.

The trial was held at Ruthin, Denbighshire, in 1960 and the evidence presented was almost

The mummy in the cupboard

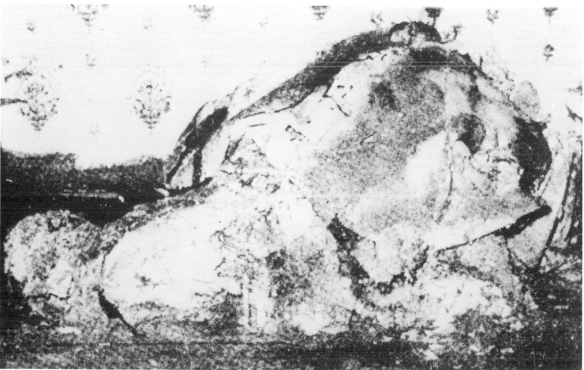

entirely scientific. Dr Francis Camps and Sir Sydney Smith advised the defence. Certainly Sir Sydney, with his experience of forensic matters in Egypt, was well acquainted with the phenomenon of mummification. While Mrs Harvey had admitted concealing the body, she denied killing her boarder, and the accusation of STRANGU-LATION was not borne out by the physical evidence. Neither the hyoid bone nor thyroid carti-lage of the corpse was fractured as would have been expected.It was concluded there was insuffi-cient evidence to sustain the murder charge, and Mrs Harvey was found not guilty. She was con-victed of fraud, though, because for twenty years she had been drawing a special pension to which the dead woman had been entitled.

Knowledge of mummification dates back to before 3,000 B.C. in ancient Egypt, when bodies buried in shallow, desert graves were found to be preserved. Dry heat and moving currents of air arrest normal decomposition, and the tissues become dry and shrivelled with the skin tightening over the bones. The corpse takes on the hard, leathery characteristics observed in the traditional Egyptian mummy. Mummification can also occur in temperate climates when the right environ-mental conditions prevail. It is not uncommon for an unwanted newly born infant to be concealed in an attic or cupboard, with the result that it becomes dehydrated and mummified. In the case of the new-born child the alimentary system is virtually sterile, so that there are no bacteria present to initiate DECOMPOSITION. Mummifi-cation is a natural process in which the tissues become desiccated and frequently retain recog-nizable features. The skin of the fingers, where it remains intact, still holds the characteristic ridge patterns and FINGERPRINTS can be taken after the skin had been softened.

Mummification of adults in temperate climates is rare, but occasionally the right circumstances combine to produce this effect. It is also a phenomenon which can occur in cases of poisoning with ARSENIC, as Sir Bernard Spilsbury noted in the Armstrong case in 1922. Following EXHUM-ATION of Mrs Armstrong's body from the grave in which it had lain for ten months, the pathologist recorded that it was unusually well-preserved and appeared to be undergoing mummification rather than normal putrefaction. In 1935 Spilsbury was presented with another mummified body, on this occasion one wrapped up in an old curtain and tied with electric flex. The mummy had been found in the coal-cellar of a public house in Southwark by the cellarman, who had been instructed to tidy up. Curious to see what lay beneath the wrappings, the man cut the cords and revealed the parchment-like exterior of a mummy.

The corpse was identified as that of an old man who had been reported missing twelve months previously. Police inquiries showed that the man had fallen asleep in the pub one afternoon and on being wakened made for the exit, but opened the wrong door by mistake. Instead of stepping into the street he plunged nine feet to his death in the cellar. The barman who found the body had reason to avoid renewing his acquaintance with the police and decided on concealment. He wrapped the body in some old curtains and tied it up into a parcel which he propped in a corner of the cellar. Having completed the task of DISPOSAL OF THE BODY, he gave notice to his employer and promptly disappeared.

The corpse had a fractured skull and other injuries consistent with a fall, and the mummifi-cation was due entirely to natural processes. The sudden manner of death, coupled with rapid cool-ing and the method of wrapping, dried out the body and caused it to mummify. Foul play was not suspected, and when the missing barman was caught he pleaded guilty to concealment, for which he received token punishment.
97, 369, 521, 632.

MURDER

The word murder is derived from 'murdrum', a heavy fine imposed on the community by the Normans when one of their number was killed and the perpetrator remained at large. In time murdrum was corrupted to murder, and signified the act of killing. (Old English *mordhor* is an alternative derivation.)

The classic definition of murder was given by Sir Edward Coke (1552–1634) Lord Chief Justice and authority on COMMON LAW:

> Murder is when a man of sound memory, and of the age of discretion, unlawfully killeth within any county of the realm any reasonable creature in rerum natura under the King's peace, with malice aforethought, either expressed by the party or implied by the law, so as the party wounded, or hurt . . . die of the wound or hurt . . . within a year and a day after the same.

By 'a man of sound memory, and at the age of discretion' is meant a person who is today neither insane under the provisions of the M'NAGHTEN RULES nor suffering from diminished responsibility, and aged at least ten years. 'Within any county of the realm' includes trial for murder outside the United Kingdom, and also for murder committed on a British ship or aircraft. 'A reasonable creature in rerum natura' includes any human being, excepting a child still in the womb. A child must have left the womb and experienced life independent of its mother in order to be the victim of murder. Independence means to have functioning breathing and blood circulation, even though it may still be attached to the mother by the umbilical cord. 'Death within a year and day' is stipulated in order to allow reasonable time to establish cause of death.

Put simply, murder is the unlawful killing of a human being with MALICE AFORETHOUGHT. Malice aforethought does not carry in law the normal meaning of those words — that is, ill-will and premeditation — but implies guilty intent (MENS REA). The clearest example is that of the person who sets out with the intention of killing another, and it is this intent which distinguishes murder from MANSLAUGHTER. The Homicide Act of 1957 abolished the concept of constructive malice whereby a person who killed another while committing an offence such as arson, for instance, could be charged with murder. The act also allowed a charge of murder to be reduced to manslaughter where the defence showed the accused to have acted as the result of DIMINISHED RESPONSIBILITY. Other provisions permitted a JURY to consider if an accused person had been unreasonably provoked to the point where self-control was lost, and accepted that death resulting from RAPE did not necessarily constitute murder. The CRIME PASSIONEL motivated by sexual jealousy is not recognized in English law, but demonstration of provocation may reduce a murder charge to one of manslaughter.

Coke's definition of murder still holds good in its essential provisions, and under common law until 1957 all acts of murder were punishable by death. The Homicide Act of that year limited capital punishment to specified types of murder, such as the killing of a police officer in the execution of his duty, and the death penalty was abolished altogether by the Homicide Act of 1965, except for acts of high treason and piracy with violence.

In the USA murder is a category of HOMICIDE, and requires malice aforethought. Murder is classed as first or second degree, depending on the amount of deliberation and premeditation. The law defining murder as a criminal act has been refined over hundreds of years. The process continues today, but the discussion has moved more into the realms of homicide, which has many aspects, both criminal and non-criminal. Interpretation of the law is being increasingly tested by medical evidence regarding the mental state of persons who have killed. In consequence, many of the traditionally accepted definitions regarding murder are under question.

Particular circumstances of death have led to the invention of some curious classes of murder, such as 'murder by request' and 'murder by omission'. In South Africa in 1961 Marthinus Roussouw confessed to killing Baron Dieter von Schauroth, a diamond-dealer who employed his services as a bodyguard. The Baron was found dead from GUNSHOT-WOUNDS, with evidence that diamonds he was carrying had been stolen. Roussouw claimed that von Schauroth — who had taken out heavy life insurance — handed him a revolver and money (2,300 rands), with instructions to kill him — 'murder by request'. It was possible that the Baron, knowing his diamond dealings were under surveillance, took out the insurance to ensure financial protection for his family, and then arranged to have himself shot. Roussouw was nevertheless tried for murder and convicted.

'Murder by omission' was the charge brought against Dr John Hill, the Houston surgeon accused of poisoning his wife with bacteria. This charge was permissible under Texan law, which recognized that if someone owes a duty to a person but fails to perform it, and death results, he is guilty of homicide. In John Hill's case his indictment read that he 'did voluntarily and with malice aforethought kill the said Joan Hill by wilfully intentionally and culpably failing and omitting to administer to her proper medical treatment'. (See under BACTERIA for an account of the case.)
49, 416, 478, **510**, *668.*

N

NECROPHILIA

A type of sexual perversion in which there is a desire for intercourse with dead bodies. Necrophilia takes various forms, ranging from intercourse following murder to offences committed on a newly buried corpse. Krafft-Ebing noted that instances of murder for the purpose of necrophilia were rare, but a number of modern cases have highlighted this type of perversion. John Christie, the murderer of 10 Rillington Place, was known as 'Reggie-no-dick' on account of his sexual inadequacy, a theme which runs through this type of crime. After GASSING his victims, he strangled and raped them, secreting their corpses in the garden and behind the kitchen wall of the house.

Edmund Kemper, American 'Co-ed' killer in the 1970s, suffered the same lack of natural endowment as Christie. Kemper had demonstrated sadistic tendencies as a child, and as an acknowledged teenage 'weirdo' shot his grandparents dead in 1964. He was judged insane, but after a period of psychiatric treatment was released in his mother's care in 1969. He drifted from job to job, and developed the habit of giving lifts to California's girl students who travelled the highways as hitch-hikers. In 1972 a number of co-eds disappeared, and when the mutilated body of one of these girls was discovered panic ensued.

In 1973 Kemper surrendered himself to the police, admitting to the murder of six girls and relating a gruesome story of shooting, knifing and STRANGULATION followed by revolting acts of SADISM. Sometimes he took the corpses home, where he performed sexual intercourse on them, and indulged in CANNIBALISM. He admitted being sexually excited by decapitating his victims, whom he later dismembered and buried. Kemper was charged on eight counts of first-degree MURDER including the killing of his mother and her friend. When asked what he considered a fit punishment he answered 'Death by torture'. He was denied this last perverted wish when the court sentenced him to life imprisonment.

Ed Gein was another necrophile, a middle-aged farmer from Wisconsin whose dominating mother made sex a taboo subject. When she died Gein took to studying female anatomy in books, but quickly graduated to the most ghoulish practices. He dug up recently buried female corpses in order to conduct his anatomical studies at close quarters. On at least one occasion he reburied the empty coffin and took the corpse home, where he performed an act of necrophilia on it.

In time he adopted murder as a means of obtaining bodies for his perverted delights. When his activities were brought to light in 1957 Gein's farm was found to contain a revolting collection of human relics — his refrigerator was stacked with human organs which, together with an assembly of other human remains, accounted for fifteen bodies. He admitted such ghoulish practices as draping his body in the skin of his victims in order to obtain sexual satisfaction, and indulging in acts of cannibalism. He was committed to an institution for the criminally insane in that same year, and his farm was so associated with evil that the local populace burned it to the ground.

Sergeant François Bertrand, a young French soldier, has been cited as the classic necrophile. His adolescent feelings were bound up with violent sexual fantasies, and he found insufficient satisfaction in normal intercourse. By the time he was twenty-four he had developed a taste for maltreating animals and mutilating their corpses. It was a short step from this practice to that of digging up and violating human corpses. This man, whose normal behaviour gave no hint of his violent nature, was arrested in Paris in 1849 for grave-robbery and violating female corpses. He professed to gain intense satisfaction from sexual intercourse with these cadavers, after which he hacked them to pieces in the course of his perverted lust.

1, 78, **115**, *129, 231, 246, 395,* **409**, *475, 477, 738.*

Christie's victims walled up in the kitchen cupboard

172

NOT PROVEN

'The jury find the panel [defendant] not guilty of the first charge in the indictment by a majority; of the second charge not proven; and by a majority find the third charge also not proven.' Thus on the third charge of administering poison to her lover with intent to murder him Madeleine Smith left Edinburgh's High Court of Justiciary in 1857 a free woman, as the case against her was judged not proven. The girl of twenty-one, whose sexual exploits shocked Glasgow society, lived to the considerable age of ninety-three, dying in another era and in another continent. (See under ARSENIC for an account of the case.)

In addition to the usual verdicts of 'guilty' and 'not guilty', Scottish criminal courts have the power to bring in the third verdict of 'not proven'. This is applied when a JURY is unsatisfied on the evidence as to the accused person's guilt or innocence. The effect of this verdict is the same as an acquittal, and allows the accused to go free without fear of punishment or retrial. It does not, however, carry moral absolution, and is regarded by some as an unsatisfactory legal compromise if not, in popular quarters, simply a formula for 'getting away with murder', or the jury saying, 'Go away and don't do it again'.

An example of the cynical view on this verdict is provided by John Donald Merrett, who was also tried for murder in Edinburgh. In his case the victim was his mother, who died from a bullet-wound in the head which defence experts maintained had been inflicted as an act of suicide. At the trial in 1926 the jury returned a not proven verdict, and Merrett escaped the charge of MATRICIDE, only to commit double murder twenty-eight years later. (See under EARS for a full account.)

Two further examples of this uniquely Scottish verdict are provided by the cases of Christine Gilmour and of Alfred John Monson. Like Madeleine Smith, Gilmour was suspected of poisoning her partner with ARSENIC. She stood trial in Edinburgh in 1844, having been extradited from the USA, to which she had fled after her husband's death. She admitted buying poison, but claimed she intended using it to take her own life. The CIRCUMSTANTIAL EVIDENCE against her was sufficient to win a verdict of not proven, and, again like Madeleine Smith, she lived to a ripe old age.

Alfred Monson was involved in a shooting incident in 1893 with a young man whom he had persuaded to take out a large life-insurance policy. Monson returned from a rabbit-hunting trip and announced that his companion had shot himself. Evidence was brought at his trial for murder to show that the manner of the shooting ruled out suicide, and that Monson had lied in statements he made about the FIREARMS and ammunition used. The judge, Lord Justice Clerk Macdonald, summed up in Monson's favour, remarking in a famous statement, 'It is the business of the Crown to prove the case, and not for the defence to prove innocence', and paving the way for a not proven verdict.

1, 249, 268, 416, 581, 582, 685, 741, 750, 752.

P

PHOSPHORUS

The Widow of Windy Nook, as she was called after she achieved notoriety, was 66-year-old Mary Elizabeth Wilson. She lived at Windy Nook in Felling-on-Tyne, and was addicted to reading romantic magazines and had a liking for the bottle. She was also greedy. Although they had been married many years, Mrs Wilson was not particularly happy with her husband, so she took the local chimney-sweep as a lover. Both her husband and her lover died within five months of each other, ostensibly of natural causes, and Mary was left a widow.

In 1957 she met Oliver James Leonard, an elderly retired estate agent, who lived in lodgings. 'Has the bugger any money?' Mary inquired of his landlady. The answer must have been encouraging, for the widow and Mr Leonard were married in September. Two weeks later Leonard was dead of natural causes, according to the DEATH CERTIFICATE. Twice widowed, Mary now set her sights on another old man, Ernest Wilson, who was looking for a housekeeper. She married him, and within two weeks he was also dead.

With echoes of George Joseph Smith (see under

DROWNING), Mrs Wilson asked the undertaker to provide a cut-price funeral for her late husband. This, together with numerous remarks made to neighbours, drew a net of suspicion around her. EXHUMATION orders were granted, and the disinterred corpses of her husbands were found to be glowing with phosphorus.

Mary Wilson was tried for murder, when it was suggested that she had fed her husbands beetle or rat poison containing yellow phosphorus, probably administered in tea or cough mixture. Phosphorus was also found in the bodies of her first husband and her lover. She was convicted, but did not suffer hanging on account of her age. The widow who murdered for gain, probably obtaining no more that £200 at the cost of four lives, died in prison at the age of seventy.

Phosphorus is an extremely dangerous material. In its wax-like, yellow form it is kept under water, as it ignites when exposed to the air. Painful burns are caused if it is handled improperly, and it has the unique quality of glowing in the dark. Yellow phosphorus was at one time widely used in the manufacture of matches and some proprietary beetle and rat poisons. It is highly poisonous, a lethal dose being as little as 1 grain (65 milligrams). The symptoms of acute phosphorus poisoning are nausea, vomiting and a burning sensation in the throat, accompanied by intense thirst. There is a characteristic smell, and the same odour is detectable in the intestines at POST-MORTEM examination. There may be internal haemorrhage which darkens the vomit with blood, and diarrhoea follows, with final collapse and death. The fatal period may last for days after ingesting the poison, or may occur within twelve hours. A feature of phosphorus poisoning is that symptoms may recede only to return after an interval often lasting several days. A startling aspect of phosphorus poisoning is that vomit and excreted matter glow in the dark!

Chronic poisoning from sub-toxic doses of phosphorus leads to a condition known as 'phossy-jaw' in which necrosis occurs in the jaw-bones, with the result that the teeth fall out. There is anorexia and loss of weight, with damage to the liver and kidneys. Phosphorus is quickly oxidized when in contact with the air, and as phosphate is found naturally in the body. Hence if ingested in small quantities it becomes oxidized in the bloodstream, and is virtually undetectable.

Rat poison was the suspected source of the phosphorus which Louisa Merrifield was judged to have administered to her victim. A shilling tin of Rodine (which in 1953, before the law was changed, could be bought over the counter of a chemist's shop) contained about ten grains of phosphorus — enough to kill several persons. Louisa Merrifield and her third husband replied to an advertisement placed in a local newspaper by an elderly widow who sought a living-in companion to look after her. On 12 March 1953 the Merrifields moved into Sarah Ricketts's bungalow to fill this role. By the end of the month Mrs Ricketts had made a will leaving all her property to her new-found companions. On 14 April the doctor was called to attend the old lady, and he found her dead when he arrived. He was puzzled as to the cause of death, and declined to give a DEATH CERTIFICATE. At the subsequent post-mortem examination 0·141 grain of phosphorus was found in Mrs Ricketts's body, and death was put down to poisoning.

Despite the clear indications of poisoning and suspicion which surrounded the Merrifields, a search of the bungalow failed to reveal any trace of phosphorus or of a poison container. A spoon found in Mrs Merrifield's handbag had some suspicious-looking material stuck to it, but there were no traces of phosphorus. A Blackpool chemist's assistant, however, identified Mr Merrifield as a customer to whom she had sold a tin of Rodine, and Mrs Merrifield's attempt to have the body cremated, coupled with several ill-considered remarks about inheriting property, created sufficient suspicion to warrant a charge of murder.

Louisa and Alfred Merrifield were tried at Manchester; both pleaded not guilty. The prosecution was led by the Attorney-General, Sir Lionel Heald, who explained that it was the custom for a Law Officer of the Crown to prosecute in cases of murder by poison because of the 'particularly heinous' nature of such crimes. His argument was that as no one doubted that Mrs Ricketts had died of phosphorus poisoning, and that the poison was unlikely to have entered the body by accident or due to suicide, it must have been deliberately administered. The defence maintained that the old lady had died of cirrhosis of the liver. The JURY convicted Mrs Merrifield, but failed to agree on her husband's guilt. Her appeal having been dismissed, Louisa was executed on 18 September 1953, and the Attorney-General decided not to pursue the case against Alfred in a retrial, issuing instead a *nolle prosequi* which declared his unwillingness to prosecute.

12, 220, 236, 256, 349, 369, 449, **491, 571,** *740.*

POISONING

The study of poisons, their effect on the human body and the law regarding their use is known as toxicology. While poisoning holds an especially sinister place in the annals of murder, in practice it is the least used method of HOMICIDE. The vast majority of fatal poisonings are suicidal or accidental, and less than 6 per cent of homicides are due to poisoning. By its very nature poison is premeditated and secret — the real horror lies not so much in those poisonings that are discovered but in those which remain undetected.

Special hatred attaches to the poisoner, who is regarded as more sinister than the gunman or knife-user. Poison has been called 'the coward's weapon', because it is administered unemotionally and by stealth, often little by little over a long period, and in full recognition of the victim's often prolonged suffering. The poisoner is thus reviled for his lack of pity and, perhaps more than any other class of murderer, carefully engineers his opportunity. It is commonly supposed that female murderers resort more readily to poison and get away with it more easily than their male counterparts. This prejudice probably arises because of the activities of such celebrated historic poisoners as Catherine de Médicis, the Marquise de Brinvilliers and Mary Ann Cotton, whose murderous ways probably accounted for a collective total of well over a hundred lives.

If any group has a predilection for the use of poison it is the medical fraternity. Britain's courts of justice ring with the names of doctors who have been convicted of murder by poison — Palmer, Cream, Crippen, Lamson, Pritchard — and North America has had its fair share too — Buchanan, Coppolino, Friedgood, Hyde, Hill, King and Waite. A whole dispensary of agents has been used, from commonplace ARSENIC to sophisticated succinylcholine chloride. Doctors have ready access to poisons and drugs, and unlike the ordinary person, cannot be suspected merely for possessing them. It is perhaps surprising, bearing in mind their professional knowledge, that so many doctors have been found out. Possibly familiarity breeds contempt and concealment is thought unnecessary, but a more sinister thought is that discovered poisoners represent only the tip of an iceberg of secret homicide.

Mathieu Orfila is regarded as the 'father of toxicology', and he set the tone and pace for the scientific investigation of poisoning. He played an important role as the expert in the Lafarge case in Paris in 1840 by adopting the new Marsh Test for arsenic. This easy method of detection should have signalled the end of arsenic as the most favoured poison, but the poisoner's attachment to traditional methods proved difficult to break.

Twenty-four years after the Lafarge case Lydia Sherman, a latter-day 'Queen Poisoner' and a policeman's wife, developed her killing ways with arsenic in New York. As many as forty-two murders were laid at her door, and she exhibited all the talent of the compulsive poisoner. Lydia had been married for seventeen years when a crisis occurred in 1864. While serving with the New York Metropolitan Police Force her husband, Edward, shirked his duty by failing to arrest a madman armed with a knife. He was dismissed for cowardice, and in her fury at her husband's shortcomings Lydia took to humiliating him in public. Poor Edward was driven to drink and despair. Lydia, who was forced to work to make ends meet, chose nursing as her occupation. It was not long before she was asking, 'What will kill a person without leaving any visible sign?' The answer was arsenic. In May 1864 she bought a quantity of the poison, informing the druggist, 'We're alive with rats.' Edward's demise followed, and he was committed to his grave, which at Lydia's request was 'a nice deep hole'.

With the urge for disposing of her family running deep in her veins, Lydia set about murdering her children. The nine-month-old baby was dispatched with arsenic added to its milk. The deaths of her husband and five children created suspicion, but all had been certified by reliable doctors as due to natural causes. Up to this point Lydia's MOTIVE had been elimination, but now she turned to gain. In 1868 she married an elderly farmer, Dennis Harlbut, who was soon persuaded to leave his savings to his new wife. The kindly farmer died an agonizing death, and Lydia inherited 10,000 dollars.

In 1870 she married Nelson Sherman and went to live in Connecticut. Stressing that 'we are overrun with rats', Lydia bought arsenic from the local drugstore and dispatched her husband and two of his family to their graves. The doctor in attendance suspected poison, and told Lydia so. She denied it, but raised no objection to the victims being subjected to POST-MORTEM examination. Organs taken from Sherman's body contained large amounts of arsenic. It took several weeks for these findings to be established, as the toxicological expertise of the time was confined to a few universities. Meanwhile Lydia absconded, although she

THE TIMELY WARNING

The timely warning

was eventually traced to New Brunswick, where she was arrested.

The 'Queen Poisoner' was tried for murder in April 1872, and faced overwhelming CIRCUM-STANTIAL EVIDENCE. The jury found her guilty of second-degree murder and, following the failure of her appeal, she was sentenced to life imprisonment. She died in prison five years later, having left for posterity a lengthy account of her activities which was strong on drama but contained no remorse.

There is a great deal of mysticism associated with poisons. This probably arises from their intriguing double nature, for on the one hand many are commonplace substances which used correctly can be beneficial, but, on the other, used carelessly or maliciously, can be quite deadly. Goethe remarked, 'There is no such thing as poison; it all depends on the dose.' Dr William Guy put this more scientifically in his *Principles of Forensic Medicine*, written in 1861, when he declared, 'the term poison does not admit of strict definition'. Indeed, it does not, for as the ancients discovered, the substance which poisons one man will leave another unharmed. As both poisoner and druggist discovered, the effect of a poison depends on its dose, the manner of its administration and the sturdiness of the victim. A popular belief in ancient times was that resistance to a lethal dose of poison could be acquired by voluntarily taking regular small doses. Mithridates, King of Pontus (120–63 B.C.), adopted the practice of taking a daily concoction of seventy-two poisons in order to nullify any attack on his life. He was so successful in this that he was unable to poison himself when he wished to take his own life following an invasion by the Romans.

Orfila led the way to the scientific understand-

177

ing of poisons, and one of his pupils, Sir Robert Christison (1797–1882), carried his learning to Edinburgh, where he was appointed to the chair of forensic medicine. In 1829 he published his *Treatise on Poisons*, which for many years was regarded as the standard work on the subject in the English language. What became apparent, despite the difficulties of defining poisons, was that for all practical purposes they were substances which acted on the body both chemically and physiologically, causing tissue damage or system malfunctions, resulting in illness or death.

It was shown too that although there were many kinds of poisons, it was possible to group them according to their effects. Thus a broad system of classification grew up which contained four categories. The first includes substances such as carbon monoxide and CYANIDE which affect the oxygen-carrying capacity of the blood with such speed as to cause respiratory failure and death, with few obvious effects. By contrast there are agents such as acids and alkalis which cause corrosive destruction at the point of entry or contact. Such corrosive poisons if swallowed burn the mouth and cause the stomach to perforate. Then there are the systemic poisons which have featured so frequently in the annals of murder — ARSENIC, ANTIMONY and MERCURY. These are absorbed by the body, causing widespread damage to the liver and kidneys and disrupting the nervous and circulatory systems. This group also includes plant poisons or vegetable alkaloids such as STRYCHNINE, MORPHINE, HYOSCINE and many others which affect the central nervous system. A great number of these substances found their way into the formularies of the pharmacist as prescribed drugs in small doses to treat a variety of ailments. A fourth category of poisons includes those which leave no trace of entry but cause destruction after they have been absorbed. Blood-destroying poisons such as RICIN fall into this class, along with nitrobenzene and arsine.

The murderer who intends to poison his victim has at his command a vast range of lethal agents and methods of applying them. Moreover, once set on the poison trail, he is aided by the knowledge that his victim's sufferings often resemble the symptoms of natural disease. Little by little he can deal out death, yet at the same time create a climate which is devoid of suspicion. Poisonous agents have traditionally been available over the shop counter in preparations sold for household, veterinary and garden use — rat-poison, weedkiller, sheep-dip, crop-spray and fly-papers.

Correctly prescribed proprietary medicines also contained poisonous constituents which have allowed the possibility of misuse — Fowler's solution (arsenic) and Easton's syrup (strychnine). In addition, countless poisons, including gases, vegetable, corrosive, mineral and organic substances, are widely used in industry and agriculture. Attempts to control the availability of poisons in Britain began with the Arsenic Act of 1851, which stipulated that the purchaser must be known to the seller. The Pharmacy Act of 1852 defined persons permitted to sell poisons, and a further Act in 1868 extended the range of controlled poisons and required pharmacists to keep registers of sales. The Pharmacy and Poisons Act of 1933 contained the first fully comprehensive controls and governed the sale, supply, labelling, storage and transportation of poisons. The increased use of addictive drugs such as heroin and cocaine and the extension of drug therapy in medicine necessitated the Dangerous Drugs Act of 1951, and further legislation was enacted in 1968 and 1971. Thus, progressively, the availability of poisons and dangerous substances has come under control, although the determined poisoner usually finds a loophole. John Armstrong, a naval sickbay attendant, was convicted of murder in 1956 using Seconal; Kenneth Barlow, a male nurse, poisoned his wife with insulin in 1957; Dr Carl Coppolino, a hospital anesthesiologist, was found guilty of second-degree murder in 1967, having poisoned his wife with the synthetic muscle relaxant succinylcholine chloride (see under UNDETECTED MURDER), while Graham Young, storeman in a photographic firm, was convicted of murder in 1972 having claimed the lives of at least three victims with THALLIUM.

The variety of poisonous agents is equalled only by the numerous methods for administering them. Food and drink have always been popular vehicles — Major Armstrong's arsenic-laden scones, Dr Lamson's Dundee cake spiced with ACONITINE, Cordelia Botkin's arsenical candies, Dr John Hill's bacterial pastries, Richard Brinkley's cyanide-flavoured stout, and Eva Rablen's strychnine-laden coffee. Poison given under the guise of medicine is a favourite device which for the murderer acting as nurse has the advantage of appearing to follow the doctor's orders. Thus did Dorothea Waddington dispose of two patients by means of morphine injections, and Carlyle Harris use the same drug, given in capsule form, to kill his young wife. Novel methods of poisoning have included Dr Arthur Waite's nasal spray loaded with BACTERIA and the RICIN pellet implanted in a convenient part of the body, such as the leg, by means of an umbrella. This was the technique used to murder Georgi Markov, the Bulgarian broadcaster, in London in 1978.

The body is vulnerable to poisoning by ingestion, inhalation, absorption, injection, and via the rectum, bladder and vagina. With every conceivable method on record — and some inconceivable — from mercury administered as an enema to thallium administered in tea or coffee, the existence of a range of highly toxic synthetic materials manufactured for military purposes offers frightening prospects for the age of the undetectable poison. There have been suspicions of gangland murders in the USA and political murders in Europe committed with toxic agents which kill quickly by absorption through the skin. Many of these poisons break down into constituents normally present in the body, and, being taken in by absorption, leave no trace of entry. *72, 98,* **148***, 200, 203, 258,* **299***, 491, 515, 599, 665, 667,* **675***, 729.*

Spilsbury at work

POST-MORTEM

At the height of his career the great pathologist Sir Bernard Spilsbury conducted over seven hundred post-mortem examinations a year. In modern New York City, the Medical Examiner's Office carries out over seven thousand autopsies annually. This industry in dissection of the dead is necessary in order to establish the manner and cause of death. It is also part of the process by which evidence is collected to assist any medico-legal inquiries which may arise. One of the most publicized and controversial post-mortems of modern times was that carried out on the body of President John F. Kennedy after his ASSASSINATION in November 1963. The failure of the pathologists to describe the gunshot wounds completely resulted in several interpretations being placed on the circumstances of the shooting, and has fuelled speculation ever since.

It has been the practice from early times for the body of a victim of violent death to be exposed to view so that its wounds might be observed. The murdered corpse of Julius Caesar was thus displayed, and a Roman physician was able to

179

establish that only one of the twenty-three stab wounds was fatal. The post-mortem examination became a regular feature of Italian medical practice in the thirteenth century, and in England at about the same time coroners and juries were required to view the bodies of suspected murder victims. Indeed, the English CORONER is still expected to see for himself any marks of violence on the body of his inquest victim.

While determining the cause of death was the province of the doctor, it was clear that many post-mortem examinations up to the end of the nineteenth century were so perfunctory as to be misleading. As medico-legal procedure developed, the post-mortem acquired greater significance, and it was realized that special skills — those of the forensic pathologist — were required if the results were to withstand the rigours of examination in court. Thus in 1861 Dr William Guy, Professor of Forensic Medicine at King's College, London, was proclaiming 'the great rule to be observed in conducting post-mortem examinations', which was 'to examine every cavity and every important organ of the body . . . even when the cause of death was obvious'. He recognized that an astute lawyer could exploit any omission by objecting that cause of death lay in some uninvestigated part of the body.

The modern post-mortem examination — also known as autopsy or necropsy — has become a highly specialized procedure, and the province of experts. However, that is not to say that mistakes do not occur, or that the experts do not at times disagree over their findings. A famous courtroom disagreement took place at Lewes Assizes in 1930 when Sidney Fox was on trial for MATRICIDE. Fox, a roguish character who moved from place to place with his mother leaving behind a trail of unpaid bills, raised the fire alarm on 23 October 1929 at a Margate hotel. His mother's body was dragged from her smoke-filled room, but efforts to revive her failed and in due time her death by misadventure was recorded. The speed with which Fox set about redeeming the old lady's life insurance created suspicion, and an EXHUMATION of the body was ordered. Spilsbury carried out the post-mortem and recorded finding a bruise on the larynx — clear evidence of STRANGULATION. By the time the pathologist had completed his examination the body, which had been kept well-preserved in an air-tight coffin, began to deteriorate rapidly. As a result, the bruise which Spilsbury had seen disappeared. The very existence of this mark was challenged by other doctors in court, who claimed that it was simply due to putrefaction. Spilsbury's reply was classically straightforward: 'It was a bruise and nothing else. There are no two opinions about it.' The great pathologist won the argument by force of personality, much to Fox's detriment — the latter being hanged for murder in 1930.

This incident illustrates the need for corroboration and for faultless handling of the chain of evidence throughout the post-mortem examination. Another alarming demonstration of the deficiencies which can occur was provided by the Croydon Poisoning in 1928–9, when three members of the same family died of arsenical poisoning within a year. The case abounded in controversy, for the coroner declined to take advice given by the Director of Public Prosecutions to hold all three inquests together. In consequence, confusion emerged at every stage of the complicated proceedings, and not least at the discovery of an error during the original post-mortem on one of the victims. It became evident that organs taken at that time for analysis were mixed up with specimens taken from another body in the mortuary at the same time. Thus the chance of establishing the presence of ARSENIC at an early stage of the inquiry was lost, and with it much of the momentum of the investigation. Officially, the Croydon poisonings remain unsolved, and represent an embarrassing reminder of the perils of inadequate post-mortem technique.

In England it is the coroner who initiates the post-mortem procedure by requesting a suitably qualified pathologist to carry out the examination. In the USA authority varies from state to state, but usually originates with either the coroner or the Chief Medical Examiner. The autopsy should be carried out with the minimum delay before putrefaction sets in, although modern mortuaries are equipped with refrigeration facilities, enabling bodies to be stored without harm to their eventual examination. After the body has been brought from the scene of the crime to the mortuary it is identified to the pathologist by a police officer or relative. Formal identification is recorded on the post-mortem report form and the body itself labelled and photographed. Then the clothing is removed and examined item by item. Stains, tears, holes and deposits are noted, and trace evidence such as HAIRS, FIBRES or fragments of paint, glass or other material are put into sealed, labelled specimen-containers. Each item of clothing after it is examined is placed in a separate plastic bag and carefully labelled. It is particularly important in cases involving gunshot-wounds to relate holes in the clothing to wounds in the body. (Failure to do this at the autopsy on President Kennedy led to serious misinterpretation of a wound in the neck.) Above all, every article and every finding is meticulously labelled and identified to preserve the chain of evidence.

The now naked body is weighed, and it is then subjected to a thorough external examination. This is made by careful scrutiny from head to toe, back to front, lifting the arms and legs and examining inside the mouth and other orifices — no part is omitted from examination. Specimens of hair are

taken from the head, eyebrows and pubic region, the mouth, anus and vagina are swabbed and fingernail scrapings are also taken. Each specimen is sealed in a labelled container. Scars, tattoos, deformities, occupational marks, birth-marks, blemishes and wounds of any kind are noted, together with the extent of LIVIDITY and RIGOR MORTIS. Injuries are photographed and measured, their position being recorded on a body-outline diagram — position is noted in relation to the parts of the body, and by distance measured from the feet to relate them to height. All wounds associated with cause of death in criminal cases are cut out and preserved as specimens. These may be required for subsequent examination by other doctors. In cases of firearm wounds the body is

Body-outline diagram used to record the positions of injuries and other marks

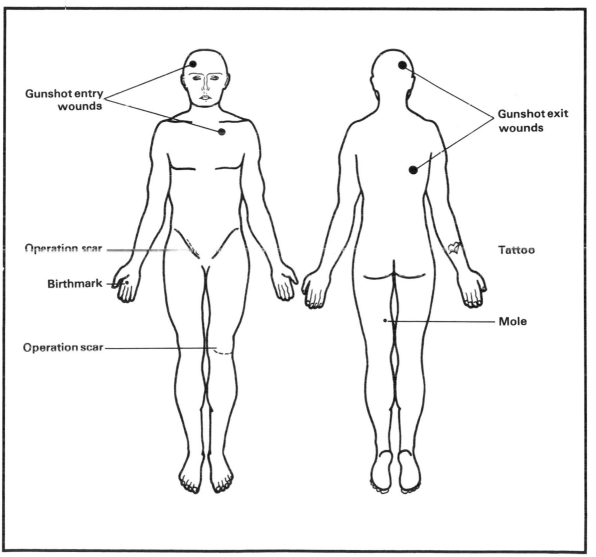

Gunshot entry wounds

Gunshot exit wounds

Operation scar

Birthmark

Tattoo

Mole

Operation scar

often X-rayed to determine the position of bullets and metal fragments before internal examination is started.

External indications of violence might lie in the presence of defensive wounds on the hands or in bruising around the neck or inside the mouth. Tiny haemorrhages known as petechiae in the EYES might indicate death by strangulation, and hypodermic-needle punctures in the arms, thighs or buttocks might denote drug-use or POISONING. KNIFE-WOUNDS, lacerations and GUNSHOT-WOUNDS all have their story to tell, and much can be learned about the type of weapon used and the direction of an assault from a close inspection of such injuries. The essence of the forensic pathologist's skill is to miss nothing, and the necessity of the detailed meticulous approach is borne out by many examples of cursory examinations which have missed a vital piece of evidence. There is also the danger, as Professor Francis Camps pointed out, of it being too easy to find what one expects, but at the expense of missing the obvious.

Once the external examination is complete the pathologist turns his attention to the internal part of the autopsy. Doctors differ in the precise technique they use, but a common procedure is to make a Y-shaped incision from throat to crotch, curving slightly to avoid the umbilicus. The structures of the neck and organs of the chest cavity are exposed to view and examined in situ by dissection and by cutting through the rib-cage. The presence and amount of any fluid is carefully noted. The whole of the neck and chest contents are then removed as one unit to preserve the integrity of the systems. This section, as it is known, is placed on another table for separate dissection. In cases of suspected STRANGULATION, for example, the hyoid bone is of particular significance, but care is needed to avoid fracturing it accidentally during dissection.

The abdominal contents are similarly examined and removed, particular attention being given to the STOMACH CONTENTS, which might afford an indication of the TIME OF DEATH or of the nature of any poisoning. The skull is also opened, and the brain inspected for any abnormality. Special procedures will be adopted by the pathologist as necessitated by the progress of the autopsy. Specimens of skin, bone, BLOOD, muscle, urine, brain, spinal cord and the more common organs may be taken for analysis. Individual organs are weighed, and the pathologist dictates his notes and findings as he goes along. These may be written up by an assistant or recorded on tape through a micro-

phone. The whole procedure is designed for thoroughness, and every organ (whether or not involved in the apparent cause of death) is examined. Negative findings are important, as Dr Milton Helpern has observed, for 'excluding a large variety of conditions that may have been suspected originally', and also in countering any speculation that may arise in court during criminal proceedings.

When the post-mortem examination has been completed the body is restored for normal burial and the pathologist completes his report for the coroner giving a clearly stated cause of death. In the case of murder, the expert's findings gleaned from post-mortem examination of the victim's body help to protect the innocent and convict the guilty — but it is a heavy responsibility which demands skill and thoroughness. The conviction of Kenneth Barlow for wife-murder is ample illustration of this. On 3 May 1957 police were called to a house in Bradford where Kenneth Barlow, a male nurse, told them he had found his wife dead in the bath. He claimed to have attempted artificial respiration, but eagle-eyed police officers noted that his pyjamas were dry, and that there were no splashes of water on the bathroom floor. Moreover, when a doctor examined the body he observed water lying in the crooks of the dead woman's arms — an indication that artificial respiration had not been tried.

Doctors suspected poison because of the dilation of the eyes, but the autopsy showed no defect in any of the organs, and there were no external marks on the body. Samples of various organs and body fluids were comprehensively analysed, but no trace of poison was found. Still dissatisfied at the negative findings, the pathologist decided to examine the entire surface of the body again. Aided by a magnifying glass and powerful illumination, he discovered two tiny hypodermic-needle punctures in the folded, freckled skin under the right buttock. Tissue from these injection sites contained insulin in amounts which suggested the dead woman had been given a massive dose of the drug.

Forensic science allied to painstaking postmortem procedure was sufficient to ensure Barlow's conviction for murder. The term 'post-mortem' has, of course, passed into the language to denote an inquiry to find out 'what went wrong' in a particular branch of human activity. That it has been so adopted is a compliment to its medical origins.

1, 97, 240, **273***, 324, 346, 589,* **625***, 626, 632, 639,* **675***.*

PSYCHIC DETECTION

When they were confronted with a multiple murder near Edmonton in 1928 the Canadian authorities decided to call in a remarkable old man to assist them. Maximilian Langsner, who had trained as a doctor in Vienna, possessed special powers which he had previously demonstrated by solving a Vancouver jewellery theft after 'reading the mind' of a suspect.

Two members of the Booher family and two cow-hands were found dead from GUNSHOT-WOUNDS on their ranch in July 1928 by another member of the family, Vernon Booher. After attending the inquest and learning the details of the killings for the first time, Dr Langsner led detectives to the hiding-place of the murder weapon. He told them it was safe to handle as it had been wiped clean of FINGERPRINTS by Vernon Booher. Up to this point Booher had not featured as a suspect, but now he was taken into custody, Dr Langsner spent an hour outside Booher's police cell, and finally declared him to be the wanted murderer. He gave police an account of how the crimes had been carried out, and described a woman who had seen Booher in possession of the stolen rifle used for the killings. This witness was found, and she confirmed Langsner's statement. Confronted with this testimony Booher broke down and made a CONFESSION, his account of the murders being the same in every detail as Langsner's reconstruction.

Despite newspaper accusations that he had confessed under HYPNOSIS, Vernon Booher was convicted of murder and was hanged. This was probably the first recorded case of a murder investigation aided by psychic detection. As for Dr Langsner, he never worked for the police again but went to live in an Alaskan Eskimo community where he died in 1931.

The phenomenon of psychic detection has been used a great deal in searches for MISSING PERSONS. There have been two renowned practitioners, both Dutchmen, Gerard Croiset and Peter Hurkos. These two men have helped police forces around the world in investigations to locate missing property, to find persons who have disappeared and to trace murder suspects. Peter Hurkos was called in by the Boston police to aid their search for the Boston Strangler in 1964.

Between June 1962 and January 1964 thirteen women died in Boston, USA, at the hands of a sex killer nicknamed the Boston Strangler. His technique was to gain plausible admittance to the homes of women living on their own, where he raped and strangled them. His 'calling card' was to tie the ligature around his victims' throats with a characteristic bow under the chin. Boston became a city of fear as the number of murders mounted. Known sexual deviants were questioned, but all the police had to go on was a spate of false confessions.

On 29 January 1964 Hurkos was asked to assist detectives working on the case. He examined nylon scarves and stockings used by the killer to strangle his victims, and he was given three hundred crime photographs of the dead women and the murder scenes. Hurkos did not look at these directly but 'read' them by passing his hands over them as they lay face downward on a table. He surprised detectives by accurately relating to them the details contained in these unseen pictures. After six days working on the inquiry — in the process of which he lost fifteen pounds in weight — Hurkos 'saw' the killer and his room in his sleep. 'I lived through the killings', he said. 'I lived through the mind of that man.'

His candidate for the strangler's identity was a small middle-aged man with perverted tastes who was connected in some way with shoes. Such a man was already known to the police, a door-to-door shoe-salesman who was receiving psychiatric attention. This man (given the alias Thomas P. O'Brien) had been known to the police since 1962. Hurkos accompanied police officers to the man's apartment, and as a result of this confrontation O'Brien was admitted as a voluntary psychiatric patient to the Massachusetts State Mental Centre. A search of the apartment revealed a diary bearing details of its owner's sexual fantasies, just as Hurkos had seen in his sleeping mind's-eye view of the strangler's room.

Convinced that the Boston Strangler was now in custody, Hurkos predicted that the killings would stop, which they did for several months. But then in October a woman was attacked in her home by a man who made off without killing her. From the woman's description police identified the assailant as Albert DeSalvo, who had been previously convicted for indecent assault. Under questioning he admitted house-breaking and rape, but denied involvement in murder. DeSalvo was admitted to Boston State Hospital, where he was judged to be suffering from SCHIZOPHRENIA and not fit to stand trial. While in hospital he confessed to the murders, although he was never charged with being the Boston Strangler.

Albert DeSalvo was sentenced in 1967 to life

imprisonment for sex offences committed before the infamous series of stranglings. He was found dead in his prison cell in November 1973 — he had been stabbed through the heart. The man whom Peter Hurkos believed to be the Boston Strangler, Thomas P. O'Brien, remains a mental hospital inmate. Since this incident Hurkos has worked mainly in entertainment, although he made an inconclusive contribution to the investigation of the Sharon Tate murder in 1969.

Pieter Cornelius van der Hurk was born in Holland in 1911. His birth was unusual in that he had a membrane or caul covering his head — a rare medical phenomenon which has given rise to a great deal of folklore. In Holland it denotes a sixth sense and a gifted personality. In the case of Peter Hurkos — the name he adopted as a member of the Dutch wartime resistance — his gift did not develop until he reached the age of thirty. In 1941, while helping his house-painter father, he fell from a ladder, severely injuring his head. When he recovered consciousness he had completely lost his memory, but found a gift for seeing things not ordinarily visible. He was a changed person, destined to gain fame as the man with 'radar eyes' and the 'X-ray brain' who could find missing objects and missing people.

During the 1950s he worked for various police organizations throughout Europe, including SCOTLAND YARD and the SÛRETÉ, and in 1957 he went to the USA. He was involved in several murder cases as a psychic consultant, and collaborated with doctors and psychologists who wished to examine his psychic powers. Hurkos works by touching things such as clothing, letters or photographs from which he can tell things about their owners — a procedure known as psychometry. It has been suggested that his gift resulted from his brain injury, which triggered off a type of schizophrenia. But after many years' demonstration of these powers, scientists are no nearer an explanation of psychic detection.
99, 227, 562, 634.

PSYCHOPATH

The term was first used in 1891 by a German psychiatrist to denote the behaviour of a person who is emotionally unstable and morally defective. The psychopathic personality is regarded as one of the greatest problems in FORENSIC PSYCHIATRY, for while the broad characteristics are recognized the condition is not a psychosis and not due to

insanity in the ordinary sense. John Bartlow Martin in his book *Break Down the Walls* described the psychopath as a person whose emotions 'are out of kilter . . he is cold, remote, indifferent to the plight of others, hostile even'.

Professor Hervey Cleckley, an American neuro-psychiatrist, defined the psychopath as one who 'can perceive consequences, formulate in theory a wise course of conduct, name and phrase what is regarded as desirable or admirable; but his disorder is, apparently, such that he does not feel sufficiently and appropriately about these things to be moved and to act accordingly'.

A murderer whose personality filled this definition was Neville Heath (see under SADISM). He was a social misfit, a plausible and intelligent man who disappointed his family and friends with his lack of persistent effort in building on a promising career. Heath was intolerant of discipline and social obligations, and developed cruel and anti-social traits which ended up in murder. He was a handsome man, whose external appearance gave no hint of the inner violence and sexual perversion which eventually surfaced.

The aggressive psychopath may commit crimes of violence with careful premeditation and a lack of compassion which his friends would find difficult to believe. This is part of the characteristic lack of true feelings for others which his conscience may allow to erupt aggressively, while at the same time appearing to court detection and punishment. This was certainly true in the case of Neville Heath, who drew attention to himself after his second murder by going to the police to see a photograph of the missing woman.

Alcoholism, drugs and sexual perversion are common outlets for the psychopath. Patrick Mackay, who at the age of fifteen was described as 'a cold psychopathic killer' and who went on to commit three brutal murders, was a classic psychopath. His father was violent to his wife and children, and died a chronic alcoholic at the age of forty-two. Patrick's behaviour rapidly went downhill as he developed bullying tactics at school and engaged in torture of pet animals. He was in and out of several approved schools, and became obsessed with the trappings of fascism. He committed numerous thefts, and took to alcohol before finally plunging into murder. In 1974 he stabbed an elderly woman to death in her Chelsea home, and in 1975, in the space of a single month, strangled one person and killed another with an axe. There was no particular MOTIVE for these murders, and Mackay's only explanation was, 'I must have gone out of my mind'.

The trial jury at the Old Bailey judged him sane, and he was given life imprisonment. He fitted the general description of the psychopathic personality, and belonged to that part of the spectrum in which mental-health specialists look for parental rejection as a causal factor. Like Neville Heath and Peter Sutcliffe, the Yorkshire Ripper, he exhibited the most dangerous characteristic of the psychopath, which is the appearance of outward normality. It is this plausibility — often combined with an impressive personality — which so bewitches their victims.
134, 250.

Q

QUESTIONED DOCUMENTS

Documents, especially wills, are often questioned in circumstances where murder is suspected. This usually arises because of a forged signature which, while it may pass at first glance, is found on close scrutiny to be an imperfect copy of the genuine article. But suspicion was aroused in at least one murder case because the forged signatures looked too perfect.

Texas millionaire William Marsh Rice had the Midas touch. He owned oil-wells and other vast enterprises, but he had no mandate for happiness. His marriages were not blessed with offspring, and when his second wife died in 1896 he gave up his luxurious life-style and retired to an austere New York apartment.

The octogenarian's only companion was a young man, Charles F. Jones, who performed every duty from valet to secretary. The old man grouched that his late wife had left a will which distributed his money among her relatives. This was permissible under Texas law, which allowed a wife an equal share of all her husband's property. Rice — who was sequestering his millions to set up his dreamed-of Rice Institute, a non-profit-making educational foundation — contested the will on the grounds that he was a New York resident.

For their part Mrs Rice's beneficiaries, in seeking to protect their benefactor's will, hired a shifty lawyer to fight their cause. Albert T. Patrick made his own assessment of the situation and decided that there were generous pickings for the shrewd operator. He met young Jones, and believed he had found a malleable and indispensable confederate. Patrick prepared a draft will in the name of William Marsh Rice in which he was left half of the estate and named as the executor. For the promise of a share in this fortune, Jones was persuaded to type the document on Rice's stationery. Patrick undertook to look after the signing and witnessing.

The plotters had assumed that old man Rice would not live long and that nature would help their plan to fruition. The trouble was that their victim remained quite healthy, so it was decided to give him a helping hand. Jones began feeding MERCURY tablets to the old man on various pretexts, and when these failed to have the desired effect murdered him on 23 September 1900 with CHLOROFORM while he was sleeping. A DEATH CERTIFICATE was issued without fuss, and Patrick made hasty arrangements for a cremation.

The next day Patrick produced six cheques each bearing a forgery of Rice's signature. He instructed

Forged signatures of William Marsh Rice

Forged signature to $65,000 check.

Authentic signature of William Marsh Rice.

Forged signature to $25,000 check.

Jones to make out the body of four of these in the style that he normally used for his late employer. All the cheques were payable to Patrick, and represented a sum of 250,000 dollars. This careful plan started to go wrong because of a spelling error — one of the cheques was made out to Abert T. Patrick, but was correctly endorsed. The bank refused to accept it, and requested that it be properly endorsed. This Patrick did, perpetrating the original mistake in his re-endorsement. Bank officials' suspicion grew, and a telephone call was made to Mr Rice's home. Jones let it be known that Mr Rice had died.

Patrick later swaggered into the bank expecting to come away richer, only to be told that payment was refused until contact had been made with the administrator of Rice's estate. Patrick informed the bank that all Mr Rice's property was assigned to him, and produced the will. This document and the four cheques were carefully examined, and as a result Patrick and Jones were arrested for forgery, and the funeral was halted.

A POST-MORTEM was carried out on Rice's body, and Dr Rudolph Witthaus, the toxicologist, found the lungs congested, probably due to the irritant vapour of chloroform. He also found traces of MERCURY. Patrick and Jones now faced a murder charge, and after attempting suicide Jones made a full CONFESSION.

The trial for murder began in 1902 with Patrick conducting his own defence and loudly proclaiming his innocence. What he could not turn aside was the evidence of the document-examiner. The will consisted of four pages, each of which was signed 'W. M. Rice'. All four signatures showed such a remarkable similarity that they might have been made with a rubber stamp. This similarity contrasted sharply with other signatures made by Rice at the same time. These showed the irregularities which would be expected in an elderly person's handwriting. The four suspect signatures were photographed under glass ruled with a squared grid. Parts of individual letters were clearly seen to occupy the same squares in each signature, as if they had been traced. That is exactly what Patrick had done, and the JURY had little hesitation in declaring the will a forgery, and convicting the lawyer of murder. He was sentenced to death, and Jones (who had confessed) was allowed to go free. After years of protracted court proceedings, and to widespread astonishment, Patrick was granted an unconditional pardon in 1912.

The role of the document-examiner has been more readily recognized in the USA than elsewhere, largely on account of the higher incidence of fraud. Examination of documentary evidence in relation to crime has gained in importance as the forger's methods have grown more sophisticated. It is an immense field of investigation, encompassing the determination of forged signatures, identifying the handwriting of anonymous letters and kidnap notes, discerning erasures and alterations and piecing together burnt or damaged documents. The document-examiner uses a full range of scientific methods from infra-red photography to thin-layer chromatographic analysis, and he has a specialist knowledge of inks, papers, watermarks, handwriting and typewriting. The versatile part played by document-examination in murder inquiries is best described by reference to a number of cases.

Richard Brinkley, for example, was brought to justice in 1907 for committing fraud and murder, by scientific evidence concerning the ink used to write a signature. His fraudulent collection of witnesses' signatures on a will was successfully unmasked by Dr Ainsworth Mitchell in the first case of its kind involving ink analysis (see under CYANIDE).

Another murderer, William Podmore, also had his guilt confirmed by documentary evidence. Vivian Messiter, an oil-company agent, was found brutally murdered by a BLUNT INSTRUMENT in a garage in Southampton in 1929. The first clue to the attacker's identity came in the form of a scrap of grease-stained paper found in the garage. After the grease had been carefully soaked from the paper a message was revealed making an appointment for W. F. Thomas, 'possibly Tuesday at 10'. On the reverse was the address of a Southampton lodging-house where Thomas, alias Podmore, had been staying.

Using his alias, Podmore had been receiving commission on sales made to fictitious persons. When his employer found out and confronted him his answer was to murder him. Fortunately, these 'sales' had been recorded in a receipt-book, and although the top copies of the incriminating entries were missing, the pencil used to write them had left indentations on the pages beneath. When these were photographed under lateral lighting the fraud, and motive for murder, were brought to light. Podmore was convicted and later hanged.

Documentary evidence is particularly important in cases of KIDNAPPING. The ransom note in the famous Lindbergh case in 1932 contained a number of spelling errors suggesting the writer was

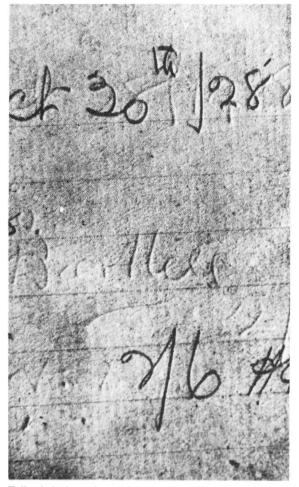

Tell-tale indentations left in the receipt book used by Podmore

editor of the *News of the World* demanding £1 million. Instructions given by the kidnappers concerning the ransom money were followed, but the Hosein brothers were spotted in their car, which was traced to their farm in Hertfordshire. The brothers denied all knowledge of Mrs McKay, and no trace of her was found at the farm — indeed, her body was never discovered. But there was ample documentary evidence to trap the kidnappers.

A handwriting expert produced visual evidence in court consisting of a photographic enlargement of the ransom note written in block letters on lined paper torn from an exercise book. When this was overlaid by a transparency of indentations found on a sheet of paper in Nizam's bedroom there was exact correspondence. Comparison of staple marks and torn edges of the letter also matched the sheet found by the police. In addition, two other notes were shown to have been written by Arthur Hosein in a disguised hand, and one of these was further identified by a FINGERPRINT. The two brothers were convicted of murder, kidnapping and blackmail, and were sentenced to life imprisonment.

The study of handwriting, or graphology, as a means of reading a person's character is not regarded as having a scientific basis. However, the examination and comparison of handwriting is an important asset to crime investigation in the hands of a specialist. Handwriting is an individualized, spontaneous and habitual skill. It is determined by early teaching, personal style and environmental factors such as stress, emotion, haste and age. The pattern of a person's writing is repetitive, and forms a recognizable style and form. Crossing the t's and dotting the i's are matters for individual expression, as is the formation of every letter. The difficulty for the forger is to emulate the free-flowing form of the genuine article and, for the person who wishes to disguise his hand, to escape an unconscious return to his own recognizable style.

Much of the handwriting expert's time is taken up by comparing known writing with questioned writing. One of the methods used is metrical analysis, which consists of measurements expressed in terms of the proportional heights of each character. These can be expressed graphically to give a visual comparison of signatures. Using this method, it was shown that Major Herbert Rowse Armstrong, in addition to poisoning his wife with ARSENIC, also forged her will.

The introduction of the typewriter in the nine-

German — as indeed he turned out to be, although Bruno Hauptmann was convicted on the strength of other evidence.

Kidnapping and murder is an unusual offence in England, but in 1970 the Hosein brothers were convicted of that crime. Arthur and Nizamodeen Hosein planned to kidnap the wife of Rupert Murdoch, the millionaire owner of the *News of the World*, by following his car to his residence. On 29 December 1969 they trailed his Rolls-Royce to a house in Wimbledon where they kidnapped a lady they assumed to be Mrs Murdoch. Their victim was in fact Mrs Muriel McKay, whose husband, the newspaper's deputy chairman, had been using the Rolls-Royce.

A telephoned ransom demand was made for £500,000, followed by numerous phone calls and letters. On 9 January 1970 a letter was sent to the

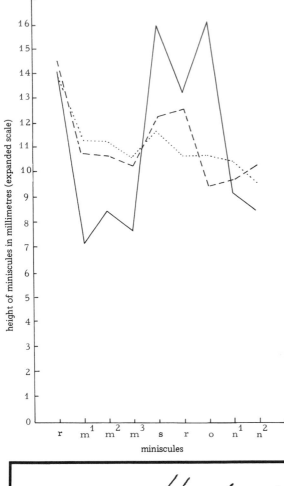

height of miniscules in millimetres (expanded scale)

miniscules

r   m   m   m   s   r   o   n   n
      1   2   3   1   2

teenth century suggested that mechanical repetition would confer anonymity on the criminal letter-writer. However, it was soon discovered that typewriters had individual identifiable characteristics, much like rifled gun barrels (see under FIREARMS). The typewriter is a mechanical device with many moving parts which are subject to uneven wear according to the manner in which the machine is used and maintained.

Manufacturers' preferences for type-styles, character and line-spacing are obvious differences, but every machine develops its own idiosyncracies which are transferred to the typed page. The state of the carbon ribbon and roller, dirt on the type-face, spacing defects, broken or damaged characters and various misalignments all contribute to a typewriter's individuality. David Carvalho, the American handwriting expert, put typewriters in the same category as bullets, fingerprints and teeth in terms of their variation. 'The history of typewriters', he wrote, 'is the record of their deterioration . . . the man who thinks he can escape detection by using a typewriter to perpetrate some written fraud is as likely to be exposed as the burglar who leaves his fingerprints. . . .' The odds of two typewriters performing identically have been put at 1 in 3,000,000,000,000.

It was typewriter evidence which brought the first breakthrough in the celebrated Leopold and Loeb murder case. The teenage killers of fourteen-

Mrs Armstrong's forged will

Herbert Rowse Armstrong

------ MAJOR ARMSTRONG

K. M. Armstrong

.... SUSPECTED WRITING
(Second Will)

Katharine M. Armstrong.

———— MRS ARMSTRONG
(First Will)

year-old Bobby Franks sent a typewritten ransom note to Mr Franks demanding 10,000 dollars. The note was signed 'George Johnson', and while checking out all persons of that name Chicago police received offers of help from Richard Loeb. A pair of spectacles found near the body turned out to belong to Loeb's friend Nathan Leopold, who was questioned about his typewriter. It was known that the ransom note had been typed on an Underwood portable machine, but Leopold denied that his machine was of that make. This story was eventually broken down when it became known that Leopold had loaned his typewriter to some fellow-students. Examination of their typed sheets showed that they came from the same machine as the ransom note. Loeb made a full CONFESSION, and there followed the sensational murder trial of the two sons of wealthy families who killed for excitement. The famous criminal lawyer Clarence Darrow successfully defended the pair against a death sentence, and in 1924 they were imprisoned for life.

97, 107, 121, 124, 264, 334, 424, 473, 489, **497, 498, 499, 502,** *520, 521, 538, 678,* **703,** *717.*

QUICKLIME

And all the while the burning lime
Eats flesh and bone away,
It eats the brittle bone by night,
And the soft flesh by day,
It eats the flesh and bones by turns
But it eats the heart alway.

Thus wrote Oscar Wilde in his *Ballad of Reading Gaol,* referring to the lime pit dug within the prison walls to receive the body of a hanged murderer. These lines illustrate a popular belief in the destructive properties of lime as a means of speeding up the decomposition of dead bodies. A number of murderers faced with the problem of disposal of a victim's body have used lime to hasten the process.

In 1847 Frederick and Maria Manning murdered Patrick O'Connor, a gauger at London docks who had made a small fortune from money-lending. Having elicited from a medical student that the weakest part of a person's skull was behind the ear, they crushed O'Connor's head with numerous blows from a crowbar, and shot him in the face for good measure. They then buried his body in a pit of quicklime beneath the flagstones of the kitchen at their house at 3 Minver Place, Bermondsey. As soon as inquiries were made about the missing man they fled their separate ways. Police forced an entry into the empty house, and soon discovered that the floor in the kitchen had been disturbed. Further investigation revealed the body of the missing man. 'So rapidly had the lime done its work in consuming the corpse,' wrote Sir Willoughby Maycock, 'that its identity was only established by the remarkable and less perishable feature of an extremely prominent chin and set of false teeth.' Only eight days had elapsed since O'Connor met his death.

Quicklime does not always work so well, and a great deal depends on whether or not the body is clothed, and on how quickly the lime is slaked with moisture from the surrounding soil, thereby generating heat. The Mannings were astute enough to throw their victim naked into the pit, and sudden slaking of the lime resulted in superficial burning of the body. The Mannings were brought to justice, and indulged in the unseemly spectacle of casting recriminations. Frederick blamed his wife as the instigator of the crime (she had been the object of O'Connor's admiration before her marriage), and Maria, who was Swiss by birth, claimed there was no justice to be had for a foreign subject in England. At any rate, a crowd of 50,000 gathered to see the Mannings dispatched by the public hangman in November 1847.

Dr Crippen made a modest use of lime in the cellar of 39 Hilldrop Crescent, London (see under HYSOSCINE), but another doctor, Marcel Petiot, at what was to become an equally sinister address, 21 rue Lesueur, Paris, made a positive industry with it. In the basement was a furnace fuelled with the dismembered remains of human bodies. The premises also accommodated a large lime-heap in the garage and a lime-pit in an adjacent stable, both of which contained human remains. Dr Albert Paul, a distinguished forensic expert and Paris coroner, hired four grave-diggers to sift the heaps of quicklime. Remains of at least ten bodies were retrieved from these sinks of decomposition and added to the charred bones and three dustbins full of other human fragments taken from the basement. Professor Henri Griffon, director of the police toxicology laboratory, was given the task of analysing some of the quicklimed viscera for drugs. The remains were shapeless, impregnated with lime and in a state of MUMMIFICATION; his quaint description noted that they emitted 'a piquant and extremely disagreeable odour'.

Sifting the lime-heaps in Dr Petiot's basement

The police discovered that Petiot's brother had delivered four hundred kilograms of quicklime to the house in February. His explanation that this was required to kill cockroaches and to whitewash the buildings was not taken too seriously, and he was charged with CONSPIRACY TO MURDER. The elusive doctor was arrested nine months after the revolting discoveries were made at his house, and he entered the ranks of MASS MURDER.

As the Paris authorities discovered, where the slaking of quicklime is achieved by taking up moisture from the bodies and their organs, the effect is often one of preservation rather than of DECOMPOSITION.
*73, 295, 441, **445**, 465, 480, 614, 753.*

RAPE

Rape and attempted rape are the most frequent forms of sexual offence. In England rape is defined under the Sexual Offences Act of 1956 as 'unlawful sexual intercourse with a woman without her consent by force, fear or fraud'. Intercourse is considered to have taken place when there is penetra-

tion, albeit of the slightest kind, and emission is not necessary to establish the offence. A boy under the age of thirteen cannot be convicted of rape, and it is a felony for a man to have unlawful intercourse with a girl under the age of thirteen.

In the USA rape is defined as carnal knowledge of a female by use of force or by threat of force sufficient to overcome her will to resist. Rape committed against under-age girls (varying between twelve and eighteen years according to the state) is classed as statutory rape, whether or not there is consent. In some states rape can be punished by death, and at one time Negro rapists in the southern states frequently fell victim to LYNCHING parties. One of the names commonly associated with sex offences is that of Caryl Chessman, who spent twelve years on Death Row before being executed in San Quentin's GAS CHAMBER in 1960, even though he had not committed murder.

Rape killings are the most common form of murder accompanied by SADISM, and virtually all multiple rapists fall into this class. The single rape killing often involves STRANGULATION, and results from excessive force used to overcome resistance. Rape killings, despite their violence, are distinguished from SEX MURDERS, in which the prime objective is mutilation. Harvey Glatman was a sadistic killer who drew women into his clutches on the pretence of hiring photographic models. In 1957 and 1958 he subjected three girls to a routine which consisted of rape, photography while they were helplessly tied up and then strangulation. He met his end in the gas chamber at San Quentin a year before Chessman.

James Ruzicka was convicted in 1973 in a Seattle court of raping two women at knife-point. The judge described him as a sexual PSYCHO-PATH, and ordered him sent to hospital to be treated as a sexual offender. Security was so lax that Ruzicka walked out after nine months, when he raped and killed two teenage girls in West Seattle and raped another teenager in Oregon. He was charged with double homicide in 1975, and found guilty. This 23-year-old habitual criminal, who had practised bestiality as a boy and had sampled cocaine and hallucinatory drugs such as LSD, was sentenced to two consecutive terms of life imprisonment.

During 1973–4 a series of nine rape murders occurred in New York City which contributed to America's annual total of over 50,000 reported rape cases. Eight of the victims were elderly residents of the decrepit Park Plaza Hotel in Manhattan, and the ninth lived in the adjacent apartment block. The first five deaths were not even rated as murder at the time because of the age of the victims! Police interest sharpened after the next four deaths, which all involved rape and murder. The hotel porter, 26-year-old ex-convict and drug addict Calvin Jackson, came under suspicion, and when he was charged with the last murder he readily confessed to eight others. There was no ready explanation why Jackson, who lived

at the hotel with his girl-friend, should have raped nine old women. The issue of insanity was widely debated at his trial, but the jury found him both sane and guilty.

POST-MORTEM examination of victims of sexual assault follows the usual procedure after full account is taken of the special aspects of such deaths. Evidence of the nature of the crime is usually obvious from the disarranged state of the clothing and the position of the body. An external examination is made for abrasions and bruises which may be found on the thighs, buttocks, shoulders and neck. These are the injuries caused by tearing at the clothing, forcing the legs open and pinioning the struggling victim. The genitals are examined both externally and internally for injuries, and to establish the likely nature of penetration. Swabs are taken from the vagina and anus to be tested in the laboratory for spermatozoa. Specimens are also taken of any fluid deposits or stains caused by blood, saliva or semen which may be found on the body, especially in the pubic region and mouth. Bite-marks may be evident on the breasts. These are carefully examined for TEETH impressions which may assist in the IDENTIFICATION of the murderer.

Rape, by the forceful nature of such assault, is likely to result in considerable transfer of CONTACT TRACES between victim and assailant. Stray HAIRS and FIBRES, especially around the pubic region, are taken as samples, together with control specimens from the victim. Finger-nail scrapings are also collected, for any vestige of skin, blood or hair may provide valuable linking evidence. The victim's clothing is carefully checked for tears, stains and any debris likely to have been transferred from the assailant. The body is photographed in the position in which it was found, and in relation to its surroundings. Footprints in outdoor crime scenes may be particularly significant, and such impressions are photographed or recorded as casts. These may provide valuable corroborative evidence of a suspect's presence at the crime scene.

The FORENSIC SCIENCE laboratory plays an important part in rape cases, especially in carrying out serological tests. A blood sample is always taken from the victim to establish her BLOOD group. Bloodstains found on the body or clothing are also grouped for comparison; saliva and semen may also be grouped if their owner is a SECRETOR. Establishing that the assailant is a secretor materially helps to narrow the criminal investigation. Stains on clothing suspected of being seminal fluid

Seminal-fluid stains

are confirmed by subjecting them to ultra-violet light, when they become fluorescent. The Florence test and acid phosphatase test are chemical reactions which provide further confirmation of the presence of seminal fluid. Spermatozoa are identified under the microscope, and this instrument is also heavily relied on for the examination of hairs and fibres.

Unless a man is quickly apprehended after committing rape and murder, there is little to be gained from medical examination of his body and clothing. In any case, prior to his arrest, such an examination may only be made with the suspect's assent. Given the opportunity, the doctor will be looking for physical injuries, such as scratches to the arms and face, and for foreign hairs on the body and clothing. The state of the clothes and shoes in respect of any soil or debris adhering to them may be especially significant in linking the suspect to the crime scene.

Colin Wilson has remarked that if a list was made of the most notorious murderers in criminal history there would be very few rapists among them. It seems to be the case that when a man is prepared to kill for sex his desire is so perverted that the normal sexual act does not interest him, and he becomes a lust murderer. It is not clear what tips the balance to turn a man into a rapist, although there is no shortage of theories. Professor James Melvin Reinhardt, the American criminologist, wrote that 'Satyriasis [grossly exaggerated sexual desire in a man, from Greek mythology's satyr] or even a mildly accentuated sex propensity may produce a Don Juan or a rapist.' Intelligent, sexually virile men satisfy their needs by guile and conquest while others resort to prostitutes and pornography. This sliding-scale of sexual fulfilment slips into forceful rape committed because the opportunity presents itself, to planned abduction and rape, and finally to rape accompanied by sadistic murder.

In the sexual tensions produced in modern society it has been suggested that the rate of sexual offences, for example, in Denmark decreased with the legalization of pornography. The scale of activity is enormous, ranging from the perverted excesses of homosexual rapists such as Dean Corll and Wayne Gacy, who murdered sixty boys between them (see under HOMOSEXUAL MURDERS), to sex and fraud on the part of a singing teacher in 1923 who convinced a pupil that the quality of her voice would be improved as a result. *261*, *410*, **569**, **627**, *738*.

REASONABLE DOUBT

It is the function of the prosecution in a criminal case to provide enough evidence to prove guilt beyond a reasonable doubt. Although juries are reminded to take account of this, the term has never been precisely defined. Probably Mr Justice Darling put it as well as anyone when he told the JURY at the trial of Steinie Morrison for murder (see under EVIDENCE), 'You know without my telling you a reasonable doubt means such a doubt not as some people "conjure up" about anything, but such a doubt as would influence a man in his own ordinary daily affairs.' English law allows no halfway house in this matter, as might be thought to exist in Scotland where a jury can return a verdict of NOT PROVEN.

A murder case with all the ingredients of a CRIME PASSIONEL which illustrated the workings of doubt in the minds of the jury was that in which Lord Erroll was the victim. He lived in Kenya, enjoying colonial life as a man of influence with an eye for the ladies. In 1940 he met Lady Diana Broughton and her husband, Sir Henry John Delves Broughton, who were spending their honeymoon in the colony. Erroll immediately fell in love with Diana, and they discussed with Broughton what should be done. Broughton had agreed with his young wife that if either fell in love with another party they would separate amicably. Diana now took him up on his promise, and he agreed to step aside.

This all seemed very civilized, until the night of

23 January 1941 when disaster struck. Erroll took Diana out to a dance, while Broughton got himself drunk. At about 2.25 a.m. Erroll brought Diana home and then drove to his death three miles away. He was found the next day lying dead on the floor of his car with a bullet through his head.

Broughton certainly had a MOTIVE to kill his rival, and he was arrested. He said that two revolvers had been stolen from his house a few days before the murder. He had used one of these for target practice at a friend's farm, and spent .32 bullets recovered from the practice shooting were believed by the police to have been fired from the same weapon that killed Erroll.

FIREARMS evidence featured prominently at Broughton's trial for murder. The Government Chemist, Mr M. H. Fox, emphatically stated that the bullet recovered from the victim matched the bullets from the practice shooting. 'I am not infallible,' he remarked, 'but in this case I think I am right.' The defence's firearms expert cast doubt on the prosecution's confident assertion by pointing out several differences between the bullets. He concluded that they had been fired from two different weapons. Moreover, the prosecution was unable to explain convincingly how a man of fifty-nine who suffered from night-blindness was able to commit the murder in the manner suggested.

The judge, Sir Joseph Sheridan, reminded the jury that they must be satisfied of guilt beyond reasonable doubt, which he emphasized was not mathematical certainty but 'such certainty as you would require before acting and coming to a conclusion in the transaction of the most important affairs you are called on to undertake'. The jury did not believe the case against Sir Henry Broughton had been proved beyond reasonable doubt, and found him not guilty of either murder or MANSLAUGHTER. Broughton committed suicide in a Liverpool hotel in 1942.
1, 50, 51, 52, 168, 244, 343, 457, 534, 659, 755.

RES GESTAE

Means literally 'things done', and refers to words or statements accompanying a crime which may be considered as part of the offence and be admitted as EVIDENCE. It is recognized that the nature of an act of MURDER may not be fully understood except by referring to statements made at the time.

After he had shot Lee Harvey Oswald, the alleged assassin of President John F. Kennedy, Jack Ruby was heard to say, 'I hope the son of a bitch dies' (an account of Ruby's trial is given under EPILEPSY). A police officer testified at the murder trial in Dallas, Texas, that these words were spoken at the time, and the judge admitted them as part of the *res gestae* of the offence. Their effect was to show that the accused man appeared to bear malice towards the victim.

Another famous Texas court affair was the trial of Dr John Hill in Houston in 1970 on a charge of murder by omission. The Robinson Hill case included among its many extraordinary incidents a controversial piece of *res gestae* testimony. Hill's wife, Joan Robinson Hill, had died mysteriously in March 1969, and after three grand juries had considered the evidence, Dr Hill was finally indicted on a charge of causing the death of his wife by omission. The implication was that he had killed her deliberately by withholding medical treatment. (The case is told more fully under BACTERIA.)

Yet again in Texas, at the trial of multi-millionaire T. Cullen Davis, central features of the prosecution case were *res gestae* statements made by two witnesses after the fatal shooting. One of these was Davis's wife, Priscilla, a petite blonde whose silicone breast implants and gold necklace bearing the words 'Rich Bitch' did a great deal to secure large newspaper headlines. She was having an affair with 6ft 10 baseball player Stan Farr, which Cullen Davis did not find amusing.

On the evening of 2 August 1976 Priscilla and Stan Farr, accompanied by a friend, returned to Davis's 'Mansion', where they were ambushed by a gunman. Stan Farr was shot dead, Priscilla and her friend were wounded, and her twelve-year-old daughter by a former marriage lay dead inside the house. Priscilla's immediate reaction was to run from the scene, and she fell into the arms of a police officer shouting, 'It was Cullen. Cullen did it.'

Cullen Davis, the richest man in America ever to be indicted for murder, hired brilliant lawyer Richard 'Racehorse' Haynes to defend him. The central features of the prosecution case were the *res gestae* statements made by Priscilla and her wounded friend in which they identified Davis as the gunman. The prosecution called them 'excited utterances', the kind of truth which comes out in the passion of the moment. After the longest and costliest murder trial in Texas history, Cullen Davis was acquitted of the charges.

With other charges of murder and attempted murder pending, this sensational case took a

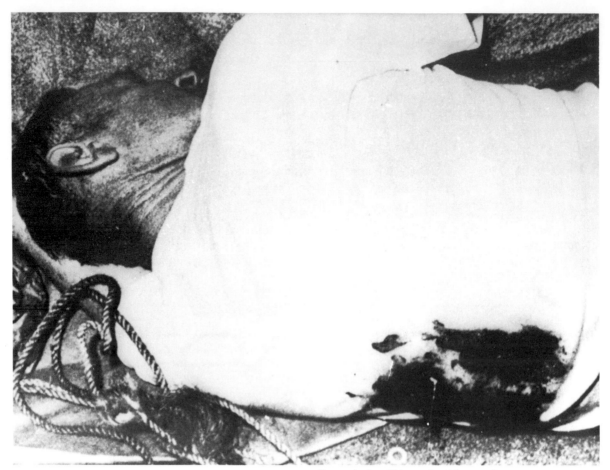

'I got Judge Eidson dead for you'

bizarre turn in August 1978 when Davis was arrested for plotting the murder of Joe Eidson, the judge involved in his divorce from Priscilla. He was alleged to have hired a man to deal with his hit-list, and a conversation in his car was tape-recorded on a concealed machine by this man, who was an FBI informant. Davis was told, 'I got Judge Eidson dead for you', to which he was said to have replied 'Good', and was shown a photograph of the supposedly dead judge. Notes to the value of 25,000 dollars were claimed to have changed hands for this evidence, which had been obligingly faked with the judge's co-operation.

After a mistrial in Houston Davis was again defended by Haynes, who argued that his client had been the victim of an elaborate frame-up. Davis himself gave evidence, and Haynes told the jury that the accused man believed he had been helping the police to set a trap for the real contract killer. The jury's verdict was not guilty, and Cullen Davis was a free man.

123, 140, 388, 547, 668.

RICIN

Georgi Markov, a Bulgarian defector who worked for the BBC in London, was waiting at a bus stop on Waterloo Bridge on 7 September 1978 when he felt a sharp pain in his leg. Turning round, he saw a man bending down to pick up an umbrella. The man apologized in a thick accent and hailed a passing taxi.

In the early hours of the following morning Markov was taken ill at home. His wife thought he had flu symptoms, but Markov told her it might be 'to do with something that happened today', referring to the umbrella puncture wound in his leg. He was admitted to a London hospital where he died on 11 September of toxaemia — his blood-count was the highest ever seen by doctors in that hospital.

Following POST-MORTEM examination, forensic experts concluded that Markov had died from a rare poison which had been slowly absorbed into his bloodstream from a tiny metal pellet implanted in his leg. The inquest, which was widely reported in the press, heard testimony from specialists in microbiology and bacterial warfare. It was clear that Markov's apparent murder was a highly sophisticated affair. The CORONER's verdict was that the Bulgarian had been 'unlawfully killed'.

The poison used was ricin, a plant toxin derived from castor-oil beans, isolated during the Second World War and considered for use as a possible chemical weapon. It ranks with botulinus among the most toxic substances known — one gram would be sufficient to kill 36,000 people, and as little as 21 micrograms (millionths of a gram) is a fatal individual dose. The poison is virtually impossible to detect in the body, although its effect on the blood — causing strong agglutination of the red corpuscles — sets up antibodies which act as indicators.

The method used to introduce the ricin into Markov's body was to implant a poison-laden pellet by means of an umbrella-gun. This pellet was a tiny platinum sphere, only 1·52 millimetres in diameter, bearing two 0·35 millimetre diameter holes which carried the lethal dose of ricin. The manufacture of this pellet necessitated use of a high-temperature furnace and sophisticated technology available at only a handful of specialized centres throughout the world. The sinister implications were that only a highly qualified scientist with access to defence secrets could have made the device.

The man with the umbrella escaped into London's crowds, and Markov's killing has not been solved. The attempted murder of another Bulgarian defector and broadcaster in Paris led to the belief that ASSASSINATIONS were being carried out at the instigation of the Bulgarian secret police. In this case the victim, who was stabbed in the back, survived because the poisonous pellet lodged in deep muscle where the toxin was released so slowly that he may have developed a partial immunity.

The World Health Organisation warned of the dangers of ricin as a chemical warfare agent in its manual on chemical weapons published in 1970. The protocol signed by Britain, the USA and Russia in 1974 banning bacteriological weapons does not include toxins such as ricin.

491, **667**.

RIGOR MORTIS

Dead bodies are known as 'stiffs' on account of the rigidity of the muscles which occurs after death. Rigor mortis is one of the classic signs of death, and as an early medical textbook put it 'is a sure indication of the hopelessness of any attempts at resuscitation'. The state of rigor mortis in a murder victim has been used in order to establish the TIME OF DEATH, but the condition is no longer regarded as an adequate indicator.

A murder in which time of death played an important role was that of Julia Wallace, which is discussed under ALIBI. When the pathologist examined the dead woman's body in the parlour of her home where she had been beaten to death with a BLUNT INSTRUMENT, he stated that she had been dead for at least four hours. He arrived at this conclusion by noting the presence of rigor mortis in the neck and upper part of the left arm. This observation was made at 9.50 p.m., which put time of death at before 6.0 p.m., thus negating William Wallace's story that he had seen his wife alive at 6.45 p.m.

The pathologist came in for some sharp criticism for failing to record the corpse's rectal temperature, which would have provided the best indication of when death had occurred. Nor did he comment on the presence of any LIVIDITY, which if his time assessment was correct should have been evident. Taken by itself, rigor mortis is an unreliable guide, and the small degree of rigidity noted in this case, bearing in mind the victim's frail physical state and the warmth of the surroundings, could have placed the murder at any time between two and eight hours before the corpse was examined. The doctor maintained his opinion about the timing of death at Wallace's trial for murder, and the accused man was convicted, although the verdict was later quashed.

Rigor mortis is a shortening of both the voluntary and involuntary muscles which stiffen and fix the limbs. This condition is brought about by the coagulation of protein in the muscles, and the earliest signs occur in the eyelids and lower jaw. Stiffening usually starts within five hours after death and spreads progressively to the neck, shoulders, arms, trunk and legs. Overall rigidity is normally established after about twelve hours. This condition lasts for about twelve hours and then recedes during the next twelve-hour period, disappearing first from those muscles in which it began. The whole process therefore takes between

36 and 48 hours, and once it has passed rigor cannot return, as irreversible chemical changes take place which initiate DECOMPOSITION.

The speed with which rigor mortis appears in a corpse depends on the conditions in which the body is left, and in particular on the temperature of the surroundings. Stiffening is delayed by cold and accelerated by heat, and by any activity which causes undue exertion or fatigue. Thus a pre-death struggle tends to speed the onset of rigor.

Three other conditions, not related to rigor mortis, cause rigidity. They are stiffening due to excessive heat or cold (see under BURNING) and CADAVERIC SPASM. Normal rigor does not occur in heat stiffening, but will appear in a frozen body once it starts to thaw.
548, **625**.

RITUAL MURDER

Ritual murder bound up with the idea of religious sacrifice is commonly associated with tribal Africa. A series of murders involving sacrificial victims occurred in Basutoland in 1947 and 1948, when a number of men and women were killed in order to procure their body organs as ingredients in protective medicines. It has been suggested that JACK THE RIPPER had a similar reason for removing organs from his victims.

Probably the most ritualistic murders of modern times were those committed by the followers of Charles Manson. On the night of 9 August 1969 three women and a man entered the Hollywood home of Sharon Tate, where they murdered the pregnant actress and four of her friends in an orgy of violence. The following night the same team of killers, helped by another girl, murdered Leno La Bianca and his wife in similar fashion. These young hippie killers had been commanded to kill by Manson, their charismatic leader, whose twisted philosophy required human sacrifices for his war against society and the 'pigs'.

Manson was interested in mysticism and HYPNOTISM, and became obsessed with ideas of universal destruction. He and his followers used LSD and moved in a semi-dream world in which he was the father figure and they were his 'family'. Manson's instructions to wreak violence were unhesitatingly followed out from devotion or manipulated obedience.

Another instance in which blind acceptance of another person's dominance led to violence was provided by Denise Labbé, a young Frenchwoman. In 1954 Denise met an officer cadet from the Saint-Cyr military school named Jacques Algarron. This dashing officer had a keen mind, and was considered an exceptional mathematician. He was also steeped in Nietzschean philosophy, and Denise fell under his domination.

Algarron regarded women as instruments of his will, and he insisted that Denise sleep with other men in order that she could ask his forgiveness. The ultimate test came when he asked the girl to prove her love for him by sacrificing her 2½-year-old daughter — the result of a previous affair. Denise undoubtedly loved her child, but she was so firmly under Algarron's evil spell that after the third attempt she succeeded in drowning the infant in a basin of water.

Friends became suspicious at the child's absence and Denise was eventually questioned by the police. 'Yes,' she said, 'I killed my daughter, but it was a ritual murder.' She and Algarron were tried for murder in 1955, and the jury listened to her desperate account of being torn between her love for a powerful man and her child. She was found guilty with extenuating circumstances for which she received penal servitude for life, and Algarron, the brilliant but evil-minded officer cadet, was given twenty years' hard labour.
44, 102, 263, 331, 551, 597, 667, 758.

SADISM

Neville Heath, who murdered two young women in London in 1946, has been labelled 'the most sadistic sex killer of all time'. While there are numerous recent contenders for that infamous title, Heath remains the classic psychopathic sadist.

Neville George Clevely Heath came from an unexceptional background and developed into a handsome young man with a compelling manner and striking blue eyes. Despite these natural gifts,

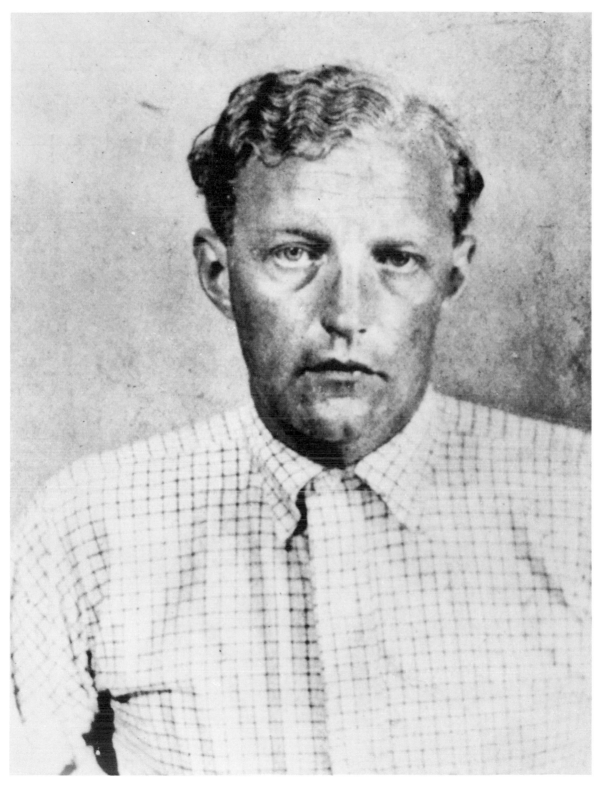

Neville Heath: portrait of a sadist

he developed anti-social habits such as petty theft, fraud and house-breaking. He was commissioned in the Royal Air Force, but after only eighteen months service was dismissed in 1937 for being absent without leave and for taking a car without permission. At the outbreak of the Second World War, Heath enlisted in the Army and within a few months was commissioned and posted to Egypt. He resumed his acts of petty crime, and as a result was cashiered and sent back to England on a troopship by way of South Africa.

In Johannesburg he joined the South African Air Force under a false name, and started training as a pilot. He also married, and appeared to be leading a stable life. His past eventually caught up with him, but the South African authorities decided to waive his murky career and offered him a commission. In 1944 he was seconded to the RAF in Britain, and flew bomber sorties over occupied Europe.

When the war ended Heath returned to South Africa but broke with his wife, who divorced him for desertion. The reprieve he had gained from the SAAF was only temporary, and when he began wearing military decorations to which he was not entitled he was dismissed from the service. He returned to London early in 1946, a rather undistinguished ex-officer, who had the remarkable record of being thrown out of the RAF, the SAAF and the British Army. He sought to regain past glories by posing as a senior officer, and lived on his wits and ability to defraud.

In June 1946 something snapped in Heath's mind and he graduated from petty crime to murder of the most horrific kind. That month he took a young woman to a London hotel, where in the privacy of their room he savagely ill-treated and murdered her. She was subjected to a whipping and a brutal sexual attack — her nipples were practically bitten off, and her vagina torn. Heath did not wait to be interviewed by the police, but wrote to SCOTLAND YARD stating that he had seen

The hotel register of the Pembridge Court Hotel for 16 June, 1946

the murder victim in the company of another man whose description he gave. He also claimed to have the whip with which the girl had been beaten.

Within two weeks Heath checked into a Bournemouth hotel, posing as an Air Force officer. He met a young woman staying in another hotel, who promptly disappeared. He body was found several days later about a mile from the hotel — she had been cruelly mutilated. Her throat was cut, and she had been beaten and stabbed. Her breasts had been bitten, and the vagina torn following the insertion of a rough implement. Before the body was found Heath offered his assistance to the police, and as a result of his craving to subject himself to suspicion he was detained. A bloodstained scarf and a metal-tipped whip were found in his possession.

Heath was tried for murder at the Old Bailey, and a defence plea of insanity won him no mercy. He was found guilty, and hanged. This charmer of women harboured sexual passions which his fellow-servicemen had recognized as abnormal. These seemed suddenly to have engulfed him, and led to his outburst of sadistic killing. There was certainly something of the exhibitionist in Heath, and while more charitable observers interpret his approaches to the police as expressions of guilt, others see only crude glorification.

While Neville Heath typifies the sadistic murderer, acknowledgment for introducing the word sadism to the language goes to a French marquis. Donatien Alphonse François de Sade (1740–1814) was born into a noble family in the eighteenth century, a period later called 'the age of complete corruption'. De Sade was part of that corruption, for he took his pleasures from perverted sexual practices, especially those in which he inflicted torture and suffering on his partners. Like Heath — a latter-day disciple — de Sade had striking blue eyes and a compelling appearance. He entered the army, serving as a cavalry captain before dedicating his life to decadence. He spent twenty-seven of his seventy-four years in prison, the last thirteen in an asylum. He was a regular visitor at the numerous brothels in Paris, and his trail of sexually abused victims brought him condemnation and prison. While he was imprisoned he amused himself with thoughts of perverted sexual practices, with torture and flagellation as the main themes, which he incorporated in his novels, *Juliette*, *Justine* and *Philosophy in the Boudoir*.

The word which the Marquis de Sade bequeathed to mankind is today used to denote the type of perversion in which sexual satisfaction is gained or enhanced by the use of cruelty. In common with other perversions, sadism differs in the degree it affects the individual, ranging from gratuitous brutality to mutilation and MURDER. Sadistic murderers experience sexual excitement by torturing and killing their victims. These acts may be sufficient in themselves, for the sadist does not always attempt sexual intercourse with his victim. Krafft-Ebing cited cases of sadism in women, although the occurrence is not common.

Perhaps the most carefully probed examples of sadistic murder were those provided by Peter Kürten, the 'Monster of Düsseldorf'. His reign of terror ended on the GUILLOTINE in 1931 after he was found guilty on nine counts of murder. His sexual life was pieced together by a noted psychiatrist, Professor Karl Berg, who persuaded Kürten to talk to him after his arrest. (See under SEX MURDER.)

In more recent times, Ian Brady and his companion, Myra Hindley, developed an appetite for a mixture of sadism, pornography and Nazism which erupted in the Moors Murders in 1964. The pleading, screaming voice of one of their child victims played on a tape-recording during their trial shocked the court, and they were both found guilty of murder. Brady's library included works by de Sade and numerous erotic publications.

1, 58, 66, 260, 308, 336, **409***, 448, 468,* **518***, 554, 640, 697, 730, 738.*

SCHIZOPHRENIA

The commonest of all forms of insanity, popularly known as 'split personality', which affects one person in a hundred. An early descriptive term for the disease was dementia praecox, meaning literally 'precocious insanity' and referring to the signs of withdrawal and delusion exhibited by some individuals in early adulthood.

No single cause of the disease has been identified, and it is not known whether the trigger is organic or environmental. One line of thought is that the schizophrenic may suffer from a defect in the sleep mechanism whereby dreams are experienced in the wakened state. Since the person knows he is not asleep, he concludes that the hallucinations are real, and acts on them.

At its simplest, schizophrenia is a withdrawal from reality and a failure to respond emotionally. The disease can progress to a catatonic stage, characterized by sudden outbursts of wild behaviour, and to a paranoid development in which violent criminal acts may be committed. Paranoid schizophrenia is marked by hallucinations in the form of imagined voices, delusions, including grandiosity and extreme religiosity, and feelings of hostility and persecution.

The classic case of the schizophrenic murderer is Daniel M'Naghten, who unwittingly gave his name to the rules used to this day to define legal insanity. (See M'NAGHTEN RULES.) A more recent example of this type of murderer highlighted a modern problem — that of the humane treatment of the psychiatric offender. In a five-month period in 1972–3 Herbert Mullin killed 13 persons in California in cold-blooded, apparently motiveless murders. Mullin came from a decent background, but drifted into drug-use and was unable to cope with the grief resulting from the death of a young friend. He became withdrawn and dissolved into schizophrenia — a mental condition for which he was diagnosed and treated in hospital. When eventually captured, Mullin spoke of hearing voices which commanded him to kill. A California jury failed to find him legally insane out of fear that the state's mental institutions would not hold him, or would prematurely release a killer into the community. Instead Mullin was found guilty and sentenced to life imprisonment.

David Berkowitz, the Son of Sam killer (see under MODUS OPERANDI), is another example of the schizophrenic personality. At times he appeared quite normal, but when madness took over he relapsed into a disorientated world in which he saw the Devil as Sam and himself as the Son of Sam. Referring to the murders, he said, 'It wasn't me. It was Sam working through me . . . Sam used me as a tool.'
389, 405, 451, 452, **518**.

SCOTLAND YARD

'Calling in the Yard' has been part of Britain's police heritage, and is a tribute to one of the world's great detective forces. The Metropolitan Police Force was set up in 1829 following Sir Robert Peel's introduction of a Bill to Parliament. Despite opposition, Britain's first official police force came into being, and a thousand uniformed men, nicknamed 'Bobbies', went on patrol in London's streets. This force was quickly expanded to three thousand men, and one of the first Police Commissioners, Sir Richard Mayne, declared that 'the protection of life and property, the preserva-

tion of public tranquillity and the absence of crime' would determine whether the police achieved their purpose. In 1856 Parliament passed an Act providing for the compulsory establishment of police forces throughout England and Wales.

The Metropolitan Police set up its first headquarters in Westminster in buildings entered through Great Scotland Yard. This focus of police activity in the capital soon became known as 'Scotland Yard', a name which was to be famous throughout the world as a symbol of the English police system. Despite changes in location, the headquarters retained its identity, simply becoming New Scotland Yard in the process. The Metropolitan Police Force is the largest in Britain, and employs about a quarter of the country's police manpower. Its area of jurisdiction covers eight hundred square miles, and in addition to policing the Greater London area, its responsibilities include the maintenance of criminal records, including FINGERPRINTS for the whole country, running the national bureau for INTERPOL, VIP protection and provision of criminal investigation expertise when requested by other forces.

The Commissioner of Police of the Metropolis is appointed by the Crown on the advice of the Home Secretary. He has a deputy and four Assistant Commissioners (ACs) working for him, each responsible for a particular branch of police organization. Up to 1878 detective work was carried out by the Bow Street Runners, but in that year the Criminal Investigation Department (CID) came into being. It became traditional for other British police forces to 'call in the Yard' to help solve difficult cases, especially MURDER inquiries. The CID operates a number of specialized activities, including a Fingerprint and Photographic branch, Criminal Records Office, Fraud Squad, Flying Squad and Special Branch. The Metropolitan Police set up its own FORENSIC SCIENCE laboratory in 1934, which with eight regional laboratories run by the Home Office provides Britain's police with scientific back-up. The Police National Computer at Hendon, which cost £50 million to install, enables the individual police officer at the crime scene to check information with great speed by way of his personal radio. The computer is linked to five hundred terminals at police stations throughout the country, and the system can deal with thousands of inquiries an hour on vehicle registration numbers, disqualified drivers, stolen cars, fingerprints and missing persons information.

The names of many great detectives have been associated with the accolade 'of the Yard', and two colourful figures who became well known to the public were Cherrill and Fabian. Frederick Cherrill headed the Yard's Fingerprint Bureau for fifteen years before he retired in 1953. He was involved in many famous murder cases, particularly those which occurred during the war years. His fingerprint evidence helped to convict Frederick Cummins, who committed four SEX MURDERS in London in 1942 which earned him comparison with JACK THE RIPPER, Bertie Manton, who killed his wife in the Luton sack murder of 1943, and Arthur Heys, an airman based in Suffolk, who brutally killed a woman in 1944. Robert Fabian, a policeman for thirty years, possessed that indefinable detective's 'nose' which enabled him to sniff out every type of crime from fraud to murder. He led the team which apprehended three robbers who shot and killed Alec de Antiquis, a courageous member of the public who tried to foil their robbery getaway. The Antiquis murder in London's West End in 1947 caused a public outcry, firstly at the murder of a citizen trying to uphold the law, and secondly at the hanging of two of the convicted murderers.

8, 59, 61, 105, 136, 137, 138, 150, 183, 198, 210, 232, 272, 280, 291, 293, 335, 345, 367, 471, 566, 611, 615, 629, 670, 683, 731, 736, 745, 746.

SECRETORS

The discovery that blood-group characteristics existed in other body fluids or secretions was made in 1925. Saliva, semen, urine, perspiration, tears, nasal mucus and mother's milk all carry the same group of specific substances as the BLOOD. This phenomenon promised to strengthen the forensic scientist's hand in the field of crime investigation by making it possible to determine a person's blood group from perspiration residues on clothing, or from saliva traces on the back of a postage stamp.

The drawback became known in 1932, when it was shown that this phenomenon did not apply to every individual. Human beings form two groups, secretors and non-secretors, of which the latter comprise some 14 per cent of the population. Nevertheless, it was established that the body-fluid group of secretors always remains identical with their blood groups, and that a secretor never becomes a non-secretor or vice versa.

The secretor principle has provided positive contributions in a number of murder investiga-

tions, but has also resulted in some setbacks. In January 1939 the sexually assaulted body of an eleven-year-old girl, Pamela Coventry, was found in a field near Hornchurch, Essex. Her legs were bound with a length of electric cable and a cigarette end, presumed to have been dropped by the murderer, lay on her body.

All the evidence pointed to the likelihood that the killer lived locally, and following house-to-house searches the police narrowed their hunt to a 28-year-old factory worker named Leonard Richardson. When questioned this man exhibited his nervousness by hand-rolling numerous cigarettes which he chain-smoked during the interview. The cigarette end which Sir Bernard Spilsbury had found at the murder scene now became the focus of a great deal of attention in the hospital laboratory of Dr Roche Lynch, a leading forensic chemist. Soiled handkerchiefs taken from Richardson's house were used in an attempt to establish his blood group for comparison with blood grouping of the saliva traces on the cigarette end. To the great disappointment of the authorities, the tests showed that Richardson belonged to the 14 per cent of non-secretors.

Richardson was tried for murder at the Old Bailey, but the evidence presented was circumstantial and REASONABLE DOUBT existed in the minds of the jury, who told the judge they could not bring a conviction.

*116, **671**, 676.*

SEX MURDER

Probably the first recognized sex murderer was JACK THE RIPPER, whose brutal killings in London's East End in 1888 made sensational headlines. The term 'sex murder' has been used in a loose sense to include almost any killing that has a sexual element, such as RAPE followed by murder. The true sex murder, however, is one accompanied by SADISM in the form of mutilation of the victim, especially of the genitals. In this respect Jack the Ripper, whose killings were notable for their savage mutilations — including disembowelment and removal of organs — was the archetypal sex murderer. Such killings are performed for sexual gratification, and the murderer is impelled by uncontrollable urges to destroy and mutilate his victim. The term sexual PSYCHOPATH has been used to define this condition, but the German word *Lustmorden*, meaning literally lust murder, is probably nearer the mark.

A number of sex murderers have been the subjects of well-documented studies. Albert Fish, whose catalogue of perversions included CANNIBALISM, was examined by Dr Frederic Wertham, a distinguished American psychiatrist, Peter Kürten, the 'Monster of Düsseldorf', came under the scrutiny of Professor Karl Berg, and William Heirens, the teenage Chicago killer, was examined by a team of forensic psychiatrists.

Peter Kürten, a 47-year-old factory worker who harboured feelings of admiration for Jack the Ripper, began a reign of terror in Düsseldorf in 1929. In that year he carried out a grim series of sex murders which included nine killings and fourteen assaults. His victims were women and children, and his violent methods included stabbing, STRANGULATION and bludgeoning with a hammer. He was caught by chance in May 1930, and readily made a CONFESSION of murder, perverted acts and sadism.

The sexual life of this mild-looking man whose wife, like the Yorkshire Ripper's spouse, had no idea of his double life, was probed by Professor Berg. Kürten was one of a family of thirteen. He was sexually aware at an early age, and in his teens made attacks on women, and also practised bestiality on farm animals. He took a succession of jobs, lived with prostitutes whom he ill treated, and engaged in theft. He had dream fantasies of killing which excited him sexually (this is often a characteristic prelude to sex murder), and he was aroused by fire. He set fire to barns and hayricks for the sexual pleasure he derived from watching them burn, and liked to imagine that tramps sleeping in them would be caught up in the blaze.

Kürten spent various terms in prison, and always returned to his life of perverted violence, which in 1929 erupted into an orgy of terror. His behaviour ran the whole gamut of sexual perversion — sadism, pyromania, NECROPHILIA, bestiality — and Berg described him as a 'king of sexual perverts'. Kürten's defence plea of insanity was rejected at his trial, and he was sentenced to death. His prime stimulant had always been blood, and perhaps it was no surprise when he remarked as he faced the GUILLOTINE that he hoped he might hear his blood gurgle when his head was severed.

William Heirens, a student at Chicago University, found sexual gratification in burglary, arson and murder. During his student days he regularly robbed apartment houses, and it was on one of these sorties in March 1945 that he committed murder. He disturbed a sleeping woman whose throat he cut. He then stabbed her several times.

In October he killed another woman, and left a message scrawled in lipstick on the bedroom wall of her apartment: 'For heaven's sake catch me before I kill more I cannot control myself.' Three months later he turned to KIDNAPPING, and demanded a ransom of 20,000 dollars for a six-year-old girl whom he abducted. Despite the ransom, he savagely killed the girl and cut her body to pieces. Like Kürten, he was captured by chance. He was spotted attempting to enter an apartment block, and was arrested as an intruder in June 1946.

He pretended to be insane at first, then made a confession, but attributed the three murders to his alter ego, whom he called George Murman. He was charged with twenty-nine criminal offences which included robbery and assault in addition to murder. Psychiatrists who examined Heirens before his trial agreed that he was legally sane, although suffering from deep sexual perversion. He was shown to be a solitary person with a hysterical personality and a low level of sensitivity to pain. He told doctors that he had been impressed by seeing the film of Dr Jekyll and Mr Hyde which gave rise to speculation as to the source of his alter ego, George. He read the pessimistic German philosophers, Nietzsche and Schopenhauer, and had pictures of Nazi leaders among his possessions. He indulged in an underwear fetish, and admitted that the act of burglary aroused him sexually. This unstable killer was judged insane at his trial and was sentenced to three consecutive life terms, never to be released from prison.

The sanity of the sex murderer has long been a matter for debate. A recent instance was the trial in May 1981 of Peter Sutcliffe, the Yorkshire Ripper. Three forensic psychiatrists believed he was suffering from paranoid SCHIZOPHRENIA, and he pleaded a defence of DIMINISHED RESPONSIBILITY. The jury, having heard the evidence of the brutality inflicted on his thirteen victims, concluded he was guilty of murder and not insane. Mr Justice Boreham sentenced him to life, which was to be at least thirty years in prison. Of Britain's post-war sex murderers Neville Heath and John Christie pleaded insanity, but the juries in both cases had little difficulty in bringing in guilty verdicts, and both men were hanged. The Homicide Act of 1957 changed the position, and Michael Dowdall, a young guardsman who killed a London prostitute in 1958, pleaded diminished responsibility, which was made possible by the new Act. The court found him guilty of the reduced charge of MANSLAUGHTER, and he was sentenced to life imprisonment. Patrick Byrne, another sex killer of this era, failed to get his murder charge reduced, and was convicted in 1960. Subsequently on appeal this was reduced to manslaughter, although the life sentence remained unchanged.

The ambivalent attitude to the sex murderer no doubt reflects public revulsion at the terror created and the atrocities committed by such individuals. There are also the difficulties faced by psychiatrists in understanding this type of mentality, and putting it into a consistent legal framework. In this sense it remains part of the overall problem of defining what constitutes legal insanity (see under M'NAGHTEN RULES).What is certain is that sex murders occupy a prominent place in the homicide league tables — about half of the MASS MURDERS committed in the USA are sexually motivated. It is said that traces of sadism lurk in the aggressive side of many human beings' behaviour. The jealousy, for example, which is often prevalent in homosexual relationships frequently erupts into violence, but only rarely does murder result. Female sex murderers are also a rarity — it is only in the male lust murderer that full rein is given to the deep-lying instincts which require destruction and mutilation to procure sexual satisfaction.

*17, 43, 58, 155, 173, 178, 230, 241, 260, 336, 395, 447, 475, 477, 551, **569**, 679, 697, 714.*

SKELETONS

That 'Dead men do tell tales' was borne out in a remarkable French murder case in which a skeleton gave up sufficient of its secrets to identify the victim and trap a pair of murderers. In 1889 police were called to a riverside location near Lyons where the badly decomposed body of a man had been discovered. Close by was a decayed wooden trunk bearing evidence that it had been sent to Lyons from Paris by railway.

Monsieur Goron, Chief of the SÛRETÉ, thought the corpse might be that of a Paris bailiff, a man called Gouffé, who had been reported missing. One of Gouffé's relatives was asked to view the remains, but as he was unable to make any identification the corpse was buried. Convinced that a crime had been committed, Goron obtained an EXHUMATION order and three months after it was discovered the corpse was disinterred.

The POST-MORTEM examination was carried out by Alexandre Lacassagne, Professor of Forensic Medicine at Lyons University. His attention was drawn to the condition of the right leg and ankle of the skeleton which suggested the muscles on that limb had been weaker than on the other. He thought this might have been due to disease, and further examination showed that the right kneecap was deformed, indicating inflammation of the joint during life. The weights of the bones in the right leg were also significantly lower than those of the left. Lacassagne's opinion was that the dead man had probably suffered tubercular disease in that leg, and would certainly have walked with a limp.

Inquiries revealed that the missing bailiff had been treated for a knee complaint and did walk with a limp. This information, together with an impressive array of evidence, enabled the Professor to announce to officers of the Sûreté, 'Gentlemen, I present M. Gouffé'! A police investigation ensued which resulted in the arrest of Michel Eyraud, a shady business-man, and his mistress, Gabrielle Bompard, who were eventually convicted of murdering Gouffé to prevent his official inquiry into their business affairs.

Except for the SKULL, few persons are able to distinguish between human and animal bones with certainty. This is a matter for the expert anatomist, and where the remains are fragmentary he may require confirmation of human origin by applying the precipitin test. Once they have been verified as human, the bones of an unidentified skeleton are examined to establish the primary characteristics of the dead person — sex, age and height. In general the skeleton provides ample evidence of its sex and age: the bones of the female, for example, are less robust than those of the male and the ridges which provide attachments for muscles and tendons are less prominent in the female. The pelvis, thigh-bones and skull are particularly noted for their sexual characteristics.

The female pelvis, constructed to meet the needs of child-bearing, has several features — notably wider hips — which distinguish it from the male. Apart from general appearance, a number of measurements can be made of pelvic bones which help to establish sex. The difference in ratio between the lengths of the pubis and ischium (known as the ischium–pubis index) is commonly used for this purpose.

Age is determined by studying a number of skeletal features, principally the skull, teeth and centres of ossification. As the young human body develops from soon after conception until early adulthood, the growth of the bones is regulated by centres of ossification which gradually fill out and fuse together to give the bones shape and size. This process is established in a regular pattern which enables the skilled anatomist to give a reliable estimate of age to within one or two years.

Examination of the growing ends of the bones (epiphyses) is especially relevant. The growth centres at the lower ends of the limb-bones permit the limbs to lengthen during childhood, and thereby increase the height of the individual. These epiphyses are soft and cartilaginous during the growing period but gradually harden into solid bone and fuse with the main shaft of the bone as adulthood is reached. The head of the thigh-bone (femur) fuses between 18 and 20 years, and part of the hip during the 24th year. Consideration of the epiphyses in the long bones of a skeleton can therefore yield reliable information about age up to 25 years. After that, age-determination depends on looking at the skull and other bones which show changes with age. As females mature quicker than males, the ageing aspects of the female skeleton are usually about a year ahead of the male.

The height of a person in life can also be determined by studying the long bones of the skeleton. An approximation of stature can be obtained by measuring from finger-tip to finger-tip of the outstretched arms, the span of which is roughly equal to the body height. The idea that a fixed relationship exists between the lengths of the limbs, especially the legs, and the total length of the body was developed by Professor Mathieu Orfila. His calculations proved unreliable, but the method was improved first by Dr Etienne Rollet and then by Dr Karl Pearson. Pearson's Formula, published in 1899, has now been discarded for the more accurate Dapertuis and Hadden formula.

An outstanding forensic investigation in which Pearson's formula played a valuable part was the Dobkin Case in 1942. Professor Keith Simpson applied the formula to the single bone available to him from the skeletal remains of a woman found on the site of a bombed church in London, and determined her body height as 5 feet and ½ inch. This was one characteristic in a case famous for the IDENTIFICATION of the murder victim by her TEETH.

When Profesor Simpson gave expert testimony at the trial of Harry Dobkin for the murder of his wife Rachel, controversy arose over the estimated height of the victim. This came about because the dead woman's sister had been incorrectly quoted in the newspapers as saying Rachel Dobkin was 5

feet 3 inches tall. Consequently the scientific evidence was severely questioned in court, but vindication was at hand when the witness claimed her dead sister was 'almost my own height', which proved to be 4 feet 11¾ inches without shoes and 5 feet 1 inch with shoes.

Provisional identification was clinched when Mrs Dobkin's dentist was traced, and he confirmed that residual roots and fillings in the teeth remaining in the upper jaw of the remains were identical to his treatment records. As a result, her husband, Harry Dobkin, was traced and put on trial for murder. He was found guilty, and was executed in 1943.

3, **117**, *276, 277, 372, 426, 436, 442, 449, 626*, **673**.

SKULLS

The human skull has occupied a prominent place in folklore since the earliest times. In association with crossed bones it has long been used as the universal symbol of death, featuring on the pirates' 'Jolly Roger' and on labels of poison containers. The skulls of criminals have been of particular fascination, and the Italian criminologist Cesare Lombroso made a study of them, 'as the seat of all the great disturbances'. He noted various ape-like characteristics in the bone structure of the born criminal's skull, a view which was later discredited (see under CRIMINOLOGY).

Frederick Bayley Deeming, a murderer who claimed victims in both England and Australia in the 1890s, was especially reviled, and his remains were used to substantiate theories regarding criminal types. He killed his first wife and four children in Rainhill near Liverpool and cemented their bodies under the floor of the kitchen fireplace. Wanted for murder and larceny, Deeming added bigamy to his crimes when he arrived in Australia in 1891. He killed his second wife and cemented her corpse under the hearthstone of their house in Melbourne. The disagreeable smell eventually brought the police in and Deeming was duly arrested. Despite a strong plea of insanity, he was found guilty of murder and was executed in 1892.

Deeming managed to excite controversy even after his execution, and there were claims that he was JACK THE RIPPER. In the early 1930s, during alterations to Melbourne Prison, Deeming's remains, together with those of a number of other murderers, were dug up from the prison yard. His skull and one long bone came into the possession of Sir William Colin Mackenzie, an eminent

Australian anatomist. He studied these relics, and presented his findings to a meeting of the Anthropological Society of New South Wales in 1933.

Mackenzie reported that the skull had a cephalic index of 82·5 and a cranial capacity of 1,400cc. The skull showed frontal and occipital development and other features reminiscent of the male apes. He concluded that in Deeming society had been confronted by a primitive brain that had turned criminal. Deeming's bones are still housed in the Australian Institute of Anatomy, apparently confirming the view that the born criminal is endowed with primitive physical characteristics.

In anthropological work skulls are classified by their cephalic index — the ratio of maximum width to the maximum length. The higher the index, the more spherical is the skull in shape, and the lower it is, the more elongated the skull. With a cephalic index of 82·5, Deeming's skull was not remarkable, but its cranial capacity of 1,400cc was below the average for the normal adult male (1,500cc).

Skulls have a number of important features which help the forensic pathologist to determine the age and sex of a SKELETON. The appearance of the sutures or seams on top of the skull can give its approximate age. The vault of the cranium is made up of a number of flat bones which interlock at the edges by means of serrations or sutures. In infants there are large gaps between these bones, which gradually close up after the age of 30. This fusing process occurs in a particular sequence beginning from the inside of the skull and working outwards. It is the state of these closures which allows age to be approximated; complete absence of closure indicates that the skeleton is less than 30 years old.

Age-determinations based on the state of the skull sutures are not exact, but in the absence of other information may be the only method of ageing human remains. This method was used by Professors John Glaister and J. C. Brash in 1935 to estimate the ages of two dismembered corpses

Comparison of male and female skulls

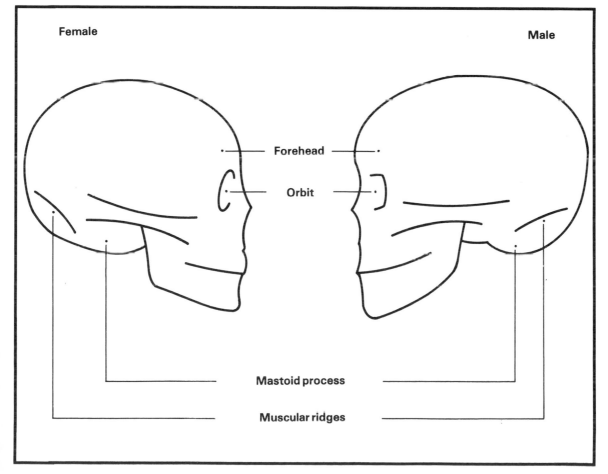

205

which turned up in a ravine under the Carlisle to Edinburgh road. The experts estimated the age of each body to within a year of its actual age, which became known when they were identified as Dr Buck Ruxton's murder victims.

The Ruxton case provided a number of challenges for the team of experts assembled from Glasgow and Edinburgh Universities, and the victims' skulls featured prominently in their scientific investigation. Sex differences are notable in the skull, the main distinguishing feature being that the female skull is smaller than the male. The mastoid processes and orbital ridges are less prominent in the female, and the eye sockets and forehead are more rounded. Sex differences are also distinguishable in the pelvis, but the skull, being one of the human frame's more durable parts, is especially significant in this respect. In the case of one of Ruxton's victims Professor Brash was able to report, 'Secondary sex characters are so well marked that I can express without hesitation the definite opinion that it is the skull of a female.'

A powerful piece of identification evidence in this case was achieved by the development of a new technique. A photographic negative enlarged to life size was made of a portrait of Ruxton's wife, and this was superimposed on an X-ray of the skull. The result was a startling match, which Professor Glaister modestly described as 'a close comparison'. The medical investigation of the Ruxton case won wide acclaim, and Glaister and Brash received an international award for their account of it.

Skulls have also featured as macabre exhibits in court-rooms. A juror fainted when the yellowed skull of Max Garvie was produced as part of the prosecution evidence against his wife Sheila and her lover Brian Tevendale, who were accused of murdering him.

Garvie's body, shot through the head, was found at St Cyrus in Scotland in 1968. This followed a stormy love-triangle which led to Sheila Garvie and Brian Tevendale electing to kill Max. The victim was shot dead while he lay asleep and his body was subsequently hidden. Garvie and Tevendale were found guilty and sentenced to life imprisonment. The case against one of Tevendale's friends who was asked for help was found NOT PROVEN.

34, 35, 53, 81, 179, 181, 248, **257***, 310, 439, 443, 530.*

STOMACH CONTENTS

A meal of turkey and vegetables followed by pine-apple cake was an unusual feature in a Canadian murder investigation. At 5.30 p.m. on 9 June 1959 Lynne Harper, the twelve-year-old daughter of a Canadian Air Force officer, enjoyed such a meal with her parents at the RCAF base near Goderich, Ontario. A quarter of an hour later, at about 5.45 p.m., she went out, and just after 7.0 p.m. she was seen with fourteen-year-old Steven Truscott, riding on the crossbar of his bicycle. When the girl did not return home at nightfall her father reported her missing, and the following day a search of the locale revealed her body lying in a copse — she had been raped and strangled.

It was important to establish when the girl had died, but as RIGOR MORTIS and body-cooling, the most reliable indicators of TIME OF DEATH, had faded by the time the body was found, a great deal depended on interpreting the state of the stomach contents. It was known that she had finished her last meal at 5.45 p.m., and the pathologist concluded from his examination of the stomach contents that it was unlikely the food had been in the stomach for as long as two hours. That put the likely time of death before 7.45 p.m.

Steven Truscott told the girl's parents that Lynne had left him at Highway No. 8, when she hitched a ride in a grey Chevrolet. This was thought implausible, as medical opinion was that the girl had been killed where she was found, and it is not usual for a murderer to move his victim's body closer to home. Steven was then medically examined, and found to have a sore penis, consistent with having committed RAPE. Grass stains were found on the knees of his trousers, and the distinctive crepe-soled shoes he was said to have worn on the night in question could not be found, making it impossible to match them with footprints found at the scene of the crime.

Steven was charged with murder and sent for trial. He was found guilty and sentenced to death — later commuted to life imprisonment — the verdict being upheld on appeal.

In 1966 a book was written about the case by Isabel Lebourdais which resulted in a storm of controversy. The author made out a strong case for Steven Truscott's innocence, which resulted in a retrial at the Ottawa Supreme Court in 1967. Such internationally recognized forensic experts as Dr Milton Helpern, Professor Keith Simpson and Dr Francis Camps were called to testify — the interpretation of the evidence relating to time of death was crucial. If the pathologist's estimate that death had occurred at around 7.45 p.m. could be shaken this would work in Truscott's favour. On the basis of this conclusion, it was possible for the youth to have committed the rape and killing between 7.05 p.m., when he was seen with the girl, and about 8.0 p.m., when he was seen alone. If it could be shown that death had occurred later than 7.45 p.m., then a jury might be convinced he did not have time to commit the crime.

In the event the weight of Simpson and Helpern's expert opinion supported the original pathologist, and confirmed the correctness of the original verdict. Truscott's appeal was rejected and he returned to prison, where he stayed until 1969, when he was released to start a new life under a new name.

In the normal course of events, after a meal is eaten it passes into the stomach, where it is partly digested before passing into the small intestine. But if physical or emotional disturbance occurs after the meal the digestion process may be affected by slowing down or stopping completely, and a well-known result of being frightened or assaulted is for the stomach to rebel by vomiting. This makes the timing of death in relation to the stomach contents a difficult factor to estimate. As in most estimates of time of death, it is hazardous to put too much faith in such findings — there is certainly no formula that can be applied to the rate of emptying of the stomach. The best that can be achieved is to relate stomach contents where they may be recognized to a meal taken at a specific time, and to conclude that death took place after that. In the Truscott case, as Helpern pointed out, the circumstances of unexpected rape and strangulation would not have produced the type of long-lasting stress that would delay the digestion process. It would have been another matter if the victim had been subjected to the type of assault which involved binding and gagging, when the normal emptying of the stomach might be affected.

Another murder investigation in which stomach contents were a feature of estimated time of death and which also involved Helpern was the Alice Crimmins case. The two children of this glamorous New York housewife were reported missing on 14 July 1965. The body of her four-year-old daughter was found the same day, and that of her five-year-old son several days later. Both children had been strangled, and it appeared that they had been subjected to a 'tug-of-love' contest between their mother and her estranged

husband. Alice Crimmins was eventually tried for murder in 1968 and found guilty of MAN-SLAUGHTER in regard to her daughter's death.

A key factor in the prosecution case concerned Alice Crimmins's statements regarding her children. She said she made them a meal of manicotti (noodles) and string beans at about 7.30 p.m. on the night she alleged they were abducted from the house. She put them to bed at 9.0 p.m. and looked in on them at midnight, which was the last time she saw them alive. When the girl's body was examined in the POST-MORTEM room her stomach was found to contain fresh-looking, virtually undigested food consisting of manicotti and string beans. As Milton Helpern rather forcibly put it, 'If she [the mother] saw them alive before midnight, how could the stomach of Missy [the daughter] show that she must have died within two hours of taking a meal at 7.30 o'clock? . . . it was evident to me that somebody was lying.'

Alice Crimmins was sent for retrial in 1971, charged with the murder of her son and manslaughter of her daughter — she was found guilty of first-degree MURDER and also of first-degree manslaughter, and she was sentenced to life imprisonment.

The nature of stomach contents is also important in cases of suspected POISONING, and samples taken for analysis may help to provide crucial evidence. In the Armstrong case (see under CHILD-MURDER), the discovery that the poison capsules were not made of gelatine but of methyl cellulose (which allowed slower absorption of the drug into the bloodstream) led to a revision of the estimates of timing.

122, 296, 324, 423, 626, 639, 681.

STRANGULATION

'A strangler's victim is usually not a pretty sight. Bluish or purple lips and ears, change of colour of the nails, froth and possibly blood-staining about the nose or mouth, the tongue forced outward, the hands clenched — these are the typical signs of death from asphyxia.' This was Sir Sydney Smith's description of one of the most commonly encountered methods of killing. When carried out with the bare hands it is a form of killing which is unmistakably deliberate, and cannot be confused with death by accident or suicide.

Strangulation results in death from ASPHYXIA due to constriction of the neck by force applied by means of a ligature or by the hands. A ligature may be any cord-like material which is put around the neck and the ends pulled tight or held with a knot. Ties and stockings are common types of ligature, and where their ends are secured the knot is usually at the front or side of the victim's neck. The knot itself may offer valuable clues to murder investigators, who always photograph it in place and cut the ligature in such a way as to preserve its fastening intact. The Boston Strangler tied the knots around his victims' necks in a characteristic way which formed part of his MODUS OPERANDI. The mark left by the ligature consists of a circumferential groove around the neck, usually at a level just above the thyroid cartilage or 'Adam's Apple'.

It is less obvious than the mark resulting from HANGING, and may be patterned in accordance with the type of ligature used and placing of the knot. The classic signs of asphyxia — congestion and tiny haemorrhages or petechiae — are usually prominent on the head and face above the ligature.

Strangulation by ligature may occur accidentally when a person's clothes, especially a tie, become entangled in machinery. Equally rarely, strangulation may be achieved suicidally if the victim adequately secures the knot, but manual strangulation, or throttling, is always murder, for the hands of the intending suicide using this

Larynx enlarged to show its structures

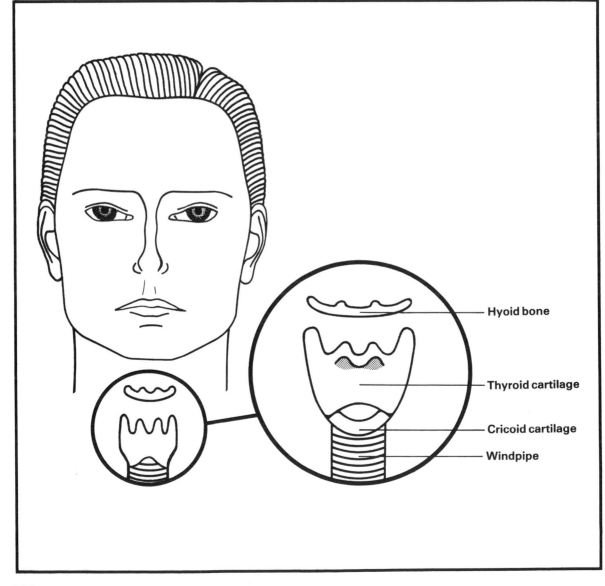

Hyoid bone

Thyroid cartilage

Cricoid cartilage

Windpipe

method would fall from his neck as consciousness was lost. Manual strangulation is usually accomplished by an attack from the front using one or both hands. The neck is gripped either immediately above or below the 'Adam's Apple', causing death as the air passage is closed off. The attacker's fingers, biting deeply into the flesh, leave external bruises, and the victim's attempts to tear away the throttling grasp may leave abrasions on the skin. The usual features of asphyxial death are evident, and there may also be subsidiary injuries. RAPE or attempted rape often accompanies manual strangulation.

Damage to the internal structures of the neck are often more severe in throttling than in other forms of strangulation because of the greater force used. The hyoid bone, a delicate structure in the throat which lies just above the Adam's Apple, is frequently broken. Damage may also be caused to the thyroid and cricoid cartilages, with severe localized bruising. The hyoid bone is of particular sigificance, as it is not directly joined to any other bone and moves freely. Consequently, considerable force is needed to break it, except in elderly persons, where it tends to be brittle. Arguments about damage to the hyoid bone and the larynx have occurred in numerous murder trials, and it is now common practice for pathologists to X-ray the internal structures of the neck before carrying out a POST-MORTEM examination. This precaution defeats any charge that damage was caused during the autopsy.

The hyoid bone is one of those tell-tale indicators of violence which survive even in partially destroyed bodies. A broken hyoid or thyroid bone found in a body in an advanced stage of DECOMPOSITION is sufficient evidence of death by strangulation. Professor Keith Simpson found such a broken bone in the partially dismembered and burned remains of Rachel Dobkin. It testified to the manner of her killing, and was part of the evidence which led to her husband's conviction for murder. (See also under SKELETON.) In his textbook *Forensic Medicine* Professor Simpson records that in twenty-five successive cases of manual strangulation in only two instances was there no fracture in the bones of the larynx.

The majority of strangulation cases are single murders, often accompanied by sexual assault. Strangulation is sometimes used to finish off a victim after an attack with knife or BLUNT INSTRUMENT has failed to kill immediately. There appears to be a primitive instinct at work whereby the kill can be achieved by going for the throat, which is demonstrably a vulnerable part of the body. It is unusual for strangulation to be chosen as a method of MASS MURDER, but Dean Corll, the Houston killer of the early 1970s, murdered twenty-seven youths in this manner with attendant SADISM and mutilation, and Albert deSalvo, the Boston strangler, is the archetype of this method. Motivated by sexual urges which he could not control, he talked his way into the homes of women living alone, where he raped and strangled them. Recounting one such attack, he said, 'I began to tie the nylons around her neck. She came to a little and she was putting up a fight now. I stuck the gag in her mouth. Now she was looking at me, right at me and I had the nylons around her neck, but she kept struggling so I had to pull them tight. . . .' (See also under PSYCHIC DETECTION.)

An unusual case of manual strangulation was that involving Harold Loughans, who was charged with murdering and robbing Rose Robinson, a Portsmouth publican, in November 1943. The dead woman had deep bruises around her throat, and scratch-marks indicated her unsuccessful efforts to fight off the attacker's grip. Some weeks after the murder, inveterate burglar Harold Loughans was caught in London selling stolen property. He admitted the Portsmouth murder, and was sent for trial at Winchester. The jury failed to agree, and he was retried at the Old Bailey.

He denied his confession and produced an ALIBI sworn to by four independent witnesses. Moreover, Sir Bernard Spilsbury, in a rare appearance for the defence, testified that it was unlikely Loughans strangled the woman as his right hand was mutilated, being short of the tips on four fingers. Loughans was acquitted, and walked from the court, only to be rearrested on a different charge of attempted murder. He was subsequently convicted of this crime and imprisoned.

In 1963, nearly twenty years after the Portsmouth murder, Harold Loughans, freed from prison where he was held in preventive detention, brought a libel action against *The People* newspaper, which he claimed had published accounts alleging he had been fortunate to be acquitted. The JURY heard a virtual rerun of the original trial evidence, and found for the newspaper and against the plaintiff. Thus he was effectively found guilty of murder as the result of a civil case he himself had brought, though having been acquitted he could not, of course, be charged again. The sequel to this unusual story came a few months later when Loughans, released from prison and knowing that

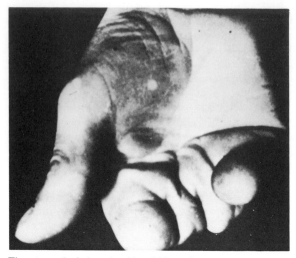

The strangler's hand — Harold Loughans

he had incurable cancer, walked into the offices of *The People* and said, 'Before I die I want to make a confession.' The man with the mutilated hand admitted that he had strangled the Portsmouth publican.

A mechanical form of strangulation known as the garotte has been used in Spain and the Spanish colonies as a means of EXECUTION. An early version of this method was used in China, where capital punishment was carried out by means of a cord placed around the victim's neck and drawn tight by the executioner. A variation of this was to fasten the victim to a stake driven into the ground and to make a simple garotte from a strong cord which looped around the neck with the ends passing through two holes in the stake. With the head thus braced, the cord was tightened to produce slow strangulation.

The method used in Spain as the official form of execution involved seating the victim in a special chair to which his arms and legs were strapped. A metal collar was placed around the neck, which by means of a weighted lever at the back of the chair could be drawn tight. This was what happened to Atahualpa, the last Inca — that dramatic moment in *The Royal Hunt of the Sun*. A variation of this device consisted of forcing the neck against an iron spike fixed into the back of the chair such that the application of pressure resulted in the spike being driven between the vertebrae and rupturing the spinal cord. As late as 1963 three men were garotted in Spain, having been convicted of treason.

21, *27*, *32*, *97*, *127*, *227*, **548**, *562*, **626**, **627**, **702**, *747*.

STRYCHNINE

'There is something to kill the little one,' remarked George Hersey to a friend as he held up a glass phial containing white powder. This incident occurred shortly after a Boston doctor had refused to carry out an abortion on his girl-friend, and had also declined to supply strychnine to 'kill a dog'. A few days later, on 3 May 1860, Hersey's fiancée, 23-year-old Betsy Frances, was taken ill after retiring for the night. Her sister found her twitching and convulsing in bed and screaming with pain. Her back was arched, and her face was bloody where she had bitten through her lip. The convulsions quickly exhausted her, and she died before the doctor could reach her bedside.

The girl's family suspected that her sudden death might be due to food-poisoning, but then they remembered that George Hersey's first wife and later a girl-friend had both died suddenly. They agreed to a POST-MORTEM examination, but Hersey objected on the grounds that he did not want the body of his loved one mutilated. He was overruled by the family, whose horror mounted when the doctors told them that Betsy was three months pregnant, and had died of strychnine poisoning. A search of Betsy's room turned up a spoon which had been thrown into the fireplace — it bore traces of jam and strychnine.

Hersey was arrested and put on trial for murder. He pleaded not guilty, and the defence argued that Betsy had committed suicide. A more sinister explanation of her death was that, learning she was pregnant, Hersey decided to help her to get rid of the child. He persuaded her to take some 'medicine', its bitter taste masked by a spoonful of jam, as a result of which mother and unborn child quickly died. Hersey was found guilty of first-degree MURDER, and he was sentenced to death. He made a CONFESSION, admitting to causing Betsy's end, but he denied killing either his former wife or fiancée.

Like many poisoners before and since, Hersey made a study of chemistry, and the effects of poisons was one of his regular conversation topics. His choice of strychnine showed his callousness, for it is a particularly violent poison. It was discovered about 1817 as an alkaloid present in the dried ripe seeds of the tree *Strychnos nux-vomica*, which is found in India. In medicinal doses, strychnine acts as a stimulant, and Tincture of Nux Vomica and Easton's Syrup were proprietary medicines given as a tonic to aid convalescence. Its lethal qualities were well recognized, and it was widely used as an animal poison.

It is in the nature of such discoveries that they find their way into criminal hands. Thus in the latter half of the eighteenth century strychnine became a popular poison for murder, and was later to be favoured by the notorious doctors Neill Cream and William Palmer. Strychnine is a colourless, crystalline powder with an exceptionally bitter taste which the poisoner who knows his subject is at pains to disguise. Cream dosed it in real medicine, Palmer in brandy, and Mr Hersey spooned it out with jam.

The drug is absorbed very rapidly, and symptoms of poisoning can arise even from external application. Once it enters the bloodstream it quickly affects the central nervous system, producing breathing difficulties and convulsions. As the motor areas of the spinal cord react to the poison the spine arches dramatically and the muscles become stiff and rigid, with only the head and the feet touching the ground. This condition is known as opisthotonus, and is a spasm which lasts for up to two minutes, during which the victim is conscious and in extreme pain. This contraction subsides as the muscles relax before the onset of another spasm. This pattern may be repeated several times, producing a tetanic spasm and a grinning effect known as *risus sardonicus*, which is accompanied by a wild-eyed, staring expression. Death may intervene within an hour from respiratory paralysis or exhaustion. Toxic symptoms can result from a 5mg dose, and 15mg have proved fatal, although 100mg is usually considered the lethal dose.

Jean-Pierre Vaquier, another dabbler in chemistry, bought his strychnine from a London pharmacist in connection with his wireless experiments. He disguised the fatal crystals in a bottle of bromo salts from which his victim made a drink. Mr Jones, landlord of the Blue Anchor at Byfleet in Surrey, died in agony and his murderer, although clever enough to wash out the bottle of bromo salts, did not make a sufficiently thorough job of it, as the dregs when analysed were found to contain strychnine. Vaquier's act of murder to dispose of his mistress's husband was successful but clumsy, and he paid the price. He was hanged in 1924.

Vaquier's implausible 'wireless experiments' as an excuse for buying poison was matched only by Eva Rablen's novel idea of killing gophers with strychnine. She bought a supply of the deadly agent from a near-by pharmacy and then dosed her husband's coffee during the weekly dance at Tuttletown, California. Her distressed victim complained of the bitter taste of the coffee before he died in great pain.

The local analyst could find no trace of a poisonous agent in the dead man's stomach, but rumours mounted that Eva had killed him for the insurance money. In due course the eminent criminologist Dr Edward Heinrich was called in, and he soon found strychnine in the dregs of the coffee-cup. Confronted by the overwhelming prosecution evidence at her open-air trial in 1929, Eva Rablen changed her plea to guilty, and was convicted of murder for which she was punished with life imprisonment.

It is one the paradoxes of POISONING that substances which may be benign or health-improving in small doses are lethal in larger amounts. Strychnine-based tonics were regularly prescribed at one time for invalids recuperating after weakening illnesses. The effect is to sharpen the senses and

Opisthotonus: violent arching of the back

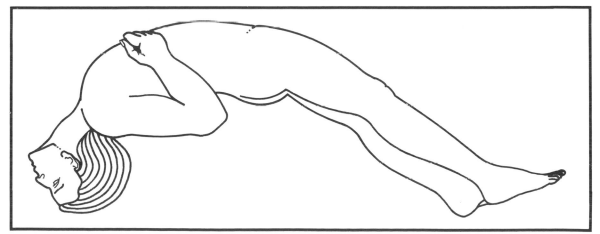

create a general feeling of well-being, but once the minimal stimulation dose is exceeded the result can be violent and fatal. Accidental deaths were fairly common as a result of patients failing to shake the medicine bottle properly and eventually dosing themselves with the concentrated liquid which had accumulated at the bottom. Suicidal use of strychnine was also common before the poison laws were made stricter.

1, 37, 67, 72, 86, 97, 103, 112, 119, 177, 196, 221, 256, 271, 275, 317, 318, 360, 370, 373, 419, 515, 523, 526, 564, 644, 665.

SUDDEN DEATH

The unexpected death of an apparently healthy person gives cause for concern as to the possibility of foul-play. Historically, POISONING has been one of the most overlooked causes of sudden death, as many toxic agents leave few if any traces in the body (see under RICIN). There are also many natural causes of unexpected death associated with the circulatory and nervous systems. Instances may occur in which fright or shock following an act of violence trigger a nervous reaction resulting in death.

One of these unusual reactions probably overtook eight-year-old Helen Priestly on an April day in 1934 when she was sent on an errand by her mother. She did not return home, and was reported missing. The next day her body was found in a sack under the stairs of the Aberdeen tenement in which she lived. She had died of ASPHYXIA, and there were marks of STRANGULATION on her throat — there were also serious injuries to her genitals, and RAPE was suspected. Her body lay on the right side in the sack, but evidence of LIVIDITY in the left side clearly indicated that she had been moved. Examination of the STOMACH CONTENTS enabled TIME OF DEATH to be established at around 2.0p.m. on the day she disappeared.

Suspicion fell on the Priestlys' neighbours, and in particular on Mrs Jeannie Donald. It appeared that tension had resulted from an incident when Mrs Donald struck Helen for some alleged misdemeanour. Stains on the floor of the Donalds' home, thought at the time to be BLOOD, led to the arrest of the couple, although Alexander Donald was released on the strength of a cast-iron ALIBI. Feeling against Jeannie Donald ran very high, and a complex chain of scientific evidence was built up against her. Human HAIR found in the sack with the girl's body was alleged to be Mrs Donald's hair, and cinders and household fluff were also linked with the Donald home. Sir Sydney Smith and Professor John Glaister spent a great deal of time in their laboratories examining FIBRES and other possibly incriminating evidence with a comparison microscope.

Jeannie was tried for murder in Edinburgh in July 1934. She was charged with harbouring malice against young Helen, and of murdering her in consequence. There were arguments about the injuries to the dead girl, which although first thought to constitute rape were shown to have been caused by an instrument such as a poker. The defence clung to the idea of sexual assault, which therefore ruled out Mrs Donald. The accused was nevertheless found guilty, and sentenced to death, which was later commuted to life imprisonment.

One former reconstruction of the events which led to Helen Priestly's death was made possible by the POST-MORTEM examination, which showed she had an enlargement of the thymus. This is a ductless gland situated in the upper part of the chest which reaches full size at about the age of two years and then gradually shrinks away. Its function is not well understood, apart from its relevance to growth. Enlargement of the thymus gland and associated lymphatic tissue can predispose a child or growing adult to sudden, unexpected death. The overgrowth of thymic tissue is occasionally sufficient to exert pressure on the heart and related nerves. This condition may not be a direct cause of death, but in association with other factors, such as shock, may result in sudden death. Doctors disagree about the nature of status lymphaticus even to the point of denying that such a condition exists, and those who do accept its existence dislike using it as a cause of death.

In the case of Helen Priestly it is just possible that Mrs Donald, who thought the child had been knocking on her door and running away, lay in wait for the child and suddenly jumped out with the intention of frightening her. Predisposed to sudden death by a combination of sudden shock and enlarged thymus, the girl was literally half frightened to death. Horrified at what had happened, and thinking the girl dead, Jeannie Donald dragged her into her house, where she simulated rape on the unconscious body. Her intention was to avoid a charge of murder by giving the impression that the assault was sexually motivated. The pain of an instrument entering her body caused the girl to vomit and choke; perhaps in panic Mrs Donald throttled the remaining life out of the girl. Thus a prank and its retaliation led to tragedy.

Another cause of sudden death results from pressure exerted on the neck. The mechanism of vagal inhibition — or reflex cardiac arrest, as it is now more usually called — lies in the compression of the carotid arteries in the neck at the level of the larynx. At this point the arteries have small pressure-sensitive areas which help to stabilize the blood pressure and signal the brain by way of the vagus nerve. If these areas are over-stimulated by force applied to the neck a stream of nervous impulses is sent to the brain, which reacts by depressing the heart action to the point of arrest and sudden death.

This is the intention of the lethal Commando punch to the throat and similar karate blows as demonstrated by a British Army sergeant who was convicted in 1955 of murdering a fellow-soldier in this manner (see under ASPHYXIA). Quarrels and struggles of various kinds may lead to a person being gripped by the neck without the intention to kill, but nevertheless causing death before asphyxia is even possible. Prostitutes gripped by the neck in violent sexual encounters have been known to die in this way, and death by DROWNING may also be prompted by cardiac arrest resulting from the shock of being plunged into cold water. The cause of death of some of George Joseph Smith's 'brides in the bath' was attributed to shock-induced heart-stoppage.

Vagal inhibition is a physiological process, and cannot be demonstrated anatomically. It is a conclusion reached in the light of particular circumstances, and after other causes have been excluded. Extreme fright is thought to play a part in inducing sudden death, and diagnosis of cardiac arrest at post-mortem examination is based on the absence of bruising, congestion or petechial haemorrhages (see under EYES).

1, **548**, *583*, **625**, *632*, **673**.

SUFFOCATION

External blocking of the nose and mouth, preventing the intake of air to the lungs, results in ASPHYXIA and suffocation. Smothering has been a commonly used method of disposing of elderly persons, whose resistance to a soft pillow pressed over the face is weak. The same method has been used for INFANTICIDE, but it is not usually successful against a healthy adult unless accompanied by other disabling tactics. Occlusion of air at the mouth and nose can result in unconsciousness

within 20 or 30 seconds, and death within minutes. The usual signs of asphyxial death are evident — cyanosis and petechial haemorrhages — but smothering with a pillow has the advantage for the attacker of leaving no marks.

Accidental suffocation can occur where a drunken person sleeps with his face pressed into the pillow, and in cases where children put plastic bags over their heads. There have been many instances of criminal suffocation when robbers or intruders have trussed and gagged a night-watchman or caretaker. The gag tied over the victim's mouth, even though it leaves the nostrils free, can cause suffocation from a build-up of saliva which blocks the air-passages. The use of adhesive tape or a gag can lead to the same fatal result, giving rise to unintentional murder which the courts may reduce to MANSLAUGHTER. There is a similar danger of suffocation in circumstances where a body is trussed and gagged and then placed in the closed confines of a trunk or cupboard. The type of asphyxia which results from inhaling smoke or gas which interferes with breathing is also classed as suffocation (see under GASSING).

Suffocation can present difficulties for the doctor, as was illustrated in 1950, when an elderly patient died at a Sussex nursing-home. Small bruises on the dead woman's arms were explained by the matron, who said the old lady had been very difficult during the night and a degree of force had been required to put her back to bed. No other injuries were evident, and a normal DEATH CERTIFICATE was issued.

The funeral was about to proceed when a junior nurse confided her anxieties to the nursing-home doctor. She related that on the night in question the old lady had been extremely tiresome, spitting out her pills, fighting off all attempts to help her, and roundly abusing the matron. In the process of restraining her patient the matron took up a pillow, placed it over the old lady's face, and held it there until she was dead. The nurse was instructed to leave all the talking to her superior, who simply told the doctor that the patient had died suddenly.

The funeral was stopped and a POST-MORTEM examination carried out. Indications of death by rapid suffocation were evident, and the nursing-home matron was charged with murder. At her trial the judge, Mr Justice Humphreys, directed the jury that the killing resulted from provocation, and amounted to manslaughter. Such a verdict was returned.
548, **571**, *626*.

SÛRETÉ

The Sûreté-Nationale is the best-known of France's four major police organizations. It is a civil police force with headquarters in Paris, and is responsible to the Minister of the Interior. The Sûreté operates throughout France, and detective squads (Brigades Mobiles) are based in the larger provincial towns.

Eugène-François Vidocq, a former convict, became Head of the Sûreté in 1811, and used his knowledge of the criminal mind in the service of law and order. Vidocq proved to be a pioneer in the field of criminal investigation, and under his direction the Sûreté became a powerful and respected organization. Today the Sûreté is headed by a Director-General, and its work is arranged under four directorates covering counter-espionage, criminal investigation, special branch and public security.

The criminal investigation branch is similar in many respects to SCOTLAND YARD's CID. It operates a detective force known as the Police Judiciaire and maintains a criminal records office, fingerprint bureau and a FORENSIC SCIENCE laboratory. Criminal investigation in France was greatly influenced by Alphonse Bertillon's anthropometric system of IDENTIFICATION. Although his system was overturned by the advent of FINGERPRINTS, Bertillon is regarded as the founder of forensic photography, which he introduced into French police methods.

The detective tradition begun by Vidocq was continued by his successors. Gustave Macé, who became Head of the Sûreté in 1879, had ten years previously master-minded the Voirbo murder investigation (see under BLOOD). Macé was a great believer in practical experience and had the detective's 'nose', but sadly, he turned Bertillon aside when the latter came forward with his new method of criminal identification.

Marie-François Goron, who became Head of the Sûreté in 1887, also featured in one of France's great murder cases. He headed the investigation which in 1890 led to the arrest of Eyraud and Bompard, murderers of a Paris bailiff. Goron developed methods of questioning prisoners which bordered on the THIRD DEGREE, and his interrogation rooms were known as 'Goron's cookshop'. Another Sûreté Commissioner who made his mark as a detective officer was Jean Belin. He arrested Henri Landru, the French Bluebeard, in 1919. Belin believed Landru strangled his victims with a thin wire ligature, having first drugged them. A book on poisoning was found in Landru's house, and when this was produced at his trial he told the judge, 'Reading is not a criminal offence.'
46, 125, 328, 330, 462, **572**, *634, 646, 695, 706, 707, 708.*

SYSTEM OF MURDER

No one ever saw George Joseph Smith in the act of DROWNING any of his brides, but the CIRCUMSTANTIAL EVIDENCE against him was strong. Sir Archibald Bodkin in the course of his prosecution listed twelve points of similarity between the deaths of three of the brides to illustrate that Smith had a system of murder.

In each case he went through a form of marriage with the victim and either insured them or arranged for their assets to be willed to him; in each case there was a visit to the doctor to register some trivial ailment on the part of the bride, and there were inquiries at each lodging about the availability of a bath; in each case the woman died in the bath of drowning, and Smith was the first to discover the tragedy. This was the essence of his system or MODUS OPERANDI which convinced the JURY that three drownings conforming to such a pattern could not be simple coincidence.

The secretive nature of the poisoner often increases the desire to show evidence of system where a series of murders is suspected. Evidence in poison cases is usually circumstantial, and this can be strengthened in arguments to the jury where testimony exists of the accused's person's involvement in similar crimes. Thus George Chapman, the ANTIMONY poisoner, was damned at his trial in 1903 as much by his association with comparable poisonings of two deceased 'wives' as by the murder for which he stood trial and was convicted. Although under English law it is the convention not to blacken a defendant's character by introducing testimony of previous offences, EVIDENCE demonstrating a system of murder is frequently admitted by the judge.
1, 14, 250, 357, 469.

T

TEETH

Fifteen-year-old Linda Peacock was reported missing from her home in Biggar, Scotland, on 6 August 1967. The following day her body was found in a cemetery near the village — she had died from head wounds and STRANGULATION. She had not been raped, but there were bite-marks on her right breast.

Photographs were taken of the teeth impressions, and the prints were sent to John Furness, lecturer in Forensic Dentistry at the Police Training School in Liverpool. He told Detective Chief Superintendent William Muncie, who was leading the investigation, that it would be possible to identify the assailant from the bite-marks, and also to eliminate suspects from the inquiry by the same means. This opinion was supported by Dr Warren Harvey, a consultant at the Glasgow Dental Hospital, who offered to take teeth impressions from suspects in the case.

In the meantime police officers made house-to-house inquiries in and around Biggar, including a near-by school for problem boys. After questioning the resident teenagers it was discovered that one of the boys was covering up for his room-mate's absence at the time the murder was committed. Seventeen-year-old Gordon Hay denied being away from the school, but CIRCUMSTANTIAL EVIDENCE pointed to his likely implication. After being cautioned, he agreed to have a dental impression taken.

Aware that new investigative ground was being broken, the police were anxious to ensure that Dr Harvey was not made aware of the identity of the suspect. Arrangements were therefore made for dental impressions to be taken from twenty-eight of the boys, including Hay. After comparing these impressions with the bite-marks on the dead girl's body, Harvey eliminated all but five suspects. Further examinations were made, and eventually the field was narrowed to one suspect — Gordon Hay. His canine teeth showed a rare condition in the presence of small pits in the tips of the teeth; there was also a filling missing from a front tooth.

Marks corresponding exactly with these features were found on the victim. Hay was arrested, and he registered a special defence of ALIBI to the High Court. He was tried in 1968, and the proceedings took an unusual turn when his counsel referred to the warrant which had been granted in order to take impressions of his teeth. It was objected that this was illegal, and consequently everything which stemmed from it was inadmissible. The trial judge dismissed the jury and sat with two other judges to consider this point. Their conclusion that the warrant was valid paved the way for the scientific evidence to be unfolded.

Dr Harvey presented his carefully prepared testimony, which showed clearly that the characteristics of the bite-marks on the victim's body were consistent in every detail with the dental impressions taken from the accused youth. In his summing-up the judge commented of forensic dentistry: 'This is a relatively new science, but there must of course be a first time.' So it proved when the jury found Gordon Hay guilty. As he was under eighteen at the time the crime was com-

Dental evidence in the Hay case

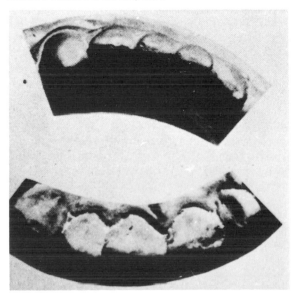

215

mitted, Hay was ordered to be detained during Her Majesty's pleasure. A subsequent appeal was dismissed by a panel of five judges, and a remarkable conviction brought about by teeth-marks made by the murderer on his victim's body was upheld.

Teeth impressions left by criminals as a result of violent assault have since led to other convictions, and bite-marks on items of food have also produced remarkable results. In 1976 an arsonist was found guilty at Southport on the strength of a bite-mark in an apple. Having caused £28,000 worth of damage to a public building by fire, he was incautious enough to take a bite out of an apple and leave it behind in one of the offices. The man was picked up five days later and his alibi was shattered by dental evidence, which showed 46 points of correspondence between bite-marks in the apple and impressions taken from his teeth. John Furness was again consulted, and he remarked, 'People can lie through their teeth, but their teeth cannot lie.' When the arsonist's appeal was dismissed Mr Justice Mars-Jones stated that dental evidence equalled that of FINGERPRINTS and FIBRES.

The contribution of dentistry to the IDENTIFICATION of dead persons by examining their teeth and records of dental treatment is an important aid to crime investigation, and has developed into an expertise known as forensic odontology.

Teeth, and some of the materials used for fillings are more durable than the rest of the body, and can withstand violence even by EXPLOSIVES and BURNING. Thus when a body has been disfigured by violence such as an air-crash its teeth can be used as the means of establishing identity. No two sets of teeth are the same. Apart from natural irregularities, there are different patterns of wear which, together with dental treatment by extraction and restoration, provide individual characteristics. The odds against two persons with full sets of 32 teeth producing identical bite-marks, for example, are calculated at 2·5 billion to 1, and fall into the same unique category as fingerprints.

The age of the body may be assessed by examining the state of eruption of its teeth up to about 25 years. After this, age-determination is more difficult, although techniques are being developed based on the study of wear of the enamel. Some racial differences may be determined from the shape of teeth, and likely social status may be indicated by the extent of restoration work, while differences in dental techniques and the materials used offer pointers to geographic origin. For example, well-to-do Orientals have a liking for gold-capping which is purely for decoration. Personal smoking habits also leave characteristic staining.

SCOTLAND YARD has set up a central index of dental records for MISSING PERSONS. Within a month of a person being reported missing his dentist is asked to provide his patient's dental charts so that a quick comparison can be made in the event of a body being found in suspicious circumstances. The comparison of ante-mortem dental records with POST-MORTEM dental examination has become a standard procedure for the identification of air-crash victims. It has also proved its worth in a number of murder cases, including the pioneering work of Professor Keith Simpson in the Dobkin case in 1942 (see under SKELETON).

As his contemporary, Professor Francis Camps, pointed out in connection with DISPOSAL OF THE BODIES, 'teeth are the most difficult things to destroy'.
111, **391**, **474**, *511*, *626*, **627**.

THALLIUM

It has been said that the imagination of the crime writer occasionally anticipates real murder. Agatha Christie's account of thallium poisoning in her novel *The Pale Horse*, published in 1961, came to be hailed as the most reliable description to be found outside a text-book. That book may have been on Graham Young's reading list when, as an inmate at Broadmoor criminal asylum, he spent his time learning about poisons. He had been sent there after confessing to poisoning his step-mother and attempting to poison other members of his family.

Young may also have read about Martha Marek, an Austrian lady who dabbled in insurance and poison. In 1932 her husband died, ostensibly of tuberculosis, followed by her baby daughter and an elderly relative from whom she inherited a valuable sum. These deaths were viewed with suspicion, and poison was rumoured. EXHUMATION of the bodies followed, and all were found to contain traces of thallium. Martha Marek was tried for murder and suffered EXECUTION by beheading in 1938.

Thallium is a heavy metal, similar to lead and MERCURY, and was discovered in 1861 by Sir William Crookes. It is extremely poisonous, and its effects have the great advantage for the poisoner of being indistinguishable from the symptoms of a number of ordinary diseases. It is also easily soluble in water, and is practically tasteless — characteristics which proved of great interest to the new tea boy at a photographic equipment factory. Graham Young joined the Hertfordshire firm of Hadlands in 1971 following his release from Broadmoor. His employers knew nothing of his antecedents, but they were impressed by his medical vocabulary.

A mysterious illness affected the firm during 1971, when many employees suffered from what they called 'The Bovington Bug'. The symptoms consisted chiefly of blurred vision and aches and pains which were put down to influenza. But in June the storeman was taken seriously ill with peripheral neuritis, and died in hospital. In October another worker died after three weeks of illness, and the manifestations of the 'The Bug' were daily becoming more serious with some workers complaining of their hair falling out, severe stomach pains and numbness in the legs. These complaints started to focus on the tea, which many said tasted bitter. In an effort to solve the firm's health problems the management called in a medical team to look around the factory. At a works meeting Graham Young featured prominently with his questions, and asked one of the doctors if thallium poisoning was suspected. The question identified Young as a 'know-all', but it also sowed seeds of suspicion which led to a check on his background — only then was his Broadmoor record discovered. He was quickly arrested, and like Major Armstrong the ARSENIC poisoner, he was carrying a lethal dose of poison in his pocket. In due course he admitted poisoning the two men who had died, and attempting to poison six others whose names were noted in his diary. This was no idle boast, for 9mg of thallium was produced from the cremated ashes of one of the dead men. At his trial in July 1972 Young denied everything, but the JURY found enough EVIDENCE to convict him, and he was sentenced to life imprisonment.

Thallium was available to Graham Young in a number of proprietary forms — for example, as thallous sulphate or acetate in ant-bait and rat-poison. Once ingested it is quickly taken up by most tissues and organs in the body and begins to interfere with the metabolism, particularly affecting the nerve cells and upsetting the calcium balance. This causes disorders similar to influenza, but has the distinctive effect of causing alopecia, or loss of hair. The poison is excreted very slowly from the body, and repeated doses have a cumulative effect. Thallium has not been widely used industrially in Britain, but it has been more popular elsewhere in Europe, where a number of accidental deaths have occurred in addition to MURDER. Its use in insecticides was banned in the USA in 1972 on account of the dangers to the public. Graham Young, the obsessive poisoner, was reported to have been flattered that his case gained a place in the history of criminology.
340, **491,** *757.*

THIRD DEGREE

In its mildest form the third degree describes intense interrogation of a prisoner by police in order to obtain a CONFESSION. In this context 'being given the third degree' has become a figure of speech denoting a severe grilling.

In its more drastic form, the third degree denotes physical intimidation of a prisoner, including putting him in an overheated cell or 'sweat-box', shining strong lights in his face, depriving him of sleep and possibly inflicting bodily assault. These methods of 'working' prisoners in order to extract admissions of guilt were first associated with the tactics of some police forces in the United States in the 1930s. The practice was condemned by the US National Commission on Law Observance and Enforcement, and strict rules have been laid down governing the interrogation of suspects and prisoners.

The use of physical torture to test a person's innocence was commonly practised in Europe during medieval times in trial by ordeal. The principle — adapted from pagan rites by the Church — was that a person's innocence in respect of a criminal accusation could be tested by his ability to withstand pain and injury. Two of the most popular tests involved contact with boiling water and red-hot metal. In cases where there was a lack of clear guilt the accused person was required to plunge his arm into a bowl of scalding water and retrieve a stone. If after three days there was evidence of burning on the skin the person was judged to be guilty. Similar tests involved walking on red-hot ploughshares or gripping a piece of hot metal in the hands without the flesh being burned. The idea was that if a person was not guilty of the accusation, his innocence would protect him.

Trial by ordeal was abolished in England in

1219, but the use of torture for other judicial purposes flourished until the eighteenth century. *Peine forte et dure*, 'Strong and fierce pain', was a procedure dating back to the thirteenth century in England whereby an accused person who refused to plead was subjected to judicial torture. Legalized torture was also used in the American Colonies, and one of the Salem witches was pressed to death in 1692.

Where an accused person remained mute — or 'mute of malice', as it was termed — he was placed on the floor under two boards with heavy weights piled on top. The weight was increased until he agreed to plead before a JURY or else he died in his refusal.

This practice was abolished in 1772, when a person who refused to plead was simply convicted, and again in 1827, when it was enacted that a person who remained mute would have a plea of not guilty entered on his behalf.
332.

TIME OF DEATH

One of the first questions asked at the scene of a murder is, 'What was the time of death?' Only in popular detective fiction is it possible for the doctor to examine the corpse and declare that death occurred at 10.30 in the evening. In reality, establishing time of death is difficult, and at best the experienced doctor will only give an estimate. But that estimate can be important in reconstructing a crime, and may help to substantiate or break a suspect's ALIBI.

Shortly after death occurs the body starts to cool, and undergoes a number of chemical changes, chief of which is RIGOR MORTIS. While the body is still newly dead it is the degree of cooling and rigor which offer the most reliable guide to the amount of time which has lapsed. The rate of body-cooling depends on a number of variable factors — whether it is clothed or not; its physical condition (with particular regard to obesity); whether it is lying indoors or out; the presence of any disease; and whether exertion preceded death. In general a clothed body will cool in air at about 2·5°F per hour. A naked body will cool half as fast again as one that is clothed, and a body in water twice as quickly. Rapid movement of air, thin clothing and poor physique will speed up the heat-loss, whereas death from ASPHYXIA or injury to the head will slow it down.

The rate of cooling also varies for different parts of the body. The extremities cool quickly, while the trunk loses its heat more gradually. Cooling slows as body temperature nears that of its surroundings. A dead body feels cold in 12 hours, and the temperature of the internal organs should be the same as that of the environment after 18–24 hours. The doctor at the murder scene feels the victim's jaw to see if it moves freely, indicating that rigor mortis has not yet begun. If the jaw is free and warmth is still present in the armpit, it is likely that death occurred within the previous six hours. If the jaw and limbs are fixed, and underarm warmth is barely detectable, the victim has probably been dead for more than six hours. The doctor next takes the temperature of the corpse with a low-reading thermometer placed in the rectum or vagina. He applies a formula to the temperature reading which gives an estimate of the number of hours elapsed since death.

$$\frac{\begin{array}{c}\text{Normal body temperature} \\ \text{37°C (99°F)}\end{array} - \begin{array}{c}\text{recorded rectal} \\ \text{temperature}\end{array}}{1\cdot5} = \text{hours since death}$$

A series of temperature recordings is taken at timed intervals and a graph plotted to show the rate of cooling. A rule of thumb is that a naked body loses 1·5°F of heat each hour.

It is recognized that this procedure does not

Estimating time of death

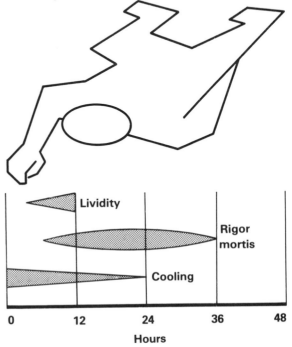

TIME SINCE DEATH	CHANGE
3–5 hours	Lividity is evident as blood drains to lowest parts.
5–7 hours	Rigor mortis begins in the face.
12 hours	Body cooled to about 25°C (77°F) internally.
12–18 hours	Rigor mortis complete with extension to arms and trunk.
20–24 hours	Body is cold with its temperature down to that of the surroundings.
24 hours	Rigor mortis starts to disappear.
24–36 hours	Rigor mortis completely disappeared.
48 hours	Discoloration of abdomen signals beginning of decomposition.

produce a highly accurate result. But in the hands of an experienced pathologist, body-cooling information can be combined with other factors to give an inspired estimate. Such was the case when the first of Neville Heath's victims was examined. On 21 June 1946 the body of a young woman was found in a London hotel room. She had been savagely beaten and mutilated. (See under SADISM.) When she was examined at 6.30 p.m., the vaginal temperature of her unclothed body was 29°C (84°F) compared with a room temperature of 17°C (63°F). By applying the normal body-cooling formula, time of death was placed ten hours previously, at about 8.30 a.m. The pathologist, the highly experienced Keith Simpson, took account of the manner of death, and adjusted his estimate of time of death. The girl died of asphyxia, which is known to raise the temperature, and he therefore calculated that the time which had elapsed since death was nearer eighteen hours. This means that the murder had occurred at around midnight. This proved to be the case, for police inquiries later revealed that a man was seen entering the hotel with the girl at 12.15 a.m. No doubt she was killed shortly afterwards.

Rigor mortis is the best known after-death effect. It is a condition brought about by coagulation of protein in the muscles which causes them to stiffen. Another process which starts after death is the draining of blood to the lowerst parts of the body, causing LIVIDITY or post-mortem staining. These changes, together with the onset of DECOMPOSITION, are part of the timetable of decay which begins with death. Their appearance and rate of progress can be charted in a manner which assists the general estimation of time of death.

Other changes after death which form part of the background enabling the pathologist to put the time of death into broad perspective are ADIPOCERE and MUMMIFICATION. Examination of STOMACH CONTENTS in relation to knowledge of when the victim last took a meal may also be taken into account at POST-MORTEM. A great deal will be learned about the likely time of death as the police investigation of a murder unfolds and witnesses' statements are collated. Nevertheless, the doctor's initial estimate is important in concentrating the inquiry within broad time limits, and thus preventing the police from dissipating their efforts.

1, **117**, **625**, *626*.

TOBACCO

Tobacco ash and cigarette and cigar butts are among the trace evidence which criminals often leave at the crime scene. While Sherlock Holmes's claim that he could distinguish at a glance the ash of any well-known brand of cigar or tobacco was a dramatic exaggeration, the smoking criminal's debris can help the investigation. Following an ASSASSINATION attempt on Hussein Pasha of Egypt in 1915 several cigarette ends were found in the room from which the bomb was thrown. The tobacconist who made the cigarettes was traced, and he told the police that they contained a special mixture made up to order. Similar cigarettes were found in the possession of the accused man, and microscopic comparison of the tobacco confirmed the presence of the accused at the scene of the crime.

Chemical analysis of tobacco ash shows differences in chloride content between different types of tobacco, but the blending of tobacco in mass-production manufacture means that even the more distinctive products are smoked by great numbers of persons. The cigarette-end itself is a far more useful piece of evidence, as it offers the possibility of determining whether the smoker is a SECRETOR. About 86 per cent of individuals are classed as secretors, which means that their body fluids, such as saliva, contain the same characteristics as their BLOOD group. Thus by testing the dried saliva on a cigarette-end, forensic scientists can determine the person's blood-group (unless he is a non-secretor), and add to the police profile of a wanted person.

The tobacco plant, *Nicotiana tabacum*, was brought to Europe from the New World in 1561. Its entry was at Lisbon, where the French Ambassador, Jean Nicot, took an interest in the new discovery and introduced the plant to France, where its medicinal use became associated with his name. It was employed chiefly as a treatment for eczema and palsy, and also as an emetic. When the most active ingredient of tobacco was isolated in 1828 it was named nicotine.

Nicotine is an alkaloid, a naturally occurring nitrogenous compound found in plants and fungi, and in the same group of classic poisons as MORPHINE, STRYCHNINE and ACONITINE. It is one of the most rapidly effective poisons known, and it was not long before it was put to criminal use.

'Gustave has fallen ill — I think he is dead. . . .' was the dramatic statement made by Countess Lydie de Bocarmé to her servants. Her brother, Gustave Fougnies, had called at the house on 20 November 1850 to announce his marriage plans. After a meal in the dining-room at the Bocarmé Château near Mons in Belgium, Gustave died suddenly. Extraordinary scenes followed in which Count Hyppolyte de Bocarmé was seen forcing vinegar down the dead man's throat, while Lydie stripped her brother's body and washed his clothes. Late in the night the servants could hear their mistress scrubbing the dining-room floor.

Count de Bocarmé, alleged by the local peasants to have been suckled by a lioness, married Lydie Fougnies, whom he erroneously believed to be wealthy. When plans to enrich himself through marriage failed his estates went downhill and he was forced to sell part of his land. Conspiring with Lydie, he realized his best chance of redemption lay with his brother-in-law who had inherited a large sum which would go to Lydie if he died

unmarried. When the Bocarmés had forewarning that Gustave was about to announce his marriage they saw their future start to crumble.

News of the strange events surrounding a SUDDEN DEATH at the Bocarmé Château reached the authorities, who sent an Examining Magistrate and three doctors to investigate. POST-MORTEM examination showed no evidence of a stroke, but the doctors' attention was drawn to signs of corrosive burning in the dead man's mouth and throat. They concluded that death was due to swallowing a quantity of ACID, and carefully secured samples of body tissue for laboratory analysis. Meanwhile Count and Countess de Bocarmé were put under arrest.

The analysis was entrusted to Jean Stas, Professor of Chemistry at the École Royale Militaire in Brussels. Having studied under Orfila, he had the right credentials for a piece of work which was to be a breakthrough in toxicology. Stas ruled out corrosive poisoning as the cause of death, and became convinced that the strong smell of vinegar in the stomach denoted an attempt to mask the real cause of death. The Professor's keen nose also detected the mousey smell of coniine, the active component of hemlock, and a faint whiff of tobacco. At that time coniine and nicotine were the only two vegetable alkaloid poisons known. The problem he faced was to prove his hunch by isolating the poison from the body tissues.

Stas's technique was to dissolve away the substance of the stomach and intestinal tissues with alkaline solution and to remove this matter from his samples by repeated washing and filtration. After this process of continual refinement the samples were treated with ether and then evaporated. Finally, his painstaking work was rewarded by the appearance in an evaporating dish of an oily substance with all the characteristics of nicotine. Chemical tests confirmed this, and the chemist reported to the police that Gustave Fougnies had died of nicotine poisoning.

The police learned from an interview with Bocarmé's gardener that the Count had spent the whole summer making 'eau de cologne' with tobacco leaves. He often worked late at night in the wash-house using a variety of glass stills and jars. The coachman divulged that his master had been to Ghent to visit a professor of chemistry, from whom the police learned that Bocarmé, using an alias, had sought advice regarding the extraction of nicotine from tobacco leaves.

Bocarmé's laboratory apparatus was eventually discovered hidden behind some wall panelling, and buried remains of animals on which he had tested his poisonous concoction were located in the garden. Nicotine was identified on floor-boards taken up from the dining-room, and the violence with which the Count and Countess carried out their plan became apparent. It was likely that the victim had been held down on the floor while the nicotine was forced into his mouth, and when he was dead vinegar was used to mask the poison.

Overwhelming evidence was brought against the pair at their trial, when their pathetic defence consisted of throwing accusations at each other. Countess de Bocarmé was acquitted, but her husband met his end on the scaffold.

Nicotine is a violent poison, and its action is more powerful than is that of coniine. It is soluble in water, and is readily absorbed by the skin. Its initial effect is that of a stimulant, but when absorbed in poisonous doses it produces nausea and cardiac irregularity, eventually paralysing the respiratory system. The lethal dose for an adult is between 40 and 60mg, and oral ingestion may result in death within a few minutes. In his text-book on FORENSIC MEDICINE Sir Sydney Smith noted that if the nicotine content of one cigar were injected into the bloodstream it could kill two persons. Homicidal use of nicotine is rare, but its inclusion in horticultural sprays has led to many cases of accidental poisoning through skin absorption.

72, 258, **445, 675,** *751.*

TRUTH DRUGS

Drugs used to produce a relaxed, uninhibited and hence truthful state of mind in persons subjected to questioning. The technique, known as narco-analysis, was discovered by a Texas doctor in the 1930s, who found that expectant mothers given scopolamine to induce 'twilight sleep' became uninhibited in their speech. Experience with the drug showed that while leaving the memory, hearing and speech intact, it submerges that part of the brain which creates lies for self-protection.

Narco-analysis has been widely used in the USA to assist criminal interrogation, and has resulted in numerous successes, including CONFESSION to murder. Information obtained in this way is inadmissible as evidence in court, as it is judged to have been gained involuntarily. Thus in common with the LIE-DETECTOR, truth drugs have yet to gain full recognition.

Scopolamine has given way to barbiturate drugs such as sodium amytal, which is administered intravenously with the subject's consent. Dosage must be carefully controlled, as individual reaction to narco-analysis varies widely. Questions must be carefully and unambiguously worded, and skilled operators are required for the purpose. It has been found that some individuals become highly suggestible and make false or misleading statements while others are able to withhold information altogether. Truthful answers may also be modified by guilt feelings and by subconscious fantasies.

The value of narco-analysis probably lies more in its power to clear innocent persons and minimize wastage of police time than in obtaining confessions. A moral objection used against the method is that it is a type of inquisition which effectively deprives a person of his freedom of mind. A case in which the French police used truth drugs on a man accused of being a German collaborator raised a storm of controversy in the years after the Second World War.

Henri Cens was charged with collaborating with the enemy, but a medical report judged him unfit to defend himself. In 1943 he had been accidentally shot in the head during a prison riot, and although his life was saved, he was reduced to a shadow of his former self, and suffered loss of speech. In 1946 a panel of three doctors declared him unfit to appear in court, but, two years later, in an incredible reversal, decided he was fit to plead. It appeared that Cens had been subjected to narco-analysis administered under the guise of treatment, as a result of which he had overcome his speech defect.

A medico-legal row quickly ensued, with Cens's lawyer complaining that duping a sick man in this way was a violation of human rights. After Cens had been three years in prison the case against him had been dropped, and legal action was brought against the doctors who administered the truth drug. This did not succeed, but bitter arguments resulted in French medical circles, and the popular view was that a miscarriage of justice had taken place.

While truth drugs have taken their place in the range of techniques available to criminal investigators, they also have obvious limitations. Codes of practice have been drawn up to avoid a repetition of the French experience, but the most reliable confessions are still considered to be those gained by conventional interrogation methods. The term 'truth serum' sometimes used in reference to narco-analysis is a complete misnomer, and owes more to popular sensationalism than to the facts.
491, *580.*

U

UNDETECTED MURDER

An American study of homicide rates published in 1958 suggested that one out of every ten murderers avoids detection. Other studies have put the level of undetected murders much higher, and it has been postulated that they outweigh the number of murders solved.

Numbers of known deaths are undoubtedly classed as accidents or suicides, partly due to the cleverness of the murderer, but also to lack of perception and, occasionally, to lack of experience in coroners and doctors. This is borne out by an analysis of causes of death stated in DEATH CERTIFICATES, which showed that up to 45 per cent of stated causes were proved to be incorrect at POST-MORTEM.

It is said that few doctors look for poison in deaths apparently from natural causes which occur in ordinary domestic circumstances. The cunning poisoner can use the similarity of the symptoms caused by his lethal agent with those of natural disease to cloak his murderous activities. The quest for an undetectable poison has taken many interesting turns, and it is to the professional awareness of doctors that most of the spectacular failures must be attributed. MORPHINE, ACONITINE and nicotine (see under TOBACCO), when little known as drugs and first used for murder, featured in notable triumphs of forensic detection. Nevertheless, it remains a chastening thought that many practitioners of the poisonous arts have outwitted the investigator and got away with murder.

While some murderers have been fortunate to escape through the chance workings of accident, most of the deliberate attempts to avoid detection have involved poison. The idea of a toxic agent which can be stealthily introduced into the human body, perform its fatal work and leave no mark or trace is for the murderer a philosopher's stone.

One such agent is succinylcholine chloride, a synthetic muscle-relaxant used in hospital operating theatres. Dr Carl Coppolino, a Florida anesthesiologist, decided that this drug would be a satisfactory means of disposing of his wife, who stood in the way of his extra-marital activities. He gave her an injection and she died, apparently of a heart attack, in 1965. Coppolino remarried within three weeks, only to have his newfound bliss shattered by accusations from a former lady-friend that he had murdered his wife. His accuser also alleged that she had injected succinylcholine chloride into her husband to procure his death under Coppolino's directions.

Both bodies were exhumed, and evidence was found suggesting foul play. Dr Milton Helpern, the New York Medical Examiner, was called in, and he found the unmistakable mark left by a hypodermic needle in Mrs Coppolino's body. Succinylcholine chloride was a subtle choice of poison, for once it enters the body it quickly breaks down into succinic acid and choline, both of which are normally found in human tissues. Extensive analytical work in this case established the presence of abnormally large amounts of succinic acid in the body organs, and also around the needle track. This strongly suggested that the dead woman had been injected with a large dose of the drug. In 1967 a Florida court found Dr Coppolino guilty of second-degree MURDER and he was imprisoned for life.

More recently, another doctor murdered his unwanted wife with an unusual drug. Paul Vickers, a surgeon from Newcastle, selected CCNU, an anti-cancer drug which combined the qualities of a potentially undetectable poison: rarity and no known method of tracing in the human body. Vickers nursed an ambition to develop a political career, and his invalid wife who was under treatment for schizophrenia was an en-

cumbrance. In the course of his political social-
izing he met a young woman who became his
mistress and who he hoped would further his
political ambitions.

Vickers decided to get his wife out of the way,
and he made out false prescriptions for CCNU in
capsule form which he had sent to him. He
changed the labels on the drug-containers so that
his wife, who received various properly prescribed
drugs, would not be able to identify them. He
administered the drug in her food, causing her to
develop aplastic anaemia, a rare blood disease,
from which she died a painful, lingering death in
June 1979.

Six months later Vickers's mistress made allegations that he had obtained drugs by criminal
deception. As the result of police inquiries the
couple were charged jointly with murder. Vickers
was examined by a psychiatrist who said that he
was suffering from induced psychosis known as
FOLIE À DEUX. The surgeon himself told the court,
'I do not really deserve to live.' He was found
guilty of murder and sentenced to life imprisonment. His mistress was acquitted.

The murder of his infant son with Seconal at
Portsmouth in 1955 by Navy Sick Birth Attendant
John Armstrong (see under CHILD-MURDER), and
of his wife with insulin by male nurse Kenneth
Barlow at Bradford in 1957 (see under POST-
MORTEM), show how easily medical workers with
access to drugs can use them for murder. Undetected murder procured by means of BACTERIA
is another problem area for investigators, and
public unease had been expressed over stories that
government agencies carry stocks of the deadly
botulinus toxin and of vegetable toxins such as
RICIN. The chief difficulty lies in the virtual un-
detectability of some of these agents, and a number
of the LSD-related hallucinogenic plants, for
example, have an unknown active principle. Con
sequently, in any mysterious fatal poisoning the
analyst has no hope of isolating the cause, for he
does not know what to look for.
26, 100, 290, 324, 341, 460.

UNSOLVED MURDERS

Perhaps the most famous unsolved murders were
those committed in London in 1888 by JACK THE
RIPPER.

Most cases offer some encouragement to the
investigators, and it is unusual to find murders so
lacking in evidence that no progress can be made.

One such was the Bogle–Chandler case which
occurred in Australia in 1963. On New Year's Day
two youths out walking in a riverside area near
Sydney found a man's body. At first they thought
he was drunk, but then decided he was dead and
called the police.

Investigators confirmed that the man — identified by papers in his wallet as Dr Stanley Bogle —
was indeed dead. Although he appeared to be fully
dressed he was in fact naked, his clothes having
been carefully placed over his body. A short
distance away was another body, later identified as
that of Mrs Margaret Chandler. It appeared that
both victims had attended a New Year's party at a
house on Sydney's North Shore. Dr Bogle had
been invited to attend with his wife, but she was
unable to go on account of nursing their baby.
Bogle arrived alone, and during the party met Mr
and Mrs Chandler. At about midnight Chandler
left the party, leaving his wife and Bogle together.
The party broke up at about 4.0 a.m., and after
discussion with Chandler (who had returned to the
festivities by then) it was agreed that Bogle would
escort Mrs Chandler home, leaving her husband to
go his own way.

Bogle drove his companion to the spot where
they were later found. Their bodies showed no
marks of violence, or signs of any organic disease.
Cause of death was given as cardiac failure. While
the man's body showed advanced signs of RIGOR
MORTIS, Mrs Chandler's body was still warm, but
it was thought that the couple died within an hour
of each other. Suspicion was voiced regarding
poison, but no toxic material was found at POST-
MORTEM. Criticism was later levelled at the
crime-scene investigators for failing to carry out
tests for alcohol, and for not taking the temperature of the bodies (see under TIME OF DEATH).

The Australian authorities did not treat the
deaths as murder, but conducted a thorough homicide investigation. One explanation offered was
that the couple, in a state of inebriation, embarked
on sexual intercourse for which one undressed, and
that one became unconscious through ASPHYXIA
associated with alcoholic intoxication and accidentally suffocated the other. This does not
adequately explain why the two bodies were found
separated by a distance of about fifteen yards, nor
why the man was covered over with his clothing.
The case remains an unsolved mystery, despite
subsequent speculation that Bogle was killed with
an undetectable poison because of his involvement with sensitive scientific research on lasers.

While some murders remain unsolved — in that

no charge is ever brought against a suspect — others remain unsolved when an accusation or even a conviction breaks down. Following the murder of multi-millionaire Sir Harry Oakes in the Bahamas in 1943 his son-in-law, Alfred de Marigny, was charged with the killing. FINGER-PRINT evidence produced at the trial which purported to have placed Marigny at the scene of the crime was shown to have been falsely obtained and he was acquitted. Another murder case solved many years after the original incident had taken place was that involving missing show-girl Mamie Stuart (see under MISSING PERSONS for full account).

70, 128, 382, 484, 537, 557, 623, 653, 656, 666.

V

VICTIMOLOGY

The study of the relationship between criminal and victim, and especially the idea that some individuals are predisposed to become victims, is known as victimology. Murder usually embraces people who are known to each other — members of a family, friends, business acquaintances or workmates — whose affairs and closeness of contact foster passion, jealousy and envy. The very existence of such links between killer and victim gave the task of criminal investigation a starting-point, whereas the recent increase in stranger-to-stranger murders increases the difficulties of detection.

The classic case is the eternal triangle, a relationship which easily distinguishes the potential victim. Mrs Phoebe Hogg and her infant child were cast in the role of luckless victims by the jealous passion of Mary Pearcey. The discovery of Mrs Hogg's body with the throat cut in a North London street in 1890, followed by the recovery of the suffocated corpse of her eighteen-month-old baby, quickly signposted a trail to Mary Pearcey. The Hoggs were not happily married. Phoebe was a sickly woman, and her husband, Frank, although a lethargic type, had the capacity to charm the opposite sex. He met Mary Pearcey before he married, and she sent him letters which showed her strong-minded pace-making. Mary nursed her rival through an illness, and in no time at all Frank was given a latch-key to her house at 2 Priory Street in Kentish Town.

On 24 October Phoebe was invited to Priory Street for tea. Leaving her perambulator in the passage of the house and clutching her baby, she entered the kitchen. There she was done to death by Mary Pearcey, who with demonic fury crushed her skull and cut her throat, almost severing the head. Police later found broken windows which indicated a struggle had taken place, and there was BLOOD on the walls and ceiling of the kitchen. A neighbour heard the noise of broken glass at about 4.0 p.m., and some two hours later Mary was seen in a near-by street wheeling a heavily laden perambulator. Thus began an incredible journey of some six miles during which she left Phoebe's corpse in a deserted street, dumped the child's body on a piece of waste ground, abandoned the blood-stained perambulator and returned home.

Mary Pearcey pleaded not guilty at her trial, but the CIRCUMSTANTIAL EVIDENCE against her was overwhelming. She was found guilty and sentenced to death, the wretched Frank Hogg, object of her devotion, failing to respond to her request to visit her in the condemned cell. Finally she left a note exonerating him from all blame. Mary Pearcey concocted an unusual triangle — it is usually the jealous husband who kills his wife's lover, but in her case it was the jealous woman eliminating her lover's wife. Poor Phoebe Hogg, a meek woman with a vacillating, wayward husband, was the dumb victim. As the murder unfolded sensation and mystery attached to the strong character of Mary Pearcey, and Frank Hogg won the unmitigated hostility of his neighbours — the innocent victims, Phoebe and her child, were forgotten.

Various permutations of sexual relationships probably create more victims than any other circumstances. The threat of blackmail in the clandestine liaisons of Madeleine Smith and Chester Gillette led to murder, as did Harvey Glatman's arousal by the flaunted sexuality of photographic models. But it is the prostitute who most clearly casts herself in the role of potential victim, as evidenced by the JACK THE RIPPER syndrome. Tennyson Jesse the crime writer coined the term 'murderee' to denote those who lay themselves open to become murder victims. For the streetwalker murder is an occupational hazard, for sex facilitates the commission of murder. Those who play with MASOCHISM have the clearest desire to become victims, and the world of drug-taking and perverted sex provides every possible opportunity for the role of victim.

There is a class of murder known as victim-precipitated homicide in which the victim is the first to show violence by a threatening gesture or by brandishing a weapon. There is also the verbal aggression of the nagging spouse which can lead to quiet elimination, as Herbert Rowse Armstrong demonstrated. (See under ARSENIC for description of the case.) The lack of awareness of children and the elderly to the potential violence in society makes them potential victims too. A child's innocent attraction to a smooth-talking but predatory stranger is the justifiable fear of all mothers.

The old person's carelessness concerning personal security makes that person vulnerable to the point where failure to take safety precautions can end in disaster. It has been suggested that to some degree victims carry blame for making themselves available as prey to marauding attackers.
142, 249, 380, 416, 421, 524.

VITAL REACTION

It is important for the pathologist to be able to distinguish between injuries inflicted before death and those sustained afterwards. For example, the discovery of a head-wound in the fatally burnt victim of a fire might have two differing explanations — a falling timber could have struck the already dead body, or a murderous blow might have been delivered with the intention of consuming the unconscious body in the fire. Alternatively, an injury accidentally inflicted on a dead body might be mistakenly interpreted as a wound sustained during life, and lead to a false trail of murder.

When the human body is injured its natural defence mechanism responds by massing thousands of white blood cells (leucocytes) at the site of the wound to fight infection and begin the work of repair. This is known as vital reaction, and is a familiar occurrence in the inflammation which is associated with cuts and scratches made to the living body. If a person receives a wound and survives for a short time before dying there is a recognizable vital reaction in the form of inflammation around the edges of the wound. This is a clear indication that the wounding occurred

during life, and confirmation is obtained by microscopic identification of leucocytes in the wound.

The phenomenon of vital reaction has also been used to determine the age of wounds. Several types of leucocytes are involved, and they appear at the wound in a regular sequence over a period of 48 hours. The first repair cells may appear within two hours of the wound being sustained, and their presence has been recorded within thirty minutes. This infiltration of leucocytes is readily apparent with the aid of the microscope.

A particular difficulty lies in distinguishing between injuries that occur immediately before or after death. Dr Milton Helpern, New York City's famous medical examiner, referred to this as 'another fertile area of trouble for the forensic pathologist'. While the heart is still beating bleeding occurs in fatal wounds sustained during life, but injuries inflicted immediately after death may also bleed for a while, especially scalp-wounds. If the victim survived the injury for less than an hour, it is unlikely that vital reaction would be in evidence. Determining the age of wounds, in common with estimates of TIME OF DEATH, is the province of experts, who invariably urge caution in arriving at conclusions.
324.

VOICEPRINTS

It is a common experience that human voices have distinctive qualities which can be readily recognized in familiar day-to-day circumstances. The problem for the investigator is to identify a voice recording relating to a criminal incident, such as a telephoned threat, compared with the voice of a suspect. American scientist Lawrence G. Kersta has developed a technique which allows this comparison to be made electronically by measuring the resonance, pitch and volume of a voice. Recordings are traced in contour form on to a paper roll, producing an acoustic spectrogram or voiceprint.

A voiceprint is made from the articulation of single common words such as 'me' or 'you'. Its value lies in a unique combination of physical characteristics governed by the shape of a person's mouth and throat structures. Attempts to disguise the voice do not affect its inherent quality, and characteristics such as loudness and speed, which can be modified by self-control, are not measured on the voiceprint.

Evidence of identity obtained through voiceprints has been presented to courts in the USA, but

Differences in voiceprints of two persons speaking the same word

like the LIE-DETECTOR, the technique has not been fully accepted. The method has been most widely applied to so-called telephone crimes involving KIDNAPPING, blackmail, extortion and terrorism. Speech scientists are divided in their opinions as to the value of voiceprints, and are most cautious to avoid comparisons with FINGERPRINTS. Some take the view that while the speech of every individual is unique, it is not yet possible to make an adequate visual representation of speech characteristics by electronic means. Others maintain that in any case the method offers little improvement on the trained ear, and is too easily distorted by emotion and other factors.

The difficulties of voice identification were demonstrated in June 1979 after the eleventh murder of the Yorkshire Ripper, when a tape-recorded voice was sent to the police. 'I'm Jack,' it began, 'I see you are still having no luck catching me. . . .' This taunting and tantalizing tape was believed to have been sent by the killer, and the police devoted a great deal of attention to it.

Specialists in dialect concluded that the speaker was from the North of England, a man probably in his early twenties, from Wearside. In the hope of someone recognizing the voice, the tape recording was played in factories and working men's clubs. It was never identified, and ultimately proved to have been an expensive hoax. Peter Sutcliffe, the Yorkshire Ripper, was arrested in 1981. Suspicions that he might be the killer were dismissed at an earlier stage because he did not speak with a Wearside 'Geordie' accent.

Despite the setbacks, voice analysis is an area of continuing technical improvement, with applications being found in industry and commerce. Psychological stress-evaluation detectors are used by many large companies for personnel screening. This equipment is based on the principle that a micro-tremor, unheard by the human ear, is produced by the muscles which control the voice during normal speech. Under the stress of telling a lie these muscles tense up, and the tremor ceases. This change is recorded graphically on the detector. These procedures are also widely used by US government agencies whose personnel work on sensitive military or political projects.
155, **399, 703.**

X̄

XYY CHROMOSOMES

A theory was developed in the 1960s suggesting a relationship between male sex hormones and aggressive behaviour. Sex and other individual human characteristics were determined by the chromosomes, which contain the genes or hereditary factors found in the nucleii of all human cells. Chromosomes are normally present as twenty-three pairs of XX chromosomes in the female, and the same number of XY chromosomes in the male. Some individuals, however, have an additional chromosome, making them either XXY or XYY.

The implication is that the extra chromosome accounts for violent and anti-social behaviour.

Psychiatric research has shown that a high proportion of XYY males are to be found among the inmates of prisons and prison hospitals. Other studies have suggested that XYY boys exhibit more impulsive behaviour than their XY fellows. The idea of the 'criminal chromosome' has been seized on in some newspaper accounts of MASS MURDERS, and Richard Speck, killer of eight nurses in Chicago in 1966, was alleged to be an XYY male. This proved to be false, and psychiatrists do not believe there is yet sufficient evidence to link possession of the extra chromosome with murder.

15, 325, 451, 555.

XYY Chromosomes

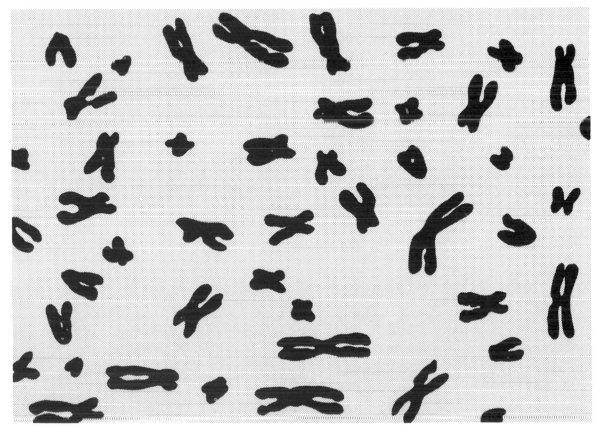

Bibliography

1 **Notable British Trials** (eighty-three titles)
2 **Famous Trials** (sixteen titles)
3 **Old Bailey Trials** (seven titles)
4 **Celebrated Trials** (six titles)
5 **Abbott, J. H:** *In the Belly of the Beast*
6 **Abinger, Edward:** *Forty Years at the Bar*
7 **Abrahams, Gerald:** *According to the Evidence*
8 **Adam, H. L:** *Police Work from Within*
9 —: *Murder Most Mysterious*
10 —: *Murder by Persons Unknown*
11 **Adams, N:** *Dead and Buried?*
12 **Adamson, Iain:** *A Man of Quality*
13 **Allen, William:** *Starkweather*
14 **Altick, Richard T:** *Victorian Studies in Scarlet*
15 **Altman, Jack and Ziporyn, Marvin:** *Born to Raise Hell*
16 **Ambler, Eric:** *The Ability to Kill*
17 **Andrews, Allen:** *Intensive Inquiries*
18 **Angelella, Michael:** *Trail of Blood*
19 **Anspacher, Carolyn:** *The Acid Test*
20 **Appleton, Arthur:** *Mary Ann Cotton*
21 **Archer, Fred:** *Killers in the Clear*
22 **Arthur, Herbert:** *All the Sinners*
23 **Ashton-Wolfe, H:** *The Underworld*
24 **Atholl, Justin:** *The Reluctant Hangman*
25 **Atlay, J. B:** *Famous Trials*
26 **Bailey, F. Lee:** *The Defence Never Rests*
27 **Bailey, Guy:** *The Fatal Chance*
28 **Baker, E. R. and Dodge, F. B:** *Criminal Evidence and Procedure*
29 **Balchin, Nigel:** *The Anatomy of Villainy*
30 **Ball, J. M:** *The Sack-'em-up Men*
31 **Ballantine, Serjeant:** *Some Experiences of a Barrister's Life*
32 **Banks, Harold K:** *The Strangler!*
33 **Bardens, Dennis:** *The Ladykiller*
34 —: *Lord Justice Birkett*
35 —: *Famous Cases of Norman Birkett KC*
36 **Barker, Dudley:** *Palmer: The Rugeley Poisoner*
37 —: *Lord Darling's Famous Cases*
38 **Barnard, A:** *The Harlot Killer*
39 **Barthel, Joan:** *A Death in Canaan*
40 **Barzun, J:** *Burke and Hare: The Resurrection Men*
41 **Battley, Harry:** *Single Finger Prints*
42 **Beal, E (Ed):** *The Trial of Adelaide Bartlett*
43 **Beattie, John:** *The Yorkshire Ripper Story*
44 **Beaver, Ninette, Ripley, B. K. and Trese, Patrick:** *Caril*
45 **Bechhofer Roberts, C. E:** *Famous American Trials*
46 **Belin, Jean:** *My Work at the Sûreté*
47 **Benedetti, Jean:** *Gilles de Rais: The Authentic Bluebeard*
48 **Bennett, Benjamin:** *Too Late for Tears*
49 —: *The Amazing Case of the Baron von Schauroth*
50 —: *Freedom or the Gallows*
51 —: *Genius for the Defence*
52 —: *Some Don't Hang*
53 —: *Murder Will Speak*
54 —: *Why Did They Do It?*
55 —: *Famous South African Murders*
56 —: *The Cohen Case*
57 **Bentley, W. G:** *My Son's Execution*
58 **Berg, Karl:** *The Sadist*
59 **Berrett, James:** *When I was at Scotland Yard*
60 **Berry, James:** *My Experiences as an Executioner*
61 **Beveridge, Peter:** *Inside the CID*
62 **Birmingham, George:** *Murder Most Foul*
63 **Bishop, Cecil:** *From Information Received*

Collections of Cases and Memoirs

American Regional Murder Series (Edited by Marie F. Rodell): *Boston, Charleston, Chicago, Cleveland, Denver, Detroit, Los Angeles, New York and San Francisco.*

Birkenhead, Earl of: *Famous Trials*
—: *More Famous Trials*
Adam, H. L.: *Old Days at the Old Bailey*
Adams, Virginia: *Human Behaviour—Crime*
Bechhofer Roberts, C. E.: *Sir Travers Humphreys: His Career and Cases*
Bennett, Benjamin: *The Evil That Men Do*
—: *The Noose Tightens*
—: *Up for Murder*
—: *Murder is my Business*
—: *Was Justice Done?*
Bixley, William: *The Guilty and the Innocent*
Blackham, Robert J.: *Sir Ernest Wild KC*
Bowker, A. E.: *A Lifetime with the Law*
Brophy, John: *The Meaning of Murder*
Butler, Ivan: *Murderers' England*
—: *Murderers' London*
Byrnes, Thomas: *Professional Criminals of America*
Camp, John: *Holloway Prison*
Cargill, David and Holland, Julian: *Scenes of Murder—A London Guide*
Carlin, Francis: *Reminiscences of an ex-Detective*
Churchill, Allen: *A Pictorial History of American Crime*
Clegg, Eric: *Return Your Verdict*
Darrow, Clarence: *The Story of My Life*
De Vries, Leonard: *'Orrible Murder*
Deeley, Peter: *The Manhunters*
Downie, R. Angus: *Murder in London*
Duke, Thomas: *Celebrated Criminal Cases of America*
Dunning, John: *Truly Murderous*
—: *Sudden Death*

Famous Crimes of Recent Times (No Author)
Fifty Greatest Rogues, Tyrants and Criminals (No Author)
Firmin, Stanley: *Crime Man*
Greenwall, Harry J.: *They Were Murdered in France*
Gribble, Leonard: *Famous Judges and Their Trials*
Grierson, Francis: *Famous French Crimes*
Griffiths, Arthur: *Mysteries of Police and Crime*
Grimshaw, Eric and Jones, Glyn: *Lord Goddard: His Career and Cases*
Haines, Max: *Crime Flashback*
Halbert, Sara: *Call Me Counselor*
Hammer, Richard: *Illustrated History of Organised Crime*
Hoskins, Percy: *They Almost Escaped*
House, Jack: *Square Mile of Murder*
Humphreys, Christmas: *Seven Murders*
Huson, Richard (Ed): *Sixty Famous Trials*
Hyde, H. Montgomery: *Cases That Changed the Law*
—: *Lord Reading*
—: *United in Crime*
—: *Crime has its Heroes*
Jackson, Stanley: *The Old Bailey*
Johnston, James A.: *Prison Life is Different*
Kelly, Vince: *The Charge is Murder*
Kennaugh, Robert Charles: *Contemporary Murder*
Kent, Arthur: *The Death Doctors*
Keylin, Aileen and Demirnian, Arto Jr: *Crime as Reported by the New York Times*
Kingston, Charles: *Dramatic Days at the Old Bailey*
—: *Law-Breakers*

MURDER: 'Whatdunit'

Knox, Bill: *Court of Murder*
Lesberg, Sandy (**Ed**): *Picture History of Crime*
Lock, Joan: *Marlborough Street: The Story of a London Court*
—: *The British Policewoman*
Logan, Guy H. B.: *Guilty or Not Guilty?*
—: *Dramas of the Dock*
Longworth, Frank: *With Detectives Around the World*
Lustgarten, Edgar: *A Century of Murderers*
—: *The Illustrated Story of Crime*
—: *The Judges and the Judged*
Lynch, P. P.: *No Remedy for Death*
Mackenzie, F. A.: *World Famous Crimes*
Massie, Allen: *Ill Met by Gaslight*
Matthews, David A.: *Crime Doctor*
McComas, Francis: *Graveside Companion*
McConnell Bodkin, M.: *Famous Irish Trials*
McDade, Thomas M: *The Annals of Murder*
Morn, Frank: *The Eye that Never Sleeps*
Napley, Sir David: *Not Without Prejudice*
Nash, Jay Robert: *Compendium of World Crime*
Nicholls, Ernest: *Crime Within the Square Mile*
Parris, John: *Most of My Murderers*
Parrish, J. M. and Crossland, J. R.: *The Fifty Most Amazing Crimes of the Last Hundred Years*
Pearson, Edmund: *Instigation of the Devil*
Postgate, Raymond: *Murder, Piracy and Treason*
Poynter, J. W.: *Forgotten Crimes*
Radin, Edward R: *Twelve Against the Law*
Rovere, Richard H.: *Howe and Hummel*
Runyon, Damon: *Trials and Other Tribulations*

Ruotolo, A. K.: *Once Upon a Murder*
Sanders, Bruce: *They Caught These Killers*
—: *Murder in Big Cities*
Scott, Sir Harold (**Ed**): *Crime and Criminals*
Seccombe, Thomas (**Ed**): *Twelve Bad Men*
Seedman, A. A.: *Chief!*
Sifakis, Karl: *Catalogue of Crime*
Singer, Kurt: *My Greatest Crime Story*
—: *My Strangest Case*
—: *Crime Omnibus*
Singer, Kurt and Sherrod, Jane: *Great Adventures in Crime*
Smith, Arthur: *Lord Goddard*
Smith-Hughes, Jack: *Unfair Comment Upon Some Victorian Murder Trials*
—: *Eight Studies in Justice*
Sutton, Charles: *The New York Tombs*
Thomas, David: *Seek Out The Guilty*
Thomson, Basil: *The Criminal*
Vanstone, Charles: *A Man in Plain Clothes*
Vincent, A. (**Ed**): *Twelve Bad Women*
Walker-Smith, Derek: *Lord Reading and his Cases*
Walling, George W.: *Recollections of a New York Chief of Police*
Warden, R. and Groves, M. (**Ed**): *America's Murder Most Foul*
Whiteley, Cecil: *Brief Life*
Wild, Roland: *Crimes and Cases of 1933*
Willemse, Cornelius, W.: *A Cop Remembers*
Wilson, Colin: *Encyclopaedia of Murder*
—: *A Casebook of Murder*
Wyndham, Horace: *Famous Trials Retold*

Individual Cases

Adleman, Robert H.: *The Bloody Benders*
Barker, Ralph: *Verdict on a Lost Flyer*
Bell, Terry: *Bitter Hill*
Bingham, John: *The Hunting Down of Peter Manuel*
Broad, Lewis: *The Innocence of Edith Thompson*
Buchanan, Edna: *Carr: Five Years of Rape and Murder*
Campbell, Marjorie Freeman: *Torso*
Cantillon, Richard H.: *In Defence of the Fox*
Capon, P.: *The Great Yarmouth Mystery*
Capote, Truman: *In Cold Blood*
Chamberlain, Sir Roderic: *Stuart Affair*
Copeland, James: *The Butler*
Curling, Jonathan: *Janus Weathercock*
Du Preez, Peter: *The Vontsteen Case*
Furneaux, Rupert: *Robert Hoolhouse*
    —: *Michael John Davies*
Gaddis, Thomas E.: *Birdman of Alcatraz*
Gibbs, Dorothy and Maltby, Herbert: *The True Story of Maria Marten*
Gibney, J. and D.: *The Galton Mystery*
Gilmore, John: *The Tucson Murders*
Giono, Jean: *The Dominici Affair*
Grosso, Sonny and Devaney, John: *Murder at the Harlem Mosque*
Havers, Sir Michael, Shankland, P. and Barrett, A.: *A Tragedy in Three Voices*
Hawkes, Harry: *Capture of the Black Panther*
Howard, Clark: *The Zebra Killings*
Inglis, K. S.: *The Stuart Case*
Kunstler, William A.: *The Minister and the Choir Singer*
Kwitny, Jonathan: *The Mullendore Murder Case*
Laborde, Jean: *The Dominici Affair*
Lambert, Richard S.: *The Universal Provider*
Langford, Gerald: *The Murder of Stanford White*
Lefkowitz, Bernard and Gross, Kenneth G.:

The Sting of Justice
Leopold, Nathan F. Jr.: *Life Plus 99 Years*
Levy, Norman: *The Nan Patterson Case*
Lindsey, J.: *Suburban Gentleman*
Lucas, Norman: *The Monster Butler*
Lustgarten, Edgar: *The Chalkpit Murder*
Machlin, Milt: *Libby*
McCormick, Donald: *The Red Barn Mystery*
McCurtin, Peter: *Murder in the Penthouse*
Meyer, Gerald: *The Memphis Murders*
Miller, Orlo: *The Donnellys Must Die*
Mooney, M. M.: *Evelyn Nesbit and Stanford White*
Nesbit, Evelyn: *The Untold Story*
Norman, C.: *The Genteel Murderer*
Packer, Edward: *The Peasenhall Murder*
Parker, Tony: *The Plough Boy*
Pearson, John: *The Profession of Violence*
Perry, Hamilton Darby: *A Chair for Wayne Lonergan*
Pugh, John: *Goodbye for Ever*
Raphael, John N.: *The Caillaux Drama*
Reuben, William A.: *The Mark Fein Case*
Root, Jonathan: *The Life and Bad Times of Charlie Becker*
Rowland, John: *The Peasenhall Mystery*
Shapiro, Fred C.: *Whitmore*
Smith, Edgar: *Brief Against Death*
    —: *Getting Out*
Thaw, Harry K.: *The Traitor*
Tullett, Tom: *No Answer from Foxtrot Eleven*
Valentine, Steven: *The Black Panther Story*
Wakefield, H. R.: *The Green Bicycle Case*
Wilkerson, Michael and Dick: *Someone Cry for the Children*
Williams, Brad: *Due Process*
Wilson, H. J. (Ed): *The Bayly Case*
Wilson, J. G.: *The Trial of Peter Manuel*
Yallop, David A.: *To Encourage the Others*
Young, Gordon: *Valley of Silence*

Specialist Booksellers

Booksellers specializing in second-hand, non-fiction crime books

C. A. Elmer, 8 Balmoral Avenue, Cheadle Hulme, Cheadle, Cheshire, SK8 5EQ, England.

W. H. Gillespie, Tutt's Cottage, Manor Close, The Street, East Preston, Sussex, England.

Grey House Books, 12a Lawrence Street, Chelsea, London, SW3 5NE, England.

J. C. G. Hammond, Crown Point, 33 Waterside, Ely, Cambridge, CB7 4AU, England.

Patterson Smith, 23 Prospect Terrace, Montclair, New Jersey 07042, USA.

Frank R. Thorold (Pty) Ltd., 4th Floor, S.A.Fire House, 103 Fox Street, Johannesburg, South Africa.

Wildy & Sons Limited, Lincoln's Inn Archway, Carey Street, London, WC2, England.

Popular Monthly Crime Periodicals

Master Detective
True Crime
True Detective

Index of Names

N.B. The headwords to articles are listed in full in the Contents, and are not repeated here.